PIERRE LOTI

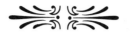

PIERRE LOTI

Portrait of an Escapist

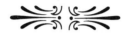

LESLEY BLANCH

COLLINS

8 Grafton Street London W1

1983

To
Sacheverell Sitwell
whom I have followed
about a world now vanished,
of which he, like Loti,
wrote incomparably

William Collins Sons and Co. Ltd.
London · Glasgow · Sydney · Auckland
Toronto · Johannesburg

British Library Cataloguing in Publication Data

Blanch, Lesley
Pierre Loti.
1. Loti, Pierre   2. Novelists, French —
19th century — Biography
I. Title
843'.8   PQ2472

ISBN 0-00-211649-9

First published 1983
© Lesley Blanch 1983
Set in Baskerville
Made and Printed in the United States of America by
Haddon Craftsman

ILLUSTRATIONS

ACKNOWLEDGMENTS

I wish to remember with gratitude the many people who by their help and interest have aided me in the writing of this book. First, the family of Pierre Loti; the late Madame Samuel Loti-Viaud, his daughter-in-law; and her son and daughter-in-law, Monsieur and Madame Pierre Loti-Viaud, and Madame le Docteur Clarisse Loti-Viaud. In Turkey, the late Count Jean Ostrorogl and Countess Ostrorogl's *yali* on the Bosphorus held many souvenirs of Loti, while at Hendaye Madame Margot Dantin's recollections of Loti's life there brought him into sharp focus. At Rochefort, I thank Madame Léonie Sauniac, Conservateur of the Maison Pierre Loti, who gave me the run of the museum in and out of visiting hours. Nearby, at La Limoise, I was made welcome by Madame Rousseau, a descendant of the Duplais family, who still lives in the old Duplais manoir, which remains much as it was when Loti spent the happiest hours of his childhood there. My especial gratitude goes to Madame Susan Train, for not only was she my hostess whenever I was in Paris for research, but she became my chauffeur when together we explored the Charente Maritime and Saintonge countryside of Loti's roots. Without another dear friend, the late Madame Blanche Sturge Moore, the chaos of my longhand manuscripts would never have reached the order of her typescript. A legion of friends have spurred me on by their encouragement: among them, I thank Gerald de Gavrey, Paul Bowles, the Baronne Elie de Rothschild, Gavin Lambert, Alaistair Duncan, Raymond Poteaux, Madame Simone de Tervagne, Leo Lerman, and Gray Foy, Jean Rauch, of the Musée de l'Homme, the late Philippe Jullian, and two more mourned friends, the late Frank Ashton Gwatkin and Monsieur Samuelian of the Librairie Orientale. General Hassan Arfa, Sir Bernard Burrows, and Monsieur Gabriel Bonneau were respectively Iranian, British and French Ambassadors about the Middle East and Central Asia, and like Mrs Edward Pope (née Princess Niloufer, of Ottoman descent) were all particularly sustaining in their specialized knowledge of Turkish affairs. Through the good offices of Douglas Cooper, my neighbour in the South of France, I have been able to study some rare Loti manuscripts including the final version of *Aziyadé*, in the collection of Colonel Daniel Sekkles, whom I thank for allowing me the freedom of his library. I also thank Monsieur Alain Quella-Villéger to whose thesis on Loti's significance during the 1914–18 war I am greatly beholden. I am much indebted to the staff of the Bibliothèque Nationale and the Musée de l'Homme, the Service d'Information et de Relations Publiques de la Marine, the Reading Room of the British Museum, and the unflagging aid of Miss Joan Bailey, at the London Library. Finally, I recall the revitalizing interest of the lamented André Malraux, encountered after many days in the Bibliothèque Nationale on one day of despondent research. 'Loti? *Quel numéro!* What a subject! Of course you must do it! The English know nothing about him – and it's high time he was re-read here.' He wished me well and, snuffling and snorting in his usual fashion, vanished, djinn-like, in a flurry of papers.

8

FOREWORD

Fantasy is the key to Pierre Loti's intricate character, for through the fantasies of his childish imagination he escaped from the schoolroom into those secret worlds of tropic radiance and adventure which, in his adult life, he was to reach. The longings of his childhood became part of that rhythm of escape which he made his own. No sooner was he in one place, or circumstance, or character – for his numerous disguises were also means of escape – than he was off again. From a life ashore he escaped into the far horizons of a sailor's life. Julien Viaud escaped into another self – Pierre Loti. He escaped from his short plain envelope ('I was not my type') by means of high heels and the paint-pot. From the Huguenot austerity of his background he sought the glow of Islam, as he escaped from the modest family house into sumptuous Arabic and Turkish interiors contrived behind the attics and parlours of his past. The mosque which crowned these extravaganzas was the ultimate escape from West to East. Here, at the heart of all evasions, he placed the gravestone of his Circassian mistress, symbol of love, loss, and longing in terms of high fantasy.

Just how much did Loti fantasize? The legends he wove round himself so assiduously were a protective barrier behind which he retreated from prying eyes and which sheltered his innermost self from the chill light of truth: though whether that inner self had remained Julien Viaud or become the *doppelgänger*, Pierre Loti, perhaps even he was not sure. The public saw him as 'the Magician', whose books held them spellbound and who lived every moment of those romantic adventures exactly as he wrote them. Only some time after his death were a few carping voices raised, hinting they were all a tissue of lies, wishful thinking, to match the changes of costume by which he played the Bedouin, the Pasha, or the circus acrobat. His

9

unpublished journals, so jealously guarded during his lifetime, are consistent with the version he offered his public. He changed little when he turned to them as material for his early, autobiographical novels. Still, it might be asked: did all those charmers of every hue really fall into his arms the moment he, the dashing naval officer, set foot ashore? How did he have so much time and the wherewithal to install himself in the local manner everywhere he went about the world? Above all, how did he contrive to filch the kadine Aziyadé from the harem of her Turkish overlord? After sifting through his unpublished journals and cross-referencing them with letters, contemporary or later, with family papers and oral legends, I have come to the conclusion – however gullible I may seem – that he did indeed live those exotic episodes and many more, pretty much as he recounted them. His life was such that he had no need to invent.

Loti began his journal early as a stand against the ultimate nothingness which obsessed him. It was an egoist's fierce determination to preserve something of his joys and sorrows as they slipped from him. His method of snaring the moment was curious: he used loose sheets of ordinary writing paper folded in half, writing on the first page only. Inside he placed letters received that day and drafts of his replies, along with bills, telegrams, visiting cards, or invitations. His entries were not always dated, but the letters, some still in their envelopes, serve as clues. Late in life Loti changed certain dates to fox prying eyes. Such mystifications were occasionally continued by his son when going through the journals and editing some parts for posthumous publication. Thus he winnowed away passages he considered too revealing of his father's nature. 'Loti loved both men and women passionately, and if there had been a third sex he would have loved that too,' I was told by one who remembered him clearly.

There are few people alive today who knew Loti; fewer still those who could recall for me the timbre of his voice, his gestures, or that indefinable but undeniable fascination he exercised over all manner of people. I have known only two persons who remembered the strange, volatile man before he was imprisoned by old age. It seems he was not always the sombre figure who emerges from his writings. His sense of fun, a noisy, jokey kind of boyish capering is impossible to convey by hearsay or in cold print. His contemporaries often referred to this gaiety, for it delighted them; but we must take it on trust, something as indescribable as his charm.

While I was working on this book, going between Loti's houses at Rochefort and Hendaye, coming on unexpected material in the tumbled cupboards and overflowing attics, my days were much enlivened by the trenchant comments of Madame Samuel Loti-Viaud, his daughter-in-law. After her husband's death she had remained in that part of the family house at Rochefort not transformed into the Maison (or Musée) Pierre Loti. This is now owned by the Municipality and open to visitors, who come there to marvel at the mosque and all those other extravaganzas Loti added to the original house. Although Elise Loti-Viaud had only known her father-in-law in his last years she became the repository of many curious sidelights on the omnipresent shade who still seemed to linger in the rooms where we talked. Through her I glimpsed the man as she had found him, the father his son remembered, and something of the husband his estranged wife, Elise's mother-in-law, had revealed.

Although Loti's books were well known to English readers during his lifetime, as they were to a wide public all over the world, they are largely forgotten today. (Even in France, although included in every anthology of nineteenth-century writers and secure in his niche, Loti is unfashionable – a romantic, not of today's mood.) For English readers, he does not translate well, nor has he, I think, been well translated. His meaning is clear but his savour is lost. Those lulling, sensuous rhythms, achieved with the simplest vocabulary, like the subtle elegance of his style, vanish. And then, it must be said, he had some deplorable habits: exclamation marks, repetitions and sentimental wallowings . . . *O! ce pauvre petit fantôme* – or child – or widowed mother – or that grandfather, in his threadbare but carefully brushed overcoat, are all maunderings which grate even more in translation. O! Loti, cut the cackle . . . let us get to the Spahi's sultry life in the desert, follow you to the Great Within, or watch the dolphins frisking round the training ship of your first halcyon voyages. Yet even through Loti's most unabashed passages of bathos his spell holds, and we read on, as Henry James the purist admitted that he did.

11

Today, one of the pleasures of reading Loti is that he, the escapist, makes escapists of us all. His first readers were largely armchair travellers and they read him avidly to reach those far horizons of which they dreamed, but which they seldom reached. Loti transposed the aristocratic detachment of most earlier travel writers into a more personal vein of intimacy, and thus his readers could identify. In the words of the enraptured Anatole France, through Loti's writings, 'they savoured to the point of intoxication, of delirium, of stupor, even, the bitter flavour of exotic loves.' We, in a less restricted age, are no doubt less stupefied by the loving, yet his travels still cast their spell. Now that the furthest points of the compass can be reached in a matter of hours, the flavour of travel is lost. We are bludgeoned by the strains and disillusions of journeys which hurtle us from one dismally overcrowded and internationalized zone to the next. By renouncing them and becoming armchair travellers like Loti's earlier readers, it is possible to travel romantically, and through his pages escape to those vanished and lovely worlds of colour, calm, and forgotten graces for which, today, we long with increasing fervour.

1

All that I was, all that I wept for,
all that I loved.

Pierre Loti

He was a provincial. For all the colour and strangeness and passion of his life, he came from austere Huguenot roots in Rochefort, on the Charente, a sober little town in Western France, the Saintonge countryside, twenty-five miles south of La Rochelle. He was born Julien Marie Viaud, but the world came to know him as Pierre Loti.

He whose writings told of a life lit by all the brilliant colours of the East, who, as an impoverished and obscure young naval officer sought adventure on the high seas, who knew love in many guises, many latitudes, who drifted into tropic indolences, savoured all voluptuousness, and knew dark melancholy without end, was to win by his writings world fame and a considerable fortune. He began his life in a narrow little house in a small street lined with similarly prim-looking white-walled houses.

Let us enter this house, No. 141 Rue Pierre Loti, or Saint-Pierre, as it was in his childhood.

We edge through the dark entrance corridor, past the unpretentious salon, with its modest Louis-Philippe furniture upholstered in plum red plush, its family portraits, its rosewood pianoforte, and its central table, where the massive eighteenth-century family Bible presides. We shall return there at evening, when the whole household is gathered round the fire, in that harmony which was the keynote of their placid existence. But first, we shall push open the coloured-glass-panelled door leading to the garden, or courtyard, for it is not much more – a narrow walled enclosure, tumbled with jasmine and honeysuckle, and ranged with pots of fragile cuttings. Under an ancient, lichen-covered wall, beside a green bench, a very small boy in a frilled pinafore is feeding spoonfuls of some pap to a very large plain cat, whom he loves and who returns his devotion. The boy is Julien Viaud, the cat, la Suprématie, one of the many

13

animals who were always an integral part of the Viauds' family life, and who, in death, were customarily buried in this courtyard. An ancestor (for several generations of Madame Viaud's family, the Texiers or Renaudins had lived here) went so far as to have his favourite black horse interred beneath the flagstones.

This courtyard garden was heart and lung of the overcrowded Viaud household. Here there was sky, sun, light and air, and here, in the long hot summers of Saintonge the little Julien was put out to play – alone for the most part, for he had few playmates of his own age. His was a solitary, but not unhappy infancy. Yet from the beginning there was something pathetic about this little creature, surrounded by overflowing tenderness, adored and overprotected, as if to make up for the fact he had not been expected, or at first, wanted. In 1850, the year of his birth, his father Théodore Viaud was forty-six, Nadine, his mother, forty: in those days an elderly couple. His sister Marie was nineteen, his brother Gustave twelve years his senior. The rest of the household ranged from fifty to eighty. There was Aunt Clarisse, Claire Texier, Madame Viaud's sister who had come to live with them when her marriage ended badly. Shy, self-effacing, childish and adorable Aunt Claire spoiled Julien to excess. Great-aunt Victorine, or Corinne in the *Memoirs* (for Loti delighted in changing the names of those he came to evoke) remains a more shadowy figure. She held a modest post in some commercial enterprise, but at one time was part of the household, before fading from view. A more emphatic presence was that of Great-aunt Rosalie (Berthe in the *Memoirs*). She was a handsome, independent-minded spinster, though not of the embittered kind, having for many years kept a suitor dangling, only to dismiss him without explanation. With her sister, Grandmama Texier, Madame Viaud's mother, she had joined the household after leaving Oléron, an island lying off the coast, where Texier ancestors, like many other Protestant families had taken refuge after the fall of La Rochelle. This Huguenot stronghold had been reduced to submission by Richelieu in 1685, and in the two hundred or more years that had passed since the exodus, the well-born, well-to-do Huguenot families of Oléron slowly sank to a proud, withdrawn impoverishment. Their spacious old stone houses – old, even before they came to occupy them, fell into decay, their possessions dwindled, sold off and not replaced, while their lands could no longer be kept up. Such were the circumstances which reduced

14

Grandmama Texier and Great-aunt Berthe to accept shelter in the Rue Saint-Pierre.

This influx of needy relatives was accepted by the young Viauds as a sacred charge. It was something that family loyalties and strict principles imposed. But it strained their already limited means to the point where Nadine Viaud's struggles to be at once charitable and economical, and above all to appear serene, played on her health, and she suffered from recurrent nervous prostrations.

Grandmama Texier, born Henriette Renaudin, was a great-niece of that Admiral Renaudin who commanded the *Vengeur* at the battle of Ushant; and, tracing her proud ancestry further, to that young French Huguenot Judith Renaudin, whose faith and stand against Catholic persecution is still recalled in Holland, at Leyden, where she took refuge, refusing to live under Rome. For the whole Viaud family their Huguenot roots were sacred, assuming legendary, even mystic proportions, and Judith Renaudin was to become the subject of one of Loti's rare ventures as dramatist. But in the 1850's, in that quiet Rochefort backwater, who could have foreseen that Julien, grown world famous, would one day thus honour the memory of his ancestress?

Grandmama Renaudin-Texier lived on the top floor of the old house, as its doyenne. She retained a charm, a prettiness and elegance reserved for few old ladies, and was rather spoiled. She lived almost entirely apart from the rest of the household, which entailed a number of errands being run, and trays taken up and down stairs, to and from her large room at the top of the house. Here Julien liked to settle with his toys, and at dusk, when they were joined by Great-aunt Berthe, he would listen to their talk; quiet chronicles which invariably returned to old and better days on the island. This was always referred to in capitals as the ISLAND, and early acquired a special significance for the child. Besides, it was on the ISLAND he had first come face to face with the sea, that immensity which was to dominate his life, and inspire some of his finest writing.

This is how he describes his first encounter. He had been taken to the ISLAND by his parents. 'I knew we had come there for something called the sea, though I had not yet seen it: I was very small, and a line of sand dunes hid it from me.' But one evening at dusk, determined to find 'the sea', he crept out, unperceived. Frightened but resolute he clambered up the dune. 'Suddenly, I stopped still,

15

trembling with terror. Before me appeared something sombre, vast, which surged forward, in a movement which made me giddy. *So that was it* – the sea! I recognized it, and I trembled. It was a very dark green, almost black: it seemed to me treacherous, sinister, wicked . . . Above it spread a sky all of one colour, dark grey, like a heavy cloak . . . From that first sight I had a presentiment that one day it would finish by taking me . . .' What he felt, standing before that sea was not only fascinated terror, he tells us, but 'some imprecise awareness of solitude, abandon, exile'. He wrote those words a lifetime later, but perhaps they were not hindsight; perhaps this child already sensed, subconsciously, his life at sea, lying in wait . . . He turned, and ran back as fast as he could, to find his mother, to be protected from the thousand fears and inexpressible presentiments which came with his first sight of those fathomless green waters which were to become, save for his mother, the most profound attachment of his life, an abiding, atavistic pull.

The child who sat so quietly beside his great-grandmother listened to her tales of the ISLAND with special intensity, for on the ISLAND were the entwined roots of his ancestry: sailors, pirates, and smugglers, admirals, cabin boys, and many more men of the sea. Already he was coming under its spell. Already those earlier Texier and Renaudin forebears who were later to summon him so imperiously in his dreams and haunt his waking reveries were closing in on the child seated by the fire, in his miniature chair. A model baby – yet, even now, marked out by these ancestors for their possession. Already that surge of tempestuous blood that had been theirs ran in his veins; already the time was coming when, with the force of some jack-in-the-box devil, all the restlessness of generations of wild seafaring men, and the furious passions that had stifled below the surface of Calvinistic restraints were to find their outlet in the person of Pierre Loti.

While the Viaud household at Rochefort were aware of turbulent elements in their ancestry, they did not dwell on them. The strength of their unshakable Huguenot convictions was a legacy of quiet pride: they did not seek more sensational legends. On the Viaud side there was also drama; Grandmama Viaud, neé Marie-Anne Morillon, whose mind was beginning to wander, was known as *la Grand'mère aux Chansons* from her habit of singing cracked snatches of the Marseillaise, le Chant du Départ or rousing songs recalling her ardent youth during the Revolution. Her husband, a young sergeant-major of artillery in the navy, lost his life after the battle of Trafalgar, dying of typhus in a Spanish port. Her eldest son, Jean, who had gone to sea at the age of fourteen, perished on the raft of the *Méduse* – where, it was whispered, he had been one of the victims of cannibalism. (This picturesque detail was something with which, many years later, Loti enjoyed titillating the Paris salons where he was lionized.)

Grandmama Viaud had been a most remarkable woman; widowed at the age of thirty-four, with no means or pension, she asked no help, but set to work, taking in ironing in order to keep herself, an orphaned nephew and her remaining son, Théodore – father of Julien, as we will call Loti, while he is still a child at home. When the child first remembered her, she was over eighty, an old lady in a crimson cashmere shawl and green ribboned cap, who spent most of her time bowing and smiling to her reflection in the mirror. *Bon jour, ma chère voisine,* she would repeat, over and over again, to the old figure who bowed and smiled back. And the child beside her would laugh delightedly – but *with* her, rather than *at* her, for he was a loving and strangely compassionate child, compassion not being an attribute usual to childhood.

In spite of a sensitivity which bordered on extra-sensory perception, making him aware of undefined, uncomprehended nuances of melancholy in the adult world around him, his childhood, as has been remarked, was a happy one. That same sensitivity made him rapturously aware of the rainbow colours of the morning. Each day some new and marvellous aspect of life was made more marvellous by this intensity. With time it was to become a torture, plunging him into excessive emotions, from the heights to the depths – mostly the depths, where all suffering, his own and that of the world around him – cruelties, injustices, the fate of the old, the lonely and animals – all animals, for whom his love and pity was boundless, caused him to seem, said his friends, *'écorché vif'* – skinned alive.

But at first, it was a radiant morning the little creature discovered in that rather sombre household, where the sunlight reached few rooms, and voices were never raised, and the only sound seemed to be the soft frou-frou of those voluminous skirts worn by the women who revolved round him: six – seven, eight, even, if his grown-up sister and his nurse were counted. Big, bell-shaped skirts over innumerable petticoats, for crinolines were not yet worn, and might have seemed too frivolous in such an ambiance. Gathered skirts,

17

flounced skirts, aproned skirts, skirts where store-cupboard keys dangled from a châtelaine, skirts where pockets held delicious surprises – bon-bons or a toy. Summer skirts of percale, or flowered indienne; winter skirts of barège, serge or merino; 'best' skirts of silk, watered silk, or satin-striped stuffs. The little Julien knew the seasons and the occasions by the skirts that moved around him in a sort of contredanse of affection and protection.

From the windows the household could keep an eye on him as he ran about the courtyard among the flower pots, inventing his own games. Such a good, quiet, *tidy* little boy – no trouble at all, in his pink or blue pinafores, his hair crimped by irons, his small shoes never muddied, his toys neatly ranged, for very early he displayed a repugnance to dirt and disorder. It was as if those habits his elders had acquired by years of ordered living were already rooted in this Benjamin on whom they doted. We see him, happy in infant contemplation of that Nature which was to become one of the wonders of his whole life. He picks a leaf, or a flower, already a baby botanist, listening to Aunt Claire's promise of splendour flowering from a packet of seedlings rather than to the fairy stories reserved for childhood. He watches the ruthless battles of small insects, and always tries to liberate the weaker; he observes the butterflies (he had not yet reached the age of collecting them, with all the cruel paraphernalia of butterfly nets, chloroform and pins). He hops and flaps in imitation of their flight, his pinafore for wings. Or he listens, rapt, to the sea's murmur sounding in the rosy depth of a shell brought him by an old seafaring cousin known as Uncle Tayeau. Everything is new, astonishing, exciting, agitating . . .

Sometimes he shared one of Great-aunt Berthe's special pleasures. '*Petit! Petit! Viens vite!*' she would call from her room at the top of the house, and wherever he was, he would rush in tumbling haste up the steep stairs to join her at the window where she watched some spectacular sunset. Together, the woman of sixty-seven and the small child would marvel at the gold-tinged clouds, and the refractions of light shimmering over the wide waters of the Charente, where the afterglow lingered, long after it had quit the low-lying green countryside. Such mysterious distances excited him. It was only from Great-aunt Berthe's window that he could glimpse the outside world of faraway, and a streak that was the Atlantic – the sea – sometimes glittering, sometimes a dark sullen line . . . but out there ships sailed, and somewhere there lay the ISLAND . . . All the other windows gave on to the quiet street, or the high-walled courtyard – confines beyond which the child rarely went. An occasional visit to neighbours, or the ritual Sunday attendance at the Protestant Temple, an austere outing, were his usual fare. Perhaps it was the call of those far horizons as much as the sunsets, which the child answered when Great-aunt Berthe called him.

Loti's father, Théodore Viaud, has remained an enigmatic figure: while we know much of the rest of the family, through Loti's journals and the beautiful memorial to his childhood, *Le Roman d'un Enfant*, or its sequel, *Prime Jeunesse*, he seldom mentions his father in one or the other. From oblique references, and mostly from other sources, we judge he was a well-liked citizen, rather didactic, but a loving, and loved head of the household, although rather overcome, if not swamped by the invasion of female relatives, whom his charitable nature compelled him to harbour. He had cultivated tastes, painted miniatures and played the flute, both accomplishments being self-taught, since he was self-educated, the fruits of long laborious nights of study. His mother, slaving over the ironing board, could not earn enough to pay for his schooling. Nevertheless, he rose to a modest but esteemed position in the Mairie, a post corresponding to that of the Town Clerk, and following his literary inclinations wrote little comedies and an excellent history of Rochefort in two volumes (which, lately reprinted, has large sales).

He had amassed every event of consequence in this quiet back-water, which had not always been so, for it was founded by Richelieu, who invested it with a strong garrison, thus to control and subdue the ever-rebellious Huguenots of La Rochelle. But grad-ually, as Huguenot resistance dwindled, the military stronghold Vauban had first fortified gave place to maritime activities. There were naval dockyards, a cannon foundry, an arsenal, a *corderie*, for the manufacture of ropes, the Préfecture Maritime and administra-tive headquarters, including training centres, besides one for such medicine and surgery as a naval surgeon would require at sea. Rochefort was always closely linked with the sea and the sailor's life. The Charente ran deep there and although nine miles inland from the Atlantic coast, big three-masted sailing ships, traders and men-o'war put in to discharge cargo or lie anchored in the roads at the mouth of the river for repairs. Below the ramparts, along the water front, there were sailors' dives and rough company, besides chain gangs of prisoners who clanked through the streets to and from their work draining the mosquito-ridden marshes. But that was a part of the town's life which had little to do with most of its citizens and was not something on which a historian of past glories wished to dwell, preferring to expatiate on the Municipality's excellent way with tax defaulters, who paid off their debt by a stint of manual work about the town.

There had been a moment, not so far distant, when the eyes of all France were turned on Rochefort, for it was there, in July 1809, that Napoleon had passed his last night on French soil, lodged in the fine buildings of the Préfet Maritime. This and other historic episodes were recounted to the little Julien as his father led him about the town on those instructive expeditions which must have early formed his habits of observation, and formed too, his later powers of seizing on the *genius loci*, the essence, or spirit of each city or country he visited. It is a quality which makes Loti's accounts of countries at once objective and subjective. The supreme egoist, he always places himself in the foreground – he is the *moi*, the I, in every scene, yet he sees and selects some vital feature, often a subtle, unsuspected detail which affects *himself*, but which nevertheless illuminates the whole for us as no amount of widespread information would do.

All his readers expected from him, he was to remark rather bitterly when late in life he had done with novels and wrote only books of travel, was to bring them the illusion of a voyage – 'the reflection of things over which my eyes have ranged'. Yet what other eyes have ranged as his? Therein lies Loti's special magic. Perhaps it had its beginning in those instructive walks about Rochefort – an unavowed legacy from the father with whom he seems to have had little else in common.

All his life, it was his mother who possessed his entire love; beside so overwhelming an emotion there was probably some complex resentment which clouded the child's relationship with his father – so that it remained to obscure later memories and evaluations. Nadine and Théodore Viaud were a united pair: their marriage had been a love match, overcoming every obstacle. The pretty, well-bred Mademoiselle Texier, from this high-born Huguenot family established on the ISLAND, had only been permitted to marry her young mainland suitor of no fortune or background – *and a Roman Catholic to boot* – on the condition that he turned Protestant. This he did, and with a convert's zeal, was to become as unquestioning an adherent to the tenets of the Reformed Church as he remained a devoted husband. In all respects an admirable man; and an intriguing one too, since throughout Pierre Loti's writings he is only glimpsed obliquely. It is as if his son wished to be all Texier or Renaudin, some immaculate conception, with nothing Viaud about him.

Of his mother, Loti has left many portraits, as he first recalled her, as she aged, and in retrospect. All love is there: to her, he was to return from the furthest voyages, cutting short travels and meetings he desired, hastening to her side as to a lover's rendez-vous. For her, as for those other *chères vieilles robes noires* (the dear old black-robed ones, as he came to describe the old ladies whose presence represented his links with that vanished youth he mourned) he forswore many more lively hours. For his mother's peace of mind he was to renounce his dream of that Oriental life he adored, and with it, as a despairing agnostic, he lost the consolations he believed he could have found in the Moslem faith. Nadine Viaud's strong faith convinced her of a life to come – of heavenly reunions after death: thus she was sustained through many bitter trials. Her son having no such beliefs became tortured by the dread of their final separation. But that grief lay many many years ahead; let us turn back from the anguished man he became to find him again, as little Benjamin of the Rue Saint-Pierre, at the moment when he first recalled his mother.

Prefacing his portrait of her, he writes, 'I would like to hail this blessed figure with words that are quite apart; were it possible, with words made only for her, words otherwise non-existent . . . My mother! the door opened, and my mother came in, smiling. She had returned from a morning's shopping in the town. She wore a straw hat trimmed with yellow roses, and a lilac shawl. She lent over my bed to kiss me and I wished for nothing more: she was there, and that was enough.'

Some toys she had brought him that morning were still piously conserved when he was a grown man. Far away at sea and in moments of danger, his mind would return to them as precious talismans in which he found once more that sense of fulfilment and protection he had known in his mother's smile, that faraway morning in May.

In this outwardly placid, united family there must have been, nevertheless, undercurrents of tension which were to have a lasting effect on Julien's already fragile nervous system. 'Nerves', tensions or stress were not then perceived, or admitted; least of all in the Viaud household, where all seemed calm and orderly. Before he could walk, his mother, for whom family love was a matter of passionate, even neurotic intensity, made a practice of carrying him to the portraits of his brother and sister who, were they absent, must not for a moment be forgotten. She wished her family to be one indissoluble, emotional whole – her mother, her sisters, her aunts, her grandmother, her husband – he too, though something of an outsider – were all swept up into this maelstrom of feeling – above all, her children (*hers*, rather than their father's, was, I fancy, how she unconsciously saw them). With an almost sacred zeal, she would inculcate in Julien this cult for all that was of the family. Marie's cup and saucer (soon he would drink from no other), an old sock belonging to Gustave which came to be cherished above any toy, a dress Grandmama Renaudin had worn as a girl on the ISLAND . . . all were sacred links. Loving so desperately, she overlaid the baby with her own perfervid sensibilities. Thus, from the beginning, he seems to have absorbed an excess of sensitivity, leaving him, as already recorded, with one skin less than others, aware of every nuance of emotion, every tremor of those around him becoming his, too. Poor little creature, a toy, wound up to weep.

Among the boxes, old trunks and cupboards crammed with the *memento mori* which he preserved as holy relics, there are one or two letters from his father. These are brief and, although a shade sententious, are full of calm affection and many outside interests which come as a breath of fresh air beside the underlinings, exclamation marks and hyperbolic declarations of devotion and possession which are the key-note of the letters with which his mother and sister pursued him throughout their life. Unfortunately, Théodore Viaud's more balanced influence was short-lived for he was to die before his son could properly appreciate his true worth or profit by his presence.

Thus undercurrents of melancholy inhabited the child Julien long before he became Loti, the anguished man. From his earliest days he seemed to sense the transitory or impermanent nature of all life. He wanted to hold on to everything – to clutch the fleeting moment in his small fist. The here and now – to where was it going? What would tomorrow bring – and after tomorrow? The flowers he loved so passionately faded; Gaspard, a cherished mongrel dog disappeared . . . But were something to be lost and then retrieved, it acquired a special value, for it had returned from that indefinable *nothingness* that was the end of everything. He had sensed that nothingness, in a confused way, when he saw his much-loved Grandmother laid out for burial. She had been there: he had liked to play in her sunny room: now she was in Heaven, they told him. But how could she be? She was there, in front of him . . . yet she was not there any more. Where was she then? In that dark void which was to haunt him all the rest of his life: in that nothingness to which people, happy hours, flowers, his favourite dog, all vanished, leaving emptiness.

But *things* remained. Things, inanimate objects, could reassure by their unchanging presence. His mother's pin-cushion, a pencil case, or the almost sacred *Ours à Pralines* – all could be loved, and held fast. This *Ours à Pralines*, a porcelain bear, possessed magical powers. It stood on the chimneypiece in Aunt Claire's room and, wonderful to relate, when its head was screwed round to the right, its belly was always full of sugary pralines; but when its head was turned to the left, there were no more sweets.

Throughout his life, *things* were a barrier standing between him and the nothingness which lay ahead – which lay in wait for him, and gradually, this obsessive attachment to objects reached fetish proportions. All these jealously preserved objects, generally of little value except by association, came to be invested with a life – a soul, even. For him, they lived, and spoke to him of a past they had known together. Each had its place in his memory – were, in short, memorials to that past he cherished, each nourished the nostalgia that was to become his drug.

While nostalgia, to that degree, only developed with time, the seed was there: even his earliest days were darkened by the anguish of partings. The most ordinary comings and goings about the house caused him misery. 'You *will* come back, won't you?' he would plead, clutching at a hand, or an apron. *'Stay! Come back!'* It was as if, already, he was aware of those wrenching farewells, those last irrevocable adieux that both life and death reserve for us.

23

There is a portrait of him, painted by his sister, just before she left to study art in Paris, which sets his age at around two. The adored infant wears a white shift falling off his chubby shoulders and he is fondling a pet bird. Even then, something strangely arresting shows in those large, beautiful dark eyes which were to work such havoc among susceptible women everywhere, and which never failed to make an overwhelming impression on everyone he encountered. ('Those eyes! that gaze!' people were always to remark.) Curiously, in this portrait, they are not the eyes of a child that look out at us. Sometimes it happens that a childlike look remains in the eyes of an adult face, but here there is a reversal: adult eyes, compelling and infinitely sad, look out prophetically from a baby's face.

Marie and Gustave vied in their ecstasies over Julien. Gustave, who had chosen this name for him, always called him Zézin or Zézinette, thus further feminizing the already dolled-up boy. When Gustave was away at college studying to enter the navy as a ship's surgeon, Marie's letters kept him posted as to the baby who was also his godson. No detail was too insignificant: every aspect of his nature or appearance was noted: his beaky little nose (later enlarged into something called Pharaonic by those who admired him, but an unfortunate protuberance by those who did not), his delicately almond-shaped nails, his adorable way of swaying in time to music, his precocity, walking and talking when little more than a year old, his marked love of beauty – 'par zoli – par zoli' – not pretty – he would lisp, when confronted by anything or anybody he thought ugly. Oh! this wonder-child! The ecstasies were never ending.

Marie observed what she took to be early signs of genius. In a letter to her mother, she writes: 'His reactions and thoughts appear to me extraordinary for such a baby! It seems as if this intelligence, already so profound, announces a brilliant destiny, a destiny consecrated to God . . . Meantime, may this darling child be brought up in wisdom and piety, and should he be marked for some high position, may he know how to turn his brilliant powers to the profit and glory of He who reigns in Heaven.'

After which, it is not surprising to learn that Julien early decided on the Church as his future. He would be a pastor; it was the proper path to follow, and for a while the child conducted himself 'like some little mystic' the grown man was to remember with longing.

Although surrounded by adulation, certain standards of conduct and discipline were gently imposed. But then, he was not an unruly child. Original sin seems to have been left out of him. Not that he was a prig: he simply seemed a child apart – if child he ever was. Old souls, it is held, sometimes inhabit young bodies. Perhaps this was so: but since he was coddled and kept away from any contact with the possibly pernicious influence of other children, there were few possibilities for original sin. Except that one dreadful occasion when Satan himself took possession. It was high summer and fly-papers were hung about the kitchen. With diabolic intent, he collected the black, glutinous masses stuck fast to the papers, and with the complicity of a jolly old peasant cook, concocted a fly omelette, intended, no doubt, to shatter for once the serenity of the family dinner table. We do not know how this lapse from grace was viewed, but it was at least – at last, one might say – the action of a normally naughty child.

Generally he was contented with more agreeable diversions. There was the model theatre he loved – it is still to be seen among other treasures on show at the Maison Pierre Loti. Aunt Claire made the costumes for these minuscule doll actors, hardly an inch high, crimping their wigs with a heated pin. Julien painted most of the scenery, and the preparation of little plays such as *Sleeping Beauty* or *Peau d'âne* occupied many months of laborious effort. When we remember that the theme of *Peau d'âne* is incest, Perrault's fairy story seems an odd choice for this Calvinistic nursery (but then most of the old fairy stories contain undercurrents of horror). At any rate, no-one seems to have questioned the suitability of this tale of a grieving, widowed king who, suddenly perceiving his daughter's beauty exceeds that of his late wife, becomes infatuated, determines to make her his bride, and is only thwarted by the ruthless machinations of the Lilac Fairy who perhaps fancies him for herself.

So, moral niceties being ignored, Julien and Aunt Claire constructed elaborate sets and Julien was transported into a wonderful world of grandiose scenic imaginings, 'moonlit glades, storms, shimmering palaces and gardens worthy of Aladdin ... All my dreams of enchanted dwellings and strange luxuries which later I was, more or less, to realize in various corners of the world' (and especially in the Arab fantasies he imposed on the old house), 'were to take form, for the first time, in this theatre of *Peau-d'Ane* ... I might almost say that all the chimera of my life were first tried out, or brought into being, on that tiny stage,' he wrote, recalling his childhood in *Le Roman d'un Enfant*.

25

Gustave's influence over Julien, both during his lifetime and forever after, makes us wish to know more about him. He emerges from his letters, the memory of his friends, as well as official navy reports as a remarkable character, cultivated and courageous, with a selfless devotion to both his family and his calling. Had he lived, it has been said, it might have been he, of the two brothers, whom the world would acclaim: his letters are in a limpid, effortless style, his observations never banal and his evocative powers often rival Loti's own. He shared the artistic and musical talents all three Viaud children inherited from their father, and played the piano, violin and cello well. Unlike his younger brother he possessed a natural gaiety; he was not morose or introspective: he did not have those excessive heights and depths which were the pigment of Loti's genius. But if Gustave was no genius, he was something almost as rare – a balanced human being – balance being a quality the Fates rarely donate along with genius. It was the admiration which Julien felt for his elder brother's irreproachable service record that was to inspire Commandant Viaud, as Loti became known to the navy, to follow suit and become, for all his mercurial temperament, a distinguished officer.

Since memories of Gustave were to remain so strong throughout the younger brother's life, let us look at the portrait of this paragon brother as Marie painted him before he left on his first expedition to the South Seas. We see a handsome, rather Byronic young man, his pale, poet's face framed in a small fringe of beard; the eyes are large, dreamy, the lips sensual, the features harmonious, the sum total romantic. In short, this would be the envelope best suited to enclose Loti's genius. There is no trace here of the swarthy looks which were those of the younger brother: no trace of that boldly hooked nose or those extraordinary black eyes. Both Gustave and Marie were recognizably Viauds or Texiers – in the European, family mould. But Julien? From infancy he was outrageously different – a changeling child, where some alien, exotic strain in both his looks and his nature set him apart. Writing of a branch of his family who had remained on Oléron, he describes a great-aunt 'whose eyes were still as black as night, sufficient testimony that once, the Moors of Spain had invaded our island'. Perhaps it was that swarthy strain left by some *beau ténébreux* that accounts not only for Loti's own dark eyes, but also explains that mysterious call of the blood to which he was always to respond when among the peoples of Islam.

Gustave, the loved and admired elder brother, so handsome, so independent, so *tall*, remained diminutive Julien's ideal. In every way he was perfection. In spite of twelve years difference in age, theirs was a deep intimacy, and ever after Julien was to miss this brotherly relationship, cut short by death; he always searched to find another brother. *Mon frère* is how he invariably addressed any favoured friend.

Between the devotion of his elder brother and Marie the sister, who was nineteen years older, the child had almost an extra set of parents rather than playmates. Marie adored him with a possessive love and the child loved and admired her wholeheartedly. She seemed different from the other young girls of Rochefort: perhaps because she had travelled more – had studied art in Paris and been as far afield as Switzerland and Germany. She knew, or divined, so much about her odd little brother who also was not like others. 'She it was whose influence removed me, even in life's smallest details, if not from all that was vulgar, certainly from all that was inelegant.' That tribute was written after her death; but for many years there were bickering scenes: her love became stifling. '*Your* life is *my* life' runs one of her letters. 'There is a sacred corner of myself for you alone – your place – and when you go away, it is empty – burnt out.'

Marie was profoundly religious, her faith never shaken by those tremors of doubt which Julien came to know so early; but while sharing so many of his secrets and understanding many complexities of his nature, she did not have their mother's more discreet approach. As time passed and the doubting child became a man without beliefs, Marie, in her own passionate exaltation, was apt to hammer at him – to hammer home her own certainties in a heavy-handed way which irked him. She lacked Nadine Viaud's intuitive awareness of every nuance in the grown man. Both Julien and Marie came to shelter their adored Maman from aspects of his nature and adventures which they thought would have been painful to her. Nadine Viaud's understanding spread far beyond Rochefort's grey ramparts or the austere tenets of the Huguenot Temple and she would have neither nagged nor condemned. But how she would have had to pray!

Just as the sober dignity of the Temple at the corner of the Rue Victor Hugo remains much as it was when the Viauds worshipped there, so that part of the house in the Rue Saint-Pierre that has not been transformed into the Maison Pierre Loti remains, in essence, as it was when the child Julien lived there. The first impression is overwhelmingly claustrophobic. All the rooms are small – some mere boxes reached by precipitous narrow stairs. Some overlook the roof tops, some give on to the walls of neighbouring houses, one or two look down, more agreeably, on the flowering courtyard. Here the whole household (and also the maid, a peasant from the ISLAND who had served the Texiers or Renaudins all her life), lived elbow to elbow, condensed into attics or a garden lean-to.

From today's easy living, where electricity, plumbing, refrigerators and central heating are accepted as necessities rather than luxuries, it is difficult to imagine the restrictions and problems of daily life as the Viauds knew it. As was customary then, there was no bathroom; jugs of water and the slops were a never-ending task. The only privy was in the back yard – a two-seated affair in a shed. Lamps had to be trimmed every day, fires lit, logs and coal carried about to replenish the grates. The big kitchen range had to be kept banked, while fresh food had to be stored in a slate-shelved larder beyond the kitchen, and was apt to 'turn' in warm weather. As the two grandmothers grew more infirm, there were more and more meals to be carried up and down, their gruels and tisanes to be prepared, and their increasingly childish exigencies to be met. There was the marketing and the cooking, the store-room shelves to restock and the household linen as well as their clothes to be kept in order. True, Aunt Claire and Great-aunt Berthe helped, though it was on Nadine Viaud that the burden fell heaviest; but in spite of her ceaseless activities, she always looked elegantly pretty, sitting night after night, under the lamp, sewing, mending, smiling lovingly at those around her. Sometimes she collapsed with nervous prostration and was obliged to keep to her bed, then the family had to limp on without her, and Julien moped.

Luxuries were unknown in the Viaud household which had begun as the ménage of a young couple, modestly endowed, and grown to compass nine adults and Julien. They lived, dressed and ate frugally: though if there was no high living, there were at least certain graces, such as the flowers and ferns which adorned every room all through the year.

In spite of Gustave's many absences, first at college and later at sea, his influence remained decisive for the younger brother. From near or far he watched over him. Zézin's health as well as his moral fibre was of concern. Chopin's music, which Julien had just discovered and fingered out in ecstasy, was thought to have a dangerously emotional hold over him. Bach would be more soothing. The child was looking sickly – he lacked exercise, so expensive riding lessons were prescribed. (The more economical solution of letting him loose among boys of his own age does not seem to have been acceptable to the family.) So much for his body. Now for his soul. Seated side by side in the family pew, the brothers bore the penetrating cold and the tedium of interminable sermons which had begun to undermine Julien's infant piety though Gustave's presence encouraged him to hold fast. But when the older brother was absent, Julien's fervour flagged sadly.

On one of his returns to Rochefort, Gustave had devised a marvellous plaything for his Zézin. This was a miniature lake and grotto that was to remain the dearest relic of all those Loti preserved. He came to attach an almost mystical significance to this Lilliputian landscape. With a collection of stones, rocks and pebbles Gustave had transformed a prosaic zinc tank into this charming fantasy. Mosses and aquatic plants lined the sides, while sandy shores were fringed with clumps of fern, hart's-tongue and maidenhair, which in so miniature a world appeared as some gigantic tropic vegetation. In the ivy-dark depths of a shell and pebble grotto, a large toad had been persuaded to settle, while four goldfish meandered about those ornamental waters and, again by the trickery of scale, appeared so many gilded whales. Zézin was transported with bliss. From then on, it was the centre of his play. Later, it was beside it, beneath the sheltering garden wall and an overhanging plum tree that he used to install himself with his lesson books; later still, it was to this corner of the garden to which the man was always to return, like some devout pilgrim, to write his books or brood. Grotto, wall and tree grew into an indissoluble whole – his Holy Mecca; the quintessential, sheltering refuge, which offered some reassurance in those doubt-ridden years to come. Gustave, who had created the grotto for him, was to vanish . . . but the grotto remained, strengthening his fetish for *things* – those *things* – inanimate objects – to which Pierre Loti, the disillusioned man clung as, one by one, the people he loved vanished and time was running out.

The family is in the snug, dark-curtained parlour; it is that enchanted hour – 'little Zézin's hour' – when, after supper and before

29

kneeling for the ritual Bible reading, they played old-fashioned parlour games to amuse him . . . *La Toilette de Madame, Le Chevalier cornu* or *Furet* . . . everyone joined in, Great-aunt Berthe displaying an irresistible gaiety. With the warm flicker of the wood fire and the lamp's glow, these were the winter evenings the child was to remember all his life. They were the source of all his egoist's longings, for then the whole world seemed centred round him, loving and giving. He was to remember too how, with the visit of the old pie-seller, he was to know those first stirrings of curiosity and longings to venture beyond the threshold he had never yet crossed alone.

Each year, the coming of winter was announced by the sing-song cry of the old pie-seller calling her wares, '*Gâteaux! Gâteaux! mes bons gâteaux tout chauds!*' The child would rush to the front door, snatching at that brief moment while she uncovered her basket and one of the grown-ups paid for the cakes, to gulp the frosty night air and look outside his cage. He would strain his eyes along the dark, empty street which sloped down towards the ramparts and those low quarters round the port – a district where the family never went and of which no-one ever spoke. And when the door closed on the winter's dark and the child returned to the warm room, he followed the fading sound of the pie-seller's voice as she went on her way towards those forbidden quarters . . . streets deserted by day, but where, from time immemorial, the sailors passed their rowdy nights, while their raucous singing and bursts of laughter could be heard many streets away in more sedate sections of the town. What could be going on down there along the water front, the child wondered. An uneasy curiosity possessed him.

The first stirrings of that lifelong hunger for '*ailleurs*' – elsewhere – and the unknown had taken hold. The child could not formulate his longings, but he wondered . . . What sort of rough play went with those loud voices? What was a sailor's life? His curiosity and some vague envy grew. A poison had entered his Eden. The familiar happiness of here and now, of the warm room, his mother's presence and Great-aunt Berthe's jokes faded . . . He wanted to join those mysterious sailors in their unknown pleasures, or to follow them to those distant ports such as Uncle Tayeau had described, where strange fruits hung on trees, and there were parrots like the uncle's scarlet and grey bird from Gabon . . . He wanted to seize all these things. He, the overprotected fragile creature, wanted to live as wild and free as the sailors – not as a little captive prince.

In 1859 Gustave had qualified as a naval surgeon and left home to serve in the colonies, about the South Seas. He was based at Tahiti which had become a French protectorate in 1843 at the request of Queen Pomaré IV who feared annexation by the English. Before leaving, a departure over which the whole Viaud family agonized, Gustave had given his small brother a picture book, *Voyage en Polynésie*, and Zézin, who felt abandoned, spent many hours colouring the engravings of fabulous blossoms, birds and fishes with loving care. After getting his hand in on them, it was the turn of the noble savages. Young Tahitian women beside the sea were the subject which had inspired the engraver. But dusky nymphs, such as these charmers were in fact, was something quite outside Zézin's imagination. He coloured them pink and white, the pink and white of the prettiest dolls, and thought them ravishing.

'The future was to teach me their colouring and their charm was quite otherwise,' writes Loti – recalling the voluptuous little Polynesian vahiné who first called him Loti. 'In my case,' he continues, 'my ideas of beauty have become modified since those childish days, and I would have been very much surprised if, then, I could have known what different kinds of faces I should come to find charming, in my unseeable future . . .'

There speaks the lover of Rarahu, the Polynesian savage; of Cora, the mulatto of Senegal; of Sulïema, the Algerian prostitute; of Aziyadé, the Circassian kadine; of Pasquala Ivanovitch, the Montenegrin shepherdess; of Madame Chrysanthème, the Japanese mousmé and a legion of other unlisted charmers whose colours ranged from ebony to ivory.

Meanwhile, there was his museum which brought him an illusion of far horizons. It had begun as a collection of fossils, beetles and butterflies, the usual natural history haul of childhood, but which, by donations from Uncle Tayeau, relics of his colonial life, snake skins, pearl shells, and bright-coloured plumage, assumed a markedly tropic flavour. The family encouraged his hobby, but none of them, seeing him so absorbed, understood that this interest in natural history was only secondary. What fascinated him, what he sensed behind those objects, was Nature itself – 'terrifying, thousand-faced Nature – an unknown ensemble of animals and forests' all contained in that magic phrase – *les colonies*. Burning suns and all beauty sounded there.

31

Sometimes family friends returned with wonderful tales of flying foxes and giant lizards or musical instruments made from gourds. Uncle Tayeau's parrot uttered frantically in some chattering Negro tongue when they rattled the coloured gourds at him; they, like the parrot, came from those African shores for which the child, and no doubt the bird too, was pining. Then there were Gustave's letters and contributions to the museum – all exotica for the longing stay-at-home conjuring the marvels and beauties of Pacific regions. Gustave dwelt at length on one of his favourite haunts, a profound valley called Fatäua which lay between two vertiginous mountains on Papeete.

'. . . a semi-darkness always reigns there, under those giant, unknown trees; cool cascades and streams carpet the ground with rare ferns . . . What a pity this delicious isle does not have a door which leads through into the courtyard of our garden – by the honeysuckle arbour perhaps, or behind the grotto of your little lake . . .' wrote Gustave.

'This notion of a door in our courtyard, linking the grotto with faraway Tahiti, affected me powerfully,' wrote Loti. 'My brother had no idea of the dangerous seduction his letters were already exercising over the child he had left so attached to his home, so tranquil, so pious, but whose tropic longings were already in his blood.'

That obsessive craving for *ailleurs* – elsewhere – which was the sovereign impulse of Loti's life (for when he was at home he longed to be at sea, and when he was the other side of the world he ached for Rochefort) was presently to change his first choice of a pastor's life. Religious beliefs instilled in him by his parents were now adjusted to his cravings for *ailleurs*. After all, exotic longings might well be combined with salvation! He would become a missionary! Thus he could reach those tropic shores which Gustave's letters were describing so lyrically. Yet, even as he unpacked the fascinating packets his brother sent home for his museum, a model canoe from Papeete, grotesque carved figures made from tropic woods, garlands of strangely scented seeds threaded with human hair, or head-dresses of rare plumage, Loti tells us he already sensed that these same tropics possessed another face, one of desolation and death (though no less seductive). Here is an echo of that same atavism which had made him, so early, know that one day the sea would come to possess him.

32

2

*Into many a green valley creeps
the appalling snow.*

T. S. Eliot, *The Waste Land*

Julien was ten before the dreaded moment of contamination was faced by the family. Their toy, their joy, must go to school. Tutors, music lessons and home instruction were not enough. He must enter the Collège de Rochefort (today the Lycée Pierre Loti), where Gustave too had studied. He was terror-struck at the prospect and insisted on wearing one of Gustave's old school uniforms as a sort of talisman – a coat of mail through which no harm could pierce. It was far too big for him and had to be cut down to his miniature proportions – not very successfully, as we see in the picture. He was entered as a day pupil, of course, as, of course, he was escorted to and from the classes, to avoid unsuitable acquaintanceships.

He hated his school days, dreading the contact with other boys and flinching from the sarcasms of the masters, while the ink-stained walls and stark ugliness repulsed him. He did not shine at school. It was already too late to overcome his inbred sense of isolation. His progress in class was fitful: Greek and Latin bored him; he was badly marked in French composition and was a laboriously slow reader, taking a year to get through *Télémaque*; but for mathematics he showed a surprising aptitude. Homework was a cross and only Aunt Claire ranged behind books of reference and lexicons dragged him along. The *Ours à Pralines* still stood on the chimneypiece, but now not even its china belly stuffed full of sweets could lighten his depression. Sunday was always overcast by thoughts of Monday morning. Only in the long summer holidays could he recapture happiness.

Gradually Julien's elders perceived that his infant piety was no more. He was not cut out for the life of pastor or missionary. In view of his aptitude for mathematics, Gustave wrote: 'Do you see our *bijou* as an engineer, with the railways – or maybe a chemist, with some

33

big pharmaceutical company?' Gustave was moving with the times. Either project was acceptable to the family since, above all, they wished to keep Julien beside them – the stay and comfort of their last years. But Julien? Other plans were now beginning to take shape, ideas as yet scarcely formed, which he confided to no-one but recorded in his first hidden journals.

He was a secretive child; not in the sense of slyness for he was of a limpid honesty, but rather, being so much alone and so surrounded by adults, he found it easier to confide in this journal which he kept meticulously. It was to become a lifelong habit and source of material for his books, since all his novels are in part autobiographical. Original in all things, this odd child conceived his first journal in the form of long narrow strips of paper rolled round a stick, in the manner of an Assyrian manuscript. It was as mysterious as he could make it, written in a code he had invented to thwart prying eyes.

Heading these cabalistic scrawls he had drawn, in red ink, a double-headed Egyptian sphinx, and more cabalistic signs. 'I invested this journal with inviolable mystery. I never wrote it at the desk in my room – that was defiled by my school exercise books: rather, I chose a minuscule old bureau which stood in my attic museum . . . It was only a year later, because of the time such characters took to write, that my journal became an ordinary note-book, with ordinary handwriting.' He usually referred to himself in the third person, as Fédin: 'Fédin got up early, to range his childish toys' . . . 'nevertheless I continued to keep it hidden under lock and key, as if it were some criminal enterprise. I did not record much of my tranquil little life, but rather, my incoherent impressions, my evening melancholies, my longings for past summers, and dreams of faraway countries. I already had the need to note, or preserve every fugitive image, and to struggle against the impermanence of both things, and myself, something which has caused me to continue my journal until now . . .' (he was to write forty years later). But in those early days, the idea that any other eyes might light on it was unsupportable; 'Were I to leave home, even for the shortest journey, I was careful to seal it up, and write on the envelope: *It is my last wish that this note-book be burned without being read.*'

Looking back, towards the end of his life, he writes 'Mon Dieu! how I have changed!' And indeed he had, for throughout the years he was forever publishing writings that dwelt, with the supreme egoist's intensity, on the agonies he suffered in loving and losing, and brooding over the inexorable passing of time. He poured out all his dreads, all his morbid imaginings. No more secrecy now: any casual reader's eye could light on his innermost anguish . . . As if apologizing for his self-exposure, he wrote that perhaps he would come to write of yet more intimate matters which had not until then been wrung from him. 'For that will be to try to prolong – beyond my own existence – all that I was, all that I wept for, all that I loved.'

It was Loti himself who came, at last, to destroy many revealing passages of his journals; thus certain aspects of the man's life remain as secret, as guarded, as the child would have wished. Even so there is much unpublished material which tells of a schizophrenic split between the puritan and the voluptuary, the agnostic and the mystic.

As Julien grew older some freedom was accorded him and he spent much time at La Limoise, an estate six miles distant across the Charente, near Echillais, where the Duplais family, neighbours in Rochefort and family friends, spent most of the year in an old, rambling stone manor house where Loti's legend is still cherished. It was sheltered by those gigantic evergreen oaks which, like vines, flourish on the warm Saintonge soil. All around was open pastoral country which erupted in strange white stones and rock formations, said to be of Druidic origin. La Limoise always drew him, held him, as if casting some special spell. It seemed to belong to another latitude, more exotic than Rochefort. *Exotic*, not then part of his vocabulary, he called *southern*. Significantly, 'La Limoise lay towards the south – in the direction of *southern* lands: I should have found its charm less powerful had it lain towards the north.' There he experienced moments of transcendental happiness: he describes this as an *elmique* spell – some kind of mystic or pagan communion with nature, a brief experience of cosmic unity, as the eastern sages he later sought might have explained.

Lucette Duplais, daughter of the house at Limoise, was a few years older than Julien and his dearest friend. Together they explored the countryside, confided their secrets to each other, collected plants and insects, and played duets in the stone-flagged salon with its charming provincial furnishings. Julien had developed marked musical talents and was already composing little pieces and playing with much feeling – or so the family thought, seconded by Aunt Eugénie, as he called Lucette's mother.

Together the two children were entirely content in the simple pattern of country life, their happiness completed by each other's presence. A childish romanticism made them watch together for the Pole-star, their own star, they said, and each vowed to think of the other, sighting it when separated. No shadows crossed their path at that time; nothing warned them then, that within a few years, Lucette would suddenly move into the adult world, leaving Julien behind, trapped by childhood.

In the open countryside of La Limoise Julien could forget the twining roots that held him captive so lovingly in the confines of the Rue Saint-Pierre. Every Wednesday evening (for Thursday was his day of reprieve from school) it was to La Limoise he hurried, generally escorted by one of Lucette's grown-up brothers. Joyously, almost too obviously happy, he would shake off the admonishments of his family. Even so, they smothered him in mufflers as they did when he went to school and forced him to carry an umbrella against sudden showers. Poor little creature, so fragile, so small of stature, he remained their idol-doll. But the boy was beginning to notice class-mates who were shooting up around him and were not coddled either.

'My hothouse upbringing' was something which was to embitter him, the resentment lingering all his life. He was only to overcome it by the hard training of a naval cadet before the mast. As a grown man, still craving the physical perfection he envied in others, there was a gruelling period at a gymnastic centre to make over, or remodel his body. But nothing was to give him height. 'I was not my type,' he was to reiterate sadly when, as an adulated young writer, he would have exchanged fame and fortune for another physique.

It was at La Limoise that he chanced on an old ship's log which was to crystallize his vague longings. This decisive moment, turning point of his childhood, was a signpost that he could not ignore. It fell on one of those Thursdays which he usually spent with the Duplais, freed from both his classes and the cribbed confines of the family house. 'As the inexorable hour of departure drew near, I had gone upstairs to the old room that was mine; I had been kneeling at the window, watching the red July sun sink . . . they were always so melancholy, those sunsets which ended my Thursdays. At the last moment, an idea I had never had before, led me to rummage in a bookcase that stood beside my bed. There, among the old volumes, their bindings dating from another century, where worms, undisturbed, had slowly eaten away whole galleries, I found a note-book, its coarse paper that of earlier times. I opened it, casually . . . and read, with a shiver of emotion: *From noon to 4 hours in the evening, 20th June 1813 by 110 degrees longitude, 15 degrees latitude australe* (consequently, in tropic zones, the waters of the Indian Ocean) *fine weather, calm seas, a fresh south-easterly breeze* . . .' He read on, learning that the sky was full of little white clouds, 'cats' tails', and that shoals of dolphins skimmed through the water to starboard. 'Dead, many years, those who noted the fugitive forms of clouds, and who watched the leaping dolphins.' The boy longed with a sudden overwhelming passion to see for himself that calm sea, those clouds across the tropic skies and the shoals of dolphins skimming those southern solitudes . . .

It was the moment of revelation, of certainty. That sailor's life which would tear him away from his mother – dread thought – and which, in any case, was a life his family would forbid, was the only one he wanted, the only possible future for him.

He kept his finding of the old ship's log, and its decisive effects from his family, though no doubt he dwelt on it at some length in the abracadabra of his journal.

Gustave had served three years in the South Seas before he was given home leave. There were tears of joy at the family reunion in 1862 and Zézin hung on the words of this tall tanned cigar-smoking brother. Yet, dutiful and loving as Gustave was, his mother was aware of a certain detachment. The idea of returning to Tahiti, of those tearing farewells all over again when his leave was up, did not seem to appal him . . . Was it possible that he was *happy*, so far away from all of them? Deeply as Gustave loved them, he had become involved, not only in his work, but in a relationship of which his family knew nothing. The young surgeon had fallen under the sway of one of those seductive vahinés – copper-skinned beauties of the South Seas, who loved as freely as they lived, and whose caresses were, in another fashion, as enveloping as those of the family. Life at Rochefort seemed dim beside this datura-scented existence. Julien noticed that when letters arrived from Papeete Gustave seized on them and shut himself away. They were letters to which he never made any allusion later. Some were from shipmates or fellow-exiles who wrote telling him of his vahiné. Sometimes, Julien, all curiosity, glimpsed cabalistic signs scrawled across a page. Gustave had learned something of the Polynesian language from Tarahu, his love, and they could communicate by both the written and the spoken word. A few of these letters remain among Loti's papers. Some employ our alphabet used to form phonetically words of the Tahitian tongue – perhaps written by some Europeans there, to Tarahu's dictation. Some appear to be written in the strangely formed lettering of the islands. No doubt all of them told Rouéri – 'the light-eyed one', as he was to the islanders – of her longing for his return.

Gustave was sufficiently versed in life there to know the inhabitants had no moral values as the West knew them, and to make love was as natural and as necessary to them as to breathe. Doubtless Tarahu was consoling herself in his absence for she was a beautiful young animal, but the ravishment of these tropics held him. Thus to leave home did not seem so sad to Gustave. The tropics' sensual spell was, for him, centred round a palm-thatched hut beside the coral seas, where he and his vahiné lived and loved, to which he returned after his doctoring about the islands, and where he had set up a primitive dark-room to develop the photographs he was the first to take of Papeete – valuable records which show the simple wooden Palace, the few houses and the luxuriant vegetation of 'l'Ile Délicieuse' as it was then.

Late in 1862, Gustave's home leave was unexpectedly cut short by a summons from the Ministère de la Marine. He was promoted and ordered to join an expedition of administrators who were leaving at once, to take up their work in the various French possessions scattered about the archipelagos of Indonesia. Adieu his vahiné; adieu the little palm-roofed hut and all the frangipani-scented shores of loving. Adieu the old house at Rochefort, too, and all the love that enfolded him there.

A gloomy autumn day found the whole family gathered in the parlour to pray together and make their farewells. It was the first time Julien had seen his mother weep and he was harrowed by this added anguish.

'When my brother had gone, but while the sound of the *fiacre* could

38

still be heard, my mother turned to me with an expression that touched me to the depths of my being. She took me in her arms, and with an air of serene confidence said: "God willing – you, at least, we shall be able to keep!" *Keep me!* They would keep me beside them! I hung my head and hid my eyes, which at that moment must have had an almost savage look.'

The sea had taken possession for everymore. He would – he *must* – go to sea. 'I would go further than my brother – go everywhere – across the whole world, even . . . But then, how to tell my parents? How could I cause them such unhappiness, how rebel against their wishes? Yet to renounce my plan, and accept to be all the time in one place, to be here, on this earth, and see nothing of it? What use to be alive – to grow up?

'I thought once more of that old ship's log. Those brief phrases written in faded ink, returned to me slowly, with the lulling, dangerous charm of magic incantations: *Fine weather . . . calm seas . . . shoals of dolphins passing to starboard . . .* with almost pantheistic ecstasy I saw in my mind's eye, all around me, the infinite, desolate, yet azure splendour of those southern seas.'

After Gustave's departure, monotony returned to the Viaud house. Julien's second year at college was lightened by the friendship of two other boys, for whom he felt a sentimental affection. This was not allowed to develop, however, for he was kept as strictly aloof as ever; they were only together during classes. Nevertheless, they managed to exchange messages which generally concerned some unknown charmer one or other had sighted in the town.

The boys launched into poetic effusions and Julien inscribed his inamorata's name on his exercise book, but he did not write poetry to her. Indeed, at no point in his overboiling romantic life did Loti express himself in verse. His school-fellows' effusions had affected him with a sort of irritated pity, he remembered. 'They were, in part, the reason why never, at any time in my life, did I have the idea of composing a single verse – something which is, I believe, rather odd: perhaps, even unique.'

What Pierre Loti was to write may not have been in verse form, but by his rhythms, repetitions and images, he was to write some of the most poetic passages in the French language.

A schoolfriend, Paul, was becoming a disturbing influence: 'He could quote verses of a forbidden poet named Alfred de Musset, which had an agitating effect on me, like something at once repulsive and delicious . . .' On the bookshelves in Gustave's narrow little study there was a thick volume of de Musset's poems, but his parents said it was unsuitable for a child of his age. So for the time being, this honourable and docile boy held off, listened furtively to Paul's recitations, dreaming constantly of some unknown vision of loveliness which haunted his sleep and, the family observed, playing Chopin with particular feeling. He was growing up.

One lovely June evening at twilight, he was in Gustave's room standing by the open window, watching the swallows wheeling about the old roof tops, their sharp cries piercing the limpid evening air. 'I was alone, no-one knew where I was . . . With a beating heart I opened the volume of de Musset. *Don Paez!* The first musical phrases seemed as if sung by some dangerous golden voice:

> *Sourcils noirs, blanches mains, et pour la petitesse*
> *De ses pieds, elle était Andalouse et comtesse . . .*

When it was quite dark, and my eyes could distinguish no more of those verses than little grey lines across the white paper, I went out alone, into the town. In the almost deserted, dimly-lit streets rows of lime and flowering acacia trees cast deep shadows and scented the air. Having pulled my hat over my eyes in the manner of Don Paez, I set out, treading softly, lifting my gaze to the balconies, pursuing some sort of childish dream of Spanish nights and Andalusian serenades . . .'

Here was the first of those play-acting sorties that were to become Loti's drug: the boy who now saw himself as a Spanish gallant was to become the man who took refuge from both the present and himself in countless guises . . . in the burnous of an Arab, adventuring in the Kasbah, as a turbanned Turk puffing a narghile on the water front at Khassim Pacha, as a Breton fisherman roistering with the sailors, or a hundred other beings far from his true self.

Early in Julien's childhood a distant cousin had been rediscovered living in the Lot, so that as he grew older, some of his summer holidays were spent away from either the ISLAND or La Limoise. *L'Oncle du Midi*, for this cousin was never called by any other name, possessed a large estate know as Les Bories. The house dated from the time of Louis XIII: it was bleached by the fierce sun of the region which beat down on the white walls and their surrounding vineyards. It was the child's first introduction to that Great Sun – the sun of southern latitudes which he came to know in the tropics, 'Baal, *le grand pourrisseur* – the great destructor', as he calls it, while yet craving its molten heat with a nearly pagan sense of worship.

It was at Breteneux in the summer of 1863 that he decided to write to Gustave telling of his determination to enter the Navy. Gustave, he believed, would be his ally in the inevitable family battle. As he wrote, he realized he was taking the first truly independent decision of his life. 'In the oppressive silence of summer heat, I wrote, and so timidly signed my pact with the navy. For the first time, the world and life seemed to open before me. I saw myself in naval uniform, under a ferocious sun, strolling along the water front of some exotic port: or returning home after perilous voyages, bringing back cases full of astonishing treasures . . . and then, with a sinking heart, I realized that these returns from perilous voyages could only be after many years, and the faces of those I loved, who waited to welcome me back, would be changed by time. I saw them, all those dearly loved faces grouped together, smiling so softly . . . but O! how melancholy to see them now, for they were deeply lined, my mother's hair quite white, and Great-aunt Berthe – already so old – would she still be there? With dread, I was making a rapid calculation of Great-aunt Berthe's age, when I reached the post office . . .

'Nevertheless, with a hand that scarcely trembled, I slipped my letter in the box, and the deed was done.'

Returning from this momentous holiday, the trials of his school days began again; but daily life was less monotonous, since his sister was to marry a cousin, Armand Bon.

'When the great day dawned my sister wished to have me beside her in the carriage, and beside her also, hand in hand, for the cortège. My hair had been frizzed up with art, I wore a coat open over a waistcoat of white satin and my gloves were yellow, "fresh butter", a fashionable colour. On our way, I overheard many compliments and I was pleased, for already my physical appearance displeased me. I was not at all my type.'

There sounds the man who, all his life was to deplore his looks, to

41

hanker after physical perfection, and finding it in others, men or women of all races and conditions, to respond unreservedly.

After Marie's departure and all the flurry of the wedding subsided, the quiet household waited, as if suspended in time, for Gustave's return. By 1865 he had been gone nearly three years and soon would be returning home for good, his letters reassured them. For Julien, all his life was centred round the coming spring: then, not only would Gustave be back, but Lucette too. She, the adored companion of his happiest days at La Limoise had married and sailed for Guyane, leaving Julien with a further sense of loss. Her husband's term of service was to finish about the same time as Gustave's, and since Marie and Armand, the newly-weds, were coming to stay in the early summer, all would be as before.

But Azrael's sombre shadow fell across Julien's path, and nothing was ever the same again.

*

'On a radiant April Sunday, full of warm breezes and the song of birds, my mother and I were returning from service at the Protestant Temple when we saw a small black-clad figure, bent and trembling, who seemed to hesitate, to come forward and then to retreat. At last she drew near, and raising her heavy veil we saw the face of Great-aunt Victorine. She had always been plain but now she was almost frightening to see, her expression that of a trapped animal. ' "You were waiting for us?" asked my mother, her voice already sounding anxious.

' "Yes, my child," replied the old lady. "Come upstairs to your room. I have something to say to you." My mother recoiled, as if she had been stabbed. "What is the matter?" she asked, her voice so hard, I could not recognize it. "What has happened? *My son is dead!*" She began to climb the stairs like one mortally wounded, dragging herself by both hands, while I fled to the further end of the garden, beside my treasured grotto. The sun shone, and the birds continued to sing serenading the spring, as if nothing had happened. "Oh God! I implore you," I prayed. "Oh God! do not let it be true! Oh God! Do not let it happen!" ' But it had happened.

Gustave's health had been shattered by conditions on Poulo Condor, yet his sense of duty had kept him there, although he knew himself condemned. He died at sea on the way home, and it was from an old abbé who had been beside the dying man on the long voyage that the family learned many harrowing details of Gustave's last struggles. Alone at his post after the death of his sole companion the Administrator, Henri Bizot, he had shouldered the whole of his work besides his own doctoring.

Together the two men had faced an overwhelming variety of tasks – the construction of essential buildings, the hospital and a new penitentiary to house the most dangerous criminals, sent there to rot. The climate was extreme, and fevers raged, for the miasmic swamps bred disease.

When Bizot lay dying, he and Gustave read the Bible together and prayed, for they belonged to that nineteenth-century breed of pious young soldiers who were so outstanding in the East at that moment of European colonial expansion. A fervent belief in the Christian mission of colonization sustained them facing life or death.

At this time an appalling kind of comfort seems to have been derived from death-bed scenes, last wishes and locks of hair set in mourning jewellery. Pompous funerals with black-plumed horses, florid tombstones, black-edged envelopes, memorial services and letters of condolences, were all part of the pattern of grieving. The Viauds accepted their sorrow in a Christian spirit of resignation, though this was something Julien could not share. There was further anguish when a large truck containing Gustave's possessions arrived and they gathered to unpack it, to unfold his uniform and put away his violin. They read and re-read a poignant farewell letter that dwelt on his belief in their ultimate heavenly reunion. The dying man had spent his fading strength sorting out his few possessions, tying on labels, scrawled in a dying hand . . . *For J . . . for bon père . . . Tante B. . .* Among these pathetic reminders was a small revolver for Julien, with a warning that it was loaded: something which was to raise his status at school when he wore it at his belt. That his parents permitted him to carry it about proves to what degree they regarded Gustave's wishes as sacred. Perhaps the dying man had hoped this dangerous legacy would help to free Zézin from the smothering domesticity of his upbringing, something he knew he himself would now never be able to combat.

Loti's lifelong sense of loss for this vanished brother, like his lifelong opposition to colonization and his bitter railings at policies which sent the youth of France to their death for colonial gains, may be directly attributed to Gustave's tragic end, just as his burial at sea produced those charnel musings over sailors and sailors' graves which recur throughout Loti's writings.

During Gustave's last hours, knowing he would be buried at sea, he had made a curious request to the Abbé Gros, who now fulfilled it, writing:

> 'Your dear son asked that I should inform you of the exact spot where his body would be confided to the deep. It is in the Bay of Bengal. 6° 11 Latitude North, and 84° 48 Longitude East.'

Loti came to believe his brother had wished the family to know the precise whereabouts of his burial in the hope that he would seem less lost to them, less abandoned or alone in the immensity of the ocean if they were to know where, in those infinite waters, he had been cast. 'Nevertheless – who among us would ever have the chance to make so hazardous a pilgrimage to this tragic spot?'

The stillness of irreparable grief had descended on the Viaud household. Even the arrival of Marie and her husband could not rouse them, nor the thought that Marie's baby, expected in two months' time, was to be born in their rooted backwater. *God gives, God takes away*: but nothing could console them for the loss of Gustave. In transports of grief Marie draped the waiting cradle with Gustave's uniform greatcoat, while Julien plunged into his work, knowing his progress at school was what his brother had desired. Soon Lucette would be home again and he longed for her presence as never before. Early in June a telegram announced the ship bringing her and her husband back had docked at Saint-Nazaire, though a certain anxiety clouded the homecoming. It seemed the climate of Guyane had affected her lungs – they were bringing her home in a *wagon-lit* . . . 'When the train pulled in, I rushed up and down looking everywhere to see her much-loved face. But an almost ghastly apparition held me rooted to the spot. Was this Lucette – this livid spectre with eyes like caverns, who emerged from the *wagon-lit* carried by two men? When she spoke to us her voice was only a hoarse whisper, hardly perceptible, a voice coming from a vault or a coffin . . .'

She died next morning.

Now he realized the full horror of death. Lucette was *dead* . . . 'no more than a poor lost sacrificed thing, that they were going to plunge into the darkness of a sealed tomb, leaving her there, to rot among other corpses . . . Anguish and desperation gripped me . . .'

Loti's lifelong horror of death dates from this moment. It is echoed again and again throughout all he wrote. In the words of François Mauriac (a great admirer of his writings, if not his agnostic sentiments):

> *Loti, lui, ne s'interrompt pas pendant quarante ans de hurler à la mort. Toute son oeuvre n'est qu'une plainte monotone, déchirante.*

An almost pathological strain always caused Loti to luxuriate in charnel horrors: later, when violently in love, he expressed a wish that he might be buried *above* rather than beside his mistress, that their decomposing remains might mingle in death as once, in life, their flesh had done.

Lucette had been the person he had loved best, outside his family world of childhood. Her marriage had come as a cruel shock, for the difference in their ages – seven years – had never appeared to him before, and he was always to rail at the unfortunate husband who had carried her off to Guyane with its killer climate. Had she lived, no doubt his boyish love would have been transposed into an adult passion. She might be older, and married, but both these obstacles would only have been fuel to his romantic nature.

Thus Lucette became a symbol of loss – irreparable loss, always so strong a stimulus. There were to be other loves – many, many other loves and losses – but Lucette's vanished, unattained youthful presence remained to haunt him in recurring dreams.

45

3

*Journeying in search of romance,
and that, after all, is our business
in this world.*

Joseph Conrad

Since Pierre Loti was destined to become not only one of the most praised writers of his day, but also a man whose voyages about the world were coloured by the most sultry and ambiguous relationships, this is the place to recount his first encounter, as a sixteen-year-old boy, with what he was later to describe as *le grand secret de la vie et de l'amour*. It was by this come-by-chance encounter with a gypsy that his taste for exotic loves was fixed. With one or two exceptions, he was always more attracted by primitive races; an unlettered Venus or Adonis whose ardours matched his own, was always to excite the man and inspire the writer. Perhaps this preference for loves that were far removed from him, in both appearance and tradition, stemmed from a sense of inferiority, brought about by his small stature and, in the beginning, his poverty, causing him to seek out those among whom he, small and poor, could cut a dash. He was timid, too; that devouring sensuality to which he was heir, pent-up legacy from generations of austere ancestors, was something to which he could give freer rein out of his class or race. Therefore, since love occupies so important a place in both Loti's life and his writings, let us follow him to his first meeting with this *belle Gitane*, the tawny creature, swaggering in her flounced skirts, selling her clothes-pegs from door to door, and up to mischief one way or another.

Julien was staying with his sister at St Porchaire, a small town twenty miles east of Rochefort, where her husband Armand Bon was the collector of taxes for the region. Their charming old house, white-walled and green-shuttered (now bearing a plaque stating Pierre Loti lived there) stands beside a stone bridge spanning a stream: it is still much as it was when Julien considered it his second home. He had his own room at St Porchaire (which for some reason he calls Fontbruant in his memoirs). All around there was wild, open country, interspersed with forests and dense woods sheltering prehistoric grottos. Some of these were on the estates of Roche-Courbon, a seigniorial castle which many many years ahead he was to write of as *le Château de la Belle au Bois Dormant*, and by so doing, save it from destruction and its magnificent forests from the axe.

Although the château of Roche-Courbon is now marvellously restored – a show place thrown open to the public – few people find their way through the woods to the ravines and grottos where Loti and the gypsy kept tryst. In my pilgrimage about Loti-land – the Saintonge of his origins – I was at Roche-Courbon on a soft grey December day (December was the month he thought these woods were at their loveliest) and followed the labyrinth of tracks he had known. By streams and ravines, in a green twilight cast by the towering evergreen oaks of this region, bouquets of gigantic ferns sprout from high branches like exuberant vegetal fountains. 'Long before I saw real exotic vegetation,' Loti was to remember, 'these ravines had already revealed it to my childish imagination . . .'

Everywhere in these woods there is lushness, greenness; the velvety mosses and lichens are thicker, more plushy than elsewhere. Entering this forest from the open countryside beyond is like coming on some primaeval zone. Tangles of unknown plants edge a stream that threads past the caverns and grottos hollowed in the cliff face, arched low and leading to subterranean galleries where Julien, exploring them with a lamp, liked to imagine a prehistoric race, sharpening their silex knives. The last grotto is beside a glade where a deep pool of unexpected blue – the only blue in all the gamut of green – is fed by a spring trickling from the rocks above. No sound from the outside world reaches this enchanted place, no distant screech of brakes, nor any picnickers' transistor radio breaks the spell: nothing here but stillness: only the soft flutter of birds, high above, where the branches open to the sky. Here I understood those magic woods old fairy tales describe. Yet here, there was nothing of the sinister oppression of northern pine forests – of Hansel and Gretel's terrors.

Gypsies used to camp in these woods, living their lawless poaching life, lounging arrogantly into St Porchaire, doing tinker's jobs as if conferring a favour on the townsfolk. One summer evening at sunset, Julien was sitting under the lime trees of his sister's garden, listening to his brother-in-law and some other men talking of the gypsies – in particular, of one young, insolent beauty – *la belle Gitane* – 'no better than she should be' was the tone of their talk; men's talk . . . 'Suddenly the garden gate opened and a bold girl – she had not deigned to knock – entered as if the place belonged to her.'

'Talk of the devil,' said someone.

Julien was transfixed. 'Even seeing her from a distance, this unexpected creature seemed incomparably lovely, and while she was offering her wares, little reed baskets, our old servant came scornfully to turn her out. Eighteen or twenty years old, perhaps, older than I at sixteen, her tawny smooth skin was the colour of the ancient Etruscan terra cottas; her dress, of cheap printed cotton, was moulded almost too close to her young bosom, that of a statue, which like her body revealed itself as completely free; her heavy black hair was pinned with clinking ornaments; at her small ears hung huge heavy gold rings and round her neck she wore a red silk scarf. What fascinated me above all were her eyes, profound and dark as night, behind which, who knows, there was perhaps nothing – but where one would have said lay all the mysticism and sensuality of India. Chased out by our servant, she went away, silent and haughty, like an outraged queen; but she had certainly understood my amazement and ardent admiration, for before vanishing she twice turned her exquisite small head to look back at me, something which was my undoing.'

Naturally, this encounter was followed by a night of agitated dreams and early next morning, Julien made for the forest and the encampment – *her* world, caravans, horses grazing, and a wood fire where an old witch was cooking something in a huge iron pot. '*La belle Gitane* was there, seated on the ground, weaving her baskets. I crept close – too close, seized with a desire to say "Here I am – I have answered your call . . . Nothing else in the world counts for me now, except you." Naturally, I went away without saying a word – but I was intoxicated by her faint, enigmatic smile, where there was at once consent and irony.'

Julien now began to haunt the ravine in the forest, for it was there she gathered the reeds for her baskets. At last she appeared, 'approaching craftily, making the detours of a cat stalking its prey'. When she reached him, he seized her hand, 'that small savage's hand, as expert at thieving as at weaving baskets . . .' Still without a word, urgent and stumbling with silent complicity, they sought some secret shelter in the green depths of the ravine.

'And there the great secret of life and love was learned. With all my scruples, I found it criminal – almost sacrilegious – but what adorable sacrilege – to be enslaved, to give myself to her wholly, and to give to her this supreme intoxication . . .

'My feast of love lasted little more than a week . . . The townspeople roundabout had begun to complain of thefts from their farms and barns, and I lived in terror the police would expel this little nomad tribe.' Which was what happened. Julien, going as usual to his tryst, found them vanished. Only some blackened lichen marked the place where their fires had been. 'They must have fled in the night . . . but by what route – towards what unknown horizon?'

All the rest of that day, Julien delayed his return home, and at evening was drawn back to that trysting place in the shadowed ravine. There, where he had lain in love with the little thieving gypsy he wept bitter tears. 'Those tears were not for her beauty, or her body – oh no! they were for some look of trust and tenderness which in those last days I had read in her eyes.'

All the ingredients of Loti's subsequent emotional life were formed then and fixed forever. An exotic setting and high passions kindled by someone of another race or class, the fury of the flesh, and then the transposition to some more spiritual or sentimental craving. Lastly, the inevitable separation which Fate (or Loti) always decreed. To Loti, an *ending* became part of his voluptuous agony, something savoured more keenly than any beginning . . . Sunsets were better than sunrise.

To his last day, Loti was to cherish his numerous nostalgias; he, the restless sensualist who had ranged the whole world, interpreting life through love, remembered to the end the hours he had known in the ravines of Roche-Courbon. 'Places where we have neither loved nor suffered leave no trace in our memory,' he wrote, 'but those where our senses have known the incomparable enchantment, we never forget. Thus the ravine of my initiation, with its ferns, its mosses, its mystery and its grottos, has kept for me, for the rest of my life, a nostalgic magnetism.'

After the feast, the fast. When Julien returned to Rochefort at summer's end, life seemed even more monotonous following the

49

blazing intensity of those few days in the forest. He told no-one, just as he did not tell his parents of his still ardent wish to join the navy. It seemed too cruel after Gustave's death. He was resigning himself to becoming an engineer and remaining for the rest of his life at home. Already the ageing relations around him were unconsciously beginning to draw in those nets of love and pity which they had cast so long ago and which were always to entangle him. But suddenly there occurred what Byron describes as *'that moment when the Fates change horses'*.

'Destiny appeared in the guise of a lugubrious individual in a badly brushed top hat. This old gentleman who had the face of a bird of ill omen was my grandmother Texier's solicitor.' Each time he called it was to announce further financial losses, following disastrous investments (which he had advised). Presently, she and her cousins who had remained on the ISLAND were obliged to sell their remaining properties, salt marshes and vineyards and, at last, to renounce the old family house, *'La Maison des Aïeulles'*, the house of the Ancestors. Henceforth the family, both on the ISLAND and at Rochefort, were to know real poverty. They had long been accustomed to living on slender means but now there was even simpler fare; no more riding or piano lessons for Julien and, last sacrifice, it was decided that part of the house must be let. Thus their already cramped quarters were pared down even further.

In 1866, Fate struck another, far more terrible, blow. Théodore Viaud, so upright, so respected, was accused of having embezzled public funds held at the town hall. He was innocent, but he could not clear himself of this grave charge. The bonds had disappeared, never to be found again: nor was the thief discovered. For a while Théodore Viaud went to prison: later, at the end of public investigations which dragged on for nearly two years, his name was cleared – but the large sums of money which had vanished had to be repaid since they had been in his charge and he could offer no explanation as to their loss. Was it an act of jealousy? But by whom and for what motive? The agonies of shame, the scandal and the slights the family suffered at that time could never be forgotten or forgiven by Julien; he became morose, bitter, and was never to refer directly to this calvary.

When his father lost his position at the town hall, he also lost his livelihood upon which all of them depended. On his release from prison some small post at a bank was found for him which testifies to the trust most townspeople continued to accord him; indeed the Admiral, chief of the Préfecture de la Marine, emphasized his esteem for Théodore Viaud by attending the trial in full dress uniform and medals and speaking loudly on his behalf. But there was still the money to be repaid – with interest. For the first time the Viauds were plunged deep in debt, their few inherited treasures sold up. The ladies of the household took orders for the fine needlework at which they excelled, and food was reduced to a bare minimum. Friends rallied round – but the debts mounted. It was from this disaster that Julien's life at sea, his travels, his fame as Pierre Loti, and the large sums his writings earned him, were to derive. Now, at last, the family agreed he should enter the navy since an engineer's training was too long and costly to be considered and it was urgent that Julien should earn his living as quickly as possible. Thus his long-desired wish was granted and, in the manner of such desires, seemed less worthwhile in the having . . . He would go to sea, would come to know the tropics, see the plume-like palms and all that Gustave's letters had described: such things he would see and much more; but the price had been cruel.

Two days after the decision was taken, he transferred from his usual classes and entered those of the Cours de la Marine where other boys, preparing to enter the navy, affected red belts, a sailor's manner, and covered their exercise books with sketches of the fleet. 'I did not draw ships – even in my earliest days; I had never asked, as most boys do, for model steamers, or sailing ships. It was not that aspect of my future career which captivated me: *it was the sea itself*' (the italics are mine), 'its vast expanses, and above all, those far shores, where we would moor beside palm groves.' Where also, he could live another life as another person. Evasions, one way or another, were the leit-motif of his life.

The crucial entrance examinations, which would open or close forever a future at sea, were to be held in four or five months' time; were he to be admitted, he must apply himself as he had never done at school, for now he had to catch up with those who had entered the Cours de la Marine some time before him. Algebra and trigonometry were terrible trials lying ahead. Aunt Claire could no longer help, but he did not need to be spurred on. He knew he must pass at all costs, go through the long cadet's training quickly, and *begin to earn* –

51

not only his own living, but to shoulder the crippling financial burdens that weighed down the family. He flung himself into the struggle, haunted by the spectre of even further disasters. What if the nightmare of seeing a TO BE SOLD notice on the door of their house now came to pass?

To be torn up from those roots he loved, for the family to creep away into some cheap, impersonal lodgings and leave to others their rooms, the flowering courtyard and Gustave's grotto, seemed profanation. It made even the present detestable compromise of letting off half the house bearable by comparison – though there were humiliating aspects of this adaptation at which he rebelled. Seeing his adored mother preparing cheap cuts in a make-shift scullery on a make-shift stove, struck him bitterly. But further humiliations reached a point where hilarity prevailed. From the poky little downstairs quarters, there was no access to the bedrooms they had kept above, for the staircase proper belonged to the part of the house now let. However, *les chères vieilles*, as stoic as ingenious, contrived to reach their rooms by a ladder balanced above the sink. 'The honours of going first devolved on Great-aunt Berthe, the doyenne of our household, since she was nearing eighty. She did not make a very brilliant ascent, and to complicate matters, la Suprématie, the adored cat of my infancy, who was still with us, thought it fitting to accompany us, going close under Great-aunt Berthe's skirts, step by step, the rest of the family following.'

Loti, who seldom found life amusing, admits that helpless laughter overcame them all at this point.

The last weeks of preparing for the examinations Julien spent mostly in Aunt Claire's room; when he was too tired to work any longer, they would turn to the distractions of *Peau-d'Ane*, the model theatre which was one of the few amusements left that cost nothing. In view of a hoped-for maritime future, they were preparing an aquatic scene. Chaotic rocks in strange ocean depths were veiled by scraps of green gauze (for Julien had yet to learn first-hand from submarine crews 'that sunlight penetrating down through deep waters is not a green gold, but sinister blood red'). To surround the green of the waves, there were corals, shells and extravagant vegetation. In these creative flights aunt and nephew could forget the strain of work for a while and later the mounting tension of waiting to know the examination results. 'These were to be announced on a Wednesday evening, and day by day, with a plaintive melancholy, I repeated the same phrase: "Oh! Aunt Claire, if only you knew *how* I long for that Wednesday evening to arrive!"

' "It will arrive, my poor child, it will arrive, your Wednesday evening: I promise you, it will arrive," she replied and her words seemed some sibylline utterance. "It will arrive, your Wednesday evening, and it will pass, and others will arrive, evenings or mornings, even more longed-for, that will give you the illusion of bringing some changes, big or small . . . but nevertheless . . ." She stopped short, and I saw her face alter; her eyes dilated as if looking back into faraway memories . . . For the first time I realized the emptiness of all life, the nothingness of my future, or our hopes.'

'As Aunt Claire predicted, it arrived – my longed-for Wednesday evening. I had passed! I was admitted to the Naval College. It had arrived, my Wednesday, and it had gone . . . I should have been overjoyed, delivered from the nightmare of overwork and examinations . . .' But no: that little phrase, so simple in appearance – *it will arrive, and it will pass* had cast a shadow over everything. Then, too, the thought of the coming partings weighed on the whole household. It had been decided that in order to catch up with pupils who had entered a year earlier, Julien should go to Paris and make concentrated studies at the Lycée Henri IV in the hopes of being admitted sooner to the Naval School at Brest, where, for a year, the cadets lived aboard a sailing ship, learning the practical aspects of a sailor's apprenticeship. In Paris he was to be under the wing of relations who wrote saying they would install him in students' lodgings near the Lycée. It was an alarming prospect, although Aunt Claire and his sister Marie both dwelt firmly on the pleasures of the Louvre.

Before leaving, Julien was obliged to give up the room that had been his precious museum: it was to be acquired by the new tenants. Feverishly, he began packing up his innumerable treasures, the fossils, shells and butterflies. But those *things* – those far more precious souvenirs to which he clung – they took infinitely longer and were infinitely more dear: old toys, souvenirs of Gustave or Lucette; above all, the small desk at which he had written Fédin's secret journal: it had come from the ISLAND, had belonged to his ancestors, and was sacrosanct. Everything must be shrouded in clean white paper: some things were wrapped in pieces of flowered muslin which had been one of Great-aunt Berthe's dresses around 1805, thereby making the packets doubly precious. Camphor and aromatic herbs were spread about, Aunt Claire assisting at these funereal or embalming rituals. When all was done and the whole collection installed in the small closet that now served as his bedroom, they closed the door, sealing it from moths or prying eyes by sticking bands of paper all round. Looking back he wrote: 'A child who took such extreme precautions and feared so much, preparing to leave the paternal roof, was really little armed for life – little armed against time and death.'

Against those two enemies he was never to be armed.

Julien had never left the family circle before, his only journeys being to the Midi. Paris seemed on another planet and he dreaded all he had heard of the city life. As well he might, for anyone less suited to that glittering and cynical metropolis would be hard to imagine. The 9th of October, 1866, was the day of his departure: 'My trunks stood ready; my poor wardrobe was composed of garments meticulously repaired and adjusted: as precious possessions I took with me Lucette's last letters and those of my brother, as well as his Bible, that had returned to us from Indo-China.' This was the Bible his mother had given Gustave on his first departure. Now she gave it to Julien. It was to be his talisman, a link with his roots – those roots which twined so lovingly – which held so fast. Beside his mother, carrying a basket of provisions, he made a painful farewell visit to his father in the town jail: the jailer had the humanity to let them meet in the prison garden rather than in Théodore's cell, but it was a harrowing moment. Sorrow piled on sorrow. As if every parting was to be an eternal one (for already this lifelong habit was formed), Julien took a last, lingering look at Gustave's little grotto and la Suprématie purring in the sun; and then, putting on a shabby pair of black gloves 'so miraculously mended by my mother, "only for the journey", I got into a train for the first time in my life.'

His childhood was over, but during the whole of his lonely, impoverished time in Paris, he lived still netted in the tangles of love and pity he felt for those he had left in Rochefort. He hated every moment of his life in the capital: he could neither appreciate it nor be integrated; the carefree student life of the Latin Quarter was not for him, so full of care. He was lodged in a small room overlooking chimney stacks and the spire of Saint-Etienne-du-Mont. It was dingy, and a broken-down cupboard filled him with repugnance, imagining what sort of garments had formerly hung there. With the old-maidish ways instilled in him by the *chères vieilles*, he now shrouded his clothes in layers of paper to avoid any contact with the cupboard's unsavoury interior.

'My Paris relations welcomed me affectionately, though without ever warming my heart. They saw to it that my wardrobe was refurbished, which touched me, but I put away my old, mended, clothes from Rochefort with pious care, and still wore them from time to time, so as not to have renounced them altogether. As for the gloves my mother had mended so carefully "just for the journey" I need not say that they took their place among my most cherished relics.' Poor, pathetic, lonely Julien, so far from home and tormented by fears he might not pass the crucial examination. Were he to fail to be admitted as a cadet officer, he knew his parents would never consent to his becoming a simple rating, and the sea would have no place in his future life.

Julien's relatives chose to regard him as an adult and, on his Thursdays and Sundays free of classes, supposed he would be off and out, kicking up his heels among the other students. Some of these were Levantines, mostly sons of rich families, smart young monkeys there to enjoy themselves rather than study, and Julien despised them, choosing to spend his free time in further study. His only friend, an equally lonely, impoverished boy, was Turkish, 'a gentle, mystic character, who died of pneumonia at the first chill of autumn'. Was the immediate sympathy which he felt for this Turk only because both were homesick exiles, or was there, already, some subconscious pull towards that race which came to mean so much to him that he wished to change his whole life and religion to live among them? In any case, Julien felt himself as much a foreigner in Paris as the Turkish boy.

When his cousins took him sightseeing, he remained aloof. 'In the middle of Paris I was like one of those young savages that are brought from their forests, and do not deign to be even astonished. Nothing amazed me, unless, perhaps, the Louvre, and the Opera, where, during my first days, they took me to hear *Les Huguenots*' (an appropriate choice). Thus, alone in his attic, Julien was bent over the hateful problems of trigonometry and abstract formulas, and when he paused to look out at the gathering autumn twilight, he imagined the life in the streets below. 'An agglomeration of labour and suffering pressed round me, taking away what little air there was to breathe. I longed to escape – anywhere, into the countryside, among fields and trees . . .'

Julien's Parisian cousins seem to have been generously disposed, for they recognized his talent as a budding pianist and engaged an excellent professor for him. The professor approved of what he called Julien's *qualité de son*, and taught him that 'lingering, singing touch' which was always remarked by Loti's listeners.

Music solaced – but even so, the life of the lonely boy between classes and the dingy student's room was gloomy. One rainy Sunday, having reached unbearable depths of depression alone among the roofs and chimney pots of the chill, indifferent city, he sought to recapture the warmth and tenderness of his childhood by writing a memoir of those days, only so lately passed yet seeming centuries away. This was not written in the code of his first venture, but a note-book was soon filled with an infinitesimally small script. It was the first of those detailed day by day journals which Loti was to keep throughout his life, his beautiful flowing handwriting filling over two hundred volumes before his death.

'That first poor little journal helped me to overcome many sad hours. Of course I had not been able to bring my *Peau-d'Ane* theatre with me, but I had brought my paint box, and this was also one of my distractions. I painted mostly landscapes of Saintonge, always under exaggeratedly blue southern skies. I now began to go to the Louvre, which fascinated me, as Aunt Claire had predicted. This was a providential outing for me, such a well-behaved boy, above all so poor, far too well dressed for my empty purse, and reproaching myself if I so much as entered a café, spending the little pocket money my relations gave me.'

Nevertheless, towards the end of his student days in Paris, there was the classic encounter with a grisette, one of those charming, feckless little creatures who, in the manner of Murger's Mimi in *La Vie de Bohème* (Puccini's version was yet to come), shared the fortunes and couch of a succession of students around the Boul' Mich. They had met, by chance, in a brasserie where Julien's companions occasionally persuaded him to join them, though he fled the prostitutes and cheap brothels they enjoyed. This girl was considerably older than he, but 'deliciously pretty', and neither she nor her clothes appeared vulgar. Julien was fastidious, lonely and ardent, and he had not forgotten the intoxications of *la belle Gitane*. Thus for some while his free Thursdays were not so dependent on the Louvre for pleasure; she showed him warmth and a tenderness which he craved.

All went well, until she began to display an enveloping, maternal side, which he found a profanation – that was not her rôle. Her way of questioning him about his family and home infuriated him; ' "I have no family – I am alone in the world" I would repeat, harshly.' At the end of one of their Thursdays together there was a scene: as usual he had been stalling her questions, when she broke out: ' "No family – no family – all the same you must have had a mother?" "*No!* I've already told you – *no!*" I said, as if just pronouncing the word *mother* was an outrage. She hung her head: "Very well, I understand, you don't want me to go near any of that." And her expression was so humiliated, so tortured, that it went right to my heart. I left her, but I promised myself to be gentler the following week . . . After all, her obstinate wish to know something of my life was only a further proof of her affection.

'Next Thursday, when I knocked on her door at the usual time, there was no answer. I knocked again insistently, and a young person who lived on the same floor opened her door. "Ah! it's you, her *petit ami de coeur*." With an unpleasant air of connivance she said: "So you didn't know? She was rushed to hospital last night – some intestinal operation – urgent, it seems." A week later I learned she had died under the surgeon's knife . . . Eight days had passed . . . by now she was nothing more than some terrifying remains, under the ground, or, what wrung my heart more, perhaps now only a piece of mummified flesh spread out for dissection in a laboratory . . . Poor girl! for three months or more of my exile she had given me all she possessed – her body, still beautiful, her lovely eyes, and the softness of her smile . . . which is why, here, among names more hallowed and loved I tell hers: *Paule*. It is in place of that devout farewell visit I was unable to make, for I could never discover to what anonymous hole they had consigned her body – no doubt some wretched and neglected cemetery.'

So ended young Julien's sole experience of *amour* in the classic Parisian terms of poor student and generous grisette.

Egocentricity and an over-developed sense of pathos were funda-mental characteristics of both the young Julien and the older Loti, their extreme sensitivity frequently edging pathos towards bathos. Yet there was one crucial event in his forlorn life in Paris which he describes simply, without undue emotion, and which is truly touching. It concerned his confirmation, an event which, in France, has always been surrounded by ceremonial conventions and domestic rejoicings.

Julien's family wished him to be confirmed at Easter, while still in Paris. He was past seventeen, the age at which Protestants were customarily confirmed. Julien, still clutching at his dwindling faith, asked that it could be postponed till he returned among them. Biblical threats against those who approached the altar unworthily haunted him, and the phantom of the dead Paule rose before him. But the family were adamant. He must seize salvation while in Paris. Downcast but still docile, Julien complied, only to be smothered in dogmas – a dusty answer to his confused spiritual longings.

'When that Easter Sunday came, I was deeply distressed . . . There was no-one to accompany me to the church: I was completely alone on this solemn occasion, while all the other young people were surrounded by their families . . . I thought I ought to put on my best clothes – an elegant spring suit that my cousins had ordered for me; black velvet jacket, tight fitting trousers, a Shakespeare collar with long points, and "ox-blood" coloured gloves. But when I saw myself reflected in the warped looking-glass, I was embarrassed. I seemed the sort of type then called a toff or swell. Was that really me – ex-lover of the girl from the brasserie who was going to present myself at the altar? In haste I tore off those clothes and put on some shabby winter things, and still alone, feeling deserted, hurried off to the church. When that first communion, on which I had pinned so many high hopes, was over, and I found myself in the Rue de Rivoli, lost, among the noisy Sunday crowds, I had that same terrible impression of emptiness – of nothingness, which, so many years later I was to know again, even more strongly, in Jerusalem.' But he was never to find faith anywhere and remained solitary and uncomforted in the great city.

Even Paris in April, the moment when it is alleged to be at its best, though this is seldom so, could not charm Julien. But, 'In May I fell suddenly in love with the Empress Eugénie and lost many hours of work waiting for her carriage to pass. Lying back in her landau, which had quite another allure to the automobiles of princes today, she was a dream of perfect beauty: no other woman's profile was comparable to hers. During the last months of my time in Paris her image alone sufficed to preserve me from the sort of women my companions frequented.'

Loti's writings show him to have had total recall, no detail of his life being too small to be remembered or recorded. Yet of the turning point – his sitting for and passing the entrance examinations for the Naval School – he had no remembrance beyond the fact that they were held in the Rue de Lille, in an oppressive silence, while in the July sunshine of 1867, the Exposition Universelle turned Paris into a fairground.

The examinations over, he was free, at last, to quit Paris. 'And I, who have so often known that tightening of the heart when leaving some quarters that I have, perhaps, only inhabited for a few days, did not even turn back for a last glance.' Joyously, he took the cheap night train to Rochefort and found the whole family waiting for him on the platform. But for a moment even that radiant morning clouded over . . . 'Nothing had prepared me for that sad impression, one so often to be experienced later in my life, when, each time I returned, it was to find them aged a little more.' How to hold back the clock? How to hold, for ever, all he loved? It was his perpetual, unanswered cry.

Paris had neither amazed nor delighted him, but now, Rochefort enchanted him. Its quiet streets, its little white houses, so calm and clean . . . the light skies, the soft air . . . As to the old house, with its flowering courtyard and Gustave's grotto . . . that was paradise regained. Nothing seemed to matter now he was home once more – even though it was only half the home he had once known.

Later in that first rapturous day Julien realized a dream he had cherished ever since his music professor in Paris had initiated him into the mysteries of the 'singing touch'. He and his mother would be alone together and he would play for her – for her alone – some of his new repertoire, *in this new manner!*

Thus, in the drowsy heat of the summer afternoon, the long-desired moment arrived; but hardly had the opening chords sounded before the door was pushed open a crack, and la Suprématie entered. He had been roused from a nap in his favourite place under the honeysuckle on hearing the piano which had been silent all the time Julien was away. He sprang onto the pianist's shoulders, ever his favourite perch, and at that moment of fulfilment, Julien plunged into the *Appassionata*, his cup of happiness overflowing.

In September the *Moniteur* published a list of candidates passed into the Naval School, Julien among them. Now the inevitable and prolonged parting loomed ahead, but it did not seem so agonizing as he had feared. Life at Brest, on the training ship *Borda*, would in no way resemble that hateful Paris exile. He made a round of farewell visits almost light-heartedly – even to his father, still in jail. The life he had chosen and worked so hard to obtain, was approaching, while the financial responsibilities he meant to shoulder came a step nearer too. One day the house would be all theirs again, his father's name cleared, and his *chères vieilles* would live in comfort and peace as before. Such were his aims.

Farewell was always a word Loti found hard to pronounce, although he often lingered over it voluptuously and it was to be the theme of so many of his writings. But now, with those beckoning tropic horizons opening before him anguish was dimmed. At the beginning of October 1867 he left Rochefort with eight other boys also going to the Naval School at Brest. For the first year they were to live aboard the *Borda*; the following year to make preliminary voyages manning a sailing ship along the coasts of France; the third year, as full-fledged cadets, to put their training into practice on a prolonged voyage across the world, in all weathers and seas.

At that time there was no railway linking Saintonge and Brittany, and the boys went by river-steamboat, arriving the evening of the second day. In the chill Breton damp the town, with its grim granite walls, seemed as alien in another way as Paris. At the naval base eighty or more cadets were each allotted a number which for the next three years would take the place of their name. Julien had never known strict discipline nor been to boarding school, and now, for the first time, realized he was no longer Julien, let alone Zézin bijou round whom his whole family had revolved – he was merely a number. Being fitted out with a sailor's wardrobe, answering to barked-out commands, struggling into rough shirts, serge trousers and sailcloth jackets as stiff as cardboard left no time for apprehension. Along with their names, the cadets surrendered their own clothes and all personal belongings; but the gruff petty officers took pity on Julien's forlorn look and allowed him to keep his Bible and the letters of Lucette and Gustave which he stowed away inside his rough shirt.

As if to welcome them, the day was warm and golden and the sea a pale blue mirror as they approached the great sailing vessel. 'It was one of those old ships, dating from the heroic days of sail: one of those majestic vessels that had kept its masts; it was painted in wide bands of alternating black and white which marked off its three superimposed decks [much as Nelson's *Victory*, in Portsmouth harbour]. It bore no resemblance to those infernal grey machines which are our present-day warships. Its masts rose into the quiet evening sky with all their scaffolding of main yards and riggings: today they are abolished, replaced by depressing steel cabling, but at that time, for those young creatures on board, they were an incomparable school of agility and health.

'The *Borda!* we had arrived – we were almost touching it, and the red sinking sun glowed over the fresh paintwork of its monumental poop, which was in the old style, with beautiful caryatids leaning out over the water, supporting the commander's quarters by their muscular arms.'

In a state of intense emotion, Julien climbed aboard. 'This floating cloister was huge and light and welcoming: it smelt of scrubbed pine, tarred ropes, salt, seaweed – and the sea.'

That night, they slept in hammocks slung high which, both to sling and to clamber into, were complicated feats for novices. In the darkness, Julien heard the ship's bell ringing the hour, and from the watch, the old cry: *All quiet to starboard*, and the answering cry: *All quiet to port*. To this lullaby he slept. The shadowed roots of his childhood were left ashore. The sea had claimed him, as he had always known it would.

4

I broke through the doors of sunset
Ran before the hooves of sunrise.

Francis Thompson

As a prelude to the kaleidoscopic brilliance of those shifting scenes which lay ahead for Julien, his apprenticeship on the *Borda* had first to be lived out in all its severity. 'That floating cloister where our youth was shut away . . . a rough, austere life,' he recalled it. Nevertheless, it was *life* – and in other terms to the swaddling of the Rue Saint-Pierre. Some of the old officers, white-bearded or peg-legged veterans, had served with the Napoleonic fleet, had fought at Trafalgar or Aboukir, and still held to the traditions and conditions of those days. Reveille sounded at 5 a.m. Two and a half hours of exercise and a round of mathematics, trigonometry and more followed, all on an empty stomach. At 8.15 there was a brief pause for a spartan breakfast. More classes followed, where much of the instruction was archaic. After a midday meal, a fifteen-minute break – the only one of the day – allowed them to walk about a small space on the upper deck. Then followed classes in practical instruction, navigation, gunnery, sailing, and such.

Three days a week small groups went out, in any weather, generally lashed by Atlantic gales, to learn the skills of handling small boats. The icy sea mists which usually roll in to envelop the coast of Brittany, drenched their rough canvas clothing and numbed their fingers. Some boys never overcame the scourge of seasickness: but this was considered self-indulgence, and not admitted. There was cannon and firing practice, and days when they were marched, in uniform, to fife and drum beat, through the streets of Brest for military drill with rifle and sabre. Swarming up and down the rigging or dragging the massive guns, their hands became raw by contact with the tarred ropes. The second year they were sent up aloft to trim the sails, though each novice was accompanied by a matelot to guide him, for the gigantic sails and booms were dangerous and such exercises did not wait for calm weather. As the ship reeled in the heavy swell, there were still the great masts (the highest was 62 metres) to be faced – to be conquered. But these and other trials Julien passed with courage; he, the little, protected creature of mufflers and fussing, proved more agile, more hardy than might have been expected, though at one point he went down with an injured knee and mumps.

The tough old captains in charge of the cadets did not think much of Julien's chances of survival. 'My boy,' said one of them, eyeing the small sickly-looking figure, 'I doubt you're the stuff to stay the course . . . but if you are, then you must learn never to be put out by the roughness of our seamen. And later, if ever you have the honour to command them, never forget their worth . . . never forget how they are, in hours of danger . . . It is we who should kneel to them!' The old salt's eyes filled with tears, remembering the men and battles of past, heroic times. The boy was never to forget his words and always to consider it an *honour* to command those sailors of whom he was to write with such understanding.

He was homesick, though never so desperately as in Paris: he missed his family, his piano, and the soft green countryside of La Limoise. From time to time the cadets were put ashore for a few hours in that perpetual Breton damp, near some harsh fishing village, where there was nothing to do but order lobster and cider feasts – expensive treats Julien could not afford. He would like to have picked the wild flowers and mosses he always loved, but there was no place he could put them on board. A hammock was all he could call his own. Thus he withdrew into himself and, in his loneliness and proud unrevealed poverty, was sometimes judged standoffish.

Nevertheless at this time he formed several friendships which were to be of long standing. The good-natured, rakish Prince Murat soon proved too undisciplined, left the service and settled in Russia, from where he kept up his friendship with Julien, following his transformation into Pierre Loti, with pride, often urging the writer to visit him in St Petersburg. Another shipmate, Lucien Hervé Jousselin (who becomes Plumkett in Loti's writings), was to play a capital rôle in Loti's literary life. This remarkable man appears as oddly placed on a warship as Loti, for he was deeply cultivated, a dilettante and lover of the arts: yet, like Loti, an excellent officer too. It seems that the French, with their profoundly intellectual traditions, were able to combine culture and quarter-deck in a manner less common to most other navies. Whereas in the British armed forces, a writer's reputation was likely to be eyed with suspicion, if not scorn, among the French it was a passport to respect and interest. Jousselin's critical faculties were to be of inestimable value to Loti; they came to share the same disillusioned Byronic pessimism and in their exchanges, such as are published in *Aziyadé, Fleurs d'Ennui*, or *Un Jeune Officier Pauvre*, it is sometimes difficult to tell them apart; although Plumkett was never so neurotic, so vibrant with emotions, and always remained with one foot firmly on the ground.

'He always saw too clearly what I tried to hide,' wrote Loti, recalling their long years of friendship. But in those early years, it was another cadet, Joseph Bernard, who played the most significant rôle in Loti's new life. They were inseparable, and Julien lavished the whole of his emotional craving for the long-mourned Gustave on Joseph, who became *'le frère chéri, frère adoré'*. To which Joseph replied by sending him 'a thousand kisses'. Joseph's family were pious Catholics, rich hidebound citizens of Lille. Nothing could have been further (except in religious fervour) from Julien's family background, just as no-one could be more dissimilar physically than the two friends – Julien so small and dark and Joseph so large and fair, the bearded Wagnerian tenor in type. But theirs was a relationship which Joseph's family, unused to the extravagant emotional terms current in the Viaud household, presently began to eye coldly – perhaps with reason.

Certain aspects of Loti's nature were wholly feminine: although he could be despotic and demanding, he also had a passive side and enjoyed being dominated. Joseph coddled him, writing to remind him about bringing his warm flannels, having his hair cut this way or that. They shared quarters ashore, while the Viaud family became 'our family', 'we send our fond love . . .' etc. etc. In short, a devoted pair.

Late in 1869 the two friends, now *aspirants de 2e classe* (midshipmen), embarked on the *Jean Bart* for a training cruise about the Mediterranean ports and those of North and South America. A halcyon voyage, it seemed to Julien. The open sea – the great ocean – spread before him, and the tropic shores of which he had dreamed drew near. Algiers was his first contact with Islam, with the Moslem people and their ways, which were to mark him and hold him, above all others, for the rest of his life. That first contact was brief, joyous, but purely touristic: the cadets swarmed about the ancient alleyways of the Kasbah, puffed experimentally at narghiles in the cafés round the harbour, bought babouches – those yellow Arab slippers which had not yet been superseded by Western shoes – and Julien collected a baby tortoise, Sulïema, who was to live on, in the Rue Saint-Pierre, for fifty years. He was always to recall those first rapturous hours in Algeria, 'the most radiant of my whole adult life . . . All filled me with a delicious intoxication, unlike that produced anywhere else . . . Those nights in the Kasbah, with the scents of orange, and strange incense, and O! the great painted eyes of the Mauresque women . . .'

Setting sail westward, making for South America, he now met the open sea in all its moods. Lulled by its shimmering stillness, challenged by its angry darkness, its tides and treacheries, its seductions and terrible powers, he saluted it as his chosen universe. And when at last land was sighted it must have seemed an intrusion, coming between himself and that element to which he was given.

From southern seas, Julien had written to his father, for the first time expressing that sense of fulfilment he felt in the life he had chosen. This was something he particularly wished his father to know, for *bon père*, of the whole family, would best understand his happiness, even though he found it so far from home roots. This letter was never read by Théodore Viaud, for it reached Rochefort a few days after his death, on June 8th, 1870. He had struggled to recover from the crushing miseries of the accusations and imprisonment, and had worked on in the lowly position which was all he could obtain after his release from prison. He was a broken man and his acquittal, like his son's letter, came too late. Julien's mother wrote harrowing accounts of his last hours when all his thoughts had been for his remaining son, and how she was certain he had been *praying for Julien with his last breath*. She was careful to underline this and harrow Julien the more.

To bind the family even closer in their grief, Marie wrote to say they were now quite penniless and would be forced to sell the house. There was not even money for a gravestone. Since their father's death no money whatever was coming in, and it was doubtful whether his widow would obtain a pension from the municipality. She reluctantly humbled herself further to apply for one: she had her sister and old Aunt Berthe to care for, and could not afford to be proud. The Viauds had remained esteemed in spite of the protracted climate of suspicion engendered by the trial: thus the Town Council looked favourably, if patronizingly, on the widow's petition and pronounced in favour of an annual grant of 400 francs . . . but even then some mysterious hatred pursued the family. When the Council voted, in secret, one of the seven-men ballot papers remained blank. Thus the vote was not unanimous and the grant was reduced drastically. The Viauds' unknown persecutor was probably the same person who was responsible for Théodore Viaud's inculpation.

Now almost the whole financial burden of the *chères vieilles* fell on Julien. Not only had he to try to provide for them as quickly as possible, but there were, too, his father's debts to be met. Although he was not legally responsible for these, he scrupulously accepted the charge though it would be another year before his first pay packet could even begin to meet some of these responsibilities. Ever since they had fallen on hard times Julien had been haunted by the spectre of having to sell up the old house in the Rue Saint-Pierre. Now it seemed inevitable. Every letter from home plunged him into deeper distress. Marie wrote frantically suggesting various last hopes. Julien was now head of the household – the man of the family, ever the undisputed master by French law and custom. He must write here or there, to cousins or well-to-do friends, proposing mortgages or loans; every letter suggested some further humiliating or impractical measure. Julien felt hunted, harassed, trapped. The Siegfrieds, a wealthy family into which Marie had once hoped Gustave would marry, were approached as a last, painfully humiliating resort. They replied by an odiously hypocritical letter still to be seen among Loti's papers. It is full of noble sentiments, though backing away from any positive help. Now Joseph, *le frère adoré*, came forward with heart-warming schemes. He and Julien, who already shared their modest shipboard expenses, should reduce their joint expenditure and put something aside regularly for Julien's family. The friends shared every aspect of life, the problems of one being the concern of the other, but to Joseph's fury the Bernard family stepped in to forbid his mortgaging an inheritance from his mother in favour of Julien.

By some miracle, and the help of the Duplais family who stood beside the Viauds as staunchly as ever, the house remained in their hands; but their poverty was desperate. Julien sent his mother a few postage stamps he had been saving so that she could buy some small luxury for her birthday. She wrote back saying she would get a quarter of a pound of chocolate creams which Great-aunt Berthe and

Aunt Claire would relish; she would keep the rest for necessities. The rest cannot have provided very much, and this poignant thought, and the picture of his *chères vieilles* in their proud penury going hungry even, tormented him ceaselessly. Where to turn for money? How to earn? The other cadets around him all seemed so carefree, had ample pocket-money, had parents who sent expensive presents, and could spend money ashore. How rich everyone else seemed! Debts – cares – debts . . . When letters from home arrived he now dreaded to open them, much as he longed for news. In a letter to his sister he writes: 'I do still hope to save it' (their old house) 'which encourages me, but I have moments of terrible anguish, so that sometimes I dash my head against the walls like a madman . . .' Julien's already fragile nervous system was over-taxed, leaving a strain of insecurity and brooding apprehension for evermore.

On July 19th 1870 war was declared between France and Germany, and the *Jean Bart* raced for French shores. When Loti left it, his apprenticeship was over. As midshipman he was transferred to the *Décres*, a corvette patrolling the North Sea and Baltic waters. That winter was a grim one for him, tormented by financial anxieties, lashed by the gales in a wretched small ship, keeping watch through long nights, searching those black horizons for the shadow of an enemy ship, from where a shell sometimes leapt at them across the icy waters. 'A useless, sacrificed time', which filled the sailors with bitterness as, day by day, they received news of France's disasters on land.

Loti's journals of this time have been lost, thus we know little of his life then except from a few letters and sparse naval records, where it is clear that one commanding officer did not note him with sympathy: '*spoilt child, sickly complexion, artistic temperament*' was the pithy verdict. As he was keeping a cat, Sulïema, the North African tortoise, a monkey, and a muddle of paint boxes and sketch-books in his cabin, it is possible the commandant's views were clouded. However, he was presently transferred to the *Vaudreuil*, where things went better. *Excellent cadet, agreeable character, very good education, will make a first class officer* was how he was next noted.

The South American ports of call he came to know from serving on the *Vaudreuil*, and later, on the *Flore* were then strange, adventurous little towns, barely imposed on the fringes of the jungle. Their harbours piled with rare merchandise, their ornate white-sugar architecture and palmy plazas were the naïve landscapes still represented so gaily on cigar-box lids. They were all part of that richly coloured world he had vowed to know as a child in Rochefort; and coming on it now was some reward for the denials and disciplines of these last years. Inland from Valparaiso lay the immense stretches of the pampas with its picturesquely clad gauchos: in the cities, there were the señoritas to be eyed as they passed, accompanied by the inevitable duenna. Did Julien recall that summer evening when, as a schoolboy, greatly daring, he had first read *Don Paez* and set out in the dusk to yearn up at the balconies of Rochefort, imagining himself a Spanish gallant seeking some dark-eyed señorita? Lima was the time and the place for such gallantry, but where was the dulcinea? Behind an overhanging mirador or along some crowded street, among the black slaves, friars, fruit vendors and carriage folk? Or was she one of those mysterious veiled women, the *tapadas* whom Moritz Rugenda's paintings of Peru have immortalized? The manner in which the *tapadas* wore their veils was as typical of South American seduction as the Spanish mantilla; of dark silk rather than lace, they were held across the face leaving only one Cyclops-like eye free to cast its invitation . . . something unlikely to have been lost on the young Frenchmen, whether midshipmen or ratings.

Late in 1871 he was transferred to the frigate *Flore*, the Admiral's flagship which was heading for Tahiti. Joseph Bernard was transferred with him, and the prospect of reaching those scented isles that Gustave had known enchanted Julien. But first they were to visit Easter Island, there to make detailed reports on this barren and inhospitable territory, for France was then taking a lively interest in its new colonies or any lands which might become such. Legends of the mysterious Easter Isle which lay lost in the immensity of the seas between Chile and Tahiti added to its sinister reputation, and the lower deck muttered of cannibals awaiting them if they went ashore. Other, less alarming stories of gigantic stone figures and monolithic heads of unfathomable origin were subjects of speculation in the ward-room. The primitive race which inhabited the island was of Maori descent, though no-one – not even they – could say how they had first reached this bleak land. Captain Cook had passed that way, and missionaries had left reports of visits, where a wholesale conversion to Christianity had been accepted as a diversion in the natives' monotonous lives, but which had given place to the old heathen gods and barbarous practices before the missionaries' boats were out of sight.

Such information intrigued Julien, who was seized with the idea that were he to write up his impressions as he did in his journals and illustrate them with sketches he might be able to sell them to one of the leading French periodicals such as *Illustration* or *Le Tour du Monde*. Were they accepted, it would augment the family budget. They *were* accepted: snapped up, in fact, editors pressing for more. Thus, before he became a novelist, he was what today would be called a roving reporter. Photographic reporting was not then daily news; there were no radio or television bulletins and few on-the-spot dispatches. The American Civil War had been superbly photographed by Brady, the Crimean campaign by Roger Fenton, where there were also the brilliant sketches of Constantin Guys, for the *Illustrated London News*. But exotic impressions of remote quarters of the globe were still rare, fascinating to editors and readers alike. Julien had become an exceptionally talented draughtsman: both his sketches and more ambitious paintings were far above amateur level. He was one of that galaxy of nineteenth-century writers such as Victor Hugo, Lermontov, de Musset, Thackeray, Fromentin and many others who could express themselves by pen or pencil. Thus Julien was able to turn his life at sea into something which had a market on land. The sea, which had claimed him, now began to reward him materially.

The following extracts are taken from his journals, rather than the published reports which were changed or edited without his knowledge, and to his subsequent exasperation.

This is his description of the *Flore*'s approach to Easter Island. Already the Loti flavour is apparent as he brings this desolate and still little-known scene before us. 'Slowly, the strange island approaches, and becomes clearer: under a sombre clouded sky it reveals reddish craters and desolate rocks. A high wind blows and the sea is covered in white spray. Rapa-Nui is the natives' name for Easter Island – and merely in the consonants of this word there seems to be the sadness, the savagery of *night*. The night of times past,

69

the night of its origins, of what obscurity one cannot say . . . but it is certain that those black clouds, out of which the island emerges, correspond exactly to my imaginings . . .'

Julien's taste for natural history and the exotic had been noted by the Admiral, who chose him to lead a small expedition ashore to make sorties about the island, reporting and acquiring objects of interest, flora and fauna, weapons or domestic utensils. Above all, he was charged to obtain information as to the possibility of acquiring one of the giant stone figures. Julien's early interests had prepared him for such specialized work – a mixture of geology, botany, ethnography and anthropology. Already his eye was a selective one, as his ear was acutely tuned to every nuance of a strange tongue. Such a young officer was invaluable, and the Admiral now detailed him for more and more expeditions ashore. He was astonished to find that Cadet Viaud seemed at once accepted, and able to communicate with 'the savages'. That was always to be Loti's especial gift. By a curious sixth sense of sympathy – or his own magic of intuition – he would contrive, within days, to be on terms of confidence, on speaking terms, wherever he went. On *sleeping* terms, cynics might add, but although this was generally true, as it was of so many European travellers, soldiers or explorers, numbers of them never acquired more than pillow-talk, while Loti came to discuss religions, philosophies, politics and local legends too. Now the young midshipman was wholly absorbed in his work, and the cares and ties of Rochefort, if not forgotten, were sublimated to this new freedom of expression. What he was doing now was an extension of those happy hours spent in his museum. This was living and working as he had always believed he should: it was quite apart from facile tourism or whoring in the ports of call, the accepted sailors' way.

Although there are now runaways all over the world, and no area is left unvisited, travellers are still seldom inclined towards the tip of South America. Easter Island's history is a cruel one. Successive ships put in only to pillage or massacre, leaving a trail of disease and disaster and the island remains an uninviting terrain, still overcast by a legacy of brooding tragedy.

Here are Loti's first impressions on landing. 'In a moment the whole shore was covered with savages. They emerged, as if by some miracle, from little huts, so low it appeared impossible they could contain a human being. In the dim morning light they were waving their silex lances, and their ancient doll-like idols . . . There it was –

Easter Isle! Rapa-Nui . . . just as I had dreamed. These men I now saw were the last débris of their mysterious race . . . I felt I had fallen into a world of phantoms. The boat that had put me ashore turned, heading back to the ship, leaving me alone, surrounded by my new hosts. It was something so unexpected, so extraordinary, that I felt, in spite of myself, filled with a certain horror. Unreasoning terror – for these figures, whose tattoo marks gave, at first sight, an impression of savagery, were nevertheless full of a soft kindness and bore an air of sadness and bewilderment.'

Here is his close-up of one of these forgotten people. 'An extraordinary, lean figure with a small falcon's beak of a nose, and eyes set too close together, too big, lost-looking, and sad! He is naked, very slim and muscular, all sinews and nerves: his skin is reddish copper colour, decorated with delicate blue tattooing, and his hair, also red, is artificially reddened, and tied with the stems of scabious flowers. Knotted on top of his head it forms a crest that stirs in the wind, and resembles a flame. He looks at us with astonished, too wide-open eyes. In all, there is the attraction of some young demon, or sprite.' Julien took a liking to him, and adopted him as one of his guides about the island. 'I would never have believed, before seeing him, that any human being could so perfectly represent a demon.' Loti was consistently attracted to the exotic, in both men and women, and this demonic, copper-coloured savage might well have aroused his passions: but there is no hint of such an embroilment.

When the French set about removing some of the giant monoliths (one of which is to be seen in Paris, in the Musée de l'Homme, another in the British Museum) Julien sent a sketch of this extraordinary scene to *Illustration*. We see the great roped figures lurching forward. Some already lay on the ground and had done so for uncounted ages . . . 'The ground was strewn with these huge deformed bodies, fallen face downwards. In the shadowy past, when this legion of idols stood upright, their effect must have been overwhelming . . . colossal heads without bodies, rising up, on long necks as if to scan the eternally empty motionless horizons. All of them were once adorned with gigantic crowns of red lava, and each had their own cult, their own human sacrifices.'

The savages of Rapa-Nui were intoxicated by the break in their dreary lives which the arrival of the French represented, and they assisted at the rape of their monuments with riotous glee, turning the whole business into a festival. Julien's sketch-book reveals several scenes of vandalism, but we do not know what he thought of it. To the islanders, accustomed to the horrors imposed on them through the centuries by passing vessels, the restraint of the French crew was both bewildering and heartening and they would have liked the visit to continue indefinitely. Julien had become quite attached to some of them, and was as usual luxuriating in melancholy as the date of departure grew near. 'In a few hours, Easter Isle will disappear forever; not only will I never see Houga and Atamon again, but no-one will ever speak to me of them . . .' When the *Flore* weighed anchor, the great sails lifting and straining in the wind, he watched the dark clouds close over the island, till it vanished . . . Gone forever: another part of his life had vanished beyond recall.

They set course west, heading for Tahiti; from Tahiti came *Le Mariage de Loti*, and the pseudonym – Loti – which Julien Viaud was to adopt and make famous. From Senegal, and the months spent patrolling the African coast and the fever-ridden rivers of that sinister scene came *Le Roman d'un Spahi*, while from Turkey came *Aziyadé*. Before he was twenty-two he had experienced a lifetime of voyaging, and by the time he was twenty-seven, he had known the love of his whole life.

It is the autobiographical nature of these first three books which make them so revealing, so haunting and so essential to the under-standing of Pierre Loti's complicated nature. His voyages brought him wealth, friendships, travels, love affairs, an extraordinarily rich pattern of loving, but never again was he to have the same intense involvement as he experienced during those earliest voyages. Loti lived by and through love, as Plumkett observed, which is why I shall dwell on these first books at length. Later ones are more in the nature of travelogues, land or seascapes with figures, seen more objectively, with more art perhaps, but there is less of the man and his life, the lover, the loved one, as he wished to remain forever. 'Forever – which for mankind means only till death . . .' he was to note bitterly, unable to take comfort in his mother's conviction of heavenly reunions.

Since I am tracing Pierre Loti's life through the autobiographical sequence his books provide rather than the order in which he wrote them, this is the place to write of his second book, *Le Mariage de Loti*.

It is a marvellous evocation of life in Polynesia as he knew it when the *Flore* reached Tahiti in 1872. So exquisite was the scene, as mountain and palm and coral reef rose up on the horizon, that he found himself uncovering his head in an instinctive, almost reverent salutation to beauty. Those were the last days of the celebrated Queen Pomaré IV's reign, when the island still preserved many of its customs and all of its local colour, untainted by tourism. For Julien, it was the dazzling morning – all voluptuous freedom and beauty were here, to be lived and loved to the full. It was here, in Francis Thompson's lovely lines, he first 'broke through the doors of sunset and ran before the hooves of sunrise'. Here, he could follow the immemorial pagan life he had craved from the confines of civilized living; here was the life which he had sensed in Gustave's descriptions of l'Ile Délicieuse. Rapturously he flung himself into this life, recording it in his journals and much of it – but not all – in letters to the family, or further accounts for avid readers of *Illustration*. Such were the sources from which, considerably fictionalized, came *Le Mariage de Loti*, which led his readers to strange lands, to savour sights and sounds and colours – marvellous colours – through the painter's palette that was Loti's page. Perhaps some of the romantic episodes do not ring quite true, but such local colour stifles criticism. What do we care when he adopts clumsy devices to avoid the censorship of French naval authorities? He twists names and nationalities, transposing himself to an English midshipman, Harry Grant, whose letters go home to Brightbury, rather than Rochefort, while the *Flore* becomes a British man-o'war, the *Reindeer*. Such is his magic that when he first introduces a character he calls Plumkett – a name no English ear can accept – we do so, though for years I had thought it a misprint for Plunket. But at this point we swallow any of Loti's tricks and follow him wherever he leads. Beside the seductive vahiné Rarahu, we wander to the stream of Fataöua, that same which Gustave's letters described to his Zézin while imagining it linked to the little grotto at Rochefort. We are by now enveloped in a languorous spell. Intense, glowing light and warmth seem to rise, shimmering, from the pages of this Polynesian book, and readers have the dizzy illusion of over-powering perfumes, heady spices, sandal and tuberose, and the datura 'which make men mad with love . . .'

Tahiti had been a French protectorate since 1843. There had been many attempts by both Spain and England to colonize the island.

When Bligh of the *Bounty* visited it in 1788 he had aided the chief Pomaré to overthrow another chieftain, and thus establish the reign of successive Pomarés. That majestic savage, old Queen Pomaré IV, had come to accept as inevitable the presence of the French in place of the British, but hers was the toleration of helplessness. She adopted certain outward symbols of civilization such as satin boots, and entertained the French administration to sumptuous feasts on the lines of European banquets; but it was not so many generations back that human sacrifice had been an integral part of Tahitian life and worship, the victim's eye being ceremoniously placed in the king's mouth by the high priest.

Here is Julien Viaud (midshipman Harry Grant in the book) acquiring the name of Loti, and since it was the name by which the world came to know him, from this point on, he will be called Loti in these pages.

'Loti was baptized on the 25th of January 1872, at the age of twenty-two years and eleven days. When this happened, it was about one o'clock, in London and Paris, but midnight the other side of the terrestrial globe, in the gardens of the widowed Queen Pomaré, where the event took place. In Europe, it was a cold and gloomy winter's day, but in the Queen's gardens, it was the calm and languor of a summer's night. Five persons assisted at Loti's baptism, surrounded by mimosa and orange trees, the air warm and scented, under a sky strewn with southern stars. These were Ariïtéa, a Princess of the Blood, Faïmana and Téria, ladies in waiting to the Queen, and two midshipmen of the British Navy [Julien and Joseph]. The three Tahitians were wreathed in flowers, and wore tunics of rose-coloured muslin, with long trains. After trying hopelessly to pronounce such barbaric European names, the harsh sounds of which revolted their Maori throats, they decided to call the two young men Loti and Rémuna, the names of two flowers.'

So begins this idyll, which however drenched in the perfumes of frangipani or datura is not sickly, for those undercurrents of tropic fatality which as a child Loti had sensed run through this book like a dark thread behind all the colour and light. It is a simple story. Loti encounters the beautiful fifteen-year-old Rarahu. They love on sight, and she becomes his wife 'in the Tahitian fashion', this union being acknowledged generally and fostered by the particular encourage-

74

ment of the old Queen, who was something of a match-maker, to use a polite label for the part she often played, pairing off her protégées among the foreigners. But fate separates the lovers: Loti sails away: Rarahu pines and ends badly. Loti never forgets, always regrets; it was the pattern he followed repeatedly in his life, as in his writings.

Since for the romantic purposes of his book Loti merged the charms and characteristics of several vahinés he had known, and centred all his changing emotions on one woman, let us leave it thus in the romantic singular of the novel rather than in the plurality of fact, and sigh over the lovers, as Loti's unsuspecting readers did, for Rarahu is the symbol of passion, voluptuousness, beauty, glowing colour, and all freedoms. In her, Loti embodies that hedonistic climate which first intoxicated him and was to intoxicate the French public, then so rigid in their conventions of loving as well as living. The Tahitian idyll was the first of this pattern of living, loving, leaving, and of course grieving. In Papeete Loti was deliberately following in Gustave's footsteps, and he lost no time establishing himself among the island people, learning something of their ways, dressing as they, sleeping on a straw mat, nourished on guavas and bread fruit, and picking up something of the language with his usual facility, the apparently unlimited leave accorded him by his chief facilitating this way of life. Vice-Admiral Lappelin's scientific and ethnographic interests were particularly strong, so that he showed a marked indulgence for the midshipman who shared his interests and whose reports of Easter Island had been so remarkable.

Although the hero of *Le Mariage de Loti* is supposed to be an English-man, it is clearly Loti, the young Frenchman, who plunges into this way of life. Perhaps, were he to set the characters of this and subsequent books relating his first voyages into more mundane or better-known settings, we might perceive they are cardboard charac-ters, foreground figures only sketched, to allow him more time with the backgrounds: and what marvellous backgrounds are here. Then such strange lore is woven round these figures. Rarahu, his Tahitian love, like Aziyadé, his adored Circassian, Pasquala Ivanovitch and others, is seen not only in his arms, but as the embodi-ment of the climate, vegetation, legends, sounds and scents that surround her. It is not only the curve of Rarahu's hips we follow, but her whispered accounts of the Toupapahou – horrible tattooed phantoms that laugh terrifyingly: we come to know the protocol, the costumes and the menus at Queen Pomaré's Court, where one old chieftain assures Loti that the flesh of the white man tastes of ripe bananas.

The moment when Loti knew Tahiti was a fascinating one: lying between two extremes – that of the primitive country which the crew of the *Bounty* knew, and today's 'civilized', mechanized pleasure resort, reached by frequent flights. Loti knew it at that moment of change between corruption and innocence. Through his eyes we see the lovely, legendary vahinés, and the vaporous garments they wore with such elegance, Head-dresses for festive occasions were fabulous confections of plumes and flowers, as if emerging from a Paris hat-box. We can imagine the effect such creatures had on European men accustomed to whaleboned brides.

Any notions we might have of Polynesian women in the terms of a Gauguin painting, large, bovine, copper-fleshed beauties in simple cotton pareos or nothing, are confounded by Loti's accounts. He describes them as being small, frivolous and very animated, rather more in terms of Tanagra figures. These charmers were in the habit of wearing a bizarre kind of green dahlia – a *tiaré miri* composed of some aromatic green leaves, pinned in their hair, over the ear. When they threw it to a man they fancied, it had the same significance as the handkerchief which the Sultan, by tradition, threw to the charmer of his choice. Papeete was very far from Rochefort.

Rarahu was ravishingly pretty. Had she not encountered Loti, she would sooner or later have found another European lover. It was an accepted way of life for these vahinés as long as their beauty and health lasted. Syphilis raged, having been first brought to Tahiti from South America, it was said. The Polynesians responded better to treatment than the Europeans, for they could support massive doses of mercury, though they did not attach much importance either to the disease or its remedies, and nothing diminished their ardours or the fatal attraction they exercised over foreigners. The sailors returned aboard in a deplorable state. No official warnings or disciplines availed. Not for nothing had earlier voyagers called the island *la Nouvelle Cythère*.

Officers and ratings on Loti's ship mingled freely with the Tahitian population. The French never had any restricting notions about caste or grade, in such respects, and in the South Seas no wives had yet joined their husbands with the fatal effects of the Mem-

Sahibs in India. When Queen Pomaré and her suite were entertained to an official luncheon washed down by pink champagne in the Admiral's cabin, the petty officers and ratings also revelled below decks, each with his own fancy lady or some seductress from among the Queen's lesser attendants, so that there too joy was unconfined. We must suppose Joseph was also tasting the delights of the island, though Loti makes little mention of his *frère adoré*, either in his journals or the subsequent book. Perhaps Loti's pace was too much for Joseph, and his Catholic upbringing weighed on him, whereas the Calvinistic rigours Loti had known merely sharpened his appetites.

Loti has left us many descriptions of Rarahu: but what of Loti himself? Early photographs of this time reveal him as a solemn, almost tragic-looking boy, dark-haired, dark-eyed, with those strange magnetic eyes that always seem fixed on some remote horizon. The faintest shadow of a moustache follows the line of his sensual mouth. His buttoned uniform, neat collar and bow tie all give an impression of that meticulous order which was part of his old-maidish upbringing as well as naval tradition. No poetic licence here: but there is something dashing in the way he wears his cap – slightly to the side, and tilted down over his eyes: a personal tilt, evidently a mannerism, perhaps a way of asserting his own personality, a gesture against the conformity of his shipmates.

Loti tells us that the year 1872 was *la belle époque* for Papeete. 'Never had there been so many fêtes, dances and supper parties. Each evening was like some madness. When the beat of drums summoned the Tahitians to the *upa-upa* [a traditional, licentious dance] they came running. Then the dances continued until morning, accelerating to the point of delirium . . .'

And here is another, more formal evening at the Palace, to celebrate the dazzling novelty of a piano. Loti is seated before this impressive instrument, the music of Meyerbeer's *L'Africaine* open before him. At one end of the ball-room, old Queen Pomaré was seated beneath a full-length portrait of herself as she had once been – a beauty among beauties. 'By her immense size the old Queen overflowed even her large gilded throne. She wore a tunic of crimson velvet and the lower part of one bare leg was to be seen, more or less imprisoned in a satin boot. In her old, lined face, brown and square and hard-looking, there was still grandeur: above all, there was immense sadness . . . Sadness to see her kingdom invaded by civilization, drifting into disorder, and her lovely country degenerating into a place known first for prostitution . . .' Over the top of the piano, Loti could see a long banquette crammed with the ladies of the Court. 'First the splendid Ariinoore, in cerise satin; beside her, Paura, a charming type of savage, with a head that might eat either raw fish or human flesh . . . Next came Titaua, who had fascinated Prince Alfred (Queen Victoria's son, the Duke of Edinburgh), dazzling with pearls, while the Queen of Bora-Bora, another old savage with sharp teeth, was draped with velvet. . . .' Loti had chosen a most appropriate extract from Meyerbeer's opera – *Pays merveilleux, Jardins fortunés*, sang the tenor, a fellow officer, while the ladies beat time with their delicate gloved hands.

One feels that Ronald Firbank must have been one of Loti's most attentive readers.

Behind all such Firbankesque interludes there is a melancholy which both Loti and Rarahu suffer, for they know their days together are numbered. The fleet will sail away, and she cannot follow him. There is no place for her in Europe among his *chères vieilles*.

Rarahu had attended missionary classes in her childhood, and now, in scented groves or on coral reefs where those 'small blue crabs that fed on corpses' scuttled, the lovers sometimes embarked on scriptural discussions, for Rarahu feared they had not been made by the same god. What if they might not be reunited in the hereafter? Alas! even if Loti had possessed what he called 'the comforting illusions of Christianity', there were other persons who would have had first claim to any heavenly reunion. Indeed, there was the entire household at the Rue Saint-Pierre, all believing stoutly in a place beside their adored Julien, all together, once more, within the pearly gates. It became impossible to discuss the protocol of spiritual reunions with Rarahu, who was single-minded. It was easier to remain in the kingdom of the flesh, where she reigned supreme.

Nearing the end of his halcyon days in Tahiti, Loti forced himself out of his lotus-eating existence to search for traces of the vahiné who had been Gustave's love, and whose mysterious letters had aroused his curiosity when they arrived in Rochefort, but of whose existence he had only learned in detail later, from someone who had known Gustave's life on the island.

Now there is no more romancing; the novel follows his journal, as Loti describes his poignant search for the vahiné who had shared his brother's exile. There were many Tahitians who remembered him, 'Rouéri – the light-eyed one'. Loti was led to his little hut under the tall coconut palms by the shore. It stood there, deserted, fallen to ruin, but still recognizable as the place Gustave had described, and shown in those faded photographs he had been the first person to take of the island.

With his customary and annoying habit of changing names from one book to another, Gustave's love (Tarahu of *Le Roman d'un Enfant*) is here called Taïmaha – her real name. But there are no rules in the game of hide and seek which Julien-Loti-Harry Grant always plays with his readers.

When at last he found Tarahu-Taïmaha it was night and she was sitting by the roadside, listless, her head sunk on her arms. 'Yes, I am the wife of Rouéri, *he whose eyes sleep*' (he who is no more), she replied carelessly. This then was the woman who was part of the legend of Rouéri, who was also Gustave, and Loti saw that, however chillingly indifferent she seemed, his brother's woman was still beautiful . . . Suddenly an idea crossed his mind, something he had never imagined before.

' "Have you any children by Rouéri?" I asked.

' "Yes," she replied, after a moment's hesitation, then, more positively, "Yes – two!" '

There was a long silence. Loti was overcome by this revelation. Gustave's children – here? He must find them! Taïmaha must take him to them at once. But this she seemed unwilling to do. Loti discovered she was indifferent to her offspring. It was a custom on Tahiti for children to be placed in foster homes, and Taïmaha even seemed uncertain where her own were placed.

His descriptions of the strange regions and people he encounters during his search are of a stark realism. His ship was to sail away for ever, within forty-eight hours, when he heard that one child was on the island of Moorea, some distance away. His only chance was to cross on a small whaler belonging to one of the chiefs. If a storm broke, he would be unable to get back before the *Flore* sailed, and so be classed as a deserter! Dared he run that risk? Yet he *must* see Gustave's child! The cult of family ties was stronger than all else.

After a stormy four-hour crossing there was a long anxious trek through forests and by small villages.

Late in the day, as the wind raged overhead, they reached their objective. Loti's heart beat violently at the thought he would at last see this unknown child, 'already loved and linked to me by the powerful ties of blood . . .'

He took Taamari, the little savage, in his arms, searching for some likeness to his dead brother. There was none. He had expected to find a boy of thirteen or so . . . this child seemed much younger. A bitter doubt crossed Loti's mind . . . Had he been duped? It was difficult to verify dates in this land where the seasons slipped by unremarked; however, certain records were kept by the chiefs and Loti asked to see them. When at last the messenger returned with the primitive records, it was almost dark. In the half-light, Loti read the inscription.

> Is born the Taamari, of the Taïmaha
> the fifth day of July 1864
> Is born the Atario of the Taïmaha
> the second day of August 1865 . . .

He knew then that Taïmaha, for her own mysterious ends, had deceived him. Both children were born some years after Gustave had left and she had taken up with another man. Loti felt an overwhelming sense of emptiness – of loss. 'I did not want to see the words. I did not want to believe them. Oddly, I was attached to this idea of a Tahitian family, and now, as it faded, I felt a profound and mysterious sorrow: it was as if my brother had died for the second time.' In spite of the joys of pagan living, it was still family ties that counted most, and any link with Gustave's Tahitian life became at once part of Rochefort, or Viaud family life.

By the stream of Fataöua Loti and Rarahu spent their last hours together, in drenching melancholy: just the ambiance to arouse his most morbid reflections.

'O! Separation of separations!' Would he ever see Rarahu again? And what would become of her? Loving Loti or no, she was of that race of women who pin the scented green *tiaré miri* in their hair, and throw it to any man they fancy for the loving game. Two heavy tears fell from Rarahu's eyes as she told her lover she would never take another husband. She would do as he wished – return to her old home on Bora-Bora, and live there in chastity and the hope of his return. With a truly appalling display of egoism Loti tells us: 'Now I could leave her! Destiny was separating us, but this parting would be less bitter, less agonizing.' She would be waiting for him. However long the wait, she would be there – all his – and removed from any likelihood of a possible successor: no doubt a conclusion Loti's male readers found as satisfactory as he did.

So ended the first and most exotic episode of his youth. All the things he had sensed in Gustave's letters, or discovered, briefly, through the brown body of *la belle Gitane,* had been given to him in full measure by his life on l'Ile Délicieuse. Like Aunt Claire's Wednesday, it had come, and it had passed. Did her voice echo now, dirge-like and prophetic? It had come, this fulfilment, and it had passed, and others were to come, and they too would pass . . . but never again those first raptures of 'the dew-dropping south'.

Gradually the Tahitian dream receded; like the necklaces of blossoms he had brought back with him, memories of those vanished colours and perfumes faded. For a while Loti tells us that he – or his hero – received letters of love and longing from Rarahu. The same kind of childish hieroglyphics that Taïmaha had sent to Gustave were now the only link with l'Ile Délicieuse. Rarahu's missives brought back something of its tropic beauty, for she expressed herself with a poetic abandon.

'O my dearest love, my perfumed flower of the evening, the sorrow of my heart is great, for I see you no more . . . O my star of the morning, my eyes melt with tears, for you will never return to me.'

Loti kept her letters, but presently he stopped replying. Sometimes he dreamed of abandoning everything and returning to Papeete, to find again his 'little savage love'. But he did nothing: as the old Queen had said: 'Of all those I have seen leave, few come back.' After a while, there were no more letters, no more cries of love and longing. He was to learn why.

In 1876, at Malta, he had news of her from the officers of another ship, lately stationed at Tahiti. They said she had picked up with a French officer, but he had deserted her . . . 'She had nowhere to live in the end, but dragged about with an ancient cat that followed her everywhere, crying piteously. All the sailors loved her, even though she had become so wild. She wanted all of them – all who were at all good-looking . . .' She was dying of consumption, and as she had begun to drink brandy, it finished her off fast. 'I stayed there, among my friends,' writes Loti, 'as we continued to talk of Oceania. Like all the rest, my tone was nonchalant. "Yes, a lovely country, Oceania – lovely creatures, the Tahitians . . . such bodies! like statues! Yet finally, incomplete as women – one loves them as one loves a beautiful fruit . . ."' Thus Loti, taking refuge in the carapace of worldly indifference, twirling his moustaches while his heart wept. 'But that night, alone, in the darkness and silence, a sombre dream, a sinister vision appeared to me.

'The gloomy wastes of Bora-Bora, terrifying in the grey, twilight sky of dreams . . . I was brought there by a black ship which, though no wind raised its sails, continued onwards . . . My eyes were fixed on the shore with an indefinable sense of horror . . . then I distinguished human forms which seemed to be awaiting me, and I landed among the trunks of the coconut palms. Women were crouched there with their heads in their hands, as for a funeral wake . . . their eyes were closed, but through their transparent lids those eyes were fixed on me. In the middle of the women a human form, white and rigid, stretched on a bed of pandanus leaves . . . I drew near to the sleeping phantom, and lent over a dead face . . . Rarahu began to laugh . . . Rarahu was lying there, her childish body wrapped in her long dark hair. Rarahu, her eyes empty, laughing that eternal laugh, that fixed laughter of the Toupapahous . . .' So ends *Le Mariage de Loti*, a book which has sometimes been dubbed sugary.

5

Loti performs so beautifully as to kick up
a fine golden dust over the question of what
he contains — or of what he does not.

Henry James

Loti's return to Europe was sombre. The *Flore* docked at Brest in the
raw half-light of a northern winter's day. O! desolation! Even
Rochefort and the *chères vieilles* could not charm him out of his gloom.
The little grotto and toy lake that had seemed l'Ile Délicieuse in
miniature now mocked him, for he had known the reality. But then –
which was real, the man now named Loti, or Julien whose roots were
in Rochefort? The family were agog to hear all about his adventures.
All? There was so much he could not tell; it was easier to sit beside
the fire with them, as of old, and persuade Great-aunt Berthe to
recount tales of another island, the ISLAND that had bound his
childish horizons.

Soon he left them to be stationed at Toulon, on manoeuvres in the
Mediterranean, now upgraded, to become *enseigne de vaisseau* . . .
sub-lieutenant's rank, with more responsibilities, and better pay.
Creditors still 'gnawed with their rats' teeth', but he had staved off
the sale of the house so far, and had no intention of relinquishing his
battle. And Joseph, who had been with him since their training days
on the *Borda*, was still beside him, as staunch as ever in the face of
family criticism. The relationship of these two young men was
typical of those romantic attachments which were so particularly
marked between men in the middle years of the nineteenth century.
Many of Dr Arnold's scholars continued, on going out into the
world, to exchange letters of lover-like devotion. The young English
officers who were heroes of the Indian Mutiny and the Afghan campaigns, men such as Laurence, Nicholson, Pottinger or Connolly,
might be described as military mystics, as perfervid in their
religious convictions as their affections, for it was a time of overboiling emotions but sublimated sex: not that either Loti's sex-life or
emotions were ever sublimated. He was one of those ardent, idealis-

tic youths who always craved such fervent relationships; Gustave's loss had left him with a permanent imbalance, and Joseph Bernard adopted something of the older brother's paternalistic care. And then, his efforts to offer solid financial aid had touched Loti profoundly. They were as one. When Bernard was posted to Senegal, Loti's letters to him were eloquent of this devotion. He continued to address him as *Frère adoré, mon frère chéri*, and fretted to be with him. From Cherbourg his tone was wretched. Bernard must have just sailed.

'I am writing from your room in the Hôtel du Nord which, in an hour, I shall leave sadly, for it is still full of you (although there is none of that disorder which proclaims your presence!). Since you left, I have been very busy, which is a good thing, for then I do not have time to think . . .'

Loti, for all his apparent fatalistic melancholy, his unappeased longings for yesterday, could be very active, very positive when determined to get his own way. Thus he set about moving heaven and earth, pulling every string, knocking on every door, including that of the Cardinal de Ségur, Bernard's uncle, to obtain a transfer to join his *frère chéri* in Senegal. By July he was writing to Bernard that all was settled: he had orders to serve on the *Pétrel*, beside him, and would sail for French West Africa almost at once. The *chères vieilles* resigned themselves to losing him once more. The sea, in all its force, had swept Julien from them. Swaying with its tides, he would come and go: but never again would he belong wholly to either them or the land.

By October he was writing to his sister from Africa, now reunited with both Bernard and the rhythm of naval life which had become his. He was noting all around him, and already his impressions were accumulating, and would, some years later, be woven into *Le Roman d'un Spahi*. As with his earlier articles and sketches from Easter Isle and Tahiti, editors were eager for his descriptions of Africa. Some of his finest drawings derive from this time in Senegal: they breathe all the sinister desolation he saw around him.

Although Loti did not write *Le Roman d'un Spahi* until 1880, six years after he had left Senegal, the material was largely autobiographical and taken from journals written while serving between Dakar and Saint-Louis in 1873. 'One of the most unhappy periods of my life,' he later described it, though he thought this book his best and strongest, until at last, embittered by everything, himself included, he was to condemn his earlier books as unhealthy. A feverish miasma of despair rings from the pages, stemming no doubt, not only from the atmosphere of Senegal at that time but also from the profound love affair which Loti had there with an unnamed woman.

Dakar was the chief seaport of Senegal, becoming the capital of French West Africa as late as 1862, a year after a French protectorate had been proclaimed in the surrounding territories. This had been an armed conquest, and was not, when Loti knew it, an entirely pacified scene. The spahis, in their dashing uniforms, high red fez and flowing cloaks, occupied a number of small forts, and made punitive expeditions against the raiding tribes, while the French navy kept a few ships patrolling the coast and the wide yellow waters of the Senegal river. Trade was beginning to stabilize; ground nuts, pistachio and indigo were of primary importance. Small trading ports had been established there since the seventeenth century, founded by Dieppois merchants. It was the oldest French African colony, but it did not flourish until a railway was constructed in 1880. This was to link Dakar with Saint-Louis, a town of some size, a hundred and fifty or more miles north. The hinterland beyond, Southern Mauritania, Timbuctoo and the Sahara, was still only reached by arduous stages, along the Senegal and Niger rivers, and beyond that, by camel. Those vast empty distances were strewn with the bones of caravans, and nothing grew and nothing lived in such wastes.

At the time of Loti's sojourn in Senegal, Europeans formed a very small colony: apart from the spahis (who counted native troops among them, like the French ships, which had mostly Negroes as crew), 'Les blancs' were composed of traders or government administrators. 'Europeans who come here are fugitives, seeking their fortune at the risk of health, or life,' wrote Loti in his journal, but he was content to find himself there beside Bernard again, and once more absorbing an extraordinary local colour.

Such fierce harshness was as far from the Tahitian scene as it was from Rochefort, and Loti was noting everything with his usual avidity, the few streets that petered out into the desert, or the great black, balding vultures swooping down from the roof tops to waddle in the filth. The buildings, the barracks, the hospital and a church were ramshackle and whitewashed, but the Great Mosque was more imposing, for the majority of the population were Moslem. Countless round, beehive-roofed native huts sprouted from the arid soil where the only vegetation was the gigantic baobab tree. The heat was ferocious: yellow fever and malaria decimated the Europeans: in the rainy season, stinking miasmas hung over everything: in the dry season a fierce wind, the harmattan, raged down from the Sahara. There was nothing to recommend this place, yet it had a curious, compelling fascination, of which Loti was soon aware.

This cumulative and dangerous spell pervades his *Roman d'un Spahi*, centred round Jean Peyral the Spahi, who rots there, thinking longingly of his return to France – to his home in the Cévennes. And yet: 'he could no longer see himself very clearly, dressed like the other men of his village . . . it seemed he would no longer be himself – the proud spahi: it was in this scarlet uniform he had learned to live, it was on the soil of Africa he had become a man, and more than he knew, he loved it: he loved his Arab fez, his sword and his horse and this great accursed country – his desert . . . He did not know what deceptions sometimes await these young men – sailors, soldiers, spahis, when they return to the village they have dreamed of, which they left while still almost children, and from afar continued to see through an enchanted prism. What sadness, what monotonous boredom awaits these exiles on their return! Those poor spahis, such as he, acclimatized to Africa, sometimes came to pine for the desolate shores of Senegal . . . the long hours in the saddle and a freer life, with its intense light and limitless horizons. In the tranquillity of home, one becomes aware of a need for that devouring sun, and the eternal heat, and one longs for the desert.'

Loti wrote this from the heart, for by now he too had come to experience that bewildering sense of exile on returning home. When he had sought to join Bernard in this harsh African scene, was he not, in fact, also seeking to escape his ancestral roots? As an exile in Senegal he was yet at home; he had already acquired the habit of faraway places. It was a transformation of which he was perhaps not fully aware at the time he was in Africa: but some years later, by the time he wrote the passage quoted above, he had travelled further and known many more ways of life, and come to realize that the native land itself can at last spell banishment.

During his first months in Dakar, Loti and his fellow officers were much ashore, cultivating the limited society, both black and white, and the half-shades of Creole ladies. Most of the spahis kept delightful little Negro girls, as mischievous as monkeys and as voluptuous as Salomé: such a creature is Fatou-Gaye, who leads the tragic Spahi, Jean Peyral, such a dance in *Le Roman d'un Spahi*. She is one of Loti's most perfect evocations. At St Louis the summit of local protocol was a visit to Mahommed Diop, the King of Dakar. 'This towering old figure was truly imposing, with his air of some ancient ebony effigy, exactly the chief for this country where the sun dries up everything, as if to preserve it for all time.'

Sometimes the fabled Touaregs swept down, mounted on their splendid camels, and it was clear these mysterious, blue-veiled men from the Sahara were the object of veneration and terror to the humbler population, whose regard for them was akin to that mixture of alarm and fascination with which, today, some people view the possibility of visitors from outer space. There has always been something daemonic, an almost extra-terrestrial quality about the Touaregs. Their allure and the mystique surrounding them were not lost on Loti, and soon a friendship was struck. To join them, going far into the desert beside them, was precisely the sort of expedition he relished: to be accepted by this little-known people and to be among them was a rare privilege, for the Touaregs did not condescend to favour many, least of all Europeans.

At Dakar, in conditions hardly conducive to comfort, Loti contrived to surround himself with a certain individual elegance. There was always ample shore leave for the young officers, as at Tahiti, and those who chose to establish themselves in a local manner during their off-duty hours were not frowned upon. Although Loti's pay packet was greatly reduced by the sums he continued to send regularly to the *chères vieilles*, the little he kept for himself had remarkable purchasing powers in the native markets. Joseph shared the expenses of their curious African dwelling and they enjoyed making it sumptuous in local terms with matting, brilliant-coloured Negro stuffs, spears, divans and a giraffe skin. There were also local pets: a huge beaked grey marabout, gravely strutting, and no doubt messing the matting; a monkey, and a lovable little green parakeet, presently eaten by the marabout. In the surrounding country there were lions, hippopotamuses, monkeys, ostriches, and in the rivers, crocodiles. But Loti was never the stuff of a big game hunter – indeed, of any hunter, once he had outgrown the butterfly net of his childhood. Once – and once only – he took a gun into the forests, and by an almost mechanical reflex shot and killed a monkey. For the rest of his life he remembered that wanton action, and never again went out to kill for what is called sport.

Among all the African flavours of the house at Dakar, there was one splendidly incongruous note: a piano. This instrument was one which, in all climates and all conditions, Loti seems to have been able to acquire. But to have come by one in Dakar, at that time, seems positively miraculous. 'It had been, originally, on the Emperor Napoleon III's yacht, and before reaching Dakar, had rolled about many seas, rather to its detriment. One evening, alone in our salon, I was trying to recapture a Negro air, very melancholy, and in the minor key, when I heard behind me a faint sound as if something smooth, but heavy was being cautiously dragged over the matting. In a brusque movement of alarm I turned and saw a large snake vanish into a hole in the wall. My music had attracted it, and afterwards I sometimes succeeded in making it return: but for that one needed absolute stillness, and one had to play plaintive airs without stopping for a long while.' Perhaps too, the serpent was not insensible to Loti's singing touch. He tells us it was always remarked.

Behind the outward calm and monotony of life in Senegal, there were undercurrents of danger; skirmishes with warring natives, punitive expeditions and sometimes small wars raged between the various tribes, the fires of ravaged villages lit the night sky, and shrieks and war cries could be heard on the still air, behind the yelp of the jackals. Then a contingent of spahis would ride out from the fort or follow the Senegal river upstream, going to battle in pirogues, by tributary streams that led deep into unknown territories, a world apart from the desert, but with the same deadly heat of equatorial Africa. 'It was something so terrible, this heat, that the black rowers were obliged to rest from time to time . . . The tepid water did not quench their thirst, and they seemed as if melted in their own sweat. As the pirogue drifted slowly on the spahis could see, at close quarters, a world which lay beneath the mangrove swamps. Crocodiles lolled in the slime, yawning with an air of grinning idiocy, their jaws gaping and sticky: delicate white aigrettes, also sleeping, rolled into snowy white balls at the end of one long stalk-like leg, or perched, to avoid sullying themselves, on the backs of the semi-conscious crocodiles.'

Above all, there were the roots of the mangroves, 'Roots, and more roots, hanging over everything, like garlands of ropes; they were all lengths, all thicknesses, twining and weaving everywhere. One might say they were like thousands of nerves, the trunks of elephants, or grey arms, striving to entwine and take possession.'

The love affair which Loti was to have in Senegal was as torrid as its African setting. By comparison the Tahitian idyll seemed childish play in a temperate zone. Most of it remains a matter of conjecture, for Loti destroyed all the pages of his journal which told of this conflagration, and there are only a few oblique references to *Elle, ma bien aimée*, or his unbearable sufferings (rather more of them). She was probably the wife of some rich merchant living in Saint-Louis, in the sort of rambling house Loti describes as that of Cora, the wanton auburn-haired Creole who was the Spahi's mistress, and briefly, Loti's also. Loti, who enjoyed his usual game of identifying himself, or transposing his own emotions from one to another of his characters, is thinly disguised as the blasé young naval officer whom Cora plays off against her other lover, the Spahi Jean Peyral, while Loti's real torments of love for the *bien aimée* are fastened onto the Spahi, suffering over Cora. What a mix-up!

Loti, who appears at first sight so revealing of his most intimate thoughts, was, in this case, particularly secretive, disguising names and dates and places, to ensure that this *grande passion* should remain an enigma. But of Cora he is not protective, and he paints an unflattering portrait.

She was a mulâtresse from Bourbon, brought up in the idle, sensual luxury of the rich Creoles; but in Saint-Louis, she was snubbed by the Europeans as being 'coloured', déclassée and immoral. Her sensuality was not the simple couplings of the gypsy, or Rarahu; in her cynical depravity, the Spahi was a plaything, to torment. 'She took him because he was handsome, tall and strong, and she liked his rough, naïve ways – even his coarse soldier's shirt . . .' But Loti was chic – an officer, and that too appealed.

Cora is the only vicious character in all Loti's gallery of women. Aziyadé, Gaud, Gracieuse, and even Rarahu, all have a basic purity: it is something he imposes on all his heroines, overlaying them with sentiment. Behind all his amorous adventures, and the mask of Don Juan, the young Julien still lurked, the loving son whose funda-mental views on women were formed by the family at Rochefort – his mother, his sister, Lucette . . . *good* women.

In a melodramatic passage, Loti describes Cora dismissing the Spahi from her room earlier than usual, so that he, though completely subjugated, suspects she is receiving another man. He creeps to the window, and sees his sophisticated rival (Loti) lounging in an armchair, and reproaching Cora lightly for her cruelty.

'He's so handsome, that boy – and then – he *loves* you!' says Loti, nonchalantly.

'That's true, but I fancied the two of you,' is the insolent reply.

Cora's new lover points to the shadowy figure of the Spahi standing outside, petrified and pallid, his eyes haggard.

Cora sees him, and goes towards him, 'with the hideous expression of a wild animal that has been disturbed in its amours'.

Just the stuff which would once have brought down the house in some provincial theatre. And yet Loti's puppet figures continue to live – perhaps because the incident really occurred – and we are touched by the poor young Spahi. It is part of Loti's magic that he can put such one-dimensional figures in settings of depth, and still disarm his critics. In any case – he disarms.

Henry James, no indulgent critic, wrote:

'Loti performs so beautifully as to kick up a fine golden dust over the question of what he contains or what he doesn't . . . To be so rare that you can be common, so good that you can be bad . . . The whole second-rate element in Loti becomes an absolute stain, if we think much about it. But practically (and this is his first-rate triumph), we *don't* think much about it.'

Just so: and we wade on, through reekingly sentimental passages on the Spahi's links with home, and his ancient, pathetic parents. Loti's characters are apt to have old, very old parents – it is one of his clichés. The Spahi or the Matelot, or any of his young men of twenty or thereabouts, appear to have sprung from septuagenarian loins, for the parents (who are unlikely to have been much more than fifty when their son is twenty or so) are portrayed as bent, quavering dotards. Thus we bear with descriptions of the Spahi's ancient progenitors in the Cévennes, pathetically awaiting his return: or accounts of how the fiancée he left behind – left too long – is pressed into marriage with an unwelcome suitor on the spot. Clichés pile on clichés.

Nevertheless, we do read on and reach, with relief, accounts of the Spahi's friend, the giant black Spahi Nyaor, who listens gravely to the complicated moral problems which torment his '*blanc*'. The Spahi is always welcome in Nyaor's hut, where, seated between Nyaor's two wives, he eats couscous and listens to their plaintive songs. Nothing cardboard here: never a false note or cliché or any sentimentality when Loti writes of the primitive peoples he understood. He is far less attuned to his European characters, unless they, too, are of primitive stock.

In all his writings, Fatou-Gaye is perhaps his most endearing portrait: he comprehends her childish yet wicked ways and the hold she has over the poor Spahi, who, tricked and rejected by Cora, solaces himself first by drink and later in Fatou-Gaye's black company. She was to become his tragic destiny, and as the story develops she grows with it into tragic dimensions.

Did the Spahi come to love Fatou-Gaye? He could not say, poor Spahi. 'He regarded her as an inferior creature, but he was touched . . . Fatou's hands, which were small and delicate, with fragile wrists, were black on the outside, but the palms were pink. For a long time this had troubled the Spahi: he did not like to see the palms of Fatou's hands . . . they had something alarming – *not human* – about them. But gradually Fatou-Gaye had grown to be a real beauty, in terms of ebony and onyx . . . When she walked she had that sway of the hips which the women of Africa seem to have borrowed from the great felines of their country. She possessed a Negro grace, a sensual charm and some power of seduction which was indefinable, something composed of the monkey, the young virgin and the tigress.'

By today's standards, black is beautiful, but in Loti's day, an ebony Venus needed all his eloquence, for his readers were conditioned to quite other standards; it was pinkness, plumpness, fluffiness, coyness, a corsetted form and a tripping step that were admired.

The real theme of *Le Roman d'un Spahi* is Africa. Although it is presented as the backcloth to the simple Spahi, to vicious Cora, or Fatou-Gaye, even she, little black wickedness, dims beside the violent African setting. It was the dark continent in all its sinister

91

and hidden ways, still a country of sorcery and magic rites, and diseases which today are cured or treated. In the white-hot dust of cities such as Guet N'Dar there was the eternal thumping beat of pestle and mortar as the women ground millet for their staple dish, a coarse couscous. It was the essential sound of Africa from Timbuctoo to the coast; thousands of graceful dark arms circled with jangling bracelets pounding in tireless monotony, the women chattering and quarrelling 'with voices that seemed to issue from the throats of so many monkeys', says Loti, conjuring all the sounds and smells of Africa, of soumaré, dusky flesh, musk, and rot; the strange cries of the baboons in the forests beyond the town's edge, the bird calls, the sound of the jackals and wild dogs disputing some dead thing, rise round us as we turn the pages.

Loti's acute musical ear made him especially aware of African music, and his descriptions of its curious rhythms intrigued his readers, for at that time there were no recordings to bring the sounds of faraway countries into every home. The frenzies of black African rhythms, now so familiar via Harlem, were quite unknown to Europe. In the Sudan, musicians were a caste apart – Griots, who from father to son were ambulant troupes, composing both heroic chants and the frenzies of the bamboula.

It was their music which launched the springtime mating rites of dance and sacrifice. Here is Loti's description of the scene: '*Anamalis fobie*! hurled the Griots, beating their tamtams – their eyes inflamed, their muscles taut, their bodies streaming with sweat . . . And the dancers repeated the cry, clapping their hands frenziedly. *Anamalis fobie! Anamalis fobie*! . . . its translation would scorch these pages . . . *Anamalis fobie*! . . . the refrain of a diabolic chant drunk with desire and licence . . . the chant of the bamboula at springtime, a howling cry of unbridled desire – of a black sap, overheated by the sun – a torrid hysteria . . . the alleluia of Negro love, a hymn of seduction chanted also by nature, by the earth, the plants and the perfumes.'

As may be imagined, Loti's readers were to find this book something of a shock in 1881 – but how agreeable! Well might Anatole France write: *It was reserved for Pierre Loti to make us savour – to the point of intoxication, of delirium, of stupor, even – the bitter flavour of exotic loves.*

In 1874, after only a few months of Loti's passion for the mysterious *bien aimée*, their affair ended abruptly. The parting did not follow what might be described as the Pinkerton syndrome, naval officer for ever loving and leaving, a girl in every port. In Senegal, it was not Pinkerton-Loti who sailed away, leaving his mistress to pine, but the lady who left, leaving Loti behind. Loti kept a last rendezvous with her in high secrecy, vowing to follow her – to marry her, to resign from the navy, to be with her forever . . . There were, for the moment, no more thoughts of Rochefort and its responsibilities. Racked with grief, standing under a giant baobab tree, he watched her boat sail downstream, taking her out of his life, as once Rarahu had watched him sail from l'Ile Délicieuse.

The next blow came from the Ministère de la Marine, and spelled his separation from Joseph Bernard. Since the beginnings of their friendship on the *Borda* he had been Loti's companion and consolation at all times, while effacing himself tactfully during romantic idylls. To be separated from him at this juncture was an added anguish. While Bernard and Loti's other shipmates of the *Pétrel* remained at Saint-Louis, Loti was abruptly seconded to the *Espadon*, lying off Dakar. Whether this was because he was considered a particularly responsible young officer, or there were echoes of his local embroilments, we do not know. There was trouble in the air; the tribes were restive and gathering, and patrol boats, the *Espadon* among them, were being rearmed, and detailed to guard the coast off Dakar. For Loti, torn from his mistress, battle promised the classic assuagement, but he now seems to have been concentrating on obtaining solace by Joseph's transfer to the *Espadon*. Once again Authority was harassed to gratify his desires.

Among the papers Loti preserved from this time is an exchange of telegrams between Loti, languishing on the *Espadon*, along the coast, and Joseph, aboard the *Pétrel*, up river at Saint-Louis. The tone of Loti's telegrams is peremptory but Joseph's replies seem oddly apathetic. Loti is planning every move – which officer to approach, what line to take, when to embark, what means of transport . . . After five days of this to and fro it appears that Joseph was not being as active as Loti expected. Had he begun to have enough of Loti's uproars – of playing second fiddle? Loti sends one more telegram to a shipmate on the *Pétrel*, asking if Bernard is really against the transfer. No reply. The matter is settled by a veto from the commanding officer. These crumpled yellow telegraphic forms which sped between Dakar and Saint-Louis a century ago, are curiously revealing of both Loti's imperious character and his violent need for Bernard.

Condemned to a solitary life aboard the *Espadon*, Loti was sunk in gloom. The *Espadon* was one of those outdated old despatch-boats that still patrolled Senegambian waters, a dilapidated affair, the disjointed woodwork of its cabins swarming with cockroaches, while the curious dried creatures and fetishes of the Negro crew were everywhere. During the torrid hours of the siesta Loti would lie on his bunk, fuming to be back on the *Pétrel* beside Bernard, while 'the conch shells of the sorcerers bellowed as they passed in their pirogues, and the warm water wrinkled lazily like oil.'

During this time aboard the *Espadon*, Loti had time to evaluate the place Bernard occupied in his life. Throughout the Tahitian idyll and especially during this last fiery love affair Bernard had been rather set aside – kept in cold storage, it would seem. But now the two beings on whom Loti's emotions were centred had vanished, leaving him with no pivot-point of passion, so that he found himself vibrating in a void, for him an unendurable state. Far sooner than his mistress had expected he was writing to say he was hoping for another transfer – now to Europe, where he would rejoin her – far sooner, perhaps, than she wished.

An unexpected order played into his hands. Since war was in the air, the *Espadon* was to leave for France, transporting a number of colonials. More agonies of farewell, more backward glances as the coast of Africa faded: more echoes of Never More! though that Africa which Loti savoured so intensely no longer held him. 'My thoughts are now entirely taken by our love, *ma bien aimée*,' he wrote, as the *Espadon* sailed. He was intent on renewing their liaison, but the secrets of that alcove were all destroyed by him: indeed, in the few pages of his journals which remain to tell of Dakar, there is no mention of *le frère chéri* either. Most of the journals of that time were burnt or cast into the sea by Loti's own hand. It was a time of special unhappiness, but unlike most other periods of suffering, he does not appear to have taken a morbid pleasure in leaving it on record.

The *Espadon* left Dakar in August 1874 and during the long voyage home fearful storms tore at the battered old ship, so that at one point it seemed improbable they would ever reach land. However, they did, limping into harbour at Rochefort, most conveniently for Loti's reunion with the *chères vieilles*, more fragile but as adoring as ever. Soon, he left them again, heading for the house in Geneva where *la bien aimée* had promised him a rendezvous. On a cold, damp night, heavy with mists, he stood, at last, before a fine old house with escutcheons over the door. 'I trembled like a child . . . there was no light, no sound within the house where my fate was to be decided. I raised my hand to knock – my head swam – I could no longer breathe . . .' Here a number of pages are missing from both the published and unpublished journals. From subsequent entries we learn that all was over. She would have no more of him. He was refused. Abandoned. 'She who abandoned me . . . *Ma bien aimée* . . . Why did you abandon me?' Abandoned, abandoned . . . he drowned in self-pity, and took his broken heart and his secret back to Rochefort. There he could not be consoled – would not be consoled – preserving his misery jealously, because it stemmed from *Her*. The devotion of the *chères vieilles* was of no avail. He could no longer paint or play the piano; nothing comforted him. Desperately he took stock of himself and decided to cultivate his muscles – to change his body, since he could do little about his face. If he could not be handsome, he could become virile in the manner of the Spahi, or any of those splendid matelots around him. His training on the *Borda*, and his life at sea had made him a wiry figure, but his hothouse childhood had been a bad start. He wanted perfection – the body of a trained athlete. Youth and love were the only things that counted in life, he decided. Thus he must make himself over, the better to seize both.

To this end, he applied for six months' leave to train at the Ecole de Gymnastique, at Joinville-le-Pont. This was a gruelling test; swarming up and down the riggings of the *Borda* was kindergarten stuff by comparison. He trained to circus agility on the trapeze, boxed, practised singlestick and fencing, and various complicated muscular manoeuvres which presently remodelled his body into the classic, if miniature, proportions of a Greek athlete. Then a severe nervous breakdown halted these activities. The doctor of the Ecole diagnosed love-sickness – *chagrin d'amour* – which seems uncommonly perceptive, coming from that hardened milieu. His state caused grave anxiety and there followed a number of delirious ravings and nightmares – always more hallucinatory with Loti than with others. The orderly detailed to sit beside his bed must have wondered at some of the images . . . Rarahu laughing the awful

95

laughter of the Topapahous, and the cannibals of Nuka Hiva being positively cheerful beside some of Loti's wilder necrophilic African fancies. At last he was restored, and returned to the trapeze; but he had to fight against sinking back into his morbid moods.

Life at Joinville was dour: there was snow, and his thoughts returned to Africa with longing. 'Ah! who will give me back the great African sun?' Give back . . . give back. It is his eternal plaint. But he was beginning to understand that nobody, nothing, could give back yesterday.

Presently he decided to try some passing distractions. Some of his fellow gymnasts formed a group, 'the Golos' (a yoloff, or Negro, name for monkey). Loti became the Golo chief, calling the tune for their various pranks. They lodged in quarters reserved for the gymnasts, and disturbing neighbours they must have been, coming in and out at all hours, penniless by the end of the month, noisily sharing the last bottle of wine and the latest mistress. Among the Golos' demoiselles was a milliner from the Rue Molière, who returned from Paris each evening with a number of hats to finish – homework much interrupted by the Golos, and Loti was always consulted as to the trimmings.

In summer, the Golos were particularly giddy, joining in every local fête. The outskirts of Paris were still green and coquettishly pretty, with gardens, woods and taverns all along the river, where boats moored and the splendidly moustached and straw-hatted rowers and their muslin-frilled companions shaded by parasols were the inspiration of many Impressionist painters; Monet, Renoir . . . scenes such as Seurat's Grande Jatte were those which Loti knew at Joinville. Indeed, Loti may have been, unknown to himself, one of Monet or Renoir's models, a dark-eyed young man in a white singlet and straw hat under the shade of the chestnut trees, ordering a bock and vying for the favours of some bonneted siren. Suburban joys, they must have seemed to Loti, after the upa-upas of Tahiti or the African bamboulas, but a youthful, carefree scene, and Loti, still paying off debts, still writing home devotedly, kept well away from the depressive atmosphere of Rochefort during this regenerative period.

On their more rowdy excursions, the Golo band were joined by their gymnastic instructors, sergeants, or quartermasters, very handy with their fists and enjoying the opportunities to get into skirmishes. They assembled at the *Lapin Sauté*, a soldiers' dive, where they changed costumes or dressed up, to set out as 'all kinds of impossible persons, ripe for all kinds of mischief'. Such evenings confirmed both Loti's passion for dressing up, odd disguises and the violent physical action which he enjoyed. Those dubious nocturnal adventures which he pursued throughout his life were easier to accomplish in disguise. The rating's blue and white became this gold-braided officer's other country, where life could be lived on different terms, bawdy, rowdy, randy . . . It was marvellously liberating. The milliner lent him her Paris work-room where he could change his clothes and indulge this passion for travesties, some of which were savoured by no less a personage than Sarah Bernhardt, for it must have been about this time that they first met. We imagine Loti in the stuffy little attic littered with artificial flowers and ribbons, hanging his trim uniform over the back of a rickety chair, getting himself up in some unlikely outfit, and stepping back from the fly-blown mirror to admire the transformation which was his ticket to *ailleurs* – 'elsewhere', or even the divine Sarah's company.

Strangely, among any of Loti's papers that I have seen, there is no mention of where and how he first encountered the great star. Even Sarah's grand-daughter, Madame Lysiane Bernhardt, remained mystified. The attachment of Julien le Fou, as Sarah called him, and *la Grande Vieille Amie*, as she came to sign herself to him, remained unbroken by time or distance. *Bon jour et mille tendresses de votre plus ancienne et plus fidèle amie* are the words of a telegram she sent him in 1906, one of so many Loti stored away, for it recalled their golden past.

This strange pair first met some time in 1875, probably during one of Loti's brief expeditions to Paris from the disciplines of the Ecole Gymnastique; certainly before he sailed for Turkey, for from Stamboul in 1877 he writes to one of the Golos, recounting the sorties he makes in disguise, 'as once, you will remember they were made for Sarah Bernhardt, made then from a fiacre, or an address in the Rue Richelieu' (which was where the actress was living at the time). In another letter to Plumkett he recalls his first sight of la Divine, playing Doña Sol in *Hernani*. 'I was in the first row of the orchestra stalls, and I shall never forget that moment when she approached the ramp, and fixed me with those great sombre eyes, her head thrust forward like some *ange du mal* . . . Twice I met those eyes . . .' The pale, panther eyes of la Divine and the dark mesmeric gaze of the young Loti had recognized each other. Or had the actress, at that first moment, only been peering across the footlights astonished to see something so unusual as an able-seaman seated in the orchestra stalls? When, later, they came face to face off-stage, Sarah, as much as Loti, must have found the ribbon round his red pomponned cap appropriate. *L'Entreprenant* – the Enterprising: just the name for a battleship: better still for the young Loti approaching the great star.

There is a little-known photograph of Loti in rating's clothes taken about this time. It catches a curious and rare expression, half content, half defiant: the cat who has had the cream. For a brief moment his face shows none of the pathos of earlier or later like-nesses, nor is he self-conscious or posing: but he is most self-assured. There is even a faint air of amusement, something very rare. It is as if, briefly, he is enjoying life – hugging to himself the fun of being favoured by the adulated Sarah B. – he, the unknown young sailor whom all might now envy.

During the years 1874 to 1876, which Loti thought the worst of his life at the time, there seemed to be more and more need to make sorties out of himself – to find forgetfulness in wild adventuring. He was still agonizing over the loss of *la bien aimée*, and made a last desperate effort to see her. By certain references in his unpublished journals, it seems certain that he believed the child to whom she had given birth some months after her return from Africa was his. In any case, her door remained barred to him, the impetuous, inconvenient suitor, who even contrived to force an entry to the house in Geneva by dressing up in the costume of a peasant from the Valais and saying he was the cook's fiancé. Not that it worked; she remained adamant.

Soon the hateful present became even more unbearable, for just as he was beginning to accept the fact he was in no position to embark on the responsibilities of matrimony and possibly fatherhood too, Joseph Bernard, who had been cooling at a distance, broke with him in bitterness. All the old ties of their youthful devotion were shat-tered. *Le frère adoré* was no longer even in the background. No-one has explained the cause of this rupture; in later references to it, Loti puts the blame on Joseph, but still seems mystified as to its cause. ('This sombre enigma which has taken him from me, irrevocably.') The draft of a letter to Joseph seems to indicate the rift was caused by

Joseph wishing to extricate himself from his former perfervid emotional ties with Loti. Joseph always moralized, and now, perhaps, saw the dangers of such a relationship continuing. Loti replies: 'I have chosen my way and I take my stand, in the strange situation which is mine, in the world . . .' At that time, and seen from the extremely narrow, Catholic bourgeois family background that was Joseph's, the uproars occasioned by Loti's tumultuous nature, and perhaps his homosexual tendencies, if no more, must have become a strain on Joseph, and to the Bernard family, inadmissible, all danger – the devil's own.

Thus Joseph was transposed into another of those lost and loved who always peopled Loti's sinister dreams. Like Lucette with no lungs, Bernard haunted Loti's sleep with fatal regularity, symbol of loss, lying dead among the lichens and dismal forests of Magellan which they had explored together. They never met again. Joseph left the navy without telling Loti, who only learned of it by chance from a gazette which recorded Service matters. Such secrecy on Joseph's part was a further shock. So, presently, was his wedding, to which he did not invite Loti, although Loti had written, asking if he might attend. His letter was sent back unopened, and the rupture was complete; Joseph followed the patriarchal ways of his family, had nine children, and came to forbid Loti's name to be mentioned in his presence. When, as an old man, some of the younger members of both families tried to heal the breach, he still refused. Loti's worldwide reputation as a man of letters, an Academician, a bemedalled officer, the companion of his boyhood, did not move Bernard. He had seen the error of his early ways. For Loti, it remained one more yesterday to regret.

The spring of 1875 found Loti's gymnastic training over, and his body remodelled most satisfactorily. He was nominated to the cruiser *Couronne,* based at Toulon, and wrote to a friend that all his free time was now spent with a circus, in company with the clowns and equestriennes who jump through paper hoops. 'I am learning all these arts, to stand upright on horseback while performing backward somersaults.' He goes on to describe how he has refurbished his cabin – 'completely in the early eighteenth century style. The walls are hung with a striped red silk, the bed covered with a heavy seventeenth-century embroidery; there are old mirrors with extraordinary gilded frames, ancient weapons and porcelain vases always full of roses. This cabin, far below deck, is a dark hole without air, but its obscurity does not displease me, it lends a rich, mysterious air to the things around me . . . All this luxury is the result of luck at the tables. One night, when I did not have ten francs in my pocket, I went to play – *et voilà*.' This was to be the first of many cabins that Loti transformed into strange settings reflecting exotic leanings. Also, it would seem, reflecting the tolerance of his commanding officers, and the devotion of the orderly responsible for cleaning and tidying what he no doubt saw as so much clutter.

As time went by, we see that Loti enjoyed special indulgence from people in all walks of life. In the navy he seems to have been generally able to get round not only hide-bound superiors, but to win the total devotion of each crew that served under him, just as he enthralled much of that coldly critical, self-satisfied world of '*le tout Paris*'. Those few people alive today who knew him have been quite unable to describe to me this fascination of which they were well aware: 'those eyes – those extraordinary eyes of his,' they all said, and then came to a standstill . . . But those eyes – no-one ever forgot those eyes: penetrating, obsessive, hopelessly nostalgic, 'the eyes of an unhappy child', 'great dark eyes which seemed to call for help', 'eyes which seemed to open on to an abyss of some profound night . . .', 'eyes which had known the infinity of the deserts and the seas'. No: Loti was like no-one else, they said; you couldn't describe the man in so many words: he was all contradiction.

So it seems, for the dutiful second-lieutenant Viaud of the *Couronne*, the brooding lover who still secretly suffered over his tragic love affair and Joseph's break, is next found performing with the Etruscan Circus, one of Toulon's attractions. Evidently he was dying to exhibit the acrobatic skills he had mastered at Joinville, and not averse to showing off his splendid new muscles. An acrobat's outfit was just the costume for this, especially if ordered from the best place – something he took care to do.

Before the performance he had come early to help light the lamps, and stood in the wings with his friend, the delicious Pasqualine, 'Star of the North'. 'She has no equal in her equestrian backward somersault number, and is engaged to one of the riders. An old hanger-on accuses her of being too intimate with me – scenes of jealousy, faintings . . . cups of tea, reconciliations, tenderness . . .' Loti tried to master his stage fright, as he peeped at groups of his friends, shipmates, and staff of the local brothel, taking their seats, amid much laughter and whispering. They were armed with enormous bouquets, oranges and squeaky toys with which they intended to pelt him.

He clutched at the stage manager and said he doubted he could go through with it.

'But Monsieur's name is on the programme,' the director replied with finality. By now, after numerous rehearsals, Loti had become one of the family and nerves were not admitted.

'It is time for me to dress,' writes Loti next day, reliving every moment of it for his journal. 'My costume comes straight from Milan, chez Carolo Lorenzi, who makes for all the fashionable acrobats . . .' (More dressing up, more escaping.) 'But the tights are a problem. I don't know how to get into them. Two clowns come to my help. My trunks are tight enough to split, which is the buffoon's extreme elegance. Bathing trunks of black velvet, so brief I tremble, big lace cuffs, a green wig with pompons, a mask and a handful of flour and I am ready. The cousins – for among circus folk all are "cousins", tell me I am magnificent.'

Once again, Loti's journals recall the painters of his age. This is a scene Toulouse-Lautrec might have immortalized: the flaring oil lamps, glittering over spangles and crudely painted faces: only this Hamlet-figure in black velvet seems out of place. It is difficult to imagine Loti as a comic; his is essentially the romantic pose. No doubt his turn was less clowning than acrobatic, despite the pompons and floury face.

The 'cousins' had no fault to find, as Loti stood before them, in his Lorenzi outfit.

' "A bit too thin, maybe?" I ask, uneasily' (*short* was what he really meant).

' "Not a bit – you're so well made, the chest so strong, the shoulders so square . . . What a pity Monsieur is not one of us!"

'With a certain complacency I contemplate this body that I have transformed by exercise. The muscles stand out in relief on the skin tight costume. An old juggler, master-hand at all the tricks of the trade, augments the effect by lightly shading in the shadows and outlines of my muscles with a crayon; this curious anatomic toilet takes twenty minutes.

'The music begins. With terrible apprehension I enter the ring. Frenetic applause. Three bows. Eight "cousins" are hot on my heels.

My muscles feel like springs . . . *Voltige*, perilous leaps, backwards or head over heels, the human pyramid, giddy balancing acts, a programme chosen to show off my répertoire in all its éclat.'

Once again, we marvel at the forbearance shown by Loti's commanding officers, who were well aware, as was the whole squadron, of these extra-service activities. He was not yet a celebrated writer, nor yet the distinguished officer he became: what then was the secret of such indulgence? There is no explanation, save that compelling charm he could exercise over so many different kinds of people, races, and classes. 'As he succeeded, I knew nothing of the whole business – but had he failed I should have bloody well clapped him in irons' is a polite version of what the Admiral was to say, recalling the circus episode, when sub-lieutenant Julien Viaud served under him at Toulon.

Fortunately Loti's act was a blazing success. Many years later he was to say it had been the happiest moment of his entire life, just as the photographs taken of him in his circus costume were the ones he preferred to give his friends. When crowned with fame he still glowed, recalling an occasion at a country fair when he had beaten a very tough adversary in a wrestling match. Physical prowess was what Loti valued most.

His mother wrote plaintively:

'It is impossible, my poor darling, for me to rejoice in the triumphs you have obtained in the circus . . . I must admit they are not the kind I had dreamed of for you.'

But he was such a generous, loving son! he could never really disappoint her. She continues:

'Why do you send me a list of your expenses? [cost of the costume from Lorenzi perhaps?] I am not criticizing. Indeed, I think there are very few young men launched in the world who spend as little as you, and I never cease to regret that you still have such heavy charges to support . . . Tante Claire and I beg you to tell us what we are to do with the giraffe skins you brought back from Senegal? They are almost rotten, and not at all an ornament for the courtyard.'

Those giraffe hides were only the first of a legion of objects, exotic, valuable, cumbersome or bizarre which Loti gradually crammed into the old house. There, in the small space left to them, the old ladies were to be seen, stacking the cupboards, smothered in gigantic tapestries, stumbling over magnificent but dangerous weapons, over Sulïema the African tortoise, or standing bewildered before the turbanned catafalque of some long-dead Emir, transported to No. 141 Rue Saint-Pierre by smugglers from Damascus.

6

For he on honey dew hath fed
And drunk the milk of paradise.

Samuel Coleridge

Sacha Guitry, the celebrated French actor, once said that a monument should be erected to the French navy for having ordered Lieutenant Viaud to sail for Salonika: 'and on the pedestal, it should read TO THE MINISTERE DE LA MARINE WHICH ORDERED PIERRE LOTI TO WRITE, ONE DAY, *AZIYADÉ*.'

That is how Guitry and countless others felt after reading this book, which recounts a series of episodes in the life of a young naval officer stationed in Turkish waters. But it is much more than a romantic tale. It is the apogee of Loti's romantic dreams and the fountainhead of his lifelong Turkophil sympathies. It is, too, an incomparable evocation of Constantinople, the city of the Sultans, before it became Ataturk's Istanbul. This was the city and the people to whom Loti felt bound for the rest of his days, a way of life, an idiom of beauty that was always to haunt him, and call him back. Indeed, this book has been described as Loti's love affair with a city, rather than a woman. But then, it was also said to be his love affair with a boy – Aziyadé being no more than one of Loti's androgynous amours, a theory which his letters, unpublished journals, and subsequent life all refute. It was this journal which he kept during his Turkish days which became the source of this, his first, book. But while his second, recalling Papeete, was lyrical, and the third, evoking Senegal, was all fiery violence, *Aziyadé* is steeped in a predestined melancholy such as both he and the city reflect. Scenes of action follow descriptions of Turkish life, interspersed with rapturous love-scenes, and accounts of local ways. A thread of tragedy weaves all into a reverie of love and loss. Whereas in *Le Mariage de Loti* and *Le Roman d'un Spahi* he presents himself and his travels judiciously interwoven with a certain amount of fiction, *Aziyadé* is otherwise. Improbable as it appears (and *inadmissible* to most Turks) Loti had lived all of that adventure, that double life, between his ship and the little house for lovers' meetings, with a Circassian mistress filched from a harem. The journals recorded it all, and needed no dramatization: but it was a dangerous game he played, for he was an Infidel – a 'Roumi', in the land of the Faithful. It was at this time he first adopted the device (also followed in *Le Mariage de Loti*) of making himself out an English officer. *Aziyadé* is subtitled *Extracts of Notes and Letters of a Lieutenant in the British Navy*. By this means of Anglicizing himself he sought to avoid any possibility that he, Julien Viaud, an inconspicuous officer in the French navy, could be involved in awkward situations arising from any admission of his liaison with a Moslem woman. Had this become widely known, it would have caused violent Turkish reactions at an international level. Not only does the book follow his journals closely, but it incorporates letters he wrote to both his sister and the faithful Plumkett. As has been told, it was Loti's habit to fold letters he received or drafts of those he wrote, between the pages of his journals, day by day. Comparing these sources, the ring of truth sounds behind the romantic imbroglio of *Aziyadé*. Only names are changed. While Jousselin-Plumkett remains Plumkett, Rochefort becomes an English provincial town, Brightbury. Loti's ship, the *Gladiateur*, anchored in the Bosphorus, becomes the *Deerhound*, the love-struck boatman Daniel is called Samuel, while Aziyadé, Loti's love, was in real life called Hakidjé.

Aziyadé, an Oriental-sounding name, was invented by Loti to protect her from scandal when the book was published, though he always maintained her real name was prettier. It has been suggested that Aziyadé is a combination of two Turkish words – *aziz*, dearest, and *yad*, memory: it also recalls Victor Hugo's Albaydé of *Les Orientales*, with her *beaux yeux de gazelle*; while Azâde in Turkish signifies 'free', surely something of which Loti was aware.

Loti's introduction to the land he was to love above all others was a grim one. On 16th May 1876 his ship left Hyères for Salonika, the Macedonian port then belonging to Turkey. An allied fleet of French, German, English, Austrian and Russian warships was dispatched to exact reparations for the assassination of the French and

105

German Consuls by some hot-headed Turkish nationalists. It was a time of tension in Europe, following Turkish atrocities in Bulgaria, then under Ottoman rule like the rest of the Balkans. Thus the arrival of Allied warships in the harbour of Salonika was designed not only to avenge the Consuls' assassination, but to assert Christian Europe's displeasure at Turkish persecution of Christian minorities. Naturally, thoughts of territorial gains lurked behind religious scruples, and Islam had not forgotten how, only forty years earlier, the French conquest of Algeria had been triggered off by a tap from the Dey's fan: a most convenient excuse for reducing and colonizing a coveted country. Thus the Turks found it expedient to bow before the Allied demands for reprisals. The book opens on the assassins' execution.

'A lovely day in May . . . When the launches of the Allied fleet arrived at the quayside, the hangmen were putting the final touches to their work: six men were performing their horrible last contortions . . . the windows and roofs were crowded with spectators: on a balcony nearby, the Turkish authorities were smiling at this familiar spectacle. The Sultan's government had not spent much on the gallows; they were so low that the bare feet of the condemned men touched the ground. Their toe-nails scraped the sand.'

The grisly business of the hangings being concluded, there followed the solemn pomp of an official funeral for the murdered Consuls, all of which was recorded by Loti. Seen from today, when life is held increasingly cheap, and violence prevails, with gangsters, hold-ups and the whole practice of hostages becoming a regular means of persuasion, the measures imposed by the Allied powers in Salonika strike an unaccustomed note of firmness. Attacks on diplomats today have become an occupational hazard, earning headlines, even the temporary breaking off of diplomatic relations, but not the show of force Loti witnessed in 1876. After the French Consul's coffin had lain in state attended by the Admirals of the Allied fleets, the Pacha, Mussulman dignitaries, and a detachment of Prussian and French sailors, all with fixed bayonets, the cortège set out, making for the Greek Chapel. 'The atmosphere was tense; it only needed a handful of hostile inhabitants to trap, and annihilate this whole procession of hated foreigners.' But the walls were plastered with the Pacha's orders for the day, orders which proved wonderfully subduing.

'Article 1 Any house from which, even by accident, an object falls on the procession will be immediately razed to the ground and the inhabitants hung.

'Article 2 Any person found among the crowd carrying arms will be hung, on the spot.'

The Allied fleets remained at Salonika for some time, anchored in the blue bay, so that Loti began his customary expeditions about the town and countryside. The hostile atmosphere had not abated, and all officers who chose to go ashore were ordered to be in full uniform, armed, and also wearing a sword. It was in this striking outfit that Aziyadé first caught sight of him. Loti had been wandering about the old Moslem quarter of the town, with its tortuous streets overhung by close-latticed mouchrabiyehs, and approaching one old house where the windows were barred, but not latticed, he experienced a strange sensation of being watched. 'Behind those heavy iron bars, two large green eyes were fixed on me. The eyebrows were drawn across, so that they met: the expression of those eyes was a mixture of energy and naïveté – one might have said it was that of a child, so fresh, so young it appeared . . . A white veil was wound tightly round the head, leaving only the brow, and those great eyes free. They were green – that sea-green which poets of the Orient once sang.

'This young woman was Aziyadé.

'Aziyadé stared at me fixedly. Before a Turk she would have hidden herself; but a giaour is not a man: only an object of curiosity, something to be observed, at leisure.'

Loti was immediately subjugated by those lovely eyes and the air of mystery, of forbidden fruit, which surrounded Aziyadé, but he could not exchange one word with her. How then could he hope to approach her, although he sensed she wished him to. Her green eyes told him that. He missed the last cutter back to his ship, and wondering where to obtain a caïque to row him out, sat in a café on the quay, surrounded by boatmen and porters. 'Among a group of Macedonians, I noticed a young man with a curious kind of beard – separated in small curls, like the antique Greek statues. He was observing me with lively curiosity. He had something of the manner of a big angora cat, and when he yawned, he showed a double row of very small teeth, white as pearls. He was in rags, barefooted and barelegged, his chemise in tatters, but he was meticulously clean, like a cat.

107

'This person was Samuel.

'These two beings, both encountered on the same day, were soon to fill a place in my existence, and, for three months, risk their lives for me . . . both were to abandon their way of life to follow me, and we were destined to pass the coming winter together, under the same roof, in Stamboul.'

No sooner had Loti set foot on Turkish soil than he was aware of an elective affinity. At once, he wished to be part of the great stream of Eastern life which surged through the vine-wreathed street markets, sprawled around the harbours, or sat in immobility and quiet, lulled by *kef*, which offered stretches of deliberate, voluptuous *nothingness*. *Kef*, or *rahat*, is the quintessential Oriental retreat from a too pressing reality. To the Turks *rahat* spelled timeless hours becalmed in fatalism, in drifts of dreams, forming and reforming, nebulous as the smoke rising from their narghiles. For Loti, who always fled the realities of life and the spectre of death, *rahat* was yet another link in the chain which bound him to this land.

By June 1876 he was writing to a friend of this dangerous, delicious life he was living. He had established a bond with Samuel, who had become his regular boatman about the harbour. They talked in Sabir, the common language of the Levantine ports. *Te portarem col la mia barca*, says Samuel, which translates as 'I will take you in my barque.' Loti now adopted his usual practice of dressing up, 'playing the effendi, as boys play soldiers', he wrote to a friend, describing his adventures. 'Act I: a dark, miserable room, but much Oriental colour. Your friend Loti is surrounded by three old Jewesses, hook-nosed, and hung with paillettes. They dress him as a Turk, putting several daggers into his sash, handsome weapons, their blades damascened in gold. The outfit is completed by a gold-embroidered jacket with wide sleeves, and a tarboosh. They panto-mime their admiration. Loti studies himself in a long mirror, and decides his new image is satisfactory (even though faintly like an operatic tenor). Such a costume could prove fatal, for were he discovered, a hated giaour, masquerading as one of the Faithful no mercy would be shown.' He left by another door: once more escaping from himself, and as Arik Ussim Effendi, an Albanian, merged into the life of the seething streets. The bazaars, mosques, and hammams – all were his, if he could pass unremarked.

'Further than this,' writes Loti, 'it would be imprudent to follow your friend. At the end of it all there is love – the love of a Turkish woman, moreover, the wife of a Turk – an insensate adventure. Beside her, Loti is going to spend an hour of complete intoxication at the risk of his head, and the heads of several others, and all kinds of diplomatic complications as well.'

Aziyadé was a Circassian, the youngest of four kadines, or legal wives, in the harem of the old Abeddin Effendi. They and their black slaves lived in a well-to-do *konak*, above Salonika, on the road to Monastir. Since it was the countryside, the harem was not very strictly guarded; even so, there were bars everywhere. Each afternoon Loti left his ship wearing the prescribed uniform and, joining Samuel, entered that mysterious house of disguises by one door, to leave by another, as another man, up to no good, on the road to Monastir.

'She did not belong to me yet: but nothing stood between us now, save material barriers: the presence of her master, and the iron bars at her window.'

At this point, one distinctly hears the opening notes of *L'Enlèvement du Sérail* . . . but it is not Mozart's airs which best suit these lovers: rather, the doom-drenched music of Wagner's *Tristan and Isolde*.

Loti was becoming attached to the vagabond Samuel, but still dared not confide his plan. To speak of a harem inmate was imprudent – inadmissible even. He hinted, but Samuel seemed not to understand. In the cafés they sat smoking *kef*, Loti yearning for Aziyadé, and, it was gradually apparent, Samuel yearning for Loti. There are only faint inferences of this in the novel, but Loti's unpublished journals reveal his ambiguous attitude to such advances. While desiring Aziyadé madly, he does not appear to have made very convincing efforts to discourage Samuel. 'By force of so much past unhappiness I had become inert, my heart emptied of all emotion. Now something that resembled love flowered in the ruins. The Orient had cast its powerful spell over me . . .' All *voluptés* beckoned. 'My evenings are spent with Daniel (as Samuel is in these unpublished pages of the journal). With Daniel I have seen strange things: strange practices and prostitutions in the cellars where they are completely drunk on raki or mastic. That is how things are in Turkey: women are for the rich, who can have many: for the poor, there are boys.' It becomes clear that Daniel-Samuel expected Loti to embark on these 'strange practices', and that he was quite bemused by the young officer. Loti writes unequivocally of Samuel's emotional approaches. 'The sins of Sodom flower everywhere in this ancient city of the Orient . . . though I do not share the unavowed physical desires of this man, chance has brought us together . . . Am I destined always to wear this mask of extreme youth? The fascination which I can exercise over a man plunges me into troubled thoughts, a vague uneasiness and even mysterious horrors . . . Yet how can I repulse some humble creature who loves me without reserve when it costs me nothing to spare him that sort of rebuff – the most bitter of all? Everything is relative. Is there a God – a moral?' Thus Loti mused, and Samuel suffered what finally became an unrequited passion. But Loti was counting on Samuel's devotion to obtain his aid regarding Aziyadé. Perhaps, in spite of lingering Protestant scruples, he was too encouraging. Samuel was bewildered. ' "But what do you want of me? *Che volete mi?*" ' he asked, as Loti turned away from his passionate embraces. 'His hand trembled in mine, and I lifted his head . . . there was a strange light in his eyes, and his whole body trembled . . . "What do you want from me?" he repeated, his voice sombre, troubled. And then he took me in his arms, and holding me close, pressed his lips on mine ardently. I had achieved my ends . . . indeed I had gone terribly beyond them: I should have foreseen his dénouement . . .' Thus the *unpublished* journal: but in the final version of the book, hero Loti gently yet firmly disengages himself from such a tricky situation, telling Samuel that kind of love is criticized – forbidden, even, in his country. ' "Never think of it again, or I shall have to send you away from me," ' says Loti in the book (and probably on the advice of his publishers). 'Samuel buried his face in his arms and remained silent. But from that night, he had been at my service body and soul . . . Each night he risks his liberty and life, to obtain entrance to the house where Aziyadé lives: to reach it he crosses, in the darkness, a cemetery which for him holds terrifying visions. He waits for me all night long . . . his being is, as it were, absorbed in mine. Wherever I go, whatever the costume I have chosen, he is my shadow, ready to defend my life at the risk of his own.'

Between the book and the journals it is clear that a tenebrous relationship continued to unite these two young men; but Loti's uneasy reactions to Samuel's advances (something he would scarcely have bothered to record in his most secret journals were it not true) refute the legend of Loti's *exclusive* homosexuality. This aspect of his nature was clearly only one side of his ardent sensuality, which, at that moment, was centred round Aziyadé: but Samuel was the way to Aziyadé. And then, 'I have the temperament of a Bedouin', Loti was to admit later to Edmond de Goncourt – and here, *temperament* is used in the French sense of physical, or sexual, appetite, rather than the literal English translation of the word – which has no overt sexual connotation.

Now that Samuel had become his unquestioning slave, Loti pressed his approach to Abeddin Effendi's harem, though by what means Samuel obtained co-operation from the Effendi's household remains mysterious. Such a project demanded heavy bribes and Loti's pay was pinched. But at last the message he waited to hear was brought to him. Aziyadé would join him that night.

So began these desperate rendezvous.

On board, Loti's fellow officers wished him good night: some were in the secret, as their later letters were to prove. At eleven o'clock there was the faint sound of oars. Samuel's barque: the watch challenged him, but Loti reassured them. For the sake of appearances a number of nets and rods, all the fisherman's paraphernalia were stowed aboard. The lieutenant was after a very rare fish. They pulled off into the darkness. Loti removed his cloak and was revealed in Turkish dress. Samuel rowed towards another barque which loomed out of the obscurity. 'In it, a hideous old Negress enveloped in a blue cloak, and an old, heavily armed Albanian guard, and then – a woman – so closely veiled that one sees nothing but a shapeless white bundle. Samuel takes the first two personages into his barque, and rows away, silently. I am alone with the veiled woman, as silent and still as a pale phantom. I take the oars and pull out, towards the horizon . . . my eyes are fixed on her, and I wait for her to make some movement, or sign . . . When we are far enough from all else, she holds out her arms to me. I reach her side, trembling as I touch her. At this first contact I am filled with a mortal languor: her veils are impregnated with all the perfumes of the Orient, her flesh is firm and cool.

111

'I have loved another woman that I no longer have the right to see: but never have my senses known such a madness as now . . .

'Aziyadé's barque is filled with soft rugs, cushions and Turkish coverlets – all the refinements and nonchalance of the Orient, so that it seems a floating bed, rather than a barque. Our situation is strange, for we cannot exchange one word. All dangers surround this bed of ours, which drifts slowly out to sea: it is as if two beings are united there to taste the intoxicating pleasure of the impossible.

'In three hours, when the Great Bear sinks in the vast skies, we must part. It is the hand of the clock which marks our hours of madness . . . In that barque, we forget all else; the same kiss, begun by night, continues until dawn . . .'

When, from afar, they heard the cock crow, the lovers rejoined Samuel's barque, where all three of their devoted servitors dozed. Aziyadé's escort rejoined her and made for the shore, while in Samuel's barque, he and Loti, shivering in the chill dawn dew, drew the covers over themselves, to lie close in sleep. Thus both the book and the journal; but the journal records further heady scenes with Samuel, who was suffering prolonged pangs, for, having brought about the lovers' union, he found himself relegated to the background, along with Aziyadé's black slave, Kadidja, and the old Albanian guard, who were also risking their lives for the lovers. Loti records watching the sleeping Samuel: 'his head was of an antique beauty. Sleep had imposed something tranquil, chaste, severe. I forgot Aziyadé, thinking of this curious fate that had united me to this man . . . Samuel opened his eyes, and half asleep took me in his arms, pressing his lips on mine. "It is you, effendi? I love you," he murmured . . . "and the Negress and the old man, are they at the bottom of the sea?" ' So saying, Samuel sank back to sleep, Loti beside him, as their boat drifted aimlessly on the still waters of the bay.

For all those rapt hours that Loti and Aziyadé shared, in the barque that was a floating bed, they still could not exchange a single word. One night, Aziyadé commanded Samuel to remain with them. She wished to know more of her lover. Where were you born? How old are you? Have you a mother? Do you believe in God? Have you seen the land of the black men? Have you had many mistresses? Are you a seigneur in your country? This questionnaire continued till, like Rarahu before her, it seemed that Aziyadé was troubled by the thought that their different religions might not allow them to be united in the grave. 'She asks if you will jump into the sea with her, and so drown together,' said Samuel. ' "Then let us do it now" I replied "and all will be over." Aziyadé understood, and flung her arms round my neck, as we leant far out over the water.' But Samuel held them both in a grip of iron. 'Ugly kisses you would give each other down there, deep in the slime,' he said savagely. 'Drowning people make hideous grimaces . . .' But Loti had understood: the journals reflect Samuel's fury more clearly: he would have consigned Aziyadé to the deep, but he wanted Loti *alive*. 'And when we were alone again in our boat, Samuel came close to me, and drew me to him, leaning his head against mine . . . That is how he remains, for a few minutes, each night, immobile and happy, overflowing with tenderness and humility. By his insidious charm and persistence he has obtained from me this strange salary for his limitless devotion.'

Such a delirious pattern could not endure, and it is likely that Loti's increasing imprudence had become known to his commanding officers, for in August he was ordered off to join another ship, stationed at Constantinople. He was to leave immediately. There was a last rendezvous with Aziyadé, Samuel interpreting. 'In the autumn,' she said, 'Abeddin Effendi, my master, will move to Stamboul with our harem: if he does not do this – I, I alone – shall come to you.' Loti cherished this reckless project, but could scarcely believe it possible.

Loti arrived in Constantinople to find his new ship, the *Gladiateur*, away on manoeuvres, so that he had time to establish himself ashore. At first, from the Europeanized quarter of Pera, he was tasting the easy ways of the Levantine quarter, cynically enjoying Armenian, Bulgarian and Greek charmers, or wandering about the cemeteries at night, where prostitution flourished among the graves – the quick and the dead. He was savouring what he calls *'les pâles débauches'*, which kept him from thinking too often of Aziyadé, as did his first explorations of Stamboul, the ancient, purely Turkish city, across the Galata bridge. There its immemorial ways remained unchanged.

No stranger has ever understood and savoured the city of the

Sultans better than Loti. Just as every historic city about the world has its quintessential moment in time (the geography of time), so it has its painter or writer who interprets it best: Turgenev for Russia, with its endless birch forests: Dickens and Cruikshank for London, with its foggy streets, snug pubs and pork pies. Constantinople finds its most perfect expression through Loti's eyes, as he found it his perfect subject. His sombre nature recognized this city which, though on the European shore, belongs to Asia. It has little of the dew-dropping south of Miss Pardoc's early nineteenth-century *Beauties of the Bosphorus*, so lushly illustrated by W. H. Bartlett's engravings. Chill winds rage down from the steppes of Central Asia, beyond the Black Sea, and it is, in essence, a winter city. Loti sensed this, describing those nights when Stamboul is wrapped in an immense shroud of snow, and through the icy mists a bluish moonlight reveals the great grey masses of the mosques with their lance-like minarets . . . Or again, those nights, hidden away in the little house for lovers' meetings, crouched beside a *mangal*, or brazier, the wind battering at the shutters . . . These are wintry scenes such as the Turkish people themselves knew, scenes unknown to dwellers in hotels, a way of life as unfamiliar to most of his readers then, as now.

Stamboul has never offered itself easily: its abiding essence has always remained hidden from those who do not search for it. However, there are still some forgotten quarters: vertiginous cobbled ways which lead down to the Marmora or lie around the Mosque of Sultan Selim are still much as Loti knew them, forbidding, withdrawn, silent. The bleached greyish wooden houses he knew are still there: the windows of their top-heavy upper storeys are sealed from prying eyes by mouchrabiyehs, and seem to conceal dark secrets. As we pass, we are aware of unseen watchers observing us, shadows lurking behind the lattice – shadows with eyes. Graveyards abound, those 'little fields of the dead', vast areas spread about this city, for death is a cult here, as it was with Loti. 'Yet a Turkish cemetery,' he wrote, 'has nothing of the horror of our European cemeteries: its Oriental melancholy is softer, and also, more majestic.' The dark spears of cyprus shelter simple graves and great turbehs alike. Sumptuous kiosks vaunt the might of long-dead pachas, but for all their brocaded and plumed catafalques topped by huge turbans such as those Loti was one day to place in the mosque he built at Rochefort, they, like the lurching, weather-beaten steles of the unknown dead, all echo his eternal *Alas!* and Never More!

Loti had not been long in Constantinople before Samuel turned up. 'I leave my friends , my country, my barque to follow you, *Effendim.*' Loti was touched by such fidelity. Could Aziyadé hold to her promise, he wondered. With Samuel's help, he decided to live *à la Turque* the better to prepare for her possible arrival. First, it was necessary to learn enough Turkish to pass as an Armenian or a Kurd – never as a European. He took lessons from an Armenian priest who marvelled at his facility, for Loti had put his whole heart into his studies and made rapid progress. 'I cherished an impossible project, to live with her somewhere along the Corne d'Or, living the life of a Moslem – her life. I wanted to possess her for whole days at a time, to read her mind and her heart, and understand strange wild things hardly imagined, during our nights at Salonika. I wanted her to be wholly mine.' Presently he decided to fulfil at least part of this dream, choosing a lodging at Khassim-Pachen, and later the remote and sacred village of Eyoub up the Corne d'Or [or Golden Horn]. This, with Samuel, was a base from which he could come and go, again as Arik Ussim, wearing Albanian costume, so that his halting Turkish was accepted.

Eyoub was a microcosm of Turkish life, with its water front, its bazaars, cafés, and cemeteries round the venerated tomb and mosque of Eyoub Ansari, the Prophet's companion. The little house intended for lovers' meetings was a dilapidated dwelling beside the landing stage. There were only three whitewashed rooms and a terrace shaded by a vine. From there the windings of the Corne d'Or could be traced as far as the heights of Pera, on the opposite shore. Beyond, the Bosphorus wound to the Black Sea, and at Dolmabagtché, Loti's ship was anchored; it was remote enough for his two lives to remain separate.

Carping voices have said that the idyll – if it was lived at all – was certainly not lived at Eyoub, the most sacred quarter of all Constantinople. But Eyoub had a thriving secular life beside its mosques and tombs, and Loti passed for an Albanian. To the citizens of Eyoub, it was Allah who had set this stranger, this mussafir Arik Ussim Effendi among them, and the Koran is specific on hospitality. Nevertheless, at nightfall Loti found Eyoub sinister. 'The Turks go to bed with the sun. All is silent . . . here and there, a lamp casts its light through the grilles of a small window. Do not look in at that opening. The lamp is a funeral lamp, to light the great catafalques. Your throat would be cut, were you seen peering in, and no-one would come to your aid. The vast hillside cemeteries are haunted by evil doers, who, having robbed you, bury you, there and then, without the police being involved.'

It was at this moment that the drama of Sultan Mourad's deposition took place. The Sultan Abdul Hamid – he who became known to Europe as the Red Sultan for his bloody persecutions – succeeded him, to be crowned, or rather, girded, with Othman's sabre, the ritual sword of rulership in the most holy mosque of Eyoub Ansari. Loti contrived to be present at the Padishah's arrival. The State caïque was an elaborate gilded affair, with twenty-six velvet-clad rowers, and a great golden bird at its prow. The new Sultan had emerged from that *kefess*, or cage, in the Top Kapou Seraglio, where princes in the line of Ottoman succession were sequestered – sometimes their whole life long – awaiting the death of their predecessor. 'My caïque touched those of the Imperial procession,' wrote Loti. 'This man they were conducting from obscurity to supreme power appeared sunk in an uneasy reverie.' In time Loti, the famous writer and Turkophil, was to know the Sultan on easy terms – if anyone could be said to be at ease, entering the close-guarded, spy-ridden precincts of his palace at Yildiz, where he skulked, trembling pale at every passing footfall, though striking terror into the hearts of all around him. Few shared the opinion of the British Ambassadress, Lady Layard, who found him 'a dear little man, though nervous, and given to biting his nails'. But that was some years ahead. When Loti watched the Sultan's historic arrival at Eyoub, the Padishah was still a young, untried ruler, and Loti only a watcher in the crowd.

Yet from the moment he reached Turkish waters, he was identifying with Turkey, its ways and its people, so that already he resented European condemnation over the thorny question of Christian minorities. Loti was never a political animal. He saw each country subjectively, as it affected *himself*. In Turkey he had found a people, a woman, a mystic faith, a land and its art, all surpassing anything he had known before. For the rest of his life he was to remain under that spell, blindly loyal.

Aziyadé! Aziyadé! He was waiting for her, always waiting . . . He wrote to his sister, dwelling on his sense of emptiness. 'I am in a

116

profound void . . . But as long as I have my dearest old mother, I shall stay outwardly as I am . . . When she is no more, I shall bid you farewell, and vanish without leaving any trace.'

In a letter to Plumkett, written from the hide-out at Eyoub, his mood had changed. He was savouring the pleasures of the moment – of the charade he was living. 'Your friend Loti is alone in his little house. Chill rain and high winds beat against the shutters. How sombre, this Eyoub, this heart of Islam!' Yet seated on a low divan, wearing a fur-lined garment, his slippered feet on a thick Turkish rug, he was tasting that sense of well-being known to the egoist at home.

As I have remarked earlier, different phases of Loti's life recall different painters: Gauguin for his Tahitian idyll; the French Impressionists for his riverside picnics among the Golos and their *midinettes* at Joinville-le-Pont; Toulouse-Lautrec for the circus interlude. And now, Liotard's Turkish scenes are summoned, as he sits cross-legged in his flowing fur-lined caftan, tchibouque in hand, in the manner of the painter's Ottoman sitters, or those noble European travellers who adopted the Turkish mode so fashionable in the early eighteenth century and commanded Liotard to immortalize them thus.

The establishment at Eyoub had now been joined by Achmet, a young man who hired out the post horses by which Loti rode about the city, going to and from his ship. He soon became dragoman, domestic and confidant, but his presence caused a certain strain, for Samuel felt himself usurped. He had come to accept Aziyadé's place in Loti's life and thoughts, but Achmet was a *man* – a rival on other terms. Achmet seems to have been rather less emotional in his relations with Loti: together the two of them went about the old city which held no secrets from Achmet, born and bred there. His was an uncomplicated nature, his companionship cheerful, and Samuel the naïve boatman from Salonika was often left behind to mope. Loti was restless, for autumn was passing and there was still no word from Aziyadé – though Stamboul was all his. Plunged into the life of the streets, Loti saw little of his fellow officers.

This is how one of them, Mongel-Bey, remembered him.

'Our luncheons in the ward-room were always lively, the talk very free. Viaud took no part in the conversation; he was cold in manner;

very short and beardless, he still seemed an adolescent, an impression emphasized by the little jackets of English midshipmen, which he used to wear ... He always went ashore alone, and one was surprised, sometimes, to see him going about Stamboul dressed as a Turk, in company of the most simple class of Turks.' It was understood that his shipmates should not appear to recognize him were their paths to cross, and this was scrupulously observed.

7

Man's pleasure is like the noonday halt under the
shady tree; it must not — it cannot — be prolonged.

Arab proverb

4th December 1876. 'She is here! Tonight, Kadidja the old Negress
from Salonika will bring her to me . . .

'And when this impossible dream was realized, when she was
here, in this room prepared for her, alone with me, behind barred
doors, I could only fall at her feet . . . I was like one thunderstruck.

'Then, I heard her voice. For the first time, when she spoke I could
understand her. But I could not find a single word of that Turkish
tongue I had learned — for her.

' "*Severim seni Lotim!* I love you, Loti, I love you," she said. Others
had spoken those eternal words to me before Aziyadé, but for the first
time, I heard their sweet sound in Turkish . . .

'I lifted her in my arms, and placed her head under a ray of
lamplight, to see her better. "Say it again," I said. "Say it once
more." Now I began to tell her many things that she could understand, for now, my Turkish returned to me.

' "Answer me!" I commanded.

'But she was looking at me in a sort of ecstatic trance and I saw
that I was talking into space.

' "Aziyadé," I said, "don't you hear me?"

' "No," she replied. And gravely, she spoke these sweet, and
savage words:

' "I would like to eat the words of your mouth! *Senin laf yemek
isterim!* I would eat the sound of your voice!" '

So began their idyll at Eyoub.

Aziyadé, who became the embodiment of Loti's Oriental mirage,
was of that race of women whose destiny was to be man's pleasure.
She had been brought from her Circassian village as a child, to be

119

sold into a Turkish harem. No disgrace was attached to this commerce; it was set rather apart from the slave trade. If a girl was well placed, her family could expect to be well remunerated, while if she proved satisfactory, her future was assured in her master's household; as his concubine, she could be ultimately married off advantageously, the terms arranged by her owner, who, after some while, might hanker for a newcomer in his harem. But were she one of his kadines, one of the four wives sanctioned by the Koran, as was Aziyadé, then she enjoyed a more assured position and further privileges in the closed world of the harems.

Here is Loti's charming portrait of Abeddin Effendi's youngest kadine. 'Aziyadé seldom speaks: she smiles often, but never laughs: her footsteps make no sound, her movements are graceful, sinuous, calm, and noiseless. Such is this mysterious little creature who vanishes with daybreak, but whom the night often brings back, at the hour of the djinns and phantoms.' She is described as wearing a long Turkish *antari* or over-dress of violet silk strewn with gold roses, a chemise of silver-woven Broussa gauze, yellow silk *chalvari* (bouffant pantaloons) and yellow slippers, to match. 'She spends much time plaiting her long dark hair into eight heavy braids threaded with ribbons, or painting her delicate fingers with the orange-hued henna beloved of eastern women. Her garments, her flesh, all are impregnated with amber perfumes.'

Loti weaves many-coloured threads: small details, old customs and beliefs and strange people are the texture of his writing. Thus it is possible to read *Aziyadé*, this most vibrantly personal of all his books, on several levels: for the love story, for the exposé of the author's own character, or for evocations of old Stamboul. Unless, like most of Loti's contemporaries, one reads it without any analysis, simply falling page by page under his spell, suffering, and, above all, journeying beside him, about the city of the Sultans.

The merchant Abeddin Effendi was often away from Stamboul on business, thus the lovers' midnight assignations developed into whole days and nights together. It seems that the ladies of Abeddin's harem took care not to remark Aziyadé's absences. 'Our harem,' she said, 'is known everywhere as a model, for our mutual understanding and the good relations between us. We have our visits to make among the hanums of other harems whom we also receive. Then we each have our turn of service with our master . . .' On those days when he was free but Aziyadé was detained by what she described as her services to her master, Loti took to haunting the quarter where she lived. Even to stand in the street in sight of the house seemed to bring her nearer. Here is Loti's description of Abeddin Effendi's konak, Aziyadé's cage.

'It was in an ancient aristocratic quarter, near the mosque of Mehmet Fatih . . . Camels pad there with their tranquil step . . . there dervishes sit, unravelling mystical problems, and nothing of the West has yet penetrated . . . The house is an old wooden one, tall and gloomy yet with a mysterious air of opulence, painted dark crimson, its iron-barred windows closed by wooden lattices. The overhanging *shaknisirs* [balconies] are painted with faded decorations of tulips and butterflies. Over the door, a star and crescent: everywhere, ancient worm-eaten woodwork . . . Never a passer-by in this street, never an open door, never a sound of life, or a light . . .'

As Loti's duties aboard were never exigent, there was ample time for him to continue studying Turkish. Soon he was speaking easily. Writing and reading remained a problem. Samuel was illiterate, Achmet and Aziyadé could write their names and read haltingly, but were not teachers, so Loti's lessons from the old mullah were increased to cramming point. Some of his Turkish scripts, exercises set by the mullah, copies of verses, aphorisms and classic Persian poetry, largely dwelling on death, remain among his papers. Loti was in love with all things Turkish, and the precarious and transient nature of the life he was leading only doubled its poignant enchantment. Already he foresaw its end. 'Who will give me back my Oriental life, my free life? Wandering without any set purpose . . . to make a round of the mosques, chaplet in hand, stopping at the cafés or Turkish Baths to drowse in the smoke of a narghile; to talk with the dervishes or passers-by; to be, myself, part of this scene, and to be sure that the beloved will be waiting for you, at night . . .'

Such was Loti's Oriental life; that life for which he was to ache ever after. Some malicious or uninformed persons would have maintained it never was: yet his letters and journals seem conclusive – at least to those who have had the opportunity to study them closely. Only the ending of *Aziyadé* is an invention. For his characters, death seemed the sole way out of a tragic impasse, and this imagined ending, which in real life was to prove, in part, strangely prophetic, was to haunt Loti with a death-wish ever after. While the *Gladiateur* was land-locked in the Bosphorus, the sea's fascination lay dormant for Loti. He too was land-locked, love-locked. Those stolen, dangerous hours beside Aziyadé and the carefree companionship of Achmet were now supplemented by admittance to another stratum of Ottoman life, an eclectic circle to which he had been mysteriously admitted. He does not tell us how. Was it as Ussim Effendi? More likely, as the enthusiastically Turkophil French officer.

'At Izeddin Effendi's one arrived at night, and did not leave till the following morning . . . His house, old and dilapidated from the outside, held within its dark walls all the mysterious magnificence of the Orient . . . In a large room where the carpets are so thick one seems to be walking on the back of a Kashmir sheep, five or six young men are seated, cross-legged, in attitudes of nonchalant, or tranquil reverie . . . Chairs, like women, are unknown in such Turkish gatherings. Not everyone is admitted to Izeddin Effendi's gatherings. Certainly not those sons of pachas who parade about the boulevards of Paris, overdressed and sottish: rather, the sons of old Turkey, brought up in the gilded *yalis*, far from that wind of equality, stinking with coal dust which blows from the west.' This was a gathering of traditionalists, having nothing in common with a rising party of militants known as the Young Turks, who, besides demanding a constitution, were becoming an agitating presence about the land: but Loti, if he were aware of them, for politics were not his strong point, would have had no sympathy with such sweeping reforms. Seated among his new friends he listened to grave talk of the coming war and 'the fatalities which Allah prepares for the Padishah and all Islam'.

What was then known as the Eastern Question centred round Turkey, for the European powers could not stomach the idea of an Ottoman Empire which continued to spread so vastly over the Christian Balkans, most of the Middle East, much of Central Asia and North Africa. In the House of Commons, Mr Gladstone thundered over the fate of Bulgarian virgins at the hands of the Terrible Turks – which was as good a stick as any other with which to beat the Sultan. Yet England as a whole, along with the Queen and Mr Disraeli, remained unmoved. Not everyone had forgotten how staunch an ally Turkey had been during the Crimean War. But Russia remembered her defeat in the Crimea; for centuries she had coveted Constantinople as the gateway to the east, and she too now began to denounce the treatment of her Christian co-religionists, minorities under Turkish rule in Herzegovina, Bulgaria and Serbia.

Russia had been at war with Turkey three times since 1828, and once again the Tsar's armies were moving south. All thinking Turks knew their days of peace were numbered, and Loti the Christian felt himself ranged beside Islam.

Meanwhile, living from embrace to embrace, the lovers were happy in their hiding-place. The winter winds buffeted the shutters, and the icy waters of the Corne d'Or slapped at the landing stage outside, where the caïques strained at their moorings. Then 'Aziyadé, in her solemn tones sings the song of the djinns, striking her little tambourine that is hung with tinkling paillettes. The smoke begins to form bluish spirals, and little by little I lose all sense of being, or the sadness of human life, as I contemplate three loved faces round me, my mistress, my servant and my cat' (Kédi Bey, Aziyadé's gift).

Although he had come to set Aziyadé apart, as a being whose duplicity towards her old master was redeemed by the fact it was *Loti* she loved, *Loti* with whom she deceived Abeddin Effendi, he could be severe in his judgement of others equally frail.

'Turkish women, in particular the more sophisticated, hold fidelity to their husbands very cheap. The savage surveillance and terror of punishment alone holds them in check. Always idle, eaten up with ennui, physically obsessed by the monotony and solitude of harem life, they are capable of giving themselves to the first comer – to a slave who is at hand, or the boatman who rows them about – if he is handsome, and pleases them . . . My knowledge of their language and my hidden house were both propitious for such enterprises. Had I wished, no doubt my hide-out could have become the rendezvous for many such idle inmates.' This complacent thought fermented in Loti's blood. Had so much honey begun to cloy on Lovelace Loti? Was he, even now, the unappeased sensualist, forever gratifying his Bedouin's temperament? Loti's character is so tangled a mass of contradictions, disguises and pirouettes that his biographer ceases to analyse and can only record.

Thoughts of the final parting hung over the lovers, and Aziyadé spent all her arts of persuasion to influence Loti to stay beside her. It would have been easy to vanish into the Turkish scene forever. Arik Ussim Effendi and Loti were two distinct separate beings. It would have sufficed, the day Loti's ship sailed, for Aziyadé's lover to remain in the house at Eyoub: no-one would have come there looking for an absconded naval officer. But Julien Viaud would have had to vanish for ever. And then, there was his mother. How could he leave her or let her face the shame of her Julien being branded a deserter? Aziyadé no longer tried to hold him when he told her that. She had the submission of true love: just what the despotic Loti enjoyed.

Allah selamet versen Aziyadé
Allah selamet versen Loti

(May Allah protect Aziyadé – May Allah protect Loti.)

It was a phrase that Aziyadé was in the habit of using, foreseeing the parting that lay ahead.

' "When you leave me," she said, "I shall go far away into the mountains, and I shall sing this song for you."

Shaïtanlar, djinnler
Kaplanar, duchmanlar
Arslandar . . .'

(May devils, djinns, lions and every enemy stay far from my love.)

'Each night, in her soft voice she sings this refrain, a long monotonous chant with curious rhythms and those melancholy oriental endings to each phrase. When I shall have left Stamboul, and am far from her for evermore, I shall hear again, in the night, Aziyadé's song.' He noted the sad little melody, inscribing the words in Turkish characters.

Aziyadé determined to give her lover something which would always recall their love. But she had no money of her own. In Abeddin Effendi's harem all her wants were supplied – gauzes, jewelled ornaments, perfumes, henna, sweetmeats and opium for her chased silver pipe – but never ready money. With considerable stealth and the aid of the old Negro slave she contrived to give some of her gold trinkets to an Armenian jeweller, who fashioned them into a massive ring with her name inscribed in Turkish letters. This became Loti's most treasured possession, something he was to wear to the end of his life.

On the 19th March 1877 Loti's ship was recalled to northern waters. As usual he thrashed about trying to circumvent an order contrary to his desires. Anything – anything to continue as Arik Ussim Effendi. Yet Loti had become a man who had accepted departure as a recurring part of his life in that Service to which he was vowed, and would hold, at whatever cost. Feverishly, he began a round of farewell calls among the European colony he had so seldom bothered to see. Protocol wasted the last precious hours à la turque. Poor long-suffering Samuel was ravaged to be ordered back to Salonika. 'He cannot understand that there is a great gulf between *his* love, and the uncomplicated, brotherly affection of Achmet . . . Samuel is an exotic plant, impossible to transplant to my orderly home' (as there had been vague talk of doing with Achmet). Were there continued, unrecorded dramas between Achmet and Samuel, with Loti standing between? Gratitude was not a marked part of Loti's nature. Samuel had played his part, had brought Aziyadé to him, and so now, adieu Samuel! 'Nevertheless I loved him,' writes Loti complacently, 'and something in his tears broke a corner of my heart.'

At Eyoub, before the porters arrived to dismantle the house of love, Loti made a drawing of the room where he had lived this strange adventure, but alas, this treasure has disappeared, like so many other relics, from the portfolios preserved at Rochefort. When Aziyadé arrived, for what was to be their last meeting, she found the walls bare. Like those condemned to death, she asked for a last favour. That night, rejoining her, he heard an extraordinary noise blaring from the house . . . singing and strange barbaric music. 'In the middle of a whirlwind of dust a chain of dancers spun round in one of those unending Turkish dances which continue, wildly, until the dancers drop by the way. Greek sailors, Moslems, all and sundry had been rounded up along the Golden Horn and were dancing furiously, and being served mastic or raki, and coffee. My neighbours and the dervishes Hassan and Mahmoud were looking on in stupefaction. Aziyadé was turning the handle of one of those deafening *orgues de Barbarie* – barrel-organs which played Turkish music stridently, accompanied by little bells and Chinese cymbals. She was unveiled, and anyone could see her face, against every custom, or the most elementary prudence. In all the holy quarter of Eyoub no-one had ever witnessed such a spectacle, nor imagined such a scandal, and had Achmet not sworn she was Armenian she would have been lost. She was turning the handle of the barrel-organ like a mad woman. Turkish music has been described as an access of heartbreaking gaiety, and now I perfectly understood this paradoxical definition.'

When Aziyadé could bear no more she tried to end it all, crushing the little coffee cup she held and opening a vein. But they staunched the blood and saved her – for more suffering. They had decided that Achmet would contrive to transmit Loti's letters to her, through Kadidja, the old slave, and Aziyadé set about preparing a series of envelopes for her lover to post from France. Achmet's address was complicated:

To Achmet, son of Ibrahim, who lives at Yedi-Koulé, near the mosque . . . the third house after a tutundji (tobacconists). At the side there is an old Armenian who sells remedies, and opposite there is a dervish.

Loti's last days with Achmet seem to have been almost as lacerating as those with Aziyadé, the two companions revisiting their old haunts one by one, while Achmet gave Loti a precious souvenir – a chaplet once belonging to his father. Even at this last moment, Loti was seized with an insensate desire to snatch Aziyadé from Abeddin's cage, but Achmet pulled him up. 'And if you succeeded? You no longer have anywhere to take her – where, in all Stamboul could you find shelter for yourself and the wife of another . . .?' (Of a Turk, above all, for neither Turk nor foreigner would risk that.) 'She would be lost,' said Achmet, 'and when you left, you would be abandoning her to the streets . . . No, Loti! Leave her where she is.'

Landing, loving and leaving . . . Once again, those last hours, last promises and last embraces which had become the pattern of Loti's romantic youth. Aziyadé wished to accompany him to the wharf at Fonducli from where he was to embark; the risks she ran, as a veiled Turkish woman beside a giaour were of no further matter to her now. They stood together in silence: there were no more words of love, no more kisses. As the cutter from the *Gladiateur* came alongside to take Loti aboard she turned away and entering a waiting carriage beside Achmet was driven out of sight. Loti likened the sound of its wheels to the sound of earth falling into an open grave. It was the end of his Turkish life, which, like all pleasure, or man's noonday halt, could not be prolonged.

Allah selamet versen Aziyadé
Allah selamet versen Loti

8

It was November when Loti reached Rochefort, and as always when
returning from other, more glowing shores, the sober little town
seemed a blighted zone where the loving ministrations of the *chères
vieilles* smothered him. He had become a foreigner in Rochefort.
Under the dripping bare branches of the little courtyard, there was
still Gustave's grotto – his Holy Mecca. But now his Mecca had
become that silent street below the mosque of Mehmet Fatih, where
Aziyadé languished and Arik Ussim Effendi, Aziyadé's lover, would
be taking up arms for Islam. How was the battle going? Was his love
menaced by the approaching Russian armies? Where were Achmet
and Samuel? In his journal he wrote bitterly: 'I adore my mother,
and it is for her I have made the sacrifice of my oriental life, though
she will probably never realize this . . .' He refurbished his room in
Turkish style with cushions of Asiatic silks and various objects from
Eyoub, to recall that faraway little room scented with amber and
attar of roses . . . Smoking his narghile he dreamed of Aziyadé's
green eyes. 'I have no-one now with whom I can talk in the language
of Islam, and I begin to forget it.' And Aziyadé? He wondered, would
the day come when some woman as yet unknown would be waiting
for him in his own home, and with his children, perhaps? 'But they
will not be yours, Aziyadé. Could I love them, if your blood and mine
did not mingle in their veins?'
  The family found him uncommunicative and clearly bored. His
favourite black and white cat, companion of several voyages, died
and was buried in the animal mausoleum of the courtyard. Another
loss. It was a relief to be posted to the naval base of Lorient.
  There he was to find some consolation by renewing his friendship
with the Breton sailor Pierre le Cor, who had sailed with him on
earlier voyages, one of the crew who trimmed the sails, a rascally

type, who could scarcely read or write, but he was tall, fair, handsome, virile – a splendid animal – all that Loti longed to be. This childish savage was to become an integral part of Loti's life, and as Yves Kermadec, the principal character of *Mon Frère Yves*. This was probably Loti's best-known book, one which, for the first time, brought the sailors' lives at sea and ashore before the public. He describes their hardships, camaraderie, courage, and that naïveté that Loti found so touching. In the company of Yves, Loti the blasé officer could once again escape from his complicated self, as well as play leader, something which soothed that deep-seated sense of inadequacy which had taken hold in his boyhood and was always to lurk behind the proud façade.

Loti was heterosexual, loving women passionately, and while he loved some men with equal fervour (though he or his son came to destroy most of his papers telling of those particular loves) it is clear that Pierre le Cor was, before all else, a *companion*. He typified the primitive, or savage, with his own gamut of vices or virtues, untainted by sophistication. This was ever Loti's ideal, and beneath his own etiolate exterior a savage always lurked, to emerge in moods of violence or sensuality, moods to which he could give rein more freely away from his own milieu. In spite of the difference in rank, Lieutenant Viaud and Seaman le Cor became inseparable, going about everywhere together in a manner which seems improbable, in the face of naval protocol, though it might be taken as a living example of *Liberté, Fraternité et Egalité*.

Like 'Mon frère Yves', le Cor was an unregenerate drinker, the legacy of alcoholic forebears, while Loti seldom drank wine, let alone hard liquor. This apparently ill-assorted pair often spent rumbustious nights round the port, all fisticuffs, gambling and brawling, or enjoying school-boy pranks, extinguishing the street lights, alarming passers-by by letting down strings of imitation bats on their heads, or throwing cardboard rats round their feet. Silly, disagreeable pranks, but which always appealed to that persistently childish streak in Loti's nature. In a quieter vein they roamed the Breton countryside, visiting the people and places which had formed Pierre le Cor's early life. Through him Loti learned the lore of the still unspoiled race and came under the spell of those austerely beautiful regions. At other times, le Cor joined Loti in his shore billet at Lorient. 'Our place', Loti called it, where they sat beside the fire, Loti flattering himself (and le Cor) that he was educating him –

Madame Théodore Viaud, 'Maman Nadine', Loti's adored and adoring mother, calm centre of his storm-tossed life.

Little Julien faces school wearing his elder brother's coat, talisman or armour against classroom terror lying ahead.

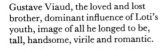

Gustave Viaud, the loved and lost brother, dominant influence of Loti's youth, image of all he longed to be, tall, handsome, virile and romantic.

Midshipman Julien Viaud and Joseph Bernard, an inseparable pair afloat or ashore: the first of Loti's many passionate involvements which ended badly.

Sub-Lieutenant Viaud, the promising
young officer, preferred wearing
ratings' clothes on leave; they were
one of the many disguises which
allowed more freedom for adventures.

Loti's drawings supplemented his journals.
Here he records some shipmates aboard the
Triomphante, a handsome, brawny lot, though
why one wears Harlequin's costume remains
mysterious. Was there a Columbine aboard?

Loti the acrobat, trained to professional pitch. The circus ring offered escape from the pangs of thwarted love besides displaying his hard-won muscles.

Loti and Samuel: the beginning of the Turkish imbroglio. Samuel yearned for Loti, and Loti yearned for Aziyadé; a triangular tangle which sealed Loti's life-long obsession with all things Turkish.

Aziyadé. Loti's sketch of his Circassian love, who embodied the Oriental chimera and paid with her life for their idyll.

widening his horizons, talking of his travels, theories and beliefs. Recounting his life in Stamboul, he found a spellbound audience in the rugged Breton sailor. '*Chez moi*, Yves has sat in an armchair for the first time in his life, and finds it marvellously comfortable,' Loti noted.

Gradually le Cor had become someone for whom he felt not only an attachment but an abiding responsibility. Their companionship was deeply rooted, for long ago on a first far voyage in South American waters the conscientious young aspirant Viaud had extracted the hard-drinking sailor from scrapes ashore, including rescue from a press-gang, and in return le Cor had paid Loti's gambling debts by selling a treasured watch inherited from his father. In Brittany, Loti encountered le Cor's mother, and swore to watch over her son for evermore. This solemn promise was faithfully kept, until, at long last, drinking and backsliding broke even Loti's infinite patience. Their friendship fluctuated with the tides of hard liquor which, again and again, undermined the sober domestic base Loti was at such pains to establish for his protégé. Standing the cost of the little Breton house where le Cor's young wife Marie, and the baby Pierre (Loti's godson) could be snugly installed, independent of le Cor's bouts of drinking, was to be only one of the many generosities which Loti came to shower on all those around him.

During this time, between Lorient and the Caserne St Maurice at Rochefort, Loti completed the first draft of his first book, *Aziyadé*. It was begun in a mood of nostalgia, re-reading his journals, trying to recapture something of that vanished Turkish life. In his own words, 'by my need to cry out my sorrow', or, in the words of the old troubadours, *mon mal je chante* (my sadness I sing), which Loti came to adopt as his motto: *mon mal j'enchante* (my sadness I enchant). (This epigraph came to be engraved on all his china, and silver in the affluent future, much as Sarah Bernhardt did with her '*Quand même*'.) Loti always needed to cry out his sorrow; it was an imperative urge, although at that moment he had no thought of publication, nor that money might be earned by such poignant personal memories.

Just to write them down brought back all the colour and radiance of those days. He detested northern waters; cruising about the sullen, sleety coast of Brittany was a penance after the pellucid blue waters of that bay where his barque had been a floating bed . . . His journal is as lugubrious as the scene. On watch, he notes: 'A wall of grey cliffs, like ramparts. Clouds, heavy and dark passing overhead rapidly, a shifting vault of lead, huge dark shapes forever forming and reforming, as if in a hurry to press on elsewhere, as if fearful of some dreadful approaching end.'

At Lorient, alone on raw February nights when his fire smoked and the wind whined under the door, he read again and again the few short messages Aziyadé had contrived to send, pathetic, almost unintelligible little scrawls of Turkish script; but they conjured the ambiance of mysterious mosques and harems which were the back-cloth to his adventure. For some while there had been no more letters, and Loti brooded. He had reached an impasse in both his life and his book. How to end his story on a high note? When he recounted the episode as he had lived it, tragic and romantic as it seemed, it petered out into anticlimax, a last embrace and the lovers going their separate ways. Only a suicide pact could properly express the anguish Loti wished his *doppelgänger* hero to suffer. Yet here he was, suffering while pursuing his naval career ably, eating three meals a day with appetite, and sitting before this unfinished manuscript . . . He decided his hero should at least have a truly doom-drenched, Wagnerian end.

Thus, under the heading 'Azrael', in the last few pages of the book, he makes his hero-self return to Stamboul in search of Aziyadé. And now a strange, dream-like veil falls between Loti and the reader. These pages, which could be described as wishful thinking, have a hallucinatory quality as they recount the death of Aziyadé, Achmet and Loti too. 'All this imaginary passage of Azrael' he noted in his journal, regretting that such a solution could not be his in reality. He makes Hero-Loti return to find the city of the Sultans sacked, and Achmet and Samuel fallen in battle before the advancing Russians. Abeddin Effendi's house stands shuttered and empty, 'tall grasses growing between the stones where the carcases of two dogs lay rotting'. Loti saw it all in his mind's eye as his hero-self searches for traces of Aziyadé. At last he finds Kadidja, the old slave go-between. She is a skeletal figure, muttering balefully.

' "Aziyadé?" I asked.

"Eûlû! Eûlû!" she replied, lingering with satisfaction on those savage words. "Eûlû! Eûlmuch! she is dead!" she repeated.' Loti stumbles away, the old slave pursuing him like a fury with her terrible cry. 'Eûlû! dead!' and Loti realizes it is he who has caused her death. Their dangerous life at Eyoub must have been denounced and Aziyadé has paid the price of an erring wife. Now author Loti indulges all his charnel visions and flings his hero dówn on Aziyadé's grave, to indulge in a monologue reflecting his own morbidity. 'Oh! to be united with her once more! To lie there, beside her!'

After the bed, the grave. Thus Loti tearing his passions to tatters, writing far into the night, alone in his gloomy lodgings. In such outpourings, Loti, a Frenchman, and certainly a romantic, though not of that breed generally known as French Romantics, comes nearer to the German Romantics. In such voluptuous grief he recalls Novalis, who wrote in his diaries: 'Our vows were not exchanged for this world. Death appears to one still alive as a nuptial night, the heart of all sweet mysteries!'

By killing off both his *doppelgänger* self, the naval officer, and his Circassian love, Loti found the solution to a situation which in real life was insoluble. *'Ah! who will give me back my Oriental life?'* There was never to be any answer to that despairing cry. It had been the peak of romantic living, the sum total of happiness. But Loti was to learn the truth of the Arab proverb, and know that man's happiness is as brief as the mid-day halt beneath the shady tree.

The circumstances of Loti's first book appearing in print are curious. He had sent the manuscript to a naval comrade who was enthusiastic and predicted it could have a great success if published. Another friend, Polignac, was equally enthusiastic: so much so that he sent it, as the work of an anonymous author, to the editor Dentu, who returned it as being quite unsuitable for publication. At the naval base of Toulon, Polignac encountered Jousselin (or Plumkett) and the talk turned on their strange shipmate, Julien Viaud, for he was always seen among them as an exotic rarity. Next Jousselin received the wandering manuscript and was at once determined his friend's talents must be more widely recognized. Jousselin was always Loti's devoted friend, and now proved to be a most valuable literary adviser. But he, too, found some of it unsuitable for publication.

He wrote his eulogies and criticisms to Loti and referred to certain scabrous passages, probably detailed accounts that centred round the prostitutes and their commerce among the graves of Khassim-Pacha, the dancing boys of Salonika or Samuel's love. The immemorial manners and customs of the East were not for the public at that time, as Richard Burton, the Arabist scholar and explorer, discovered in England when translating *The Thousand and One Nights*. Jousselin wrote: 'It is enchanting, but in its present form absolutely impossible to print . . . You have committed the greatest imprudence in exposing so openly your phenomenal nature, so difficult to gauge, so incomprehensible to most people, who have neither the perspicacity nor tact to read aright what could be interpreted deplorably!' At the risk of quarrelling with Loti, Jousselin ventured to cut and reform some chapters, 'veiling certain traits' while preserving what he thought 'valuable in its originality'.

The part which Jousselin played in the publication of *Aziyadé*, and launching Loti as a writer, has been generally passed over in the most ungrateful silence. It was he who laboriously corrected errors and generally reformed the final version, all of which Loti left to his judgment. He presented it once again to Dentu, who, while conceding its merits, again turned it down. Nettled and still convinced of its value, Jousselin now offered it to Calmann-Lévy, a fortunate choice though made at hazard, for he was not in the publishing world. Calmann-Lévy seized on *Behidjé* as the book was then entitled. 'Here is a Writer!' was the publishers' verdict. They offered 500 francs for it, and would double this sum for all subsequent works by 'the author of *Behidjé*', as Loti was known to them, some anonymous figure far from Paris. It is impossible to reckon what such a sum represented then, for its purchasing power was far greater: perhaps around the modest sum Flaubert had received for *Madame Bovary*. To Loti it seemed a fantastic windfall. He left all negotiations to Jousselin, still maintaining his anonymity. The devoted Jousselin was left to deal with a lot of small details as well as major decisions, these responsibilities obliging him to set aside a book he himself was writing and had obtained leave to finish. (Careless, ungrateful Loti, always accepted his friend's devotion as his due.) Jousselin urged him to illustrate *Aziyadé*, for he had been extolling Loti's talents as an artist to the publishers. 'All sorts of small vignettes throughout the text . . . You could do them easily enough – why don't you?' He also urged Loti to come to Paris to meet with his publishers, but Loti did nothing; a strange inertia seemed to have gripped him now that the tide of his fortunes was turning.

Aziyadé has always been surrounded by mystifications, scandals, polemics and theories as to its autobiographical verity. In 1892, referring to Loti's election to L'Académie Française, Goncourt wrote of *'this author, whose love, in his first book, was a Monsieur'*. It had also been said that Loti made the transposition from feminine to masculine in the first manuscript, since he well knew the temper of Islam in any matter touching the inviolate harem. Whereas this adventure could have been countenanced in Turkey, between the author and some Ganymede boy, it would have been unthinkable with a kadine from a harem. This substitution of he for she would have been a most daring notion on Loti's part, showing, moreover, his naïveté in matters of both publishing and French public opinion: in short, not a theory to be considered seriously, and certainly not to be taken as an indication that the whole amour had been a homosexual one, and the hanum Aziyadé had never existed. There are too many letters, too many references to her throughout Loti's life in his journals and elsewhere, references both at the time, and later, by others too who knew something of the affair, which refute this theory. The first manuscript has disappeared, but there remain his journals, flimsy yellowing pages with a Turkish watermark, with letters and notes folded beside them in his usual manner, so that the journals may be read as first draft of the book; and indeed, there is little difference from the published version, save that in the journals and letters he received from friends of that moment, Aziyadé is called by her real name, Hakidjé, and is certainly no Ganymede boy.

Once the adjustments were agreed, and the corrected manuscript accepted, the contract was signed by Jousselin. Loti seemed curiously indifferent, beyond stating that he wished to dedicate the book to Sarah Bernhardt, and that he would agree to make a sketch of Aziyadé for the cover. Both these suggestions came too late to be followed. Nevertheless, the original edition, now a collectors' piece, *'l'édition mauve'*, has the drawing of a veiled kadine, printed in violet for its cover: it was a gauge of the publishers' uncertainty as to the book's appeal that they provided a picture-cover: no established author was then considered to require such embellishment.

Loti's withdrawal from anything to do with the publication of his book – even to correcting the proofs – remains inexplicable. Was it feigned indifference – a screen behind which to hide his inbred timidity, and his dislike of coming face to face with his publishers, to whom he had revealed so much of himself? To stand naked in the market place, a sensation known to every writer of autobiography, was perhaps not so disagreeable to him: he had a strong streak of the show-off, many of his poses resulting, no doubt, from the humiliations and austerity of his childhood. He appears to have felt no particular excitement or pride as the day of publication drew near: though in view of the family debts, which he had shouldered so honourably, and which were still 'gnawing with their rats' teeth', at least the money he had earned so unexpectedly must have been a source of gratification.

The loss of his Oriental life still overwhelmed him. He writes to Jousselin-Plumkett, 'I wear my oldest uniforms. I have done with curling irons and rice powder.' There were so many losses to haunt him. Nostalgia for the lotus-life on l'Ile Délicieuse and torments over *la bien aimée* had seemed unendurable at the time, and then there had been more, much more, to bear with Bernard's break. Yet he had to admit, life at Joinville, his muscular prowess, and all those circus triumphs had been wonderfully reviving . . . Gradually thoughts of entering a monastery began to take shape. Could he, as it were, build up his *spiritual* muscles? He saw himself shut away from the world, seeking regeneration at the feet of the Saviour. It is typical of his excessive nature and that craving to dramatize that he selected a Trappist brotherhood, the most severe of all orders. 'An eternal silence – this cold peace, where the uproar of the world is stilled, fascinates me. Behind those high grey walls, the words of Solomon are inscribed: *Vanity of Vanities, all is Vanity and emptiness of spirit.*'

The Trappist (and Papist) solution appalled his Huguenot family. Marie wrote in a frenzy: 'I beg you, on my knees, for your mother's sake – at least wait till she is no more . . . all these emotions are killing her.' (She was to live another eighteen years, weathering many more of her son's emotional tempests.) 'Her Huguenot heart suffers terribly. Can you not hear the agonized beating of a mother's heart? Never mind, if we are of no more account to you – if only all this was leading you to truth, to happiness! What are you searching for, in a monastery? You know well enough, you will mortify your flesh only to emerge with your passions more unbridled, more overboiling than ever.'

However maddening his sister's letters were (and this is a fair specimen of her style) she read her brother shrewdly enough, but to no avail. Loti entered the Trappist monastery of Briquebeck for a period of trial, and was well received by the Abbot, who talked to him with understanding. 'But I saw only too clearly the inanity of their means to lull, even for a moment, one's misery. And then, this life here is too sombre for me, who does not have that support which can hardly sustain the Trappists themselves . . . All day long, all night funeral chants to make one shudder, faces from another world, processions of phantoms. And this damp, icy cold, this dark sky of winter, the wind that moans along lugubrious corridors . . . In the refectory I eat with the erring brothers sent to La Trappe for a period of penitence. Beside our table a monk with a cavernous voice intones Saint Bonaventure's lines.

'I said to Putrefaction, you are my mother: and to the worms, you are my father and my brothers.'

Before long he had left the monastery to rejoice in village inns, cider and cigarettes: the hedonist had overcome the monk. Still, he brooded. 'I would pay dear to have the faith of Islam' – what he calls 'the radiant illusions of Christianity' have failed him. But Islam! – that mystic, fatalistic acceptance of both life and dreaded death lying ahead, that dark nothingness that came closer each day and night. Islam! Islam! his spirit yearned for its peaceful certainties, as his flesh longed for Aziyadé. What was the use of sacrificing his Oriental life for his mother's peace of mind, when his present life did not contribute to her peace either?

In March 1878, while serving on the *Tonnerre* based at Toulon, there was bad news from Turkey. 'Yesterday by what means I do not know, I received another letter from Aziyadé my beloved: a letter of despair, a solemn appeal to my past vows, and calling on my love and pity for her plight.' As Loti had foreseen, the Russian armies were converging on Stamboul and every man was called to the Sultan's banners. *Jehad!* Holy War! Crescent against Cross! Abeddin, Aziyadé's master, courageous and fanatic, was likely to be killed in the front line. If so, Aziyadé, as a widow, would be sought in marriage by his friend Osman Effendi. (He, being posted to military headquarters was unlikely to be killed.) Osman Effendi was well known in Stamboul: 'young, audacious and jealous', Loti's journal noted. 'If Aziyadé becomes his wife she will be as lost to me as if she were dead . . . She wishes to escape him at any price . . . The disorder reigning in the city might favour this, but she must get away from Turkish territory at once: and then – she cannot speak any Christian language, not even a word of Greek. She has no idea of other ways, of journeys, of how to take a train or a steamer ticket . . . nor even of any geography . . .'

What to do? Seizing his pen he wrote a long and impetuous letter to Loganitz, a Hungarian and good friend from Stamboul days, who still lived there, and had known the details of Loti's Eyoub existence. A draft of this letter remains among Loti's papers and tallies with that which was published after his death, in *Un Jeune Officier Pauvre*. It was a letter to make any friend, however loyal, hesitate, for Loti asked him to rescue Aziyadé – *'mon odalisque*, as you used to call her, smiling at my folly. But today, don't smile.' Indeed it was no light matter Loti proposed. He cannot undertake the rescue: he has no ready money, he cannot get leave – he cannot desert, he has his honour as a French officer. He pleads with Loganitz and says he is writing to various friends at the French Embassy, outlining his plan. Naïve Loti! How could he believe the Embassy could help him make off with a Turkish wife? We imagine the stunned Loganitz reading on to know what else was demanded of him. Now Loti was at his most cloak and dagger. 'Do not lose a moment. Put on a fez, go over to Stamboul by the Kura Kevi bridge. Just before the little mosque of At Bazar-Bachi there is a blind alley: at the end of it, an old house painted red – the others are yellow. Beside the door, there is a barred and shuttered window. Knock on it – six short raps. It used to be my sign . . .'

And so on, not a detail is omitted in pages of minute direction for this dangerous enterprise entrusted so coolly to another. The red house in the blind alley was where Kadidja the old slave lived. 'Trust Kadidja, she is the most cunning old creature imaginable. She will find a way to get Aziyadé out,' writes Loti, and then announces that it must be in Loganitz' own house at Galata in which Aziyadé should be hidden till she can be got out of the country. 'It may be necessary to buy some European women's clothes . . . will your mistress make these purchases in memory of me? . . . Don't ask for explanations at present. You may need money. Go to Villiers, at the Embassy: he will give you some he is holding for me . . .' He goes on to say he wishes Aziyadé to sail on one of the Compagnie Fraissinet boats leaving for Marseilles. 'Use my name – I know all the captains.' (More risks, for them too, harbouring an escapee from a harem!) 'At

Marseilles I shall be waiting for her. Have no fear, this is no romantic adventure. On my honour I swear that, once in France, Aziyadé will be my wife.'

Next Loti wrote to Villiers, and no doubt plunged him, too, into confusion and alarm. The overcast March day was wearing on: Loti had begun these startling letters at dawn, and now an early dusk was falling. The last, laboriously written in Turkish, was to Aziyadé. Twilight was the proper moment for a letter of such love and longing, but this one had also to be of a practical nature. He plunged: he loves her more than life, more than sunlight, or Stamboul! 'That which I swore, I swear again, by the God of the Christians and the God of the Moslems, by my soul, and the soul of my dead – I hold to that which I have sworn' (not to abandon her). 'I swear again: you have only to speak, and I obey. But this is a grave, a terrible moment for us both. Before deciding our fate, listen to the loving counsels I send you now. As long as the old Abeddin, who still cherishes and respects you, is alive, O thou! my beloved, *stay beside him*, awaiting what the mysterious future prepares for us. We are young – a long life stretches ahead . . . But if he dies – listen again, my beloved, to what I tell you in anguish, for it destroys half my own life. If he is killed O! my adored! *marry Osman Effendi!*'

If Loti's letter to Loganitz would stun him, what effect would this letter have on adoring Aziyadé? 'Forget Loti,' he writes, 'Loti brings unhappiness to all who approach him.' He now saw himself as *l'amant fatal*, whose love inevitably brought destruction with it. By Fate the pattern was formed – he was condemned to eternal separations, forced departures, or those brought about by death: it was all in the romantic tradition. 'With Osman,' he told Aziyadé, 'you will have slaves, gardens, rank, and your place as wife in the invisible world of the harems . . . But with me – even if all the difficulties were overcome, have you thought of what it would be like, to be my wife? To come alone, a fugitive, to a distant land, where not one soul understands your language . . . to go unveiled, to share my poverty, to take your part in the hard work of the house?' He painted a sombre picture of her, left alone at Rochefort during the years when he must be far away on the high seas; long winters, far longer and gloomier than those of Stamboul . . . where she would never see the blue sky of her own land again, nor any familiar faces . . .

It is clear that even if he had arranged his room at Rochefort *à la Turque* and dreamt of her, he did not envisage her there in the flesh. A

Circassian odalisque as daughter-in-law for his venerated mother? Aziyadé, among the bourgeois French wives of his naval colleagues? It was inconceivable. Nevertheless, he glided back into high romance . . . 'If you accept all that, my beloved, if you love me enough to endure all that, then come to me. I adore you, and I am waiting for you . . .'

When the letters were sealed, he stared out, watching the rain lashing down on the dark street below. 'I had taken my decision and acted as I should: a feeling of peace enveloped me. Now I had only to wait.' Strange, contradictory Loti, loving, sensitive, despotic, blind, selfish Loti. Which was the real man? Had he no idea of the effect these letters would have on the recipients? Scarcely peace: bewilderment and alarm for Loganitz: bewilderment and exasperation for Villiers; disillusion and tears, bitter tears, for Aziyadé, who would realize that, in spite of all the protestations of love, Loti no longer had a place for her in his life. 'When my letters were posted, and all was irrevocable, I went to find Yves, and we spent the evening together.'

No doubt they were carousing in the bars along the water front and behaving in a fashion which more than once resulted in brawls that the port authorities opposed energetically, but which Loti found wonderfully restorative. Their odd relationship, like others Loti was to pursue with other ratings, was tolerated but not viewed sympathetically by his superiors, and cost him certain promotions. Officers did not generally mingle with the ratings. But for Loti, such friendships were an expression of democracy; let protocol go hang – a curious attitude for one who set such store by all that concerned the navy and its traditions.

Loti now renounced a flying visit to Paris to meet his as yet unknown publishers, preferring to join Yves for a visit to the sailor's Breton village, Plounès-en-Goëlan. He was beginning to find a certain exoticism in Breton customs, language and clothes. His mother had, by chance, sent him a blue jersey; a red sash and a Breton beret completed a costume suited to the festivities for Yves' return home. He had begun once more his old ways of escape, of dressing up, of playing a part among people of another race or class. The old craving for disguise, for escaping from himself, was the best way to forget realities.

His mother wrote lovingly, reproaching him that his daily letters were falling off . . . 'Until now, I have been so spoiled by your

138

regular news . . . I received your photograph safely, you are dressed as a Breton fisherman, no doubt? You know how I always love to see your darling face reproduced – that is, when not too distorted. This one pleases me particularly because your cheeks look nice and plump. But I *would* have preferred you in another costume to the jersey and that beret . . .' No doubt she longed to have a series of portraits of her darling boy, handsome and trim in his officer's uniform: it was so difficult to explain to neighbours, all those ones of him as a Turkish sailor – with that turbaned Turkish friend – Daniel, was it? – or dressed as an Albanian guard in a spahi's cloak, or in Tahitian pareo and little else . . . Such *outlandish* outfits . . .

At the end of March 1878, an imperative telegram from the publishers summoned Loti to Paris, to discuss and sign contracts for further books. 'Two extremely active days, which at least shook me out of my gloom.' He was fêted by his old friends the Golos, who had shared his life at Joinville. But nothing really lifted his spirits: there was no word from Stamboul, neither from Loganitz nor Aziyadé. Had something gone wrong? In April, in a letter to a friend, he described his continuing depression. 'To lie down, to await the end – that is already my wish . . . and nevertheless, there is one thing which counts above all else in life – love. I have had ravishing mistresses, and no doubt shall have others. There have been women I have adored, and I have been in agony, dreaming that one day, death will separate us, that all will finish in the dust. I have even dreamed that we might lie together in the same grave, for our dust to mingle . . . And then, I have forgotten those women: I have loved others, and woven the same dreams round them. Friends? I don't believe in them – yet I, more than anyone, have had them in plenty . . . but everything passes . . . When love is no more possible, except that which is bought, when I am abandoned, like some worn out, broken object – what will be left for me, except suicide? All those whom we think of, you and I, as simple, naïve, who still kneel at Christ's feet – they are the happy of this world. They are confident and calm. I would give my life to possess their radiant illusions . . .'

Loti was twenty-eight when he wrote that but it was the pathetic cry of a lost child, frightened of the adult world lying outside his own world of make-believe.

In a letter to Plumkett there was further despair, for time went by without word from Stamboul. He describes how his roistering nights with Yves and the horse-play of a band of sailors were no more: instead, he accompanied Yves to the house where Marie, Yves' new bride, was cooking, ironing, or sewing bonnets for the baby. A domestic scene, and Loti found comfort there. But he was tense, apprehensive. Still no news from Stamboul. Presently he learnt why. Loganitz was dead: he had engaged in a battalion of Hungarian volunteers marching against the Russians. Thus he never received Loti's letter – nor the enclosure for Aziyadé. A curtain had fallen over Loti's Turkish life.

There were never any other ways to reach her, and now that she was lost to him irrevocably, he was consumed with remorse. Now began the cult of Aziyadé the loved and lost, Aziyadé the beloved above all others, Aziyadé the symbol of his vanished Oriental life, the chimera of true love, which was to lure him back to Constantinople repeatedly to search for her traces, or pray on her grave, and to take up an impassioned defence of all things Turkish when the world turned against 'the sick man of Europe': at last, to place her tombstone in the mosque he came to build at Rochefort.

Loti's next appointment was to the *Moselle*, cruising between Cherbourg and Brest, ports that revived painful memories of Joseph Bernard. As those he loved disappeared, to be followed by others who in turn vanished, the old pains that had once racked him did not diminish; they simply accrued or were gathered together in one agonizing whole. Gustave, Lucette, *la bien aimée* of Senegal, Bernard, and now Aziyadé. He wallowed in misery. To think that in that last letter he had advised her to forget him and marry Osman Effendi! As if either of them could ever forget . . . He thrashed round, trying (half-heartedly, I fancy) to put such thoughts out of his mind, for his journals dwell luxuriously on his misery. But Yves' companionship always helped.

Yves was his prop, his companion and confidant – above all, another version of the ever-desired *brother* – but the friendship always seemed incomprehensible to the fragile *chères vieilles*, when their precious Julien brought him to Rochefort. Yves, on his best behaviour, remained sober and marvelled at everything, tiptoeing about the modest rooms like some huge, half-tamed wild creature anxious to please, carrying Great-aunt Berthe, then rising ninety, down the narrow staircase for her birthday party with touching solicitude. Gradually he became part of Loti's family life, as Loti became in Yves' home. To Plumkett, Loti wrote: 'With Yves I can be simple, and that is what rests me. In me, there is layer upon layer of dissimilarities. People who surround me know one or another of these artificial layers, acccording to what they are themselves. The deepest layer has only been reached by this primitive companion, who has not passed through all the exterior layers and is not cultivated enough to understand them, though he senses them, and ignores them . . .'

There was one notable exception to the attractions of simplicity, however, for there was nothing simple about Sarah Bernhardt, with whom Loti was now on familiar terms. He records going to the Théâtre-Français, to see her play Dõna Sol once more, again taking a first-row orchestra stall, and again wearing the blue and white seaman's outfit. The star made a sign to him across the footlights, while the public craned to see the sailor who had obtained this mark of favour. At this moment Sarah Bernhardt was at her zenith, sizzling with emotions. The theatre, sculpture, painting, multifarious interests, lovers and a passionate public, headed by Victor Hugo – such was her life. Yet there was time for the obscure young admirer too. He wrote to her, dwelling on the rapturous hours he had spent at her feet . . . 'something unhoped for, unimaginable, since you have admitted me close to you'. The drafts of Loti's letters to her show he was already well acquainted with the bizarre black-hung bedroom. 'When my letters reach you, you won't read them . . . you will give them to Lazare (the celebrated skeleton) who will read them to the vampire bat.' These unpleasing objects were part of the décor, along with a coffin, upholstered in white satin, in which the actress sometimes reposed. 'In the middle of all this funereal richness, three persons stand out against the dominating black satin,' Loti's journal records. 'Three persons stand before the mirror looking at themselves, and holding hands. One is a skeleton whose bones are white and polished like ivory – chef d'oeuvre of the anatomist's skill, for it knows how to stand upright, or strike various attitudes. Beside it, a young woman wearing a long white satin train, a young woman of delicious prettiness with large sombre eyes, a grace, a distinction and

141

a supreme charm . . . a strange creature – Sarah Bernhardt. The third person is a young man in an Oriental costume embroidered in gold as for a fête at Stamboul – Pierre or Loti, or better still, Ali Nyssim . . . as you please. What insanities we three have said here, in this room belonging to this courtesan, who is unique in the whole world.' In a loose page, attached to his journal, where some further details were noted, the word *said* – (*dit*) – reads *known* – (*connu*) – which was not printed in the more discreet *Journal Intime* published after his death by his son. But I fancy it was nearer the truth. Were they ever lovers? Briefly, perhaps. It would have been in character for both of them, so to crown their meeting. Throughout their long series of quarrels and reconciliations, Sarah and her Julien le Fou understood each other perfectly. Their taste for the fantastic as well as their sensual appetites tallied. Loti's description of his friend Yves had intrigued Sarah, so he made a drawing for her of this Breton Adonis in the nude – a bronze statue of masculine perfection, something both of them could appreciate with a connoisseur's eye.

While the family at Rochefort glowed at the prospect of their Julien's book being accepted for publication, his mother felt a certain alarm when Sarah Bernhardt's name was mentioned. Loti had written home asking his *chères vieilles* to make some small alterations to one of his Turkish costumes. His mother replied that these were done. 'Was it to visit Sarah Bernhardt you wanted it? I hope I shall not annoy you if I dare to say, O my darling, do not lose your head over this woman!'

But when some years later, the great actress arrived in Rochefort to play in the exquisite little blue and gold eighteenth-century theatre which strikes a note of such sophisticated elegance in the small town, she visited Loti in his old home. 'June 1888 . . . we went into the Turkish room and I posed her on the divan at the far end of the room: then I stepped back, the better to see how lovely she was, and how well she looked in this setting, with her white dress and scarlet cloak.' They dined à deux, but Madame Viaud joined them for coffee. She wore her best black satin for the occasion, and both ladies enjoyed the meeting, Madame Viaud pronouncing the Divine Sarah to be *tout à fait comme il faut*.

9

To want a world is fire – to obtain it, smoke.

Tzigane saying

Aziyadé was published in January 1879. It was unsigned, simply marked *Stamboul, 1876–1879. Extracts of notes and letters of a Lieutenant in the British Navy*. It did not have a brilliant start; the general public did not know what to make of this sombre romance over which Azrael brooded, from its first page. Sombre stuff indeed, but the stuff of high romance. Maxime Gaucher, one of the book's first critics wrote: 'very romantic, this adventure . . . and very strange, very unpleasant, this hero, this "Loti" – and yet, one must admit there is great talent here – fine descriptions . . . colour . . . *style.*' However, Loti's publishers did not regret their further contract; nor was he particularly downcast. He sensed a left-handed career might open before him, writing further novels based on his voyages and experiences. At that moment, no-one could foresee *Aziyadé* would become world-famous, though there was some speculation about the anonymous author in the literary salons of Paris. Loti was not tempted to approach this formidable world, and still remained aloof. He could not foresee the blazing triumph his next book (*Le Mariage de Loti*) was to be. He had asked his mother not to read *Aziyadé*: did he imagine its amorous content would shock her, or did he, rather, dread her coming on certain iconoclastic and cynical passages affirming he no longer believed in man or God – or indeed, in anything but love and youth? It was a denial of all he had been raised to respect.

In Paris, talk continued about 'that strangely flavoured book *Aziyadé*'. Madame Juliette Adam, a distinguished figure in Paris literary life, had just founded her *Nouvelle Revue* in conjunction with Georges Calmann-Lévy (Loti's publisher). She was casting about for new material for her *Revue*, and when he told her he had just

143

received this unknown author's second manuscript, she asked to read it. At first she held back, for *Rarahu* was such curious, original material, falling into no known category . . . Moreover, it could have seemed repetitive, following the Turkish story. Again a young naval officer (English) and his exotic mistress live out their ill-starred love against an unfamiliar, marvellously evoked background. When Loti's publishers had asked for a second book, he had turned to his Tahitian journals for inspiration: but now there were none of those 'pâles débauches', ambiguous loves or iconoclastic railings against conventions and morality which had displeased some of *Aziyadé*'s critics. This second book was of a softer key and Madame Adam published it in two parts, in January and February 1880, retitled *Le Mariage de Loti* and signed 'by the author of Aziyadé'. With it, Loti became famous overnight.

Thus it was through her *Revue*, and her growing enthusiasm, that Madame Adam launched this unknown author in style. She constituted herself his literary godmother, encouraging, guiding and protecting him, becoming in time, in her own words, his second mother – something his real mother acknowledged with gentle generosity. 'He belongs to us both,' she said. 'I kissed your letter of this morning, where you call me *your son*,' Loti wrote to Madame Adam, as usual overboiling with emotion, although here, on a strictly filial plane. Juliette Adam was fourteen years older than he, handsome, charming and rich, the widow of Edmond Adam, politician and journalist. Together they had been part of the boiling lava stream of French political life. She had become an outstanding personality in Paris, as distinguished in the world of high politics as letters; and Loti could have had no better sponsor for his literary debut. As their association developed, so their friendship deepened; sometimes she gave her turbulent protégé unwelcome but sound advice, or lectured him lovingly on the errors of his private life, and he who was always intolerant of criticism took it meekly from Madame Chérie as she became to him.

Calmann-Lévy were delighted with public reaction to *Le Mariage de Loti*. Its voluptuous dream-like quality stole over the materialistic French readers like some insidious spell. Even its ingenuous sentimentality, something usually abhorrent to them, was accepted. This

144

most static, untravelled of people, now rediscovered *Aziyadé*, the book they had largely overlooked, and found in each that magic carpet by which Loti transported them, not only to unknown horizons, but to equally unknown emotions. The young Proust was among those who fell immediately under Loti's insidious spell, spending long days in the Bois, reading *Le Mariage de Loti*. Later he was to electrify a dinner table, at the mention of *Aziyadé*, by quoting whole pages, on the spur of the moment.

While Nadine Viaud rejoiced unreservedly in her Benjamin's success, his sister Marie, though rejoicing, nourished a certain bitterness. She had played a formative part in the development of his childish talents; now, far from Paris, and his triumphs, she was shut out – and felt herself a forgotten provincial housewife, her own career as a painter outshone forever. There remained for consolation the beauty of her daughter Ninette. She had been brought up in the Viaud tradition of overwhelming family devotion, and was becoming excessive in an emotional cult for the young and famous uncle, who was only fourteen years her elder. In time, this adoration was to be another of those twining family roots from which Loti was never to be freed.

While he was not yet to sign his name, or rather the nom de plume of Pierre Loti, the young naval officer Julien Viaud was now becoming well known. Anatole France, Edmond de Goncourt, Alexandre Dumas *fils* and Ernest Renan were among the eclectic circle who acclaimed this '*débutant de génie*'. The critic Philippe Gille of *Figaro*, who had been especially eulogistic, recalled their first meeting, when the young author had seemed astonished at his own successes, taking the praises for politeness, and even questioning their sincerity.

Both *Aziyadé* and *Le Mariage de Loti* were now reprinted, edition after edition being in gratifying demand; though they still remained anonymous, the mysterious author was the subject of lively speculation. Shops sold Rarahu ribbons and Loti bonbons – Turkish delight perhaps? Money began to accrue agreeably, and Loti was able to make life easier for his *chères vieilles* in their rusty black dresses. For himself, money was never of any consequence. His generosity was limitless. No charitable appeal ever went unanswered, no-one in need was ever overlooked. Always, he was to give, right and left, explosions of reckless generosity, asking no return.

The contrasts, or contrapuntal rhythms, which were so marked a characteristic of Loti's life, were never more apparent than during the years 1880–1883. They were the first years of fame, of freedom from money problems, and the first years he tasted real independence and was liberated from the humiliations and patronage under which he and his family had smarted for so long. Those years saw the obscure young provincial's reputation established in that jealous world known (to themselves) as *le tout Paris*. It was a small closed world which postulated its own rules of admission or rejection. It was bounded by the aristocratic salons of the Faubourg, where the *gratin* lived in style, and those circles, equally elevated, of the world of letters. There was also that marginal world of *la haute galanterie* which was acknowledged, but not received everywhere. Loti did not seek any of these overlapping strata. Thus while his writings, those 'voluptuous reveries', aroused their senses, the writer himself aroused their liveliest curiosity. Just when the salons thought he was captured, he was gone – to sea? To the provinces? He had escaped again. Reassuringly disguised, he went rioting about Belleville or dancing the java at the apache dives, where other seamen, though few officers, liked to racket.

Not only did the disguises Loti adopted give him more freedom, but he knew he looked better in them. On him (his officer's uniform apart) all suits, stiff collars and hats seemed absurd. Wearing them he cut a faintly ridiculous figure, 'like a dressed up organ grinder' was one unkind opinion. All his life he was to remain faithful to the local tailor at Rochefort, so perhaps this loyalty was in part responsible for the fatal effect. But as soon as he resumed the various disguises he enjoyed, he was at ease, as if safe in his own chameleon's skin, Loti the Turk, Loti the rating, the Berber, the Basque smuggler . . . By his nomadic journeys, his seeking to live among the simple people wherever he went, and his adoption of local costumes or casual clothes – something then quite unknown except among working men – he foreshadowed the casual life-style of today.

Loti always knew himself to be more of an exile in Paris than anywhere else about the world. He never sought to put down roots there. Most Parisians made him aware how uncultivated he was by their standards. His classical education had ceased at fifteen, when he crammed to enter the navy. He had been brought up on the

146

majestic cadences of the Old Testament, which often sound in his writings. He had the usual French child's background of La Fontaine and Bernardin; he had read Chateaubriand's *Les Natchez* for local colour, as later he read Victor Hugo's *Les Orientales* for exoticism, while it was de Musset's forbidden fruit which had first cast the romantic spell. But of contemporary French writing, or the giants, Shakespeare, Goethe, or Dante, he had only the most superficial knowledge.

Those first years of his ascendancy were marked by some imperishable milestones of European culture. Ibsen's *Doll's House*, Zola's *Germinal*, Wagner's *Parsifal*, Dostoievsky's *Crime and Punishment* were among the subjects then discussed with passion. Thus the cosmopolitan culture of Paris put him at a disadvantage. In spite of the eulogies which surrounded him, he felt himself an outsider, and withdrew behind a mask of extreme reserve. 'I never read,' he would say, shrugging off this failing, while adding to the legend already forming round him, so that he came to be known as Anatole France labelled him – 'the sublime illiterate'. But what a paying proposition to his publishers!

Paris, 19th March 1880. 'At Calmann-Lévy's. An agreeable surprise. A thousand francs more than I had hoped: on all sides praise for *Le Mariage de Loti*. He [Calmann-Lévy] smothers me with his attentions and proposes I should sign a ten-year contract.' It was time to begin thinking about his next book – and the one after that. Perspectives of prosperity opened.

He was now receiving quantities of letters from ecstatic readers. A fellow officer recalled how he would occupy one end of the long ward-room table and settle down there, surrounded by a post which often made him laugh uproariously. He would read extracts aloud, sometimes inviting suggestions as to how they should be answered. He was generally popular with his fellow officers, who took a pride in his success, while the lower deck had always appreciated this officer who was so appreciative of them, who took an interest in their problems and welfare, wrote letters home for the illiterate, boxed with them, took charge of their sports and physical training, and knew how to be authoritative without being overbearing. The navy was his chosen life: 'I could not live, were I to be deprived of that,' he wrote. When in Paris, and continuing to avoid the hostesses who sought him so assiduously, his adventures in seamy quarters were gradually known, and aroused acid comment; however, it seems that le Ministère de la Marine were becoming inured to both his bizarre ways and indifference to naval protocol. His personal charm and growing reputation as a writer accounted for much of the indulgence accorded him, though jealousies were aroused by the money he was earning which far exceeded his service pay.

This golden time of achievement, of success and financial independence, was also a turning point. This was, at last, the moment when he could have set about carrying out that long-desired plan to rescue Aziyadé. He could have applied for leave: he now had the means to make the journey and try, himself, to execute the desperate scheme he had been obliged to entrust to Loganitz and others. Did he even contemplate such a hare-brained scheme? I find no mention of it in his letters or journal, although yearnings for Aziyadé are a constant thread. We must suppose that prudence and common sense overcame the yearnings. But from this moment dates the cumulative remorse and self-torment with which he became saturated. Henceforth he was to live with the knowledge that, however much he protested to himself or others that the cause of his perpetual sorrow was his loss of Aziyadé, he took no positive action. Henceforth, in the words of Pushkin's poem, he was to live with the serpents of remorse.

Alphonse Daudet had become a trusted friend in the barbed mazes of the literary salons. One of his letters reached Loti at sea: 'Do you realize, my dear Loti, that you are becoming a celebrated man? Do you read the newspapers? Do you want these articles sent on to you? . . . Your name is everywhere. Charming articles, heavy articles, and academic ones . . . the whole world is mad on Rarahu. Goncourt asks me to tell you your talent is a rare one . . .'

Here is Edmond de Goncourt on the young Pierre Loti: 'a thin, slight skinny man with the big sensual nose of Karaguez' (the Eastern punchinello) 'and the faraway voice of a sick man. A silent fellow who admits to being terribly shy. Words have to be dragged out of him. He gives us horrifying information about Calmann-Lévy's usurious contracts . . .' For six more years Loti was bound to share fifty-fifty with the publisher all he was paid for contributions to newspapers and periodicals. Such cut-throat contracts were – and are – often imposed on debutante authors.

Although Loti often railed at his lonely state, he savoured solitude. At sea he writes to Daudet: 'Nine o'clock at night. Shut in my cabin I enjoy that quiet, that egoist's peace that only sailors can know, that of the officer who has finished his watch. One hears, from below, the sound of the engines: above, the masts straining, and the melancholy sound of a high wind rising. Bad weather on the way – and it's all the same to me.' In this 'egoist's peace', he echoes once more that sense of well-being which he enjoyed shut away in the little house at Eyoub. It was always one of Loti's deepest needs, to know that inward-turning secretive pleasure of being alone – alone with darling self, away from any intrusions, in some setting where he had achieved a reflection of his own personality to keep him company. It was as if he was forever setting the stage for a dialogue between himself and that other self – the *doppelgänger* who liked to dress up and escape to other ways of living which the two selves could recall later, when alone together.

Loti's bouts of despondency and his unsettled way of life caused his family growing anxiety. Whispers of their Julien's adventures must have reached Rochefort, for they redoubled their pressures, urging matrimony. *If only he would settle down!* They lined up several suitable brides but their machinations were cut short by Loti's sailing orders. He was escaping again – now to ports along the North African coast.

In the spring of 1881, the *Friedland* lay at anchor off Algiers. Blue skies! Mediterranean waters 'the colour of melted turquoises'. Palms! Aloes! Islam once more, and the long chant of the muezzin reaching him on deck, calling to him, across the bustle of the water front. But now, since his first dazzled glimpse of Algiers as a midshipman on the *Borda*, he found much to criticize in the Frenchified city. The feasts and Arab fantasias which welcomed the fleet had become no more than organized theatricals. 'Zouaves, chasseurs and spahis are a travesty of local colour – the simplest Bedouin now speaks the slang of the faubourg. They [the French colonizers] have almost succeeded in making Algeria insipid . . . little that is genuine remains except the sunlight, and the houses.'

He looked round and resented what he saw. 'Poor citified Arabs! Poor creatures, already gangrened by our manners; thieved and exploited by us, existing on the débris of their ancestors' riches, becoming a bastard race which a mutual scorn separates from the colonial French society but who accept all with their fatalistic indifference. Mektoub! It is written!'

From this moment in North Africa – much of it spent about the Kasbah, the fortress heart of Algiers – Loti drew two of his most perfect pieces of evocation – the tragic *Suliema*, an Oriental Tale, as he calls it, and *Les Trois Dames du Kasbah*. This is in a less sombre vein with its descriptions of the profligate westernized town, Babel, sprawling at the feet of the ancient Arab city where, aloft, far above the blue bay, the women of the roof-top terraces still lived traditionally. Loti describes their dreams, as they rise at sunset from their long siesta. In this passage he has caught all the shimmering poetry of an Oriental legend. 'They returned from those enchanted lands where the fumes of amber and kef, and the perfume of certain flowers had the power to lead them, these sequestered women of the harems. They had seen Mecca and the green veils of the Holy Kaaba on which the Koran in its entirety was embroidered in silver letters by the hands of angels . . . They had seen Stamboul, and the gardens of the Grand Seigneur, where groups of women covered in precious stones danced in the vapours of ambergris, under the shadows of the dark cyprus trees . . . They had seen El Borak, that winged horse with a woman's head, on which the Prophet travels over rosy skies where the mysterious zodiacal signs cross and recross in the vertiginous distances, like vast golden rainbows . . .' And then, descending from such distillations of Arabic legends, Loti makes one of those volte-faces which he contrives so cunningly, describing a cheerful, almost childish, drunken band of Basque and Breton matelots plunging noisily about the alleys of the Kasbah, and the Trois Dames – prostitutes – who entice them into the shadowy, arcaded courtyard where they languish among their cushions, their perfumes and glittering adornments. Loti sees the sailors' spree as an immemorial ritual, like the traffic which these sumptuously painted and perfumed women knew how to invest with an almost hieratical splendour. Whatever Loti wrote concerning Islam was always written with indulgence. 'Everything that touches Islam, near or afar, casts a spell over me, and likewise, the Mussulmen of every country seem to accept me, and welcome me differently to others, as if, somehow, I am one of them.' Did he, seeing his own, strangely Arab-dark eyes regarding him from the looking glass, remember those jetty eyes of the old great-aunt on the ISLAND, and how, once, the ISLAND had been stormed by the Moors, leaving behind their heritage of another, darker, blood?

As usual, all his free time was spent ashore, absorbing the local life, listening to the plaintive Arab music he loved, because it reminded him of Turkey. Once more the old spell.

At night, a change of key. 'Dinner at the Cercle Militaire . . . after dinner, a small ovation in honour of the author of *Le Mariage de Loti*.' But Islam beckoned. 'At ten o'clock I change my clothes in the street, under torrents of rain, send my uniform back to the ship by the cutter, and climb the Kasbah. The mauresque Zohra, rue des Abencerages . . .

'Zohra does not understand why Loti likes to rearrange her hair and tie her veils in Turkish style; to place her in certain attitudes, to contemplate her sadly, covering with his hand first this part of her face, and then another; to try out the effect of different lights, as if to trace in her, some other . . . But Zohra accepts it resignedly, on account of the little gold pieces Loti puts in her hand, and she gives him her commanded kisses which he hardly takes the trouble to return: and then, being a practical girl, as soon as Loti leaves, so as not to waste any more time, she receives a Zouave . . .'

Behind such cynicism, blasé Loti always preserved a youthfully sentimental view of this traffic. He writes elsewhere of hours spent with another such as Zohra, where 'that kiss she gave me on parting – that was not bought'. He found such women of the Orient infinitely more seductive than their European counterpart. And then – how could the needs of the flesh be ignored? And why should they be? In a short piece entitled *A small world which has not yet reached our dizzy pace*, he describes long hours of siesta spent among the Ouled Naïlia in the desert, gold-hung, tawny beauties 'with their allure, half panther, half Queen . . . who aroused that eternal need which can seem some divine urge to merge two souls in one . . . but which is, rather, only a snare by which matter obstinately pursues its urge to reproduce'.

Loti was an excellent horseman (something rare among men of the sea) and the Caïds and tribal nobles arranged that he should take part in a fantasia, all charging horses and gunfire. Splendid trappings were provided for him and he was eager to cut a dash among the princely riders.

151

Unfortunately the *Friedland* received unexpected sailing orders, and Loti missed both the fantasia and his Arab apotheosis. 'Instead of galloping on a black horse in the suite of Caïd Ibrahim, I shall be on watch; I shall put on my oldest tunic,' noted the disillusioned diarist.

Not that Loti ever regretted land for long. The sea was a whole planet in itself, his chosen life. Like Conrad, Loti sailed the seven seas and wrote of that sailor's life he had lived. All he had seen and known and feared and loved of that life rises from his pages with such force that the reader seems to taste the salt spray, to be lifted with him on the swell, or to hear the great masts and ropes battling the waves which are hurled against them. Loti has the power to involve his readers physically, as well as emotionally. With him, we come to *feel* 'the great circle of blue' around us, to see that 'limitless mirror of water, still, heavy, polished, like melted silver', to watch moonlight 'sparkling over the water, as if mysterious hands were waving thousands of little mirrors', while from atop the highest mast, he shows us the ship's deck, seen dizzily through a network of riggings.

In southern waters, across 'the great blue solitude', he shows us something vague forming on the horizon '. . . a coral island that as yet no navigator had charted. Century after century it had been slowly rising from the depths, patiently pushing up its stony branches. From afar it was still only an immense crown of white spray in the middle of the sea's absolute calm, and now it was heard making the sound of some living thing, a sort of mysterious and eternal roaring . . .'

Loti writes of the sea as some great creature, a breathing entity whose changing moods he knows, fears, and loves. 'There was a heavy swell, but lazy and gentle, which passed and re-passed under us, always with the same tranquillity, arriving from one infinite horizon to lose itself in the opposite one: long undulations; smooth, immense masses of water slowly and rhythmically succeeding each other like the backs of giant beasts, made harmless by their indolence. Little by little, lifted by no volition of our own, we would reach one of these passing blue summits, then, for a moment, one could see magnificent empty distances all flooded with light . . .'

The sea was that other dimension which in its infinity offered him an escape from his inbred melancholies. The discipline and monotony, the comradeship, physical efforts and dangers of life on the high seas overcame those anguishing thoughts which haunted him ashore. The sea's horizons were infinite, for ever retreating and renewing: were timeless, unlike land, which was finite, and for ever marking the passing seasons. The sea was not only a drug but also a challenge. Hurricanes or a becalmed passage were challenges that he could meet. There was no way of overcoming old age and infirmities. They always won in the end. Thus, enticing or menacing, the sea lulled him, inspired him, and possessed him entirely.

Each night at sea, as ashore, even after a particularly onerous night watch, he would shut himself in his cabin to enter up his notes, describing the drama of sunrise or the loss of a man overboard, the passage of a strange bird or the character of his sailors, at once tough and innocent. He noted their way of swaying as they walked, their delicate cat-like manner of stepping about the deck, and how their bare feet assumed something simian, from long habits of swarming up and down the riggings, as their hands were forever bleeding and torn from battling with the sails. Sometimes he fell asleep as he wrote, only to be roused next morning by a solicitous orderly, or the scuffling of his petted jackal, keen for breakfast.

Loti was always subject to the slightest variations of climate, his mood changing with the skies. In the long chill winters of northern ports he was as downcast as he was elated in torrid equatorial zones. His journals are full of meticulous recordings of weather, where his own poet's vision is strengthened by the naval officer's eye, trained to study climatic conditions as well as charts. I have been told that some of Loti's descriptions are still regarded as a kind of unofficial text book by meteorologists, who even now can rely on the accuracy of his minute observation of atmospheric conditions in remote areas where he had sailed. Cloud formations, the ranges of temperature and the sea's reaction foretelling storms or calms were all noted, and are often woven into the texture of his books. Standing watch on the bridge he not only recorded the speed of knots, or the gale, but also observed the subtle, fugitive gradations of colour and light around him in passages which transform Loti's pages to paintings. As he sailed about the world, always noting the shifting skies, were there sometimes echoes of a vanished voice? '*Viens! viens petit!*' – the voice of Great-aunt Berthe, summoning him to marvel at a sunset gleaming over the flat Saintonge countryside.

Only in one book did Loti write by hearsay, that is, of conditions he had not personally experienced. To describe the extreme northern latitudes of Icelandic waters, where the Breton fishermen went each year for long lonely months at a time, he was at pains to obtain the facts from those who had lived that life. The harsh monotony, the changeless, livid pale days and nights which merge, like the terrible storms, are the canvas of *Pêcheur d'Islande*.

While stationed off Algiers Loti received a letter which was the reward for all those years during which he had shouldered, so honourably, the family's cares and debts. 'My dearest old mother writes to say I have no more debts! We are free! Everything is paid up. I have told Plumkett to repeat, every hour, with the regularity of a cuckoo clock *You have no more debts!* NO MORE DEBTS.' He determined that his next leave should be devoted to taking his mother to Paris: this had always been one of her fondest dreams, something she had never hoped to realize. Now Julien's celebrity and earnings made it possible, and he wrote to her, announcing this delicious project.

By September, the dream was realized. Madame Viaud, almost overcome with anticipation, had a new black satin dress and bonnet for the trip. 'In eight days here, Maman has become quite Parisian,' Loti writes. 'She is transformed, enjoying everything like a young and intelligent girl, finding it quite natural to have her box at the Opéra Comique or the Comédie Française, and a carriage all day long: we stop at various shops to buy this or that, or at the pastrycook's to eat *babas au rhum*. Nothing tires Maman, she wants to see everything . . . It is costing me a crazy amount of money, but I throw it around happily, to give her pleasure.'

There were a number of preoccupations lurking behind his determination to give his mother this splendid treat. In his journal he notes: 'I ought to go on to Lille, to see Joseph . . . to Geneva, to *see my son* and then, perhaps, as a rest from all that . . . to go to the lake-side, at Annecy, with my poor friend François . . . Ah! if only I had the time to go further – to Stamboul, to search for those lost traces . . . Yet how to combine everything – to take Maman about, and live my own life too, the life of Pierre Loti, and then, returning at night, work feverishly to finish my article for *Le Temps?*'

This was *Le Roman d'un Spahi*, his third book, but the first to be signed. He chose the pseudonym of Pierre Loti, keeping the name given him by the vahinés of Papeete. Pierre was perhaps in honour of his paternal grandfather who had died after fighting at Trafalgar. Again he drew on his voyages; now on his memories of Africa. All these first three exotic novels were written under northern skies, very far from the glow of their original settings, though no doubt the exile's longings for those climes sharpened his retrospective vision. One Parisian critic had advised him to abandon primitive people and place his characters in a more elevated milieu (that of *le tout Paris*, rather than Fatou Gaye's desert?). Fortunately, he went his own way. On the rare occasions when he was in the capital he had taken to staying under a false name at the Hôtel Bon La Fontaine, a modest establishment on the Left Bank much frequented by the clergy. There, as Monsieur Denis, he believed his comings and goings went unremarked. Mystification again: the most piquant contrasts too.

'Saw Mme Juliette Adam, Sarah Bernhardt, Daudet, Octave Feuillet and Jules Sandeau,' Loti notes. 'Journalists, chic *cocottes* and that "*devoted*" lot who crowd round as my fame grows . . . Walked in the Bois with my friend B. Through my books, I am already well known to all these cocottes . . . I receive the compliments with an indifference that is not play-acting.' But how his mother must have enjoyed knowing her darling boy was the centre of attention. He had always been that to her.

10

Aye, in the very Temple of Delight
Veiled Melancholy has her sovran shrine.

John Keats

In the summer of 1881, the colourless life Loti was leading at Rochefort was abruptly broken. He had been shuttling between administrative work at the Préfet Maritime and the monotony of the old home, accepting it patiently since shore postings avoided long absences on the high seas which his mother dreaded increasingly. In February he had been promoted to the rank of Lieutenant-Commander, something which might have come earlier had he not accepted shore billets so often. Sometimes he spent a few days in Bordeaux, the nearest approach to urban life and its distractions, without being tainted by Parisian sophistication. In Bordeaux he had encountered a siren of '*indescribable* loveliness' – as he wrote to Plumkett, nevertheless describing her in detail. He now began agitating his faithful friend with accounts of his new passion. This incomparable beauty had instantly become his mistress, although she had another lover – richer, younger, better-looking – whom she intended to marry. Yes! she was brazen, calculating, dishonest – but never mind. Her ardent flesh transported him into a sensual delirium. Similar protestations over those palpitating nights with Aziyadé in the barque that was their floating bed were now forgotten.

'When I think of the rapidity with which she abandoned herself to me I tremble! Her lovely head falling back . . . a long look, and her great dark eyes close . . .' And so on: several more close-packed pages of ecstasy. 'Her divine beauty should be sculptured in a marble which is faintly amber, like alabaster in sunlight . . .' Then follows the inevitable transposition to charnel musings: he wishes them to be together in the grave, and she should be placed above him, so that the decomposition of her body should filter through his own . . . 'What I have written is banal, I know, my dear

156

Plumkett . . . but you asked for my thoughts, and here they are, both delicious and terrible.'

Though scarcely banal.

Plumkett replied to this paroxysm of passion in a bracing tone; 'what you call your news – is simply Literature . . . for it goes too far beyond reality to be taken seriously . . . but you see all through prisms which magnify and colour everything, and your style works on this again, so that you intoxicate yourself, and could intoxicate me, too. These episodes always pass: exteriorize them, put them all down in pages that may become the finest yet written on love – then put it all out of your mind.'

What an idea! Loti was nourished on such pulsations. More rendezvous of a delirious nature were followed by more rhapsodies. 'O! her sovereign beauty – her corruption too! She has chosen to stay with her other lover. *Why? Why?*' Plumkett urged him to come to his senses, to become again *le bon petit Julien,* to return to his mother and friends, making of them living talismans to rescue him from the Venusberg. In vain: Loti was off again, remembering *la bien aimée's* similar decision to end their affair. 'It is always like that, always, I am loved as some sort of plaything – an amusement of the moment', he wrote, forgetting Aziyadé's devotion.

Plumkett analysed Loti with acumen. The instability of his character, he wrote, had its reflection in the transitory nature of such love affairs, and derived from the *multiplicity of different beings* all concentrated within Loti himself. (The jack-in-the-box of his ancestors springing out after generations of repression.) 'Thus if one of your multiple selves or even several, inspire a profound or violent attraction, to which a woman cedes irresistibly, others of your multiplicity emerge in turn, so that this woman who gave herself to you in a moment of passion, now draws back from uniting her life with some other being of whom she knows nothing – to some *beings* even, and unknown to you, too.' Plumkett had discovered the key to Loti's life: he could only live through and for love. Better the storms than the calms which for him were always the doldrums.

Loti obtained a last midnight assignation with the siren on the eve of her marriage. He reached the garden door by stealth, surprised to see, contrary to the agreed darkness, one candle flickering at a window. Was it some signal of danger? But no, only a light placed beside the body of an old servant who had inconveniently died that day, and was laid out upstairs. However, there is no more mention of

157

this dampening fact. Loti is locked in love with the bride to be, when he spies a cardboard bandbox: 'A sudden extraordinary certainty made me tear it open. There lay her bridal veil and orange blossom. "Put it on!" I said. "Wear your bridal clothes *for me!*" O! that night – our *last*, what fevers, what frenzies of tears and despair . . .' The curtain falls on yet another of those episodes by which Loti usually contrived to keep the emotional pot boiling.

Late in the autumn of 1881, Loti and Plumkett were serving together in the cruiser *Friedland*, which was part of an international fleet dispatched by the big powers to patrol the Adriatic coast of Dalmatia, Montenegro and Albania. There had been incidents over the town of Dulcingo and both Turkish and Russian interests were involved, with Greece, Austria and Serbia on the sidelines. The small population of that unruly region was divided between Islam and Orthodoxy. They were shepherds, fishermen, and bandits, a wild lot, forever simmering or skirmishing, engaging in conflicts which could, overnight, develop into international war, as Sarajevo was to prove in 1914. Thus the international fleet lying in the bay of Bazoich was a forbidding assemblage, their guns trained on the savage countryside which rose sheer from the water. As usual, Loti was spending much time ashore, exploring a land new to him, cultivating the few inhabitants he found at the primitive inns and collecting copy for articles on these unknown Illyrian shores, for he still contributed to various French periodicals. But now there was no more question of living and loving as once in Stamboul or Papeete, though there was a brief idyll with a peasant girl from Herzegovina.

Pasquala Ivanovitch was simple, illiterate and comely; 'she smelled of fresh hay, the wild plants of the mountains, and something of the sheep she guarded, too.' No tearing passions were involved here: only a gentle sadness for Loti when he sailed away; for Pasquala Ivanovitch – who knows? She was an orphan; the peasant couple to whom she was in bond were her masters, and she slept in a stable. She was proud, for all that, and would not accept her lover's money. There is a muted charm about this brief encounter which Loti describes in *Fleurs d'Ennui*, a book warmed by an autumnal sun, which is in keeping. Never again that exquisite pattern of landing, loving and leaving before the glow faded. That pattern which had inspired his earlier books was only faintly echoed here. Never again was Loti to be deeply involved with the numerous women with whom he continued to dally on faraway shores.

When *Fleurs d'Ennui* was published in 1883, it broke new ground by being written in collaboration with Plumkett. The two friends had decided to venture on some sort of dialogue where they exchanged their disillusioned, *fin de siècle* views in a gallimaufry of dreams, incidents, and ruminations of a cynical or morbid nature. Besides the piece entitled 'Pasquala Ivanovitch,' there is an account of a journey they made into the fastnesses of Montenegro. This book – perhaps because of its odd format – has never enjoyed a wide success. Madame Adam believed the public wanted Loti's former manner – unadulterated Loti, and no Plumkett. *Fleurs d'Ennui* conjures the special, now vanished flavour of the Balkans. Loti has seized on its curious duality of torrid south and boreal north, of minarets and ikons, political violence and pastoral calm.

Here he is, evoking the Montenegrin scene . . . 'A savage desolation of rocks . . . the landscape of a dead planet.' Climbing higher, ever higher, by precipitous tracks, he is led by swaggering, ferocious figures wearing an arsenal of splendid daggers and firearms stuck in their ragged sashes. Cettingne, the microscopic capital, was composed of several streets, a miniature palace, a post office boasting Montenegrin stamps and a primitive inn. In the frost-powdered main street was 'a personage wearing a sky-blue and gold embroidered costume – Prince Nikita, a patriarchal ruler who was in the habit of holding audience in the open, pacing up and down, followed by a gathering which turned and returned at his heels, bowing, offering gestures of submission and veneration'.

However much Loti enjoyed the primitive and the picturesque around him he could not forget that these people were Southern Slavs – hereditary enemies of the Turks – *his* Turks. High on a crag, there was a round tower where it had been the custom to expose the heads of Moslems, stuck on long poles. 'One senses the savagery of this fiery nation, their notions of religion mingled with thoughts of war and vengeance, severed heads and disembowelling.' He longed to cross the mountain frontiers that divided him from Turkey to reach again its fatalistic calm – perhaps to find Aziyadé once more. All roads led to her. On some wild pathway, he overheard two cloaked figures speaking Turkish, and followed them . . . '*Siz Osmanli* – you are Turks?' he pressed. One was an uliema from

Constantinople, and asked what Loti wanted. But Loti, master of words, was silent: he wanted only to hear that loved language – *her* language. A whole dead past had come to life at its sound. He strained his eyes beyond the cloaked figures to where her country lay. He could not, would not, forget, and this his anxious mother knew.

While in Cattaro he received her letter . . . 'If you should return to Constantinople, which I dare not wish for you, however much you yourself desire it, may you never recommence the follies of your first time there! . . . I would be so unhappy, so tormented. And tell me, my child, was it happiness that you brought back from your first visit to Turkey?'

The late nineteenth century was still an age of voluminous correspondence, the telephone not yet having established its sway over private life. The Viaud family, in particular, were given to unburdening themselves at length among themselves, even from room to room. Notes were regularly pushed under doors, containing comments on the day's events or midnight reflections of an uplifting nature such as Marie, especially, addressed to her brother, a series of emphatic comments on his ways or character. More tender messages were those of his mother, written in pencil on economically doll-sized folds of paper, all of which he preserved. 'O! that my prayers may fall on you like a dew of benediction . . . My darling, you know there is no child in the world more loved than you.' He knew it, he returned her love unreservedly, but at times it overwhelmed, though she never jarred on him as did his sister. Marie was heavy-handed, and sometimes, in her devotion, came too close – dangerously close – to problems which Loti kept hidden.

His unpublished journals for the spring of 1882 reveal that there were, indeed, some dark secrets in his life at this time. Loti was in the habit of marking certain dates or entries in the journals with signs bearing sinister implications. A heavily scored cross, or a double triangle, crudely drawn, as if under stress, is found beside initials or cryptic entries. There is rarely any clue or details as to their significance. An entry for 28 March 1882 is more explicit. Under a heavily inked cross he writes: 'Beginning of the *Souveraine* affair. The Admiral has warned me officially that my honour has been attacked in the most odious manner from aboard the gunnery training ship

160

[the *Souveraine*] where he wished to appoint me. I was turned down by a vote of thirty *for having lost the esteem of my fellow officers.* I understand the accusations are terrible. I don't know of what I am accused, or yet, who accuses me.' The Admiral took Loti's part against all the rest until the accusations were proved. 'Lightning has fallen on me,' writes Loti. 'I suppose, as is natural, they have put their finger on *that sombre thing which I believed to have been well hidden from everyone . . .*' (the italics are mine) 'I feel lost . . . I face the only thing that in all my sufferings I have not known – dishonour.' More dark crosses follow.

Two days later the cloud lifts: 'March 30th. Thank God, I now know of what I was accused, and I breathe again! It is all so childish, so easy to disprove; I hold up my head. Of that dark stain which exists in my life – of that they have no suspicion – neither they, or anyone else . . . In their stupid jealousy, they brought the most absurd accusations that eleven years ago, on the *Jean Bart*, I had been too involved with Joseph and had taken advantage of our intimacy to extort money from him!'

There was much sympathy for Loti among his comrades at Rochefort. 'Their indignation has done me good. I shall confound my enemies, and get even with them by a duel or two' but we learn no more of any challenges being sent, or accepted. It was perhaps the nature of Loti's friendship with Joseph, rather than a question of money, which his accusers remembered, wishing to avoid the risk of any more of those perfervid emotions which Loti might have engendered among the novices on the training ship. Thus 'that sombre thing' he believed hidden remains unknown, as he would have wished.

Barely a month later there are further despairing entries and more cabalistic marks spelling disaster, this time centred round Geneva, and probably referring to the 'dark stain'. Loti must have been continuing to pursue or harass '*the beloved*', for he remained obstinately convinced that the child born after his return from Senegal in 1874 was his – a means, too, of coercing the mother to join him. In spite of all the tempests of emotion which engulfed him at regular intervals, *She, the beloved*, remained an *idée fixe*, while he saw the child – a boy – as a companion for his declining years. Crazy, unrealistic Loti! How could he, with his way of life, and the old, old ladies, have assumed this charge? Yet there are references in both the journals and a letter to Plumkett which dwell on this possibility. No doubt the lady, or her husband, who must have accepted the child as his own, as perhaps it was, took drastic steps and even legal aid, to put an end to Loti's persistence. What those steps, or counter threats, were are not disclosed. In an entry for April 1882, Loti writes: 'Saved! almost saved! Finished, for the moment, this terror which comes from Geneva. I am saved, but *I no longer have a son*, and I feel, now, that I have committed another infamy by abandoning him, so that they will let me live in peace, and I am even more wretched. I have done all they wanted and now I am free. Now it seems the past is truly dead, and no-one can any longer throw it in my face . . . I have also taken care of such papers as could destroy me . . . letters too. I ought to have burnt the lot, but' (words indecipherable) 'I have sealed, and put in a safe place . . . And all that which is not *She*, has no more meaning for me.'

Between the more agitated passages of his life, Loti was now finding the tranquil rhythm of the old house, which he had once found monotonous, was giving place to a disturbing atmosphere of invasions, chatter, and constant demands on his time and purse. With prosperity, numbers of people crowded round, uninvited. Family friends, distant relations and hangers-on became a further drain on his generosity, besides distracting him from his writing, without which there could be no further prosperity.

Unlike most people who have known poverty, Loti attached no great value to money when at last he acquired it. Money was for using: for paying back the family debt first; then for giving, lending and helping those around him, even the most casual acquaintances. It was also for spending lavishly on more and more sumptuous additions to the old house, for arranging special treats for his mother and Aunt Claire, or to indulge the whims of his niece Ninette. She had early insinuated herself into her young uncle's affections, and at seventeen, a spoiled beauty, was forever engaging his attentions, or making extravagant demands on his purse. Nothing was too good for this capricious miss, and Loti could deny her nothing. There seems to have been some emotional undercurrents on both sides, some undefined relationship which led to more complications for Loti. He was also under constant pressure from his sister, who was for ever carping, arriving suddenly to din marriage and morality into his ears. More and more he craved calm – something he naïvely began to believe might be found in matrimony – the conventional panacea. Marriage then – but with whom? He flatly declined the advances of a rich widow, Madame Roberti, whom his sister favoured; she was far too bourgeois, he said, and indeed, throughout his life, he preferred aristocratic or humble people. The same criterion applied to various young girls, again selected by the family. Where was he to find that simplicity and peace for which he longed? He was to find it, unexpectedly.

While stationed at Brest, aboard the *Surveillant*, he noticed a Breton girl, one of a crowd of sailors' families visiting the lower deck. Something about her calm beauty stood out, and Loti was again enslaved. Her brother was serving aboard; her father was one of that race of Breton fishermen locally known as Icelanders for they spent six or more months of the year fishing in northern waters. Loti knew of their harsh lives, both the monotony and the danger, and the lonely waiting of their womenfolk, from whom, each year, the sea claimed its victims. Such lives, such tragedies, were to become the theme of his *Pêcheur d'Islande*. Meanwhile, there was this Breton girl to fix his attention. 'She was remarkably beautiful,' he notes, 'of an antique, sculptural beauty, with large, proud eyes which charmed me.'

Next day, Lothario-Loti followed her to her village near Paimpol, set on conquest. 'I might be excused, for I had succeeded many times before, without putting myself to so much trouble: but I was defeated by a nobility, a disdain I had not imagined . . .' The rebuffed Lothario took it hard, 'for I loved her . . . Strangely, I *loved* her!' he notes ingenuously. But was it so strange? He craved her simplicity as talisman against those neuroses which racked him. He believed that this Breton girl embodied all those high ideals and values he had known round him as a child, but from which he had drifted.

In that Brittany which both she and Yves personified, Loti had glimpsed something eternal which seemed to promise the final refuge or tranquillity that was the answer to those spiritual yearnings which haunted him.

Next day he rushed back to the primitive granite house where her family lived. 'There, before her brother, who had learned of my game, and was seething with anger, and before her father, I said: "*Eh bien*, it's true. But now I ask you to give her to me as my wife, for I love her as I could never love a young girl from my own world." '
This declaration dumbfounded the family, but while she realized her

163

impetuous suitor spoke in earnest, she still refused him. She was promised to one of the Icelandic fishermen, and so it must remain. Still, her brother might call on Loti next day, to give her final answer.

Loti spent the night wandering about the frosty countryside in a ferment, at last taking refuge in a church where, 'for the first time in many years, I knelt in prayer . . . All night, praying and dreaming of this marriage the world would call madness, but to me – salvation.' Next morning the brother arrived bearing lavish offerings, 'the kind fisher-folk give each other – all their wealth, in the form of lobsters and crayfish. But the reply was still no.' Though her brother and father had wished otherwise, she would remain loyal to her fiancé. As Loti watched her brother leave 'it seemed my last honest dream went with him.'

In those first years of Loti's Parisian triumphs and emotional uproars one woman stands apart – Oirda – Madame Lee-Childe. She occupied a unique place among the women in his life. If Juliette Adam became his godmother in the world of letters, Blanche Lee-Childe became his good fairy in the exclusive world of the faubourg. The aristocratic, cultivated and fragile young woman, born Blanche de Triqueti, was married to a wealthy Parisian of American origin. She had fallen under the spell of Loti's writings, and on an impulse, wrote to him, signing herself Oirda (the rose). She had never done such a thing before, and hid behind a poste restante address. In his journal for 1st January 1883, Loti noted that the year had finished sadly: rain, the old people . . . his usual reflections. 'Curiously, the only message of friendship on this 31st December was from an unknown person who sent me a médaillon of St George, to wear as a talisman.' He replied, and the correspondence flourished. Loti unburdened himself of his eternal griefs and Oirda replied comfortingly, but remained mysterious. 'What do you want to know of the Masque signed Oirda . . . who admires your talent passionately, who knows no painter to equal you, and who loves the extremes of your personality?'

They grew closer with each letter, discussing his books, his moods, himself, but little of Oirda. Presently he began to press for a meeting. Oirda dwelt on the perils of this . . . 'Coming face to face one is pleased – or perhaps displeased. That is all: but it is everything. Never mind, coquetry and I bid each other adieu long ago . . . and really it would be far more comfortable not to have to reckon with that ennui . . . Loti, one does not fall in love with Oirda, but one loves . . . at least, that is what I have been told, sometimes.'

Such was the protective barrier this beautiful and still young woman put up to conceal her true feelings. She had fallen in love with the man his books revealed, but she chose to transpose her emotions to a less complicated plane. She was a wise, well-schooled woman of the world, and in her splendid house on the Champs-Elysées, the centre of a small eclectic circle, she was dreadfully lonely. She might have risked losing her name and fortune – but Loti? She would not risk losing their friendship. Love, she divined, he found elsewhere, on his own strange terms.

After a while it was Oirda who took the first step towards a meeting. With a rare independence, or indifference to the conventions of the time, she visited him at Rochefort. Yet although attuned when they corresponded, on coming face to face their perfect understanding seemed tinged by a curious reserve. Loti the sensualist, the vagabond, held back, and Oirda the sensitive woman could not, dared not, risk that first lover's step towards him. Instinctively she must have been aware of that 'Bedouin's temperament' which would have torn like a hurricane across her life, and which, as a woman, she knew she could never satisfy. Her husband appears to have been always appreciative of Loti's friendship, but is unlikely to have been a *mari complaisant*.

Through Oirda's guidance and tact, Loti was steered through the labyrinths of Parisian social life. She saw him clearly, and knew just how to help the secretly timid provincial to overcome his sense of inferiority among the critical Parisians. *Never forget there is only one Loti in all the world*, she wrote, though it must have tried her when she learned that her protégé, this strange genius – for so she thought him – had ignored her counsels, and caused a scandal by appearing at a particularly exclusive gathering accompanied by the stalwart Yves, in rating's blue and white. Loti never brought his sailors into her orbit. He neither showed off with Oirda, or teased, but he wrote to her from every far shore to which he sailed, and Oirda, counting the hours till his return, replied faithfully with delightful letters, written from the palmy groves of her boudoir overlooking the Champs -Elysées, which was crammed with precious bibelots in the fashion of that moment. Through the taste of this luxurious woman, who was also a connoisseur, Loti was to develop his own sense of luxury, and his passion for acquiring *objets d'art* with an expert's eye.

'Then you do care for Oirda a little?' Oirda wrote, when one of his letters showed special warmth. But she never overstepped the bounds of their close, yet almost disembodied friendship. That he, the most perceptive of men where the emotions were concerned, a man forever craving love, could never read between the lines of her letters is inexplicable. But perhaps he did: perhaps he too knew they could never come together otherwise than as friends, however insatiably his nature craved love.

Wherever his service took him she wrote: of his latest manuscripts, with both praise and criticism, for she was the first to read them; of publishers' gossip; résumés of the latest plays and concerts and the Paris scene from which she thought he should not be too removed. Their relationship was cut short by her death barely four years after their meeting. In those four years letters flowed between them, and it was to her memory he dedicated *Propos d'Exil*, which is in part his letters to her, telling of his life aboard and ashore during campaigns in the Far East. As an introduction he wrote a loving Memoir of Oirda, which reflects something of her charms, and courage facing death. All Loti's pirouettes and poses vanished before Oirda's verities. Together, they had seemed to move to the rhythm of the *Valses Nobles et Sentimentales* such as Ravel's music expresses.

11

Those dark enchantments that were my life.

Pierre Loti

Early in 1883, Loti's life was lit by a glow of fame and bolstered by a sound bank balance. The pendulum swung between Rochefort roots and life at sea – that sea which he thought a whole planet in itself, and to which, fundamentally, he belonged: though there were continued excursions into both high and low life in Paris by way of change, and Oirda and Madame Adam were there, for comfort and counsel. Even so, there were pangs over the lost salvation of a Breton marriage and tormenting memories of those pagan delights offered by the Bordeaux siren. For the moment it seemed the perennial sufferings over both the *bien aimée* of Senegal and Aziyadé were set aside: as it were a reserve of melancholy on which to fall back should happiness threaten.

But in May, the established pattern, or any further repinings for Breton purity or Bordeaux corruption were interrupted by an order to embark on the cruiser *Atalante* for action in the Far East, where, in the campaign of Tonkin, the French were fiercely defending large colonial territories in a region now familiar through the disasters of America's Vietnamese campaigns. In Loti's day all the great powers saw such expansion as a perfectly legitimate expression of nationalism. North Africa, South Africa, German East Africa, the Belgian Congo, India, Burma, Indo-China and the Marquesas were all Promised Lands for Imperialism then. The French bombardment of the forts of Hué and a number of landings occasioned hand-to-hand fighting of fearful ferocity on both sides. While Loti was an ardent patriot, he was always violently opposed to policies of colonization: thus the brutalities of this campaign were to revolt him particularly.

On his way east his journal notes the light and dark of the voyage. In Indian waters: 'Returned on board very late after a night of

167

adventures . . . The Indian dancing girls . . . the perfume of plants that intoxicate . . . Even more intoxicated by those great velvet eyes which all the women here have – even the most abandoned. Intoxicated by the pleasure of such creatures, perhaps the most beautiful and voluptuous of all races . . . Returned the worse for wear, after all kinds of escapades; obliged to fight my way out, like a sailor in a tavern brawl, finally making a run for it like a criminal.'

He could be lyrical: 'One of those equatorial moonlight nights that resemble some vast, rose-coloured day.' Sometimes he was starkly factual, as when he told of a sailor washed overboard in heavy seas. 'There being no hope of rescuing him, the chaplain was summoned to give absolution from the deck, and the wretched man was abandoned, disappearing from sight, clinging to his life buoy . . . Such are the decisions a commander must sometimes face with courage.'

Wherever he found himself, Loti contrived to maintain unlikely contacts, obtained by his entire disregard for the conventions. Even aboard the *Atalante*, between Port Said and Suez he still contrived to pursue his own path, by hiring and bringing aboard a down-at-heel Arab taxi driver, to fan him as he worked through a night of oven-heat so that he might finish *Mon Frère Yves*, which was due to catch the courier at Suez.

As the cruiser left Suez for the Red Sea, Loti spent the night watch beside the Arab pilot, one Mahmoud, 'who wears a rose-coloured gandourah and regales me with stories of his harem at Aden and his harem at Suez . . . The watch finished I sleep almost naked, stretched on a straw mat, beneath starry skies.'

Once again, we marvel at the freedom from naval protocol which Loti was able to achieve while retaining the respect of his fellow officers and the crew.

In the Indian Ocean the *Atalante* passed close to that latitude which was graven on the hearts of the whole Viaud family: latitude 6°11′ North, longitude 84°48′ East, the spot where Gustave's body had been buried at sea. Here was an occasion for all Loti's sense of drama and grief to prevail, and the captain indulged him by altering course.

'I was not on watch that night, but they woke me about 2 o'clock. When I left my stifling cabin to go up on the bridge, it was is if we were sailing through some marvellous equatorial phosphorescence of aquamarine blue, a sort of brilliant dew. Nothing but a tranquil stillness; one scarcely heard the propellers turning . . . But on each side of the ship we saw, beneath the warm waters, a continual luminous spray – the wake of big, fast fish, sharks or others, man-eaters, devourers of the dead, circling beside us, in the hope of some prey . . . Ah! in those same waters, on other ships bringing back our wretched sick from Indo-China . . . how many were cast overboard, poor dead men, sacrificed by the criminal folly of colonizing politicians.' From the bridge of the great cruiser Loti recalled the brother whose loss he mourned all his life. 'Just to have passed that way gave me the impression I was near to him once more.' But Gustave's life had been sacrificed for those same 'criminal follies', and he could never resign himself to that.

They reached the Straits of Malacca, and entered the mouth of the yellow hell . . . 'All this life is *yellow*, scurrying, rapacious, apelike and obscene . . . a smell of yellow sweat, incense and filth, over all, the stench of musk, irritating, sickening, intolerable.' A more sympathetic note sounds when he writes of the rats. 'They scurry swiftly across my path, uttering little cries, *Kwic! Kwic! Kwic!* – joyous little bird-voices – but they too leave behind them a musky trail of odours.'

Goncourt had already marked a new trend among writers of the day – that of describing acutely the smells as well as the sights around them. Loti was first among these, absorbing every nuance, fetid or frangipanied, through that large nose that Daudet classified as a sponge. In the Goncourt Journals for 1884 we read:

'In order to depict Nature, Gautier used only his eyes. Since then, all the writer's senses have been called into play in the rendering of landscape in prose. Fromentin used his ears, and produced fine passages on the silence of the desert. Now it is the turn of noses, and with Zola or Loti we have the smells and perfumes of a place whether it is the Central Market or a corner of Africa. Both men, come to think of it, have curious olfactory organs, Loti with his sensual Punchinello's nose, and Zola, with his pointer's nose aimed inquiringly . . .'

It was in a mood of bitterness that Loti reached Tonkin. From there he was to continue his old practice of sending back reports to the eager newspapers at home. His unvarnished accounts of battle and the taking of Thuan-an (published by *Figaro* and later reprinted in *Figures et Choses qui passaient*) were to raise a storm and cause his recall. The fighting had been ferocious, the ships gunning forts and villages alike, while landing parties of sailors with fixed bayonets fought the Annamites along the beaches, where, as they tried to escape into the water, they were picked off by rifle fire from the boats. No quarter was given after the French had seen what happened to any of their own men who fell into the enemies' hands. Loti's all-seeing eye did not spare his readers the gruesome details of that 'yellow hell', and public opinion was outraged.

Loti was accused of exposing the barbarity of French sailors in battle. (Barbarism was of course expected of the Asiatics, but simply did not occur when brave French sailors fought for their lives.) The Government shuffled uneasily, for the French and foreign press fastened on the uproar, and as is their habit, distorted all to make headlines, and in some cases to embarrass the Government. Loti himself was also attacked as having denounced the sailors' brutality. *Denounced?* Nothing could have been further from his intentions: he had simply described the war as he saw it. Nevertheless the uproar continued, and the Admiralty recalled him in disgrace.

The effect this recall had on him may be imagined, for he put his naval life before all else. The crew of the *Atalante* smarted for him, his men coming one by one, 'as if to wring a martyr's hand'. They knew the true face of war: but he now realized his report should have been nothing but all-glorious accounts of chivalrous combats for the motherland, as he wrote bitterly to Daudet, Madame Adam and Oirda, all of whom were marshalled to intercede for him with the Government.

He sailed for France on the transport ship *Corrèze*, his uncertain fate hanging over him. They docked at Aden, and his painter's eye saw it all. 'The crimson rocks, the bony camels with their slow tread, the men with their fierce gaze . . . the colours of everything intensified, as if by a sun too near, an air too pure . . .' In the city he noted a passing encounter.

'An Abyssinian woman, called Ambar Igal, with the profile of a tigress, great painted eyes, and strange African ornaments too heavy for her lovely arms. She smelled of benjoin, myrrh, the sun, and the savage . . . She danced for me. It was in a little Arab courtyard, its square of white walls open to a sky too blue, against which climbed the peaks of rocks the colour of blood and sulphur.'

At Suez, a reassuring letter from Oirda awaited him. His recall would have no more consequences, she wrote. 'Courage, Loti. You will find nothing but good news on your return, and such a welcome

170

as you cannot imagine in advance. For ten friends you left, you will find a hundred. If only you knew how you are talked of everywhere, and in what excellent, flattering terms.'

On reaching Rochefort, in grey weather, he began to unpack 600 kilos of baggage, filling the courtyard with porcelain and mandarin's robes. 'Why did I encumber myself with all this?' He was petulant; as usual, everything at Rochefort soon irked him. Extracting himself from the web of home (and the problems of unpacking) he left for Paris, where Oirda's predictions proved correct. The brouhaha and official censure were forgotten. The good offices of his friends, his excellent service record and, no doubt, the brilliant nimbus now surrounding him as an author, had dispersed the clouds. The Admiralty closed the matter by appointing him to administrative work in various naval bases: a polite way of barring him temporarily from further active service.

16th February: 'Ten days in Paris. My name everywhere.' He renewed his old ties with Sarah Bernhardt, and was privileged to watch her rehearsing *La Dame aux Camélias*. 'Tonight I shall play for Renan, and for you, because you are back from Tonkin, and you will see how it is,' she told him. Later, 'flinging a fox cape over her cambric chemise, she left her dressing room for her big landau, giving me her hand between two hedges of admirers who blocked the way.'

Nevertheless Loti's recall and his shore posting – in unjust ignominy, he felt – preyed on him, for he knew the matter was not, as Oirda had assured him, forgotten. He fretted to be again beside his comrades in the 'yellow hell' of Tonkin. 'I am ashamed to be here, in such comfort – and useless,' he wrote to Madame Adam, and went on to revile a government so hot to trade at any price. 'This Republic, this *grocer's daughter* that sends the bravest and best of our nation to die far away . . . May the blood of our sailors be on our politicians' heads . . . What have I said to be so misrepresented? To pretend that I have denounced *my brave sailors – my comrades*! You, of all people, know what I feel for them – I, who know them to be so fine . . . In the middle of war, they were, naturally, compelled to kill, to undertake terrible tasks,' he continued, 'but I am beside them – one of theirs. It is enough of a punishment to be recalled: but to be obliged to leave them, just as the decisive moment of action approaches . . .' Loti was writing nothing at this time, feeling himself an outcast – a leper – and shutting himself away, not even replying to the letters of anxious

171

friends. At last Madame Adam's affection and the belief she had in him, as a man and a writer, dragged him from the slough of despond. She wrote tenderly, showering on him the affection he craved so insatiably: he was her adoptive son, she his literary mother, she told him. Thus this profound relationship was sealed, and 'Madame Chérie' was to watch over him for the rest of his life.

About this time, the Viauds saw the last of those tenants to whom they had been obliged to lease half the house during those long years of poverty. Loti and his mother went over their regained territory, blissfully rearranging everything just as before: 'It seemed that happy moment would never come. Yet it has!'

He now had the means to realize a cherished project, to transform another room into an Oriental idiom. The first had been the Turkish room (once that of Great-aunt Berthe) where Aziyadé's portrait reigned supreme; this had been executed in colour by Marie, from one of Loti's pencil sketches, and was sumptuously framed. As if for a shrine, Loti amassed all loveliness around the portrait: Turkish rugs and embroideries, and now he added a marvellous crimson and gold fretted ceiling (not strictly Turkish, being more Moorish in its stalactite form, but all exoticism). There were silken divans, amber chaplets and damascened weapons on little pearl and cedar-wood coffee tables. It was Byron's East rather than Loti's, for the lovers of Eyoub had known a simpler interior. Nevertheless it enshrined all Loti's memories of his Oriental life.

The next transformation was his Arabic room, little more than a closet leading from the Turkish room. Loti worked with the masons, he and his niece Ninette up to their elbows in plaster. The thick clotted white walls were interspersed with ancient tiles, Arabic and Persian, gravestones, chased silver lamps and mouchrabiyehs, all collected from Middle Eastern souks or the rubbish heaps of ancient quarters in the Kasbah. In this nostalgic setting, wearing a burnous and smoking his narghile, Loti spent timeless hours conjuring up the past. Such transformations were his apprenticeship to further splendours. Not yet the porphyry pillars, the mihrab, nor the turbanned catafalques of his mosque.

Cats were always an integral part of the Viaud household, as they were Loti's cabin companions at sea. 'One has the feeling for cats, or

172

one has not,' he said: there were no half measures. He adored his long succession of felines. There were la Suprématie of his childhood, Moumoutte I and Moumoutte II, and their offspring; Kedi Bey, the Turkish kitten of Eyoub, Tu-duc, Belkis and Mahmud, to name only a few of those who sat beside him while he wrote, curled at his feet when he slept, and had their place beside him at the table or in his cabin. They were his faithful friends. His toys, too. This grown-up child enjoyed dressing them up, having them photographed seated in armchairs, wearing frilly robes and bonnets, like the beaming tabby, Moumoutte Blanche, whose picture is to be seen in his Museum, among a gallery of personages such as Queen Elizabeth of Belgium, or Annie Besant. Some of the cats had their own visiting cards. On a yellowing pasteboard, we read: *Madame Moumoutte Blanche, 1ère chatte chez Monsieur Pierre Loti.* Besides a playful card where Loti emphasizes his athletic prowess, *Monsieur Pierre Loti. Pointe, Contre-pointe, Canne et Boxe,* there is another yellowing card: *Madame Moumoutte-Chinoise, 2ème chatte chez Monsieur Pierre Loti.* She is the picture of whiskered content, dressed very lacily with a frilled European baby's bonnet, but was, in fact, a survivor of the Boxer Rebellion, souvenir of the time Loti served in China, at the sack of Peking, when he removed Moumoutte along with other treasures from the Great Within. He generally preferred cat society to any social round. 'Here we are tyrannized by cats,' he would remark, when visitors saw them occupying chairs and sofas complacently. One of his most heartrending pieces of writing tells of the drowning of a kitten. The pathos of animals was something to which he could never become hardened, nor could he forgive those who harmed them, such as a shipmate who wantonly killed a young seal frisking joyously in the wake of their ship.

About this time he was working on several short pieces with the Far East as subject. *Pagodes Souterraines* appears in *La Revue des Deux Mondes* and marked a new phase. It was a vein in which, through the years to come, he was to recreate the many strange faraway places he had known. Editors were now ravening for anything the author of *Le Mariage de Loti* would give them, from pen or pencil, for he still employed that other talent to advantage. His sketch books were filled with records of his voyages, of places and people; above all, of his shipmates, afloat or ashore, and a brawny, handsome lot they appear. Some of these sketches, such as that of his crew aboard the *Triomphante* (where one is mysteriously dressed as a Harlequin), are now in the Archives of the Ministère de la Marine. Loti's genius had first found expression through his life at sea, and it is fitting that he, the man of letters, is recalled there as a man of the sea.

Throughout 1884, his life continued to swing between his duties at the Caserne St Maurice at Rochefort and the old home, with short spells in Paris. 11th May 1884: 'All night racketing about the *bas fonds* with the brothers Nopein, once my crew, today the toughs of Belleville. The bal Kolbus, the bal Sauvage, and Auvergnat taverns, dancing to a *cornemuse*. Overturned tables, sang around the streets till dawn. The Nopein brothers, their mistresses and friends, a united band . . . Parted at Les Halles, embracing: they will be devoted to me till death, they told me. Vows of eternal friendship, vows to meet again . . .'

Monday, 12th May. 'Dined at a table which disappeared under garlands of white flowers: on my right Oirda, on my left the young Duchesse de Richelieu, glittering with diamonds. The Duchesse de Grammont, the Comtesse de la Rochefoucauld, the Marquise de Nadaillac, etc. etc. . . On separating, promises of enduring friendship, promises to meet again – as yesterday, in the lower depths of Belleville with the Nopeins.'

At this time it was Loti's habit to go about Paris accompanied by one or other of those young handsome sailors who became his protégés. He writes of Pierre Scoarnec's delight in a jaunt to Paris, and the admiration his fair Breton handsomeness aroused in the capital. Loti always felt himself free to flout the conventions when on leave, and expected his friends to welcome each unusual protégé of the moment, whom he would introduce into the most rarefied circles without a qualm. There were many cruel comments, but one wonders, what were the feelings of the brawny blue-collared sailor, standing dumbly beside his little painted patron?

It was with *Mon Frère Yves*, the book on which Loti had been working during much of 1883–4 that his true stature was to emerge. It marked his break from the earlier, exotic, autobiographic novels, and although everything Loti wrote always had strong personal derivations, he was no longer the central figure. The lover of Rarahu and Aziyadé has become the companion-in-arms of the matelot

Yves, and we follow their life ashore and at sea, with naval tradition and discipline, and Yves' back-slidings into alcoholism, until his final regeneration is brought about by Loti's mixture of harsh discipline and understanding. Most of it followed the true pattern of their relationship: but in life it was alcoholism which finally claimed Yves, ruined his marriage and broke Loti's infinite patience.

Loti is generally dubbed an exotic writer. In his earlier books, certainly. Yet the exoticism of the first three was never to be repeated. Travels in exotic lands continued to produce some of his finest writing, but in a detached rather than romantic vein. For Loti, exoticism and romance now became transposed into northern terms. Brittany had its own exoticism; it seemed remote from France, and was yet another '*ailleurs*'. The Bretons still wore their distinctive costumes, marched in the solemn penitential processions, and followed the stoic pattern of their ancestors, living and dying at the will of the sea – that sea which held Loti too in bond. In finding inspiration there, his writing took on another, more disciplined note, which was to reach perfection in a later Breton novel, *Pêcheur d'Islande*. Gradually the professional novelist had taken over from the amateur diarist, but without losing any of those marvellously evocative powers. Papeete or Paimpol – he cast the same poetic spell, and now that the egoist lover who had set certain critics' teeth on edge had disappeared, there were praises, praises all the way. But for Loti himself, some magic had vanished. Life as he had once known it and dreamed it should be – love and the romantic East – was over, while the regeneration he sought in the Breton marriage was unrealized.

Oirda, the recipient of his inner conflicts wrote: 'How I wish I could see you happier, Loti, less tormented by this perpetual, unquenchable thirst which devours you. Work is the sole remedy worth anything . . . Only, to be calm, you have need of storms.' (Something Jousselin-Plumkett had already divined.) 'In the calm, you yourself create interior storms, as you accumulate boredom on boredom. But a breath of tempest – a real storm – and you are again alive, vibrant, suffering – and happy!' And *writing*, she hoped.

Soon, he was off again, heading into the storm.

Rochefort, 4th October: 'I have returned from a dash to Brittany; the daughter of the Iceland fisherman, she who refused to become my wife, she whom I desired and adored without hope for two years –

175

she will be mine at last!' That she was now married, she, the symbol of unattainable purity who was proving frail, did not disillusion Loti. He had forgotten the myth of regeneration through marriage to her: that had merely been a rationalization of desire. Now desire would be fulfilled. 'I know very well this can finish in a real drama. So much the worse . . . Now all past sufferings are swept away in a whirlwind of youth, and some savage breath of the sea.'

In November, when he was counting the hours to their next rendezvous he received her letter. 'Remorse, black remorse has possessed her proud and naïve soul – perhaps, too, love for her husband,' he grudgingly adds. Nevertheless he wrote, imploring another meeting.

While awaiting her reply he was in Paris, his arrival there announced by all the journals in royal style, though such marks of fame left him unmoved. Dinner with Daudet, Goncourt and Zola – the talk continuing till the small hours – was no distraction. He could bear no more! He rushed back to Paimpol, only to find his love inflexible.

Thursday, 11th December. 'That terrible day when all was shattered! I had never imagined anything so fearful as our parting. *And I love her in this desperate way which is my way.*' At this point the journals positively throb, like an aching tooth. For Loti, custom never staled the infinite variety of his torments. De Musset's Don Paez, who had influenced the schoolboy, was the man's latter-day portrait.

> *'Ce n'était pas Rolla qui gouvernait sa vie*
> *C'étaient ses passions; il les laissait aller . . .'*

Returning to Paris from the Breton rebuff, he clung to misery, still wearing his rough blue fisherman's jersey. 'It seems she will be further from me, when I leave off this costume which I wore for *her*,' he notes.

Dressing up was perpetual, if limited distraction. 'Dined with the Duchesse de Richelieu; afterwards to see *Théodora*. In the entracte, with Sarah Bernhardt, and amused myself trying on the Imperial Byzantine costumes.' In one scene, Sarah's dress was of cerulean blue satin with a four-foot-long train, the whole embroidered with peacock's feathers of emeralds and sapphires, her head-dress a casque encrusted with more jewels topped by a strange edifice of crescents and further explosions of glitter. It must have been a very long entracte for Loti to get himself in and out of such intricacies; and to this pair of show-offs it must have recalled old times, when 'Julien le Fou', the unknown young sailor wearing rating's blue and white, or Arik Ussim Effendi's Turkish costume, was received in the black satin-hung bedroom where the skeleton Lazare presided.

In the spring of 1885 Loti was ordered back to Tonkin for active service, and spent his last days at Rochefort working on *Pêcheur d'Islande*, which was then appearing in *La Revue des Deux Mondes*, in extracts entitled *Au Large* – At Sea. He wrote in the narrow strip of garden where as a schoolboy he used to dream of those fabulous voyages he would make – one day. Now he wrote of seas he had come to know, of great storms that tore at the ships and claimed their victims, and of the women who waited for their men in vain. Such a woman was Gaud, heroine of *Pêcheur d'Islande*. Yet this book, which has come to rank among French classics, was written without the zest of his earlier work. For all his cult of home, the torpor of the old house oppressed him dreadfully. 'Today, all day long, the street door has remained closed: not one sound of the bell . . .' Moumoutte, his seafaring cat, companion of many earlier voyages, kept him quiet company, but she showed signs of age. Suliema the tortoise wore better – would live to be sixty or more . . . but watching the frail, black-robed figures of Maman, Aunt Claire and Mélanie, still busying themselves between kitchen and flower beds, he knew that time was running out fast . . . That thought came between him and his writing.

On the eve of his departure for Tonkin he received a few lines of tender farewell from Oirda. Her days were numbered, and she knew it, but she made no drama of it. 'Write to me when you can . . . and on bad days remember that as long as I am in this world you have a place in my affection from which nothing can take you.'

   The old ladies thought it would be the last time they would be able to pack for their Julien, but insisted on panting up and down the stairs with his belongings, which added to the melancholy. Last times, last moments, last embraces, last backward glances . . . Loti was in his element. 'Now it is the last evening, our last tea together, and we linger there. We have nothing more to do, nothing more to say . . . we await the omnibus that takes me to the station . . . How long, this wait . . . It is at the door. Quick! I embrace them, and as I do so, I am torn with grief . . . yet I long to be gone.'

Loti's return to active service and the life aboard which he loved best was crowned by the warmth of Vice-Admiral Courbet's greeting when he joined the cruiser *Triomphante* in the Asiatic oven of Ma-Kun'g. Yves was also aboard, and once more the two friends were together as much as their free time allowed.

For the next six months the *Triomphante* was in Japanese waters. Anchored in the roads, or at Nagasaki, Loti was able to spend much time ashore, observing the Japanese closely. From this moment came his first Japanese book, *Madame Chrysanthème*. It recounts his 'marriage' – a business-like contract, with one of those doll-like *mousmés* whose families leased them out as a pastime for any gentleman desirous of their submissive company. They should not be confused with the geishas, who were a more exclusive band trained to subtle arts of diversion as hostesses, musicians, dancers, and conversationalists. Their graces and intellect were the geishas' fortune, rather than their bodies. The *mousmés* Loti knew, Mme Chrysanthème and her friends of the same calling, were half-way between geisha and prostitute, more available than the former, less promiscuous than the latter, but one and all schooled to please.

There was never the slightest emotion in this arrangement, either for Loti or his *mousmé*. He entered into this 'marriage' (arranged by the agent – Kangarou-san, and registered by the local police) the better to acquaint himself with Japanese life. He found himself installed in a little paper-screen dwelling high above the city of Nagasaki in the quarter of Diou-djen-dji. It was of glacial cleanliness, bare of anything except two cotton mattresses, a dark blue mosquito net tied with yellow cords, a lacquer tray with tea pot and cups of delicate porcelain, a gilded Buddha and the doll-like *mousmé*, who did her best to satisfy her new master. She prostrated herself before him, sang plaintively to a long-handled guitar, and took her place beside him under the blue mosquito net, her elaborately lacquered dark head resting on a small wooden block, for this coiffure was never to be disturbed. Yves was sometimes a guest at the little paper house, his giant's stature reducing it and Mme Chrysanthème to even more toy-like proportions. Loti fancied 'mon frère Yves' was rather inclined towards his *mousmé*, and she to him. The thought intrigued him, and he played with the idea of being jealous. It was all part of the coquettish scene.

Although Loti acquired a smattering of Japanese, it did not bring him closer to the people. Impatience and an amused detachment sound behind all he wrote then. 'I knew it all, long ago, from scenes painted on the bottom of a tea cup,' he wrote; and those are the scenes his book reflects. For all his perspicacity, there is no echo of that fierce warrior violence of mediaeval Japan, which remains a characteristic of the nation. Loti's Japan is very far from those angry grimacing gods, the Samurai, or the courtly *Tales of Gengii*.

Japanese art had come to occupy a prominent place in Europe about this time: though it seems unlikely that Loti was blindly following the fashionable cult for all things Japanese, for his own instincts as a collector proved his fine sensibility. The influence of Japan on Whistler's art and Lord Leighton's study of Japanese art published in 1869 are unlikely to have been known to him: but by 1875 Edmond de Goncourt's *Albums Japonais* had aroused the interest of the French intellectuals, who followed Princesse Mathilde's lead, so that *Japoneries* were collected avidly. Loti now had the rare chance to seek them at source. But he never really responded to this people's fragile genius: nothing of them spoke to him as did every aspect of Islamic culture. Nevertheless, he is not forgotten in Japan, and although he described their women as insect figures, his brief sojourn in Nagasaki is commemorated by a statue, erected '*to the author of Madame Chrysanthème*' in 1950, the centenary of his birth.

179

12

The man was married: the officer less so – Loti never.

Sacha Guitry

In 1886, *Pêcheur d'Islande* was published, and through it the French public learned something of the strangeness, drama and tragedy of Breton fishermen's lives, with the eternal struggle between man and the sea and the abnegation of their waiting wives, with Gaud as their symbol. This book is generally thought to be Loti's masterpiece, though there are some, and I am one, who consider his travel pieces more perfectly achieved than his novels. With *Pêcheur d'Islande*, the simple yet violent love story of Gaud and Yann, where the sea disputes Yann's earthly love and at last reclaims him, is obsessive in its stark tragedy and poetic beauty. After reading this book, Goncourt wrote: 'You are an admirable, a miraculous painter, and when you write of reality, your vision is of an intense poetry – something no other has seen . . .'

Ernest Renan, who was from Brittany, and knew the country and characters of Loti's book at first hand, wrote to him: 'These Icelandic fisherfolk are my cousins and second cousins . . . Bréhat, Paimpol, Lézardrieux and Plourivo are peopled with the ancient clans from which I stem. You have painted them marvellously, dear and admirable artist that you are.' Renan's praise meant much to Loti, for it was not easily won; nor did Renan belong to the fluctuating world of Parisian *belles lettres*. There were some curious similarities between these two outwardly dissimilar figures, who became close friends; small, dandified Loti and Renan, who appeared a rather elephantine old sober-sides. Both were from the provinces, adored sons of an adored and pious mother for whom both had made many sacrifices. Both had grown up in an atmosphere of unquestioning religious beliefs – Renan's being of Rome and Loti's of Luther. Both had much older sisters who influenced their youth. Both lost their faith, and travelled about the Holy Land in search of it, only to become reluctant but confirmed atheists; both were oppressed by the grief their atheism caused their mothers. 'I loved him [Renan] with a particular respect and affection, and how his genius enchanted me,' wrote Loti, recalling their unclouded friendship.

Just as Loti's romantic life in Turkey had been the apogee of all happiness, so *Pêcheur d'Islande* might be seen as the peak of his achievement as a novelist. He had reached the watershed of life, love and fame, and in his eyes, only a slow descent lay ahead. The image of that exotic *doppelgänger* self on faraway shores, landing, loving and leaving had vanished forever.

It was time to try out the husband's rôle, and in so doing, gratify his mother's wish to see him, as she fondly hoped, safe in harbour before she died. He eyed matrimony without enthusiasm, but as a means of ensuring that through his children something of himself would remain, a flesh and blood version of those journals which, from Fédin on, had recorded his life as a stand against the impermanence of all things. And yet – children – whose children? Aziyadé stole between him and reality, or even past repinings over a child in Geneva. 'They would not be yours, Aziyadé. Could I love them, if your blood and mine did not mingle in their veins?' he had written long ago, on his return from Turkey.

He began pressing Madame Adam to discover some suitable bride, stipulating that she must be Protestant, well off and smaller than he (this last condition being the most difficult to fulfil). He himself had asked for the hand of a distinguished magistrate's daughter and was brusquely turned down by her father. *Unlikely to attain Admiral's rank* was the pith of the refusal, Loti's lustre as a man of letters being ignored. That he was unlikely to make the grade as a satisfactory husband does not seem to have troubled Loti nor his family: nor, presently, the family of Mademoiselle Jean-Blanche Blanc de Ferrière, upon whom his final choice rested.

The Ferrières were known to Madame Viaud, and Loti when serving in the Far East had known one of Jean-Blanche's brothers who was also in the navy. The family was one of the oldest among the Protestants of Bordeaux, wealthy, and with estates in the Lot. But Loti was not going to be pushed into any conventional mould. On his first visit to his future relatives he was careful to wear the fisherman's coarse blue jersey and red neckerchief he cherished in memory of his abortive Breton romance. How this was viewed by the Ferrières or the girl who her family had decided should link her life and fortune to his, we do not know. It was not always easy, in France, to find husbands for Protestant daughters, for they were not considered desirable in Roman Catholic families (nor were bridegrooms of the Catholic faith welcomed by Protestants). Blanche de Ferrière met all the requirements, being of the Reformed Church, an heiress, and of doll-like proportions. She was gentle, well-bred and well-read too; she admired her suitor's books and the man they revealed, who, of course, was very far from the husband whom the future would reveal to her. She had fallen at once under his spell, yet another of those willing victims who always strewed his path.

If the announcement of his forthcoming marriage appeared to Loti as something still improbable – even unbelievable – it came as even more of a surprise to his friends.

The wedding was fixed for October 21st at the Protestant Church in Bordeaux. For a few days before, Loti was with his fiancée, assisting with the preparations and sending out invitations. Numbers of guests, family friends, Loti's shipmates and Parisians of the literary world, headed by Madame Adam and the poet François Coppée, were all about to converge on Bordeaux. The press were already there, for Loti, hero of those romantic novels, and also the sailor-author who had brought the courageous lives and deaths of the matelots before the whole nation, was now a personality who interested a wide public. His wedding promised splendid copy.

'October 10th. My little fiancée wants all that I want,' Loti notes complacently. 'She is prepared for anything, nothing surprises her, she who knows nothing about anything . . . She is like someone who draws near to a whirlwind, and throws herself into it, head first. What will her tomorrow be? We spent the evening addressing the invitations for our wedding. I was in a hurry to leave, because *she* awaited me.' '*She*' was the Bordeaux siren who had proved so inflammatory some years earlier. The fact that she had married another had not prevented her from showing a renewed interest in Loti after his rise to fame. Now, 'some demon placed her once more on my path. She begged me for one more night. I said no – but she reminded me how she had granted me, out of pity, one more night on the eve of her own marriage.' (That night when Loti had made her put on her veil and wedding dress for him to agonize over.) So Lothario-Loti agreed to another meeting, and leaving his fiancée to continue addressing the invitations, was off again. His journal continues: 'A fevered night, almost painful. Now she loves me as once I loved her! She suffers as once I did. The same desperate caresses that I had given her she now gives back to me. I am avenged!'

On 17th October, the Viauds and a contingent from Rochefort arrived. The old pastor Puaux was to perform the ceremony – he who had once made a curious suggestion that Loti should look no further for a wife, since in Ninette, his niece, he had all he needed at his side. It was noticed that Ninette seemed gloomy. She had not shown much enthusiasm for the engagement of her famous uncle, who had always indulged her and with whom she continued to spend much time, even after her marriage. She had always nourished a possessive jealousy where Loti was concerned. 'I would have liked *you* for my bridegroom, ton-ton,' she wrote, 'but Mama would not hear of it.' Yet even without the kill-joy Marie, it seems unlikely that Loti would have married his niece; the perils of consanguinity were great, and he wanted a son.

Madame Viaud and Aunt Clarisse were accompanied by the family servants, devoted old Mélanie and Pierre Scoarnec, a favoured Breton matelot. The day before the wedding, the complications of bureaucracy gathered. The trap was closing. '20th October. Agitation: some papers missing, without which we cannot marry. 3 p.m. Civil marriage at the Town Hall. It seems I am taking part in someone else's wedding. In the evening, a big dinner, Blanche and I at the centre of the table. I am astonished to read, on her place card: Madame Julien Viaud . . .

'21st October. Gloomy overcast weather. I miss the family luncheon party to go round the hotels where Mme Adam, the Durands etc. are dispersed. Went right to the end of the town, by the St Jean station, and booked rooms there in a rather dubious kind of hotel [*un hôtel suspect*] for my wife and me, before we leave for Spain.'

Why Loti had not booked rooms earlier and why he selected a dubious hotel is not known. No doubt psychologists would pronounce it proof of his inability to face the marriage, and a determination to make the whole process as disagreeable as possible for himself – and Blanche too.

Before the momentous day was over Loti had noted it all in his journal; not even his wedding night appears to have stopped him keeping to this lifelong habit.

'I start to dress. When I see the bride in her bridal toilette I begin to understand – to realize that it is *I* who am the groom, and I grow giddy. 4 p.m. At the church: a huge crowd. Music, an address, everyone looking and listening religiously. I should do likewise. I understand nothing. I hear nothing. My eyes are fixed on Ninette, sitting near me, and so lovely in her beautiful dress . . . It is all very long . . . Blanche and I go out to the porch, but I see no-one except my dear Samuel [one of his particular sailor favourites] who is wearing his seaman's clothes. I give him my hand, to show publicly the especial feeling I have for him.'

At the dinner that night, Loti was the spectre at the feast. 'I am anguished, giddy . . . Everyone anxious, for I have turned livid-pale, my heart constricted with regrets for my Breton love' (the Iceland fisherman's unattainable bride haunts him still). 'My heart beats horribly . . . there are speeches, toasts, and I glimpse my dear old mother smiling so happily. About midnight, when I have seen off numbers of guests, I put on travelling clothes, Blanche likewise, and we get into some sort of omnibus and are off into the sad, cold night, chained together for life.'

For the bridal pair to leave in an omnibus was perhaps more of Loti's Freudian determination that both of them should be wretched from the start.

Descriptions of the honeymoon, only the briefest notations, read like the itinerary of some Cook's tour. 'Sat. 23rd. Leave for Spain. Day and night in train. Sun. 24th. Madrid, 8 a.m. Mon. 25th. Museums. Tues. 26th. Toledo for the day . . .' In Granada they pause. 'We get on very well, my little wife and I' is all Loti vouchsafes on this new state. They are photographed in the courtyard of the Alhambra, Loti with a Velasquez beard, strikes a proud pose, very much the grandee in wide Spanish hat and cloak. Blanche stands meekly beside him, prim in her dark, bustled costume, her neat little gloved hands folded, button eyes staring out with a faintly apprehensive expression. As well she might have had, were she to realize what married life would be like at Rochefort.

In their absence, the old house had been slightly rearranged. His mother's bedroom was now made over for himself and Blanche. He had chosen the white and gold Empire furniture in Bordeaux; the panelled walls and a charming little marble cheminée were also in the Empire style, while the entire ceiling was oddly dotted with sparrow-sized Napoleonic bees, gilded and in high relief. They are still there, those ceiling-stuck bees, and disturbing they must have seemed to the young bride, generally alone in the alcoved Empire bed, while Loti spent uncounted hours elsewhere – in the Turkish room sustained by memories of his Oriental life, or in the port among his sailor friends.

Since Loti was head of the family, Blanche was, in theory, head of the household, but no-one saw her as such. She yielded passively to the *chères vieilles*, who were affectionate and attentive but who, in turn, yielded unquestioningly to Loti's slightest wish, obeying those commands that were issued in that soft caressing voice that was yet so authoritative. It was still a perpetually overcrowded household, for Marie Bon and her husband, and Ninette and her Duvigneau in-laws came and went incessantly, increasingly possessive. Then there were numbers of lesser relatives and old friends such as the Durands, inexplicably now treated as part of the Viaud family, as well as some of Loti's shipmates, usually from the lower deck, not all of whom mixed well, though Léopold Thémèze, *'le beau Léo'*, was a frequent presence liked by everyone. Loti was commanding the *Ecureuil*, in the port at Rochefort, and Thémèze was one of his crew, extraordinarily handsome in a dark, Arab way. Loti was besotted by him. 'It is Léo I would like to have near me when I die,' he was fond of repeating. His journals contain several rhapsodic descriptions of *le beau Léo* asleep on the rugs in the Arab room. Thémèze was a nonchalant, agreeable character of some education, who had endured many hardships uncomplainingly. His family were modest jewellers from Antibes, but Léo's patrimony had been lost by his brother's negligence. Unlike most of Loti's seafaring friends, Léo never exploited him, and never seems to have been resented by the Viaud family – not that it would have made any difference. He became an almost permanent welcome presence at Rue St Pierre, sometimes accompanying Loti on his travels.

Loti was writing little, except his journal, at this time. Between his duties at the Port, and the harrowing novelty of married life, he was in no mood even to play the piano, hitherto one of his greatest pleasures. He and Blanche made excursions into local social life, evidently depressing ones: 'Reception, the Préfet Maritime. Blanche in red velvet . . . Dinner at the D's, Blanche in blue.' He always took a dictatorial interest in her clothes, insisting she went to the best couturières of Bordeaux. Not for her the local tailors to whom he remained faithful with such unfortunate results.

For the young, inexperienced girl who had been brought up in considerable comfort, if not luxury, in Bordeaux, life at Rochefort was claustrophobic and very uncomfortable. No-one seems to have considered attacking the question of plumbing. There was no bathroom, and still only the antiquated closet at the end of the garden – the old two-seater of Loti's childhood. There was no gas or electricity. Lamps and the old lavatory had been good enough for everyone all these years was Loti's view, so nothing was done. Blanche was far too timid, and far too much in love to demand that some of her dowry should be used to obtain comfort. Meanwhile she stole about the house like a little changeling, conscious that all those around her were primarily interested in her waist-line, waiting for her to produce the desired heir. Once, trying to rearrange her room, she smashed a yellow china candlestick. It was of no great value, but it was a souvenir of Loti's childhood, and the storm that broke quite crushed her. She, the intruder, had destroyed a sacred relic, one of those fetish possessions which to him were bulwarks against the terrible passage of time. Nevertheless, since she was dutifully pregnant, he tried not to dwell on her clumsiness. But how fearful the tedium of his life! 'I am bored – bored to death, bored as never before,' he confided to Madame Adam.

He was shaken out of such moods in May 1887, for just seven months after her marriage Blanche stumbled, fell headlong down the steep stairway of the old house, and miscarried. Loti was summoned from the Bureau de la Marine and rushed back, frantic with anxiety. The baby was a boy, barely alive, but it lingered for a few days. Loti could not bring himself to look at the poor little thing. At last his mother persuaded him: 'I did not want to see him, fearing some horrible, malformed creature. I turned my eyes slowly sideways, as if to look at some terrifying corpse, and I was amazed. What anguish, what tearing grief, to see this little being already formed, already living . . . this little mouth which opened in an effort to breathe – to live. It was my image, this tiny child – myself in miniature, with a likeness that was almost terrifying . . . And it was going to die! Nothing to be done, nothing but to watch it die. What profound mystery was there! This little model of myself, who would have had *my* thoughts, *my* problems, *my* agonies, and who was already returning to dust, the dust of eternity . . .'

Made in his image: for Loti this loss was unbearable. His journal reeks with grief. There is only the briefest mention of Blanche, lying upstairs, half dead herself, after a terrible labour which had been grossly mishandled by the old family doctor. She had developed

186

puerperal fever, generally fatal then, and only struggled back to life more fragile than ever, her sight and hearing affected, and bitterly disappointed that she had failed her husband – clumsy again – in his ardent wish for an heir. From this moment dates the deafness which was to develop so tragically, and set her even further from him.

The night the baby died Loti took him to the Turkish room, there to give way to grief. 'I laid him there like a little prince of the Orient, lying on gold embroideries, surrounded by flowers. He wore his peaceful smile of tranquil mystery . . . he was so pretty, like some delicious wax doll . . . How could he be so beautiful, this little Samuel? . . . I said to Léo, "come and see my son" . . . and then I wept – wept, and life seemed finished, for me, as for my child.' Loti had insisted on naming the baby Samuel, probably after a Huguenot ancestor – though possibly after his sailor friend Samuel Greusiller, who was as unknown to Blanche as the rest of his family. It was this same Samuel whose hand he had wrung at the wedding; and now perhaps offered a further proof of his affection for the mysterious seaman. It was also proof of his indifference to any name Blanche might have liked. But then he saw the baby as *his* – all his – a part of himself, already gone to dust.

For five harrowing days the baby lay in the Turkish room, beside Aziyadé's portrait, and the family, who were so seldom encouraged to penetrate this sanctuary of memories, were now admitted to mourn. In the gruesome fashion of the age, photographers were incessantly hovering, taking innumerable pictures of the tiny cocooned corpse, and on the last afternoon, a plaster cast was made of one minuscule foot. 'We had to hurry. I laid him in the pine box myself and shut the cover on him. At six o'clock they took away my little son to the cemetery, to the tomb of my father, which we opened for him.'

For a long while Loti was sunk in apathy, and now there was no longer Oirda the consoler, to whom he could have poured out his misery. Even his nomination for the Légion d'Honneur left him indifferent. Instead of a scrap of scarlet ribbon, he would prefer to be covered by a black sheet, he said. Writing to Ninette, some time later, and still lingering over his loss, he wrote: 'I would be less unhappy if I had not *seen* him – so pretty, poor little thing.' Would he have been a better husband to Blanche had she been beautiful? She was not even pretty, by the full-blown standards of those days, though she had a certain quiet charm, with her soft, round brown eyes, and small retroussé nose. Everyone who knew her recalled her air of distinction, her gentleness, and touching solicitude for her difficult husband, and all those around her. She was tactful to the point of self-effacement, alone in this household of egoists ('a nest of vipers', as it was described to me by one who had known it at a later date), all of them, except his mother and sweet Aunt Claire exploiting Blanche's fortune while snubbing her as an outsider.

I have sometimes wondered how Blanche and her conventional family viewed her husband's constant use of make-up. He is described as entering a Paris salon almost on tip-toe, from the height of the heels he had adopted, to add to his stature . . . 'his moustache frizzed and dyed, a touch of rouge on his grease-painted cheeks'. He could never realize how absurd he appeared. If only his mother, the one person for whom he was prepared to renounce what he held dear (long voyages, or the Islamic faith), could have persuaded him to abandon such conceits. Probably she was too innocent, too myopic to be aware of those prejudicial aids: but his wife – equally innocent and myopic – had neither she nor the Ferrières ever questioned her husband's strangely blooming appearance? Had his sister Marie never spoken out, as was her wont? If so, it had been to no avail. He had turned early to the artifices of paint and dye pot in that desperate quest for physical perfection which haunted him throughout his life. To be tall and handsome – '*un bel homme*'! As the years began to leave their mark he felt himself disgraced and humiliated, and suffered increasingly, and so redoubled his artifices with an ingenuosity that was touching. It must have seemed singular to the navy, confronted with such audacious non-conformity.

In the archives of the Ministère de la Marine, Lieutenant-Commander Julien Viaud's dossier for 1890 contained the following entry by the Préfet Maritime at Rochefort: '*Is made-up in a ridiculous manner. I shall not propose him for a command.*' Yet such was Loti's curious ability to overcome prejudice, that only a year later, the same Admiral noted glowingly, '*Excellent officer. Repays knowing better. I shall propose him for a command.*' It is clear that Loti's true worth gradually emerged from behind the painted façade. He was *le bon Julien*, the infinitely kind, generous, loyal companion, whom both his friends and shipmates came to accept unquestioningly.

In the autumn of 1887, four gloomy months after his dashed paternity, Loti's spirits were slightly revived by an invitation from Queen Elizabeth of Romania to visit her at Castel Pelesh, deep in the Carpathian forests. He accepted with alacrity. A voyage would change his ideas; and then, he always found royalty irresistible, admitting that the sight of a Crowned Head sent shivers of delight through him.

The Queen had been born a German princess, Elizabeth of Wied. She was unhappy in her marriage to the stern King Carol I and, having lost her only child, was a frustrated mother. She solaced herself by various artistic pursuits, was an amateur pianist of merit, illuminated vellum missals for the church, wrote Romanian fairy tales, poetry and other pieces which were published under the pseudonym of Carmen Sylva, by which she became widely known. She overflowed with grace, was full of sentiment and generosity, and was gullible to the point of silliness. In the turreted castle, her rooms were hung with dark velvet, and there she gave readings of her own works as well as those of other poets, and played the organ with emotion, her ladies clustered round devotionally. She was also an inveterate poseur affecting vaporous white robes often woven with silver which, with her aureole of prematurely silvery hair, gave her the air of some incorporeal being, or so beholders told her. 'Silver locks,' she wrote in her *Pensées*, 'are the spray which covers the ocean after a tempest.'

When Loti arrived in this rarefied atmosphere, 'the enchanted castle of a fairy being,' as he described it, poseur met poseur head on. But there was no collision; rather, a collusion. Together they walked through the sombre pine forests, weeping over their sorrows and lost babies and exchanging high-flown compliments, for were they not literary confrères? The Queen had just translated *Pêcheur d'Islande* into German and proudly displayed the manuscript: she cherished hopes of being elected to the French Academy and Loti was encouraging. It was Carmen Sylva, entranced by his memories of childhood, who first urged him to write them down, and this he came to do, in the beautiful *Roman d'un Enfant*, which is dedicated to the Queen.

Loti's arrival at Bucharest had been awaited by the whole Court with bated breath. They had expected some dashing man of the sea, this husband of Rarahu and countless other charmers from diverse latitudes. Instead, a diminutive, shy figure appeared, dressed in

189

those conventional stiff clothes in which he looked his worst. He had not risked the fisherman's jersey or the matelot's blue and white before royalty, and we do not know if he toned down his make-up (not that paint would have astonished the Romanians: men there used heavy perfumes, attar of roses or patchouli, though in the army, officers under the rank of major were not permitted make-up). Loti and the Queen formed a lasting friendship, and he was later to visit her once more, during her banishment in Venice, and to write of her at length in his book *L'Exilée* before she was sequestered and any further visits became impossible.

Meanwhile, at Castel Pelesh, the mixture of protocol, intrigue and Literature, with a capital 'L', occupied Loti to the exclusion of all else. He scarcely left the Queen's side except to visit her dead child's tomb, and so did not travel about this picturesque land as his readers would have wished. For the first time, he made a journey to an unknown country without attempting to look beyond the windows. He was not appreciated by the King, and after an ill-timed practical joke – one of Loti's infantile pranks – he prudently took leave of the Romanian Court.

But not to head homeward. On the contrary, he turned east, making for Turkey. Constantinople lay beyond the Black Sea, and he had determined, before leaving Rochefort, to return there to search for traces of Aziyadé. It was a pious pilgrimage; perhaps it explained the alacrity with which he accepted Carmen Sylva's invitation, for Bucharest was three-quarters of the way to Constantinople, though it is unlikely he mentioned this nostalgic project to Blanche, or any of the family.

Fantôme d'Orient, the book which describes Loti's return to Constantinople is the sequel or coda to *Aziyadé*, telling of his despairing search for his lost love. He described it as being neither the recital of a voyage nor a romantic novel – rather, the end of a romance.

In spite of a succession of emotional uproars, listed and unlisted, and the chimera of marriage and children, only two women (his mother apart) touched the profound springs of Loti's perpetually unappeased craving for love: *la bien aimée* of Geneva and Aziyadé. But since Aziyadé had become indissolubly one with the city that had held him in thrall from the beginning, he now sought two phantoms – the woman and the city. As his boat sailed up the Bosphorus it rose before him once more in all its haunting beauty of great mosques and shadowy cyprus groves. A ghostly spell overshadows both this book and the passages in his journal where he noted his fevered wanderings, tracking down his past through forgotten by-ways. His caïque skims the waters of the Corne d'Or and, as in a dream, he again draws near to Eyoub. Who would remember him there, and where could he find those who might give him news of Aziyadé? A dreadful sense of urgency pervades these pages. There were only two more days left before he must turn westward and resume that other life, now more unreal to him than any charade once played out in Stamboul. Lieutenant-Commander Julien Viaud and Loti the writer were reminding his *doppelgänger* self (Aziyadé's lover, rather than Blanche's husband) that here he was only a ticket-of-leave man.

Once more wearing the treasured Turkish costume of Ussim Effendi (which he had been careful to pack), he went feverishly from one scribbled address to another, deciphering the scraps of yellowing paper, precious souvenirs where those of his Turkish friends who could write had inscribed some improbable address. *The blue door beyond the seller of babouches at Balik Bazaar . . . the copper-smith's house at Buyuk Otloupdji* . . . Could they lead him to Kadidja? There was an Armenian woman whom Achmet had trusted to deliver letters to Aziyadé . . . If he could find her again – and if she could find Achmet . . . ? He did find the Armenian woman, and through her, Achmet's sister Eriknaz . . . but not Achmet. And now he was to learn that the truth was almost as he had imagined the end of his adventure. Those hallucinatory last pages of *Aziyadé* had been extraordinarily prophetic. Written in loneliness and despair, they had foreseen the true end. Samuel had vanished and Achmet had died of wounds received in battle. Dead, the companion of those joyous days, and buried in a pauper's grave, the family having fled before the Russian armies' advance. *But Aziyadé?* As in a dream he waited to hear again that dread dreamed phrase '*Eûlû! Eûlû!*' – dead!

'It was about three years after you left,' Eriknaz told him. 'They took her away one evening, almost stealthily . . . though old Abeddin her master ordered a tombstone for her.'

That was all she knew, or all she would tell, though she knew where Kadidja was to be found and agreed to take Loti to her next day.

That night, fleeing the chatter of his hotel, Loti found his way through the silent streets of old Stamboul to reach once more the Fatih quarter where Aziyadé had languished in Abeddin's harem. Again, as he had imagined this return in his book, so it was in life. Ruins and silence: where the konak had stood, only a waste land of rubble and charred beams. Fire had razed the old street. By now Loti had realized what was the real object of his return to Turkey. In his heart, he had always known that Aziyadé must be dead, but his sense of melodrama, his morbidity, demanded he should find her grave and, like his hero, tell the cold earth above her that he had come back. Thus Loti, preparing to live out the last prophetic chapter of Aziyadé, and suffering to the top of his bent.

When he reached the miserable hovel where Kadidja was stretched on a heap of rags like a sick animal, there was none of the hatred with which she had pursued him in his imagined ending. Instead there was compassion in her old eyes as she held out her wrinkled hands to him. 'She, the last of the last, born a black slave, now a piece of débris, hardly human, ending miserably on a dung-hill.' She had understood his remorse, and however much she had once judged him for abandoning the mistress she adored, he had returned, and she understood that he still sought and loved Aziyadé.

For a year or more, Kadidja told him, Aziyadé had believed he would return . . . but presently, when there were no more of his letters, she lost hope.

'Why no more letters? – I sent many,' said Loti.

'Into the fire! I threw them all into the fire, like her letters to you,' said the old slave defiantly. She had been dismissed from the harem, for she was suspect. She believed the letters represented some evil force. Danger for herself and her mistress! Into the fire with them!

As Loti had feared, their rash conduct during those last days had come to Abeddin's ears and some of the harem ladies had talked . . . Aziyadé was neither chased away nor ill-treated. She was simply set apart as something impure, shut away in an obscure apartment giving on to the north, where no ray of sun ever penetrated, and only the chill of Stamboul winters passed the bars. She sickened rapidly. And then, said Kadidja, the other hanums sent her remedies . . . 'Ah! Loti, it was those remedies I doubted . . .' Yes, she would lead him to Aziyadé's grave. It would be a last pilgrimage for her too, one she no longer had the strength to make alone.

Loti hired a kind of sedan chair for her, something then much in use about the steep streets, but its porters refused to lift the abject old figure into its plush-lined luxury. However, a little Jewish booth nearby supplied an orange wool coverlet. Kadidja was wrapped in it, patting its softness with childish glee, and the porters sullenly accepted their strange passenger. (It is by these small details, the *Jewish* booth, the *orange* coverlet such as Loti noted in his journals, and generally incorporated in his books, that he obtains such a vivid, visual impact.) The little party set out for the ancient city walls by the Seven Towers. Beyond, lay desolate fields of the dead, strewn with gravestones of all ages, upright, lurching or fallen about the arid ground. Another hallucinatory search began, the old slave gesticulating with her withered mummy's arms. At last she led them to a tomb where an inscription in faded gilt letters was still visible. After the Fâtihah, the ritual prayer which opens the Koran, *In the name of Allah, the Beneficent, the Merciful,* Loti made out the following lines:

Alas! O Death!
The fragile body that rests in this lonely tomb
Faded at a tender age. Allah knew her to be
Not for this earth and took her to his side.
In the name of Allah the Beneficent, the Merciful,
We pray for the soul of Hakidjé hanum,
Daughter of Abdullah Effendi the Circassian.

19. Zilkadé. 1297   [23rd October 1880]

Although Hakidjé-Aziyadé had died in May, October was probably the date when the tomb was erected. Kadidja crouched down beside it, mumbling and caressing it with her wrinkled black paws, 'those of an old monkey'. Suddenly she turned on Loti, her voice strident in the silence around them. '*Bourda! Bourda* Aziyadé! – Aziyadé is *here!* And it is *you* who brought her here,' she cried, tears pouring down her raddled cheeks. For once, Loti had no tears. He bent over the tomb trying to read again the loved name – the name engraved on the ring she had given him and which he had worn ever since. By now he saw

193

it, and no other, as his wedding ring. He had quite forgotten it was the anniversary of his wedding to Blanche.

Loving, leaving and grieving. It is no good reading Loti unless you are prepared to be torn. Thus, in the last pages of *Fantôme d'Orient*, we follow him to the cemetery yet again. He was alone now, and on reaching Aziyadé's grave, flung himself down for a last lacerating farewell, just as his hero had done. A fine rain misted this lugubrious scene, yet Loti tells us he experienced a radiant sense of peace and fulfilment . . . 'an exquisite illusion that Aziyadé's phantom was beside me, that she knew I had returned, and she understood everything . . . Then all the bitterness and remorse which clung round my memories of her vanished forever,' Loti confided to his journal.

But Aziyadé's phantom knew otherwise.

He returned to pick up that other life again, as Blanche's husband, and wrote: 'In this life there are periods of boredom which we plod through – *clopin-clopant*, accompanied by la Dame Réalité.' Married life stretched before him in greying perspectives. Whichever way he looked, he saw himself pinned down like the night moths and tropic butterflies he had once collected. Married life, provincial life, all was intolerable; the simple expedient of being transferred for a long voyage on the high seas could not be, for he was still held back by his love for the *chères vieilles*, so tranquil in their acceptance of his presence. What Blanche felt, with this restive and morose figure beside her but never *with* her, is not known. She, like so many other women, was in love with him, and small change she obtained for all her proffered devotion. He always treated her with the greatest respect (a dusty answer to one in love) and continued to dictate her wardrobe, preferring very rich materials and elaborately trimmed formal garments, for after all, she was the wife of Julien Viaud. But Loti the writer had settled into a narrow slip of a room leading out of their bedroom: it had been his as a small child, and now he had another door made which gave directly on to the stairs so that he could come and go as he pleased, to roam the town, brood in the Turkish room, or write up his journal where he entered pages he would not have cared for other eyes to see and which he locked away scrupulously, as once Fédin had done.

194

Blanche remained very frail after her miscarriage, her deafness and eye trouble worsening day by day. It was a trial and a humiliation for her to try to follow the rapid-fire of French conversation. Not even her efforts to lip-read helped. She remained an outsider in the Viaud household, as elsewhere. Yet for all her timidity, her sense of guilt over the dead baby, and her continuing ill-health, she was determined to give Loti what he wanted – the only thing he wanted from her – another child, and in defiance of the Viauds' family doctor she left for Paris to consult specialists on her future chances of maternity.

During this stagnant time, while Loti was not at work on a new book, he sometimes responded to editors who continued to press him for travel pieces. He always saw things differently from other travellers, always carried his readers away with him. Not for nothing was he called the Magician. Some of these short pieces are to be found in *L'Exilée* (his memoir of Carmen Sylva, when later he joined her in Venice) together with more impressions of Japan and, notably, Japanese women, now seen even more objectively than in *Madame Chrysanthème*. In the Japanese room, a further transformation he had imposed on the old house on his return from the Far East, his memories were sharpened, and he weighed up Japanese women and the arts, religion, manners and morals surrounding them; a wide range, but he goes straight to essential characteristics, whether writing of the wrinkled, blue-cotton-clad workers or the exquisite aristocrats. 'The slanted eyes of these women have an expression at once youthful and dead ... Tiny little creatures living among tiny little objects as fanciful and light as they ... They laugh with an excess of amiability, or by long habit: they laugh in life's most solemn moments, in their temples or at funerals ... In Japan nothing is taken seriously ... a curtain of levity cloaks the most unpardonable acts ... there are so many nuances of morality, so difficult to seize, above all, scabrous to touch on ... In short, these women resemble certain bibelots of an extreme delicacy, but which it is prudent to examine carefully before bringing back to Europe, for fear of some obscenity lurking beneath a stem of bamboo or a sacred stork ... One might also compare them to those Japanese fans which being opened from right to left, reveal the most charming branches of blossom, but when opened inversely, reveal revolting indecencies ... *Voilà!*' he concludes, 'I have been asked to write on Japanese women, but in a manner that can be read by anyone, and thus I must leave aside certain of their ways.'

Madame Chrysanthème had been the first of Loti's Japanese trilogy: the second, *Japoneries d'Automne* was published in 1889, the last, *La Troisième Jeunesse de Madame Prune*, not until 1905, after his return from Nagasaki. Both the latter were accounts of travel, but in a more remote mood: no more *mousmés* or the presence of Yves. *Japoneries d'Automne* reveals an aristocratic milieu, and there is an enthralling description of Court circles at Yeddo, on the occasion of the Chrysanthemum Viewing Ceremony, where the Empress Harou-Ko and her retinue of ladies were to be seen for the last time wearing their fabulous medieval Court costumes, as stylized as a pack of cards. On this splendid occasion a Japanese band was rendering Berlioz' *Symphonie Fantastique* from behind a clump of bamboos when the Empress and her suite appeared. They had nothing of the kimono'd coquetry of Madame Butterfly, who, to the West, was the prototype of all Japanese women, and until that moment, Loti's image too. He describes these hieratic figures advancing, rigid in stiff silks, with brilliant coloured scarlet trousers, each leg as wide as a huge skirt, their pagoda sleeves trailing, their tunics embroidered with heraldic blazons. Their lacquered hair was gummed stiff, and arranged to stand away from their faces like great black wings, with nothing of the chignons and pins of lesser women. The Empress carried a violet parasol, and as the frou-frou of her heavy silks came nearer Loti saw she was smiling, the remote fixed smile of an idol, her eyes two oblique black slits, narrower than the line of her eyebrows. She passed before him, so close that her shadow fell across him – and he longed to seize it, this Imperial shadow, to become a treasure among his many others. The combination of majesty and mystery was irresistible.

It was about this time that Loti began enlarging or reconstructing the old house far beyond his Arabic, Turkish and Japanese conceits. Blanche's money aided such developments, and it proved a splendid way to kill time. It would be impossible to describe here, or even indicate by blue-prints, the architectural intricacies that Loti contrived, year after year. Like a Chinese puzzle, rooms were conjured from others, were superimposed, reached by outside stairways, by plunging levels or hidden doors, or appeared to be suspended where no room had been before. The Japanese salon was to be followed later by a superb Chinese pagoda, while a salon, strictly Louis XVI, designed to satisfy Blanche's conventional tastes, opened into a monumental Gothic-cum-Renaissance hall which appeased Loti's seigneurial longings. There was also a peasant interior holding Breton souvenirs and furniture from the ISLAND, while all was to be crowned by a superb mosque, dearest of all Loti's fantasies.

His mosque! His own private mosque within his own walls! This audacious project only took shape by degrees. The original structure was Sunnite, and about to be demolished in Damascus. It was a rare chance, and he seized it, purchasing the whole mass of pillars and arches and prayer niches for a song. With the aid of Léo Thémèze and 'honest smugglers', it was shipped to France, where a band of Arab and French workmen reconstructed it, stone by stone. The problem of finding space, for it was large and lofty, was solved by acquiring two adjacent houses, and on their site, joined to what was formerly his sister's studio, this fabulous dream took shape.

Loti had too much veneration for his birthplace to impose any visible Islamic architecture there, and so the prim grey façade of the street remained unchanged. Only behind it rose this Moslem shrine, above or beside the polyglot rooms that he, the Magician, had conjured. They were around but apart from the settings of his childhood; the red parlour of those winter evenings round the fire, the narrow yellow dining room opening on to the courtyard, and the bedrooms of his mother and Aunt Claire were little changed, part of that past to which he clung, tangible expression of the roots which held him. But later fantasies, hidden warrens of exoticism, reflected his true nature, so extravagant, yet secret. In the words of the spellbound Sacha Guitry: 'Nothing tells the passer-by that this is the house a genius has made his own.'

Meanwhile, running counterpoint to planning the mosque, the best part of a year was spent preparing for the sumptuous fête he gave to inaugurate his medieval room, designed to evoke the epoch of Louis XI. This was contrived above the old family dining room and had, at first, to be reached from the courtyard by an outside staircase, for Loti had overlooked the necessity of one and, too late, thought of consulting an architect. There were dark panelling, leering gargoyles, unyielding carved chairs, a cavernous fireplace, much iron work, grilles and ogival windows – all authentic. The stone work came from a ruined Gothic church at Marennes, the splendid tapestries and blazons being sought far and wide. Such lugubrious settings were then much in vogue: Sarah Bernhardt imposed rather less authentic medievalism in the Avenue de Villiers, and cluttered it with plushy divans and outrageous draperies. Loti's passion for authenticity allowed no concessions to comfort. 'Blanche's medieval room,' he said airily, when questioned as to its purpose. Perhaps he saw her as one of those patient ladies of the missals, seated rigidly at her tapestry, awaiting, for years, some lord and master gone to the wars. It made the perfect setting for the medieval fête he had planned in meticulous detail.

This was the first of many other sumptuous entertainments he was to give during the next twenty years; *fête Arabe* (for his mother), *fête Chinoise*, and *fête Paysanne*, besides numbers of theatrical or operatic evenings. In Meyerbeer's *Les Huguenots*, an opera which the Viauds always regarded as peculiarly their own, Loti's light tenor was taken very seriously, like his dramatic powers. A photograph taken at this time reveals a rather sheepish figure in doublet and hose, dwarfed by an ample soprano. But all dressing up was an escape, and his weakness for masquerading persisted. 'It was always my favourite amusement. These transformations were my great resource against the monotony of life,' he admitted, thus justifying Edmond de Goncourt's unkind remarks about his life being one long carnival, dressed as a Breton in his Japanese room and as a Turk in his Breton room . . .

Preparations for the medieval fête excited Rochefort and the whole countryside, echoes of it reaching *le tout Paris*, who eagerly awaited their invitations. Guests were bidden to come in costume and bring their own silver goblet and knife, since such was the usage at the Court of Louis XI. Plates were replaced by flat rounds of specially baked bread, and a stuffed peacock and lampreys were part of the banquet, for which a chef had been coached to prepare a strictly authentic menu. Photographers, never long absent from Loti's life, were the sole anachronism, and recorded him receiving his guests in wig and ermine, as the King, while Blanche, overbalanced by a steeple headdress, was the Queen. Rushlights flickered, and were eclipsed by the photographers' lamps as they caught the famous faces gathered there to celebrate Loti's latest eccentricity. Everyone was expected to converse in medieval French – the language of Balzac's *Contes Drolatiques* – and were out of favour if they did not rise to the occasion. Madame Adam did not, and her stumbling speech seemed quite a gaffe. Tumblers and jesters (probably some of Loti's sailors) capered convincingly, and there was music, pipes, lute and rebeck, reviving ancient airs. Above, a narrow minstrels' gallery was crowded with a succession of strange figures peering down at the revellers below. Following the old kingly ways, Loti had admitted the rabble to his feast . . . at a distance. Thus, the lesser citizens of Rochefort were permitted to gape, provided they wore the correct costumes. These were hired or sewn up locally and distributed free. But since the *hoi polloi* were only visible above the waist, their costumes were sketchy – ragged jerkins and hoods sufficed, and were worn with the citizens' everyday trousers and boots at this almost perfect realization of *les joyeustés du roy Loys le onzième* of the *Contes Drolatiques*.

Sometimes there were urban distractions – a few days in Paris, which briefly took Loti's mind off the matrimonial trap into which he had walked. Visits to Sarah Bernhardt proved that neither time, distance nor marriage spoiled their rapport. 'February 23rd, 1888. Lunch with Sarah B. Many interruptions, Louise Abbéma, Comtesse de Béthune: at last we shut ourselves upstairs in her room. Downstairs, a mass of people are awaiting an audience, and I have all sorts of business appointments for the rest of the day. I miss them all. It has been night for a long while when I leave her, taking with me her smile, her look . . . How exquisite she is, when she takes the trouble to be *herself* with one.'

On March 18th 1889, the hopes of the whole family were fulfilled, and Blanche and Loti were united in the shared happiness of a son. He was a strong baby, and was given, like his predecessor, the name of Samuel, the seaman Samuel Greusiller being named his godfather, a choice which neither Blanche nor the Viauds dared contest. However, he seems to have been an invisible godparent, never seen at the house or known to his godson, and Loti's motives for choosing this particular sailor remain a matter for conjecture.

This was the son Loti had wanted, and had married to obtain. But paternity was not so strong an emotion as he had believed. There is a curiously revealing letter to Madame Adam written during the anxious hours of Blanche's labour. Loti appears to have been in a fever of anxiety – not over the imminent birth or Blanche's sufferings, but over the matter of Léo's future, and the *absolute necessity* of Madame Adam's intervention at the Ministère de la Marine to obtain for *le beau Léo* the right to sit for a Merchant Navy examination, which would enable him to become captain of a merchantman, something Loti had planned for him, and for which he had spent many hours coaching him through the intricacies of hydrography. But owing to some administrative error, Léo's time at sea navigating had not been correctly counted, and by two months he now missed the right to sit the examination. Loti was distracted and, as usual, turned to Madame Chérie for help. He had already petitioned the Préfet Maritime and governmental big-wigs without result. 'Only the Ministère de la Marine can decide the matter . . . Time presses . . . Will you give me this proof of your affection?' writes Loti. 'Will you, Madame, make a *real effort* . . . I know you will succeed . . .' Almost as an afterthought to this long detailed letter, he adds: 'While I am writing this to you in the middle of the night, my child is about to be born. Tomorrow morning he will surely be here, arriving among all the agitations of my departure' (for Morocco). But back to Léo. 'Won't you send me a telegram, to catch me before I leave, telling me what you can do at the Ministère?' Later: 'My little boy was born at three o'clock this morning, a strong baby with a loud voice . . . Now I can leave, my mind at ease . . .' But no: he is back on the same tack, over the question of Léo's future. 'The matter is urgent, the examinations will be next month . . . Please do *all* you can.' He signs himself, 'Your son, Loti'. In the nature of a postscript, there are a few pleased words about his own newly-born son. 'I can't believe he is real and belongs to me.'

The devoted, long-suffering, and influential Madame Adam did indeed pull the right strings for Léo's future, and within days of the baby's birth, Loti left France, reassured, to accompany the French Minister on an official journey through Morocco to Fez, where the Minister was to present his credentials to the Sultan.

Since Loti's reputation as a man of letters was now international and undisputed, it was he who was chosen to represent the French Navy, together with four high-ranking army officers, part of the

Minister's suite intended to impress the Sultan. The press made much of this mission, for French interests in Morocco were important. That sombre and lovely land was still unspoiled, little known and very dangerous, for religious fanaticism, brigand bands and tribal warfare flourished. Nothing could have been more to Loti's taste. Once more, in the words of Sacha Guitry: '*The man was married, the officer less so, Loti not at all.*'

Joyously the traveller headed once more for those Arab lands which held his heart. Morocco – *Maghreb!* – which signifies the West, the hour of sunset and the evening prayer, and also, Morocco itself, most westerly point of all Islam; 'the point of the earth where that great faith given to the Arabs by Mohammed subsides, coming at last to rest beside that ocean where Africa herself ends'.

At Perpignan on the eve of embarking, the journal records Loti's eternal craving for youth and beauty: it is a passionate wish to please, to appear pleasing, rather than mere vanity. '20th March 1889. I have stopped the rouge I used to wear; in a spirit of obstinate contradiction, it aged me, made me appear haggard. My colourless face is more distinguished, younger, and my eyes are finer in this pallor. Over there, I shall enlarge them a little, in the Arab fashion (with a dark surrounding line of kohl) that will be my desert coquetry.'

Loti's impressions of this journey were later distilled into one of his best travel books, *Au Maroc*. There is a freshness, a sense of wonder at all around him, which probably derives from his unexpected escape from domesticity. That sense of wonder was to dim progressively. *Au Maroc* lies between his first, violently felt books of love and travel, interwoven with personal involvement, and the later chronicles where no emotions are involved, nor so much real sense of wonder; only the painter's eye still records in his own manner. (As he came to say bitterly, 'all my readers want from me is the reflection of things over which my eyes have ranged.') If, as Loti suggests in his preface to the Moroccan book, he might be accused of undue partiality, 'it is because I know not by what remote atavistic phenomena I have always felt my soul to be half Arab.'

Loti's chronicle of this time of honey is not so much a rhapsody, all colour and picturesque customs, as a sober account of a journey where harsh travel conditions were matched by dark skies and dangers, the party usually lashed by rain, in sodden clothes, and with uneasy nights spent in bandit country. He does not minimize the discomforts: it was all part of the adventure.

Au Maroc records one spectacular occasion where Loti's pen matches Delacroix's brush as he describes the Sultan's reception of the French Ambassador. There are the high crenellated walls of Fez, the vast Court of the Ambassadors, the superb Caïds, the gaudily uniformed soldiers and Negro musicians. Yet over all, an air of sinister desolation; the frowning walls shadowed the huge court where, in muddy puddles, innumerable frogs croaked. This court was so vast that the massed figures seemed lost Lilliputians. At one end the gold-laced and bemedalled French mission waited expectantly beside a giant mulatto, a magnificent bull-necked figure, hugely turbaned, whose sole function was to present foreign emissaries to His Majesty the Sultan.

Presently, the great doors to yet another inner courtyard opened and a gilded coach pulled by six splendid white horses appeared – 'something quite unexpected in such a context'. (It was the only carriage in all Fez and had been presented to the Sultan by Queen Victoria, the party learned later.) 'It might be supposed the Sultan rode in this coach: but it was empty, and merely a forerunner, or presage of his glory.' After another long, palpitating pause, the musicians brayed on their trumpets and clattered their cymbals and tambourines. 'The black slaves scattered, and a shiver of religious terror seemed to pass across the lines of soldiers.' Then, in the shadowy depths of the archway, Loti saw a superb white horse advancing. Four black slaves held it in check, for the rider was a mummified figure swathed in white muslin. 'Above his head, more slaves held a scarlet parasol, of an ancient, pointed form, such as the Queen of Sheba would have recognized.' (And we too can recognize it from Delacroix's paintings of such scenes.) 'Two gigantic Negroes, one in a rose-coloured robe, the other in blue, waved fly-switches around the Sultan's head ... As he drew near, the music, as if exasperated, groaned louder and louder, sounding notes that were more and more strident, seemingly a religious chant, slow and melancholy, accompanied by the counterpoint of fierce drum-beats. The white mummy's horse pranced and plunged with rage, and was scarcely held in check by the black grooms, until, finally brought to a halt before us, we saw this last authentic descendant of the Prophet – bastardized by Nubian blood, yet the great Sultan himself – the very personification of ancient Islam.'

13

No matter what, I am always a déclassé, playing a part.

Pierre Loti

Although Loti continued to dislike Paris life, cloying domesticity and the monotony of his shore posting at the Préfecture Maritime drove him there more and more often, seeking livelier company. He still hid out under the pseudonym of Monsieur Denis at the Hôtel Bon la Fontaine, and chose an even more modest establishment for his meals, one of the Bouillons Duval, a chain of simple restaurants then spread about the city (first taking care to remove his decorations, if in uniform, thus appearing less noticeable among the rest of the clientèle). But he was also frequently to be seen, now glittering with decorations, in those elegant, super-sophisticated circles where every calculated dissipation or variation of *mœurs* was encouraged. This decadent society also enjoyed a thriving intellectual life, celebrated *poules de luxe* following every new expression of the arts. Loti was always fêted in the capital, yet he remained lost there, as lost as when he was an unknown débutant of letters. And now there was no more of Oirda's loving guidance so that he often fell among a mischievous, if not malicious set of second-rate persons who exploited him. There were few Parisians he could count as true friends, but Alphonse Daudet was such, thus it was chiefly by his promptings that Loti became candidate for election to l'Académie Française.

For more than three centuries, l'Académie has enjoyed an almost mythical prestige, election to its ranks being considered the apotheosis of glory. Under the noble cupola of the former Palais Mazarin on the Quai de Conti, once the great Cardinal's dwelling, the Immortals or Members meet in solemn conclave to elect a new member who will fill the chair left vacant by a death in their ranks.

There are forty of these *Fauteuils*, and no-one has yet been considered lofty enough for that number to be exceeded, and tradition broken. Admission to this élite is not limited to men of letters, though they form the majority: there are also scientists, statesmen, historians, though few poets, a sprinkling of grands seigneurs and men of the Church. There are certain responsibilities attached to the honours. Members meet to vote, and discuss various literary questions, award prizes, and above all work on the Dictionary. To define or co-ordinate the French language was the initial purpose of the Académie when it was founded in 1634. Letter by letter, word by word, through the centuries, successive Academicians have laboured to define, modify or clarify the language, also to include new definitions, for words have come to change their meaning according to their usage (and their resistance to, or absorption by, the influx of Anglo-Saxon speech). Thus the Académie is at once a bastion of classic tradition and an innovator of language as it is correctly spoken today.

On being elected each new Immortal must deliver an inaugural address at a ceremony widely attended and splendidly formal, members filing to their places through lines of the Garde Républicaine, and to the solemn roll of drums (the same as formerly performed for the execution of criminals). In France men of letters command respect, and by the intricate shadings of protocol and precedence Academicians were placed at table before Papal Nuncios and other high ranks: thus a great deal of jockeying and intrigues both political and social have always surrounded the process of election, the candidates themselves making numbers of 'Visits' which resemble canvassing calls. The final choice should be approved by the President himself; this tradition dates from the Académie's beginnings when the Monarch's approval or veto sealed the candidate's fate. Yet, while some of the most distinguished figures of French literature have been elected, there have been dismal omissions, and manoeuvres sometimes place quite second-rate persons among the élite.

When Daudet, doting Daudet, urged Loti to pose his candidature, he was intrigued. He, the most unacademic of writers, the most unconventional of beings, an Academician? Why not? It would gratify his two mothers, Madame Viaud and Madame Chérie, the Juliette Adam of his first success, besides being a distraction from the awful ennui beside Blanche. The father rôle was proving a disappointment too, and the infant prattle and nursery capers of his little son, so ardently desired, merely grated on his nerves. Watching him toddling about among his Ferrière cousins. Loti was heard to remark bitterly that the child seemed all Ferrière – there was nothing *Viaud* about the fair-haired, placid child. How could that have happened? The first, lost baby had been his own self in miniature, and some vague resentment lingered, creating a barrier between the critical father and the devoted son that Samuel would prove to be.

Loti's candidature aroused mixed reactions. Anatole France, who dubbed him *le sublime illettré*, supported him enthusiastically; Renan, who fondly admired him, shrugged when asked his opinion on Loti's chances. 'He's a child,' he said, and indeed, those childlike naïvetés which endeared Loti to his friends were not generally appreciated by the sophisticated Parisians who influenced the voting. But Renan agreed to be his sponsor. *'I will be your godfather at this academic baptism with the greatest joy, and it will be a fine day for the Compagnie,'* he wrote warmly.

In general, however, he had the support of many literary figures, and all-powerful hostesses such as Mme Carnot, the President's wife, or Mme Armand de Cavaillet (Anatole France's Egeria); her salon made or broke reputations. These French literary salons were palmy groves where the butterfly women whom Boldini or Helleu portrayed fluttered about, but were in fact so many wasp-waisted birds of prey, fastening on the hero of the hour. Laced and scented, with puffed-up coiffures topped by vastly plumed hats, their pouter-pigeon bosoms were offered seductively to the distinguished men who gathered there. Such extravagant figures as Boni de Castellane, Proust, D'Annunzio or the young Reynaldo Hahn were to be found at these gatherings, along with more robust personages; Clemenceau, ecclesiastical celebrities, or the Grand Duke Vladimir, who, between *les tournées des Grands Ducs*, sometimes lent Romanov majesty to the scene.

Yet even in that exquisite atmosphere of mutual admiration there were undercurrents of vinegar. Loti was far too successful, too unorthodox, and aroused rivalry among both men and women. 'The wives had eyes only for Loti,' noted a guest at some gathering graced by the President and other big-wigs. His reputation as a great lover, and the questing pathos of those extraordinary dark eyes subjugated them. 'He had a special way of kissing one's hand, as if he wished to draw out one's very soul' was how one of the ladies recalled his spell. In all ways 'the Magician' was a mysterious rarity, and implications

205

of homosexuality were of small account in elegant Paris at that moment, where it had become fashionable. Unlike the England that prosecuted Oscar Wilde there was no criminal condemnation in France, and persons of that inclination frequently left England for the more indulgent climate across the Channel, as did Wilde, on his release from Reading Gaol.

Loti had always been an exhibitionist, indulging himself by wearing the exotic costumes he had collected on his travels, or concocted for the fancy-dress parties to which he was addicted. The publicity which buzzed round his Academic candidature gave him every occasion to pose before both press and public. When newspapers requested a photograph, he teased them by sending one of himself in a fez or burnous, as a Persian archer, or even naked, superbly muscled. '*En Algérien de Mardi Gras*,' Goncourt noted, having no sympathy with dressing up, or the Arab interiors Loti often chose as backgrounds for his portrait.

During the period of uncertainty – to be or not to be an Academician – Loti obtained two months' leave and left for Romania, where once again he was the guest of the Queen in her turreted palace. It is unlikely he would have returned to that small Court of intrigue and affectation had he not received word, if not a direct summons, from the Sultan Abdul Hamid or his ministers inviting him to Constantinople. For what precise reason is not known. Loti's discretion can be extreme (except over his own emotions): though where anything touches Moslem sensibilities or taboos he is mute. His youthful escapades were by now well known and overlooked by the Sultan, being outweighed by the world-famous author's proclaimed affection for all things Turkish. The business of public relations was then unknown, but Loti's value to the Sublime Porte was exactly that, and it is probable that it was the Sultan himself who proposed that Loti should write some personal description of Stamboul, some sort of eulogy, which would express his feelings for the city, and which, coming from his pen, would be read far and wide. It was from this visit that the beautiful pages entitled *Constantinople 1900* derive. They are to be found in Loti's book *L'Exilée*, and are among his finest.

Loti had no sooner arrived at his hotel than he was drawn into the golden web of palace life. At Yildiz, surrounded by a vast park and forbidding walls, the Sultan, Allah's Shadow on Earth, skulked, fearful of assassination but ruling with an iron hand, 'seen nowhere, yet knowing everything'. At Yildiz Loti spent several privileged hours closeted with Allah's Shadow on Earth.

What an odd pair they must have appeared, the Grand Turk, with his scimitar-nose and livid rouged cheeks, and his guest, the would-be Turk, also lightly rouged. The Sultan was the thirty-fourth Ottoman ruler – that race of princes born by custom of slave-women of non-Turkish birth, in the *kefess*, or Cage, and brought up by eunuchs who guarded the harem. Some emerged only to continue their indolent life: but Abdul Hamid was otherwise. From the beginning he had shown fierce ambition for his country and an astute grasp of world affairs. With this key figure in Middle Eastern politics Loti was as one, the two men united in their suspicions of Western perfidy, and their opposition to any modernisation, as interpreted by the Young Turk movement. Yet when asked to write something expressing his feelings for Constantinople Loti hesitated . . . Would he not seem too partial? But to refuse would be a sort of betrayal. Reluctantly, he agreed, though 'I would be incapable of writing an impersonal description, with the detachment of the artist . . . Those who follow me must resign themselves: it will be through *my soul* that they will see the Great Stamboul . . .'

It was probably at this point, now secure in Palace protection, that Loti dared to set about his long-held plan, not only to repair and gild Aziyadé's neglected stele but to obtain the tombstone, to be beside him for evermore, centrepiece of his mosque, and focus of all his prayers and longings. Turkish views on the defiling presence of an Infidel anywhere near their graves, especially that of a woman, would have made such a singular enterprise impossible on any earlier visits. But now? He makes no mention of this undertaking, certainly known to the authorities, but this visit remains a likely moment for it to have occurred. Loti always enjoyed playing hide and seek with his readers – with his friends – with himself too. In later books he speaks of having a *replica* of the cherished tombstone made, in another, of the *original* being beside him at Rochefort, the replica being substituted for the original in the cemetery of Top Kapou in 1905. Either came to assume symbolic status, representing all love and loss. There are no clues left in the journals – discretion again, or were they removed later for the sake of further mystification? Thus the substitution or duplication remains an enigma, tantalizing to anyone studying Loti's intricate character. Even his family remained uncertain of the truth, though it seems probable that it was the original he removed to Rochefort. Less than three years after his audiences at Yildiz, the stele was seen *in situ* at Rochefort by Antoine, who, as the leading theatrical producer of the day, was appreciative of the *coup de théâtre* this lugubrious object produced.

1890 had ended in misery for the whole household at Rue Saint-Pierre, for Aunt Claire died, fading away slowly on the last night of the year. For Loti, keeping watch through that icy night, it was a grief beyond measure. She had been his nearest and dearest after his mother, and now *'les chères vieilles'* were no longer a loving plural. Recalling all the selfless devotion she had shown him throughout his childhood, he found himself weeping, broom in hand, laboriously sweeping out her room, hoping by such a task to express something of his humility and love. For the rest of his life he kept this room and her few possessions as she had known them, with fresh flowers on her table, so that should her spirit return it would find a welcome. In his poignant book *Le Livre de la Pitié et de la Mort*, which is all sadness, all suffering for man and beast, there is a chapter entitled *Tante Claire nous quitte*. It makes agonizing reading for those who have known loss and despairing regrets. He dedicated this book to his mother, Aunt Claire's lifelong companion, whose faith had always sustained her, but which he could not share.

> *A ma mère bien aimée*
> *Je dédie ce livre*
> *Sans crainte, parce que la foi chrétienne lui*
> *permet de lire avec sérénité les plus sombres choses.*

(I dedicate this book to my beloved mother
without fear, for the Christian faith allows
her to read of the darkest things with serenity.)

In January 1891, Loti was appointed to the *Formidable*, a cruiser on manoeuvres in the Mediterranean. This was something he needed to make up the requisite amount of service at sea to obtain promotion. It was a relief to be able to escape from the tearing grief that hung over the old home, for Aunt Claire's gentle presence lingered everywhere. Aboard ship, in Mediterranean sunlight, among some of his old shipmates, his loss became less agonizing, and he was once again living the life he had chosen but had so often set aside for the sake of the old ladies.

The *Formidable* was stationed at Algiers in May 1891 when the result of Loti's candidature to l'Académie Française was to be announced, and as the appointed day wore on, and no news came through, he showed signs of strain. He was on watch when at last telegrams came flooding in, and he knew he was elected. The whole ship fêted him. In the wardroom there was champagne, toasts, a speech by the Captain . . . Loti spent the next three days and nights celebrating in his own, secret way, vanishing into the warrens of the Kasbah, which always lured him back, and where he never felt an outsider, as he did so often in the cities of the West.

His inauguration was to take place the following year, on April 7, 1892, the intervening months being calculated to give time for the candidate's inaugural address to be prepared, the traditional green, gold-laced uniform to be fitted, and his ceremonial sword handle to be worked with the design he had selected.

Among the letters of congratulation Loti received was one from Carmen Sylva, Queen of Romania. They had been in the habit of exchanging letters of an exalted nature, dwelling on their problems of loss, faith and authorship too. Now Loti learned that the Queen had been banished from Bucharest by her husband, King Carol I. Her romantic meddling in affairs of State was becoming dangerous, for she was fostering the union of one of her young ladies-in-waiting with the Crown Prince Ferdinand, and behaving very indiscreetly. Thus she was packed off to Venice in disgrace, and installed at the Hotel Danieli, accompanied by a small household. There she fretted, under strict surveillance, cut off from the outside world. All Loti's chivalry and compassion were roused by her pathetic situation, and he decided to visit her, however unwise this might appear to the King's advisers. In August, they shared a few days of melancholy reunion, gliding along stagnant canals, passing under bridges, each one a Bridge of Sighs, so sombre was the mood he and the Queen shared, as the Queen read aloud the book she was then writing, *Le Livre d'Ame*. But almost at once Loti was requested to leave the Queen to her loneliness, ill-health, and the poetry in which she poured out her unhappiness. They were never to meet again and letters were barred, for the Romanian Court considered Loti's championship of Carmen Sylva a cause of embarrassment. Loti was to commemorate those brief Venetian meetings, the Queen's perfervid romanticism and the spiritual exaltation of *Le Livre d'Ame*, in his book *L'Exilée* (the Queen herself), which recounted their last meeting.

Six months before Loti's official entry among the Immortals, he was appointed to command the *Javelot*, a gun-boat stationed at Hendaye, from where he arbitrated on maritime disputes, controlled such fishing fleets and Atlantic shipping as put in to the wide estuary, and where, too, smugglers were active. It was not an arduous post, and held diplomatic status, the *Javelot* being in the nature of a floating consulate, with many Spanish contacts. It also left plenty of time to write and to enter into the life of the country, as he now did with special passion. It was as if he sensed, from the first, what this land and these people would come to mean to him for the rest of his life. It was with a marked lack of enthusiasm that he tore himself away from his new-found life which straddled land and sea, and headed for Paris, to face the inauguration ceremony under the cupola of glory.

As the auspicious day approached, some of Loti's well-wishers became apprehensive that his usual eccentricities might cause offence. Madame Adam urged circumspection, imploring him to avoid those pranks which irritated or laid him open to ridicule. 'To be an Academician calls for a certain discretion. This is something your admirers expect from you.' Unfortunately Loti did not consult her over his inaugural address, preferring the advice of a rackety personage, Comtesse Diane de Beausacq, who leaked the speech to the press, so that the most malicious reports circulated. However, he heeded Madame Adam up to a point, eschewing rowdy escapades with his sailor friends, inappropriate clothes or make-up.

A day or two before the ceremony, Goncourt (who admired Loti as a writer, but thought he lost caste by becoming an Academician), noted: 'Most extraordinary! Loti is not made-up . . . looks quite pale, and devil take me if he hasn't stopped wearing, inside his shoes, those mechanical devices that lift him several inches while making him walk on tip-toe.' Poor Loti! All such childish subterfuges had long ago been discovered and mocked. But he persisted in his hopeless quest for height and romantic youthful looks – he, who had achieved towering stature as a writer, and was, through his books, the symbol of all youthful romanticism.

Naturally the entire Viaud family was in Paris for Julien's reception among the Immortals, and Loti now took some pains to be seen in the most select circles, accompanied by his wife, and on one occasion was heard to suggest she take his arm, so that they should appear as a devoted couple. He was also at pains to stage-manage the ceremony to his advantage: after all, he was the star performer. He thought the green and gold-laced uniform unbecoming; it was probably the only fanciful outfit he never enjoyed wearing. However, the sword, which was such a trial to most civilian Immortals, was in no danger of tripping him up, and must have seemed a friendly presence, reminder of his service life. He was determined to achieve a suitably dramatic setting by changing the customary green draperies behind the rostrum for scarlet – a better foil, he thought. Nevertheless his journal for May 7th is dank. 'The day of my reception, but I cannot take it seriously. I accept it like some obligation . . . it hardly touches me.' Although he had wished to be elected, for it appealed to that persistent snobbish streak where public honours or crowned heads were concerned, he described the whole Academy and its rituals as a macabre puppet-show, worth nothing beside youth, freedom, and the sun, those three things which remained for him the sum total of mortal bliss.

The press, which had whipped up a palpitating climate for or against his candidature, was present in full force, noting the assembly of distinguished spectators. Madame Carnot, the wife of the French President, Lord Dufferin, the British Ambassador, and large numbers of socialites had gathered to hear Loti, so that *Figaro* described it as a victory for the salons. Loti was introduced by Renan and Sully-Prudhomme, and as his friends feared, launched into an address that was unconventional, if not downright provocative. He began by stating his confrères would seldom see him among them, as he disliked life in Paris. After a banal appreciation of Octave Feuillet his predecessor ('I never read' being one of his stock phrases when questioned as to his tastes in contemporary literature) he had, nevertheless, some scathing things to say on the sordid themes chosen by the realist or naturalist writers then in vogue, and headed by Zola. Loti denounced the lives they uncovered as so many manure heaps. Zola, who was present, and once more a defeated candidate, was observed to smile sardonically. It was oddly insensitive of Loti to hit a fellow writer, an unsuccessful rival, though he had not known Zola was among the audience. When, that night, he was told, he at once wrote, expressing his regrets, and saying he would have removed the offending passage had he known of Zola's presence. He had seized the occasion, he explained, believing it his right to state publicly that his own view of life, of humanity, was not that of the great naturalist.

Loti has been described as a romantic upon whom a realist was grafted, and much of his writing, war reports, or descriptions of poverty, loneliness, cruelty to animals, old age and death are as strong as anything by Zola; but their realism has a less cumulative effect for they are interspersed with passages of luminous beauty, colour, and descriptions of nature, as well as being, it must be said, sometimes of a reeking sentimentality unknown to Zola. Loti's letter was accepted by Zola in good faith: 'Your letter touched me profoundly,' he wrote. 'My only regret is that one of us' (men of letters) 'should be so unaware of the grandiose movement of contemporary literature . . . I have the strongest sympathy for your talent, so great, and so personal . . .' Not everyone was so large in spirit, and Loti was angry with himself for the blunder.

Although he was the youngest Immortal, something that should have comforted him in his perpetual cult for youth, he was forty-two, but he confided in his journal that no-one would take him for more than twenty-eight, as he had kept himself in such good trim. Perhaps that consoled him, for glory seemed a dusty answer. Throughout the week of his Academic triumph, Paris fêted him. 'I am like a god, or a strange animal, everyone wishes to see, or touch!' At the lavish soirée given for him by Madame Adam three hundred guests were crowded out and stood on the pavement below. 'My photographs are everywhere, even in the newspaper kiosks, and now there is a crescendo of comic attacks by the press, on account of my speech.' Maurice Barrès, writing in *Figaro*, accused the new Immortal of sensuality and a lack of culture, who had only scraped in because de Maupassant and Bourget had declined to stand. But such attacks did not trouble Loti: if he was unsure of himself, as a man, he was sure of his writing, and these vituperations only served to send up his sales. But his glory among the Immortals could not raise his spirits.

He still believed he had become one of the middle-aged puppets . . .
O! to where had Arik Ussim Effendi vanished?

Loti did not linger to bask in the limelight. By now, he had fallen
completely under the spell of the Basque country, a region as remote,
as apart from the rest of France, as that Brittany he had loved in
earlier days.

Like Brittany, the Basque country – Eskual Eerria to its inhabitants – was a land apart, holding to its own customs and strange
language – Euskaro, something which baffled even the most learned
philologists with its Xs, double Rs, and Zs in profusion; where the
musician's flute and tambourine are *xürüla* and *ttunttun*, and names
such as Oxocelhaya, Urruty or Ybarnegaray are typical. The
Basque race was fiery, hardy, proud and pious, a people of the land
rather than the sea, unlike the Bretons, though the same Atlantic
tore at their cliffs, and ebbed and flowed into their rivers from the
Gulf of Gascony.

The roots which Loti put down at Hendaye, though not as profound as those of Rochefort, were without the sad, clinging memories
which assailed him at every turn in his home town. It was a more
vigorous, uncomplicated life at Hendaye, and though Blanche and
the child Samuel, and his old mother too, spent much time at the
house he had leased there, he was not enmeshed as in the tangled
Viaud atmosphere of Rochefort, where all the ramifications of relatives and hangers-on confused his days, and drew heavily on him
financially. At Hendaye there were fewer lacerating souvenirs, no
Turqueries (though he always wore Aziyadé's ring), no brooding
over Aunt Claire's death. His mother alone remained to represent
those figures of the past, the black-dressed old darlings who had
always been there to fuss over him. If Hendaye was not – yet – a
shrine to the past, it became at once a root, so that Loti swung
between the old and the new, coming and going, a restless pattern,
following the rhythm of his contradictory nature. He could not love
without roots, but while he sought to escape them, he was for ever
putting down more: in cabins he had only occupied briefly, or a room
at an inn where he had experienced some tearing passion . . .
wherever he believed he had left a part of himself became a root to
haunt him, pull him back, when he had left it.

The house which he leased, and was later to buy, was known as

213

Bakhar Etchea – the Solitary House: the House of the Solitary would have been better suited to Loti's secret self. It was unpretentious, white-walled, with beams and shutters painted a dark reddish brown in the local manner. The small garden was a tangle of tall palms, magnolia trees, bamboo thickets and gigantic hydrangeas, for the soft damp air bred a tropical profusion which Loti encouraged. The special charm of the house was, and still is, three rounded terraces which jut out over the wide estuary of the Bidassoa, facing the ancient town of Fontarabie on the far Spanish shore. From there the bells of its churches and convents, like the fife and drum of its fiestas, still sound across the sheen of water. Standing on one of the rounded terraces high above the water, one has the illusion of being on the deck of a ship, an impression strengthened by the sound of the tides below, sometimes lapping, sometimes lashing, but ever with the sea's eternal pulse. Perhaps it was the sea before all else which called him back there. The sea, and this illusion of being on the bridge of a ship. Once again, as it had claimed the child, so it held the man.

Then there were the Basque people, the race that became, after the Turks, the people of his predilection. They too had a sombre strength, and that unquestioning faith for which he ached. Although the Basques have been defined by Voltaire as *un petit peuple qui danse au sommet des Pyrénées*, they were, in fact, far from carefree; their lives were stern, frugal, and they prayed more often than they danced the fandango. In their darkly wooded hill countryside crops were poor, but flocks of sheep – *txotx*, in the Basque tongue – throve. Shepherd families alternated with those of the smugglers, for smuggling was regarded as an honourable necessity, its risks seen in the nature of a national sport. To Loti there was something irresistibly picaresque in those stealthy midnight sorties, which he sometimes joined, as sure-footed as the rest, carrying the heavy sacks of contraband by precipitous paths where one false step of man or mule could let loose an avalanche of stones and alert the frontier guards who would fire without more ado. Loti, romanticizing as usual, saw such conflicts as though so many Robin Hoods and Merry Men were defying Authority for the benefit of the needy. That he, the symbol of Authority in the region, could join his smuggling friends in their nefarious ways typifies the special standard of conduct Loti reserved for himself. True, he joined those expeditions in a spirit of camaraderie and never for gain, but what did the Customs men think, both sides of the frontier? In so small an area, 'le Commandant's' little game was well known. It could have been denounced with unfortunate international repercussions – yet it never was.

Basque smuggling was a highly structured system, *la grande contrebande*, and *la petite contrebande*. Brandy, silks, tobacco and copper, in the form of small French coinage, were the most usual goods transported by this essentially God-fearing race, who never failed to kneel in prayer before the primitive stone crosses and shrines which were strewn about the mountain paths they used. Did they ask for forgiveness? Rather, a blessing on their enterprise. There was time to confess, on Sundays. Their ancient churches are richly gilded, in the exuberant Spanish baroque manner, and often strike a note of violence, by their painted, blood-red walls. They are generally constructed with two or three wooden-railed balconies running round the nave where the men assemble; women are below, in the body of the church: many are darkly veiled figures, whose old family houses still bear a white cross above the lintel. Loti respected all religions and through his many friends of the Roman Catholic faith had come to lose much of his early, Protestant prejudice so that in this devout countryside, he was to give lavishly for the churches, endowing their charities, aiding the priests, and providing new bells for one impoverished village. Such practical help was only one example of the many ways in which he came to be integrated among the Basques. Pelota, their national game, was another.

In this furious sport a hard leather ball is hurled against a high wall, or *fronton*, by six players wielding a curious, curved wicker basket, the *chistera*, which is strapped, claw-like, to their wrist. Loti was soon accepted at the *fronton*, playing with an agility which belied his forty years. Off duty, he adopted the heavy cloak and beret worn by the people, and carried the *maklia*, a lead-weighted stick with a steel tip, a formidable weapon much used for both defence and attack. There was an undercurrent of primordial violence here, to which that savage lurking below Loti's dandified exterior reponded. Anything of primitive force attracted him: a tempest at sea, 'the blind fury of all, as if before man's creation', Baal, the great sun god, life giver and destroyer, whom the ancients worshipped with 'terrible, mysterious rites', and which he too adored, the spell of la Limoise, Druidic and remote, or the seaman Pierre le Cor, 'savage and superb' . . . all drew him. And now, the Basque land and its people, where something untamed remained. Today, this has exploded into the struggle for Basque independence, a movement Loti would certainly have supported.

On his return to Bakhar Etchea, after his triumph under the Coupole, he recorded standing on his terrace facing Spain, that extreme point where France ends. 'There, for the first time, the real soil of this Basque land appeared to me . . . there I became aware of what this country had kept within itself – something mysterious, which impregnates everything – the primitive Basque force' – the genius loci, its echo sounding in the *irrintzina*, that wild cry by which the Basques greeted a victory at the *fronton*, the birth of a son, or shepherd called to shepherd across the mountains. Its echoes no longer reached those nearby, international watering-places such as Biarritz, which, barely forty years earlier, had been discovered and made chic, in terms of an Offenbach operetta, by the Empress Eugénie and her frothy Court.

Loti's friends in the Basque country were many and varied. Among the most remarkable were the d'Abbadies, who lived in a turreted château designed for them by Viollet-le-Duc down to the last machicolation or portcullis. Antoine d'Abbadie was a savant, astronomer and explorer, who had spent much time and money trying to preserve the Basque language, which was already threatened with extinction. (*No spitting or speaking Eskaro* was a notice in the local schools.) Madame d'Abbadie was a no less striking personality; loving and defending all animals, she was surrounded by them, and as she trailed about the park, in rather ragged but immaculate white draperies often cut from ecclesiastical robes, a balding eagle she had tamed would clamber on and off her shoulders affectionately, while terrorizing her visitors.

An iron-beaked macaw snatched at the plates during meals, and in the library rats darted about unchecked, wreaking havoc among rare books. Madame d'Abbadie had been a fervent admirer of Loti's writings long before he became a neighbour; it was she who opened many vistas, many doors for him in the Basque country, and it was to her that he was to dedicate *Ramuntcho*, his novel of Basque life which was published in 1897.

For all his sympathy with the people and the region, this rather sickly story, founded on fact, verges on the romantic novelette. Loti wrote much of it in the village of Ascain, where he had many friends among the pelota players. It tells, very simply, the history of the

216

young smuggler Ramuntcho and Gracieuse, his faithful love, who refuses to give him up to marry another and is forced into a convent by her harsh mother. When at last Ramuntcho returns from soldiering afar and plans to abduct her, it is too late. She holds to her vows. *O crux ave spes unica!* These beautiful words are inscribed all over the Basque countryside, and were to haunt Loti, the despairing agnostic.

Beside Loti's immediate attraction to all things, all people Basque, notably such stalwart creatures as the smuggler Otharré, or yet another virile figure, the sailor Joseph Brahy, there was the perennial fascination of crowned heads often to be encountered at Biarritz. Close at hand the ex-Queen Natalie of Serbia lived in exile at the château Sashino, which she built on a crag overlooking the Atlantic, not far from Saint-Jean-de-Luz. There she had withdrawn in proud solitude. Her husband King Milan Obrénovitch had divorced her, taken away her son, and later was to abdicate. Later still, she was to suffer the assassination of their son, the young King Alexander. He had insisted on marrying her lady-in-waiting, a mature commoner, Draga Machin, whose fate was to be hacked to pieces beside him, their bodies flung from a window of the palace in Belgrade. When Loti first knew the ex-Queen that drama lay far ahead, and she was not yet surrounded by an aura of martyrdom, but an air of romantic melancholy and her dark beauty, as much as her rank and her loneliness captivated Loti and they were often together. A room was always kept ready for her at Rochefort, and was known as 'The Queen's Room': it gratified Loti's weakness for crowned heads. Sometimes he visited her at Sashino, and sometimes she came to Bakhar Etchea; then Loti was at pains to achieve a perfect setting for majesty with bowers of flowers and a delicate menu. The small dining room had inlaid mother-of-pearl furniture of Moorish origin, and sometimes he arranged the flowers in a manner copied from the Arabs: a whole row of identical vases, with identical bouquets would be placed side by side, giving the delightful but unexpected impression of some indoor flowerbed. 'Don't you think the absurd has a certain charm?' he would say, wistfully, when his décor was criticized.

It was ex-Queen Natalie who first introduced Loti to the celebrated clairvoyante Madame Fraya, who was to foretell the place of his death. Loti was much impressed by Madame Fraya. He was always superstitious and fascinated by dark enchantments, presages and dreams – above all, by the inexhaustible fount of his own dreams. He wore almost as many charms as jewellery, his pockets being stuffed with the amulets of many nations. When, much later in life he visited India, seeking the solace of eastern wisdoms, he came into possession of an ancient necklace reputed to have occult powers. It was known as the Necklace of the Goddess of All Favours. But even the Goddess of All Favours could not grant Loti the one thing he craved above all else – perpetual youth.

At the Solitary House Loti had installed himself in a top-floor room overlooking the Bidassoa, which, as a precaution against interruption, was reached by a rope-ladder, up and down which he swarmed with sailor's agility. There was, of course, the staircase, but this was not shown to unwelcome visitors who, wishing to visit the famous writer in his lair, were faced with the dangling ladder, and whose frantic efforts to ascend were much enjoyed by Loti. It was here, thus isolated, that he wrote *Matelot*, which was published in 1893, and dedicated to Queen Marie-Christine of Spain. It is a mixture of fiction, autobiography and biography, which blends the pathetic tale of the young sailor Jean Berny with something of Loti's own early experiences at sea, and much of the character and family background of his adored friend the desperately handsome Léo Thémèze. Through Loti's influence he later became master of a merchantman, and flourished, unlike the poor Berny who ends his wasted youth at sea, dying on his way home. Accounts of Gustave's death must have inspired Loti, for his descriptions of the young sailor's last hours, carried up on deck, from the stifling sick bay below, are among his finest pages. There is a poignant simplicity in his account of the dying boy among his comrades, seeing once more their faces, hearing their songs, watching the great sails overhead, and the sea all around . . . all life – that life he must soon leave for ever.

Of all those who represented Basque life to Loti, it was Doctor Etienne Durutty and his wife, Berthe, who came to play the most significant rôle. The doctor, who practised at Hendaye, was widely known as an opthalmic surgeon. He shared Loti's infantile love of practical jokes, and together they enjoyed many passing adventures. Berthe Durutty was the most charming of women, though not strictly pretty, and was to become Loti's last true love. She was considerably younger than he, and adored him with selfless devotion, though she must have been one of the few women who refused his wooing, for she was never his mistress, though local opinion thought her so. 'Don't you want a child by me?' he would demand, insistently, and she, childless by her husband and overcome by religious scruples, would turn away in tears. Many years after Loti's death, she continued to talk of him at length whenever she was with his son and daughter-in-law, precious links, to whom she confided that it was fear of her rigid Spanish mother, rather than her husband, which had caused her to refuse 'The Magician' – the man she adored.

Long years of frustration tortured Loti's *petite Madame amie*, as he called her, and as she signed herself in the innumerable letters that passed between them. While he came and went, travelled far afield, and had other affairs and distractions, she remained at Hendaye, letters their only link. Hers are pathetic outpourings of passionate longing, rather monotonous plaints, peppered with terms of love in the Basque language. '*Maïté, Maïtia*! my dearest, my darling,' she writes, 'when shall we meet – when will you return, so that I can tell you how my heart reaches out to you, always to you. Nothing else counts for me. *You, maïté* – only you!' A packet of these old letters remained at Hendaye, stuffed in a cupboard, where they had escaped the bonfire to which Loti, at the end of his life, consigned such outpourings. When I looked through them, with that painful feeling of eavesdropping which is known to every biographer, I wondered once again – *what* was this curious power which Loti could exercise over so many women? To be famous was not enough. He was egocentric, and no Adonis. I put the question to a very old lady at Hendaye, who, nudging a hundred, was still elegant, and perfectly able to recall Loti, whom she had known well. 'Those eyes – he could make you his slave with those eyes,' she told me. 'I was afraid of his eyes – they looked right into your mind and heart . . . He knew all about you, he noticed everything you wore, too . . . and then, those eyes of his *undressed* you!' She smiled roguishly, and I realized what a prolonged pleasure this must have represented for all concerned, in the days of starched petticoats, cache-corsets, corsets, camisoles, frilled drawers, black stockings and garters . . . layer on layer of anticipated voluptuousness.

Life at Hendaye offered many degrees of distraction. Below the rounded terraces of Bakhar Etchea there are curious little dungeon-like rooms, gained by steps going down to the water, once said to be used by smugglers coming in from the sea. Loti transformed one of these into a most convenient hide-out, all cushions, divans and Oriental ease. Here he retreated to smoke his narghile or enjoy 'the midnight's kind admittance', unperturbed by the proximity of the family and servants. In a sense, such rendezvous were another kind of smuggling.

Then there was the circus: Hendaye was on the frontier; several of the best circuses passed through during the year, and Loti's acrobatic prowess was well known to them. They asked nothing better than to have him join their troupe for a performance. The clown Béby of the Cirque Frediani remembered Loti at Hendaye. 'He loved us circus folk,' Béby told a journalist: 'he was an amateur who really understood our work. He had iron muscles. His speciality was the rings. Once he did a number for a charity gala we gave at Hendaye. It was marvellous! You've never seen '*le Christ*' performed so easily . . .' Béby struck a pose, his arms stretched out, as on the Cross, to display Loti's position when suspended from the rings. 'And Monsieur! he stayed like that for five whole minutes!' Evasions again. As once Julien Viaud had escaped into the person of Pierre Loti, the adulated author, so now that celebrated figure escaped, briefly, into the acrobat's body.

In the autumn of 1893 Loti's term of duty on the *Javelot* came to an end, and once more he was agonizing over a round of farewells which ranged between royalty and smugglers. His mother, Blanche, Samuel and the domestics had been dispatched to Rochefort, but still he lingered. His journal for September records a number of last meetings. Queen Natalie came over for a farewell dinner, and he garnished the little dining room with swags of fishing nets, at that time a most unconventional decoration. '*September 24th:* Pelota at Abbadia – the last, no doubt . . . Sombre weather, already dead leaves, autumn in the air. To leave this country wrings my heart. All night smuggling with Simon and Ramuntcho. O! the sadness of endings!'

14

All they expect from me is the illusion of travel —
the reflection of a thousand things over which my
eyes have ranged.

Pierre Loti

Leaving the invigorating Basque life for Rochefort had plunged Loti
into a twilight zone of old memories and greying skies. If he walked
in the little courtyard, he stepped on the graves of vanished pets: the
jasmine flowering on the old walls had been planted by Aunt
Claire . . . Gustave's grotto and the little pond were still his Holy
Mecca, but the long-living goldfish were no more, and although the
Algerian tortoise still shuffled towards him affectionately, the palms
and aloes he had planted were growing tall, and his little son played
about the courtyard as he had once done — all were reminders of
passing time. Then, although there was Léo's companionship and
perfect beauty to console him, Yves had vanished, leaving a bitter
taste to cloud memories of old, rumbustious days together. Yves had
left the Navy and sunk into alcoholic immobility at Rosporden, so
that all Loti's regenerative efforts had been in vain. At the Préfecture
de la Marine, Loti was no longer his own master as on the *Javelot*;
now he was a cog in the wheels, with much paper work, and he felt
middle-age taking possession, but without the numbing effects of
resignation. Each day he watched his mother moving closer to that
fearful, final separation. If only he could have kept his childhood's
faith with which to face the parting ahead! It was as much for
self-protection as spiritual fulfilment that he yearned. The 'radiant
illusion of Christianity', the fatalism of Islam, the serene beliefs of
the Hindus or the Buddhists, the renouncements of the Brahmans,
all accepted death as no more than an opening door leading to
various new paths, while to Loti, death remained an end — the
terrifying, final end of all those he loved, of himself, and all the
loveliness of the world around him. Contradictory as ever, he could
never quite accept the idea of oblivion for himself. 'It would be
impossible to imagine that someone like myself could simply vanish,'

he remarked. Yet stronger than everything was the belief that all must perish in eternal darkness.

As the shadows came closer, dull day by dull day, he decided to make one last effort to recover his lost faith – his mother's faith. For many years he had wished to visit the Holy Land: it was a journey she had hoped for him, too. There perhaps the miracle might be wrought. Sunrise rather than sunset.

In the spring of 1894 he applied for leave, and set about organizing his departure. Léo was to accompany him, and together they planned to follow the slow stages of a camel caravan. The old familiar intoxication of travel had gripped him, now strengthened by the spiritual goal to be attained. He would go to Jerusalem – to Bethlehem – would pray at Gethsemane, and kneel humbly, imploring the Saviour's mercy. Surely his despairing cry must be answered? Through all the vicissitudes of his life, Loti the atheist had continued to seek faith with the fervour of an illuminé, for the atheist was, in reality, a profoundly devout man whose intellect had overcome his original, ancestral beliefs, leaving him stranded. Yet how he prayed to pray! Always, he haunted places of worship, churches, chapels, mosques, temples . . . By no matter what creed or cult, he sought that Presence. So, forever seeking, his travels were gradually to become pilgrimages, hopeless, nostalgic quests, never fulfilled.

For this crucial approach to the Holy Places Loti planned a circuitous route to prepare himself slowly, reverentially, rather than arriving directly, still stained by cities and civilization. Thus, instead of sailing direct to some Palestinian port and following an easy journey inland, he chose to go overland, from Egypt, via Sinai, Aqaba, and the deserts of El Tyh and Petra, reaching Jerusalem from the south, by the old, abandoned caravan routes. There in the stern solitude of the desert he believed he might better prepare himself, like those devout Russian peasants who trudged, praying, across the world, carrying their shrouds with them, to dip in the waters of Jordan before turning back, blessed, for the cruel homeward trek.

By this journey or pilgrimage, which he recounts in the trilogy, Le Désert, Jérusalem and La Galilée, Loti was fulfilling his mother's lifelong dream of seeing Jerusalem the Golden before she died. For her, the means to go there had come too late. Old ladies did not move about much then. But she, the patient stay-at-home, could still travel through her son's all-seeing eyes, and Loti must have been aware of her spirit beside him as he set out on his own journey of the spirit.

On February 4th 1894 he left for Cairo, accompanied by *'le beau Léo'* and the Duc de Talleyrand-Périgord, who was to leave them on reaching Jerusalem. For all Loti's love of simplicity, he no longer travelled as once when playing Arik Ussim Effendi, young, penniless and carefree. Now he was to travel in the splendid comfort of patriarchal Arabic ways, with a whole caravan of camels, tents, carpets, servitors, armed guards, and even musicians with plaintive flutes to charm his evenings by the camp fires. In Cairo, a *laisser passer* had been obtained from a powerful Sheik of the Senoussi tribe, his co-operation made possible through the French Embassy, for wherever Loti went he had now become a person of consequence. The deserts they were to pass through were dangerous, controlled by thieving murderous bands, but the Sheik Omar's *laisser passer* was reassuring; picturesque, too, in its stately Arab rhythms.

Before Allah the compassionate on High,
these words from the most humble Seïd Omar, son of
Edriss, in favour of his friend Pierre Loti,
recommending him to the Chiefs of all the tribes
of Arabia, to aid him during his journeys in the
land of the Arabs, for he venerates Islam and is
inspired by the noblest feelings for our religion.
Know that I shall be gratified by all those who
respect and aid him, for such he merits.

Omar, son of Edriss El Senoussi El Mosni

Loti had studied the Biblical foundations of his journey well in advance, though no doubt he was aided by recollections of those nightly Bible readings of his childhood. Throughout this journey he cites the appropriate Scriptures; the Prophets and Saints accompany him, and are a basis for his vivid descriptions of each scene, so little changed from its Biblical past. Indeed it is rewarding to read this book as a visual supplement to the passages of the Old Testament which he cites. He shows us the great sweep of the desert and the small, unchanging details; nomad tribes in their camps, desolate rock regions scorched by the khamsin's fiery blast, strange insects and almost colourless desert plants which have a violent peppery odour; the grave beauty of the Arabs, swathed in their white robes, crouched in groups, silently awaiting the holy hour of Maghreb – hour of the evening prayer, when the muezzin sounds in the dusk. This call of the muezzin has been described by Loti many times over, but never with more poetry than here . . . 'that voice, which hung on the air, like a great flight of sound, as if with a trembling of wings . . . Before the splendours of the earth and the sky, which confound mankind, that voice called, called, a psalm to the god of Islam, who is also the god of the great desert.'

Moving ever deeper into the desert, Loti tells of a track they follow by El Tyh, 'the dread land' of Great Arabia to earlier travellers, the desert of the Amalekites to students of the Bible. Loti sees it blooming strangely with what appear to be myriads of small blue flowers, which prove to be crushed fragments of those turquoise glass beads with which the camels are traditionally hung, amulets against the evil eye. 'Through countless centuries the passing caravans have shed these strange desert flowers, even to the cortège of Sheba's Queen, going through the Nabataean fastness of Petra, to visit Solomon.' Such unexpected details animate the scene as no purely historic or ethnographic accounts can do. The reader, who is beside Loti or has followed him to share that romantic nomad's life, lulled by beauty and timeless hours of sun, suddenly senses an icy chill, that which creeps beneath the tent-flaps at nightfall, and hearing the jackals prowling near, grows uneasy. Then, reading on, discovers that Loti too, although the most seasoned of travellers, is uneasy and aware that he is on alien ground. 'One comes to realize one is never completely *a man of the tents*, in spite of the charms of nomad life. *The man of the stone houses* formed by our ancient atavisms must always feel a vague uneasiness, to be without roof or walls; moreover, to know there are no such things anywhere in all this vast desert.' Did he, alone in his tent, when the sinister shadows pressed round, hear again the talismanic song Aziyadé used to sing for him so long ago?

> *Shaïtanlar, djinnler*
> *Kaplanar, duchmanlar*
> *Arslandar*
>
> (May devils, djinns, lions
> and every enemy stay far from my love.)

'Jerusalem O! the dying radiance of that name!' is Loti's perfervid opening to the book which tells of his search for faith there.

Loti and Blanche honeymooning at
the Alhambra, Loti striking a proud
Spanish Grandee's pose, while Blanche
maintains her timid, wifely role.

Loti the bemedalled officer. No fancy
dress, here: such decorations tell
of his long, distinguished career at
sea and ashore.

Loti puffs his narghile voluptuously.
Beside the Bosphorus, with Choukri
in attendance, he once more
'plays the Effendi'.

Loti, a willing victim, beside
the veiled impostors who styled
themselves *Les Désenchantées*, and
tricked him cruelly with a farrago
of romantic bliss.

Loti in yet another change of costume. Syrian or Algerian, the bedouin or the Effendi . . . all were escapes into another shell.

141 Rue St-Pierre, now Rue Pierre Loti, birthplace of Julien-Marie Viaud, his deepest root, remaining outwardly unchanged, though within, wild Oriental fantasies lulled his longings for Islam.

Loti at home: the poseur poses amid the gorgeous trappings of the East: prayer rugs, divans, coffee tables and narghiles lead through to the mosque in all its serene grandeur. There the would-be Moslem prayed.

Loti with his three sons.
The paterfamilias role, for Loti
abhorred hypocrisy, and acknowledged
his left-handed family whatever
the scandal. Samuel wears uniform,
Raymond Gainza stands to the left,
Edmond to the right.

Pierre Loti: the last picture.
Paralyzed, the puppet figure leans
against a wall. Only the eyes still live,
those strange, compelling, haunting
eyes – 'the eyes of a lost child'.

At the time of his visit, Jerusalem was under Turkish rule, Palestine having been part of the Ottoman Empire since 1517. Yet through the centuries, the Holy City remained essentially international by virtue of the spiritual significance it held for so many races and creeds. Lethargic Ottoman administrators had left it largely to its immemorial ways and babel of worshippers: but while doing little to preserve its monuments, a Turkish militia ensured that the various cults, their processions, prayers and shrines were respected. Thus, for all its sombre decay, Loti found it shimmering with faith, something intangible yet overwhelming, which illuminated churches, temples and mosques alike. He saw it when it was neither a political pawn nor a business proposition.

As Loti went from one sacred site to another, from the Via Dolorosa to the Mosque of Al Aksar or the Wall of Lamentation, all was faith. Christians, whether Armenian, Greek, or Russian Orthodox, like the Copts, Roman Catholics, Calvinists, Ethiopians, and Sephardic and Ashkenazic Jews were all met there to worship their God, as did the Arabs and the various denominations of Islam, for Jerusalem is a most holy city to Moslems too. The Dome of the Rock is the holiest place on earth after Mecca and Medina. That great gold-domed, turquoise and lapis-tiled mosque which remains a glorious centre-piece and landmark of incomparable beauty was built by the Caliph Omar, to commemorate the Prophet's ascent to Heaven on a ladder of light, there to learn God's word. He was held to have returned enjoying, among other things, veneration for all the Prophets of other faiths, Abraham and Moses, and Jesus the Messiah. In the words of the Koran (Surah XLII)

> God is our Lord and your Lord
> We have our deeds and you have your deeds;
> There is no argument between us and you:
> God shall bring us together, and unto Him
> Is the homecoming.

Those lovely words were known to Loti through his affinities with Islam: and if he was now vainly seeking a homecoming in the faith of his ancestors, it was surely because he had forsworn that other faith – the faith of Islam, which he had set aside for the sake of his mother, but which he continued to believe would have brought peace to his doubting heart.

Thus this book reflects the contrapuntal emotions which swayed

225

him as he went about the Holy City. If Christian sites often moved him to easy tears, they sometimes left him with a cold sense of desolation: yet when he approached the mosques, he felt his whole being drawn towards their less harrowing ambience: '. . . they speak of acceptance, they are a refuge of peace.' Yet that peace was to remain forsworn, while he continued to hunger before the Holy Sepulchre or spend long night hours alone in the Garden of Gethsemane. This was his last hope of some Divine revelation, and a certain, perhaps unconscious, sense of theatre made him choose the site of Christ's agony for his own desperate prayers. There, surely, he would be heard – be answered? But no: in the shadows under the olives the Lord did not come to the rescue of this lost sheep who, in his self-centred longings, had believed he – Loti, *must* find a response. 'Empty as never before, bitter to the point of revolt, I returned to the City of Faith.'

I have heard Loti criticized as being anti-Semitic for his descriptions of Jerusalem's Jewry; but he was recording them as meticulously as he recorded all around him – as he saw them then – in their mixture of rags and medieval splendour; of filth and fur-lined velvets, with 'appraising, needle-sharp eyes under heavy hooded lids'. It is not a prepossessing picture, but as always with Loti, a very exact picture of what he saw. Because he was drawn to Islam by memories of Aziyadé's city or, as he believed, by some remote atavism, it did not make him automatically anti-Jewish. He was to be as harsh in his descriptions of the Chinese, whom he held in horror: and one might remark his rabid criticism of the English, too.

At the time of Loti's visit to Jerusalem there was no Palestinian question over which to take sides, while the Zionist Movement was not founded until the following year, in 1895. In his day, the Jews of Jerusalem were only a small accepted colony, taking refuge from the ghettos of Poland and Russia, the mollahs of Morocco, or the Pale of settlements in Eastern Europe.

He describes the scene at the Wailing Wall thus: 'It is Friday evening, the traditional moment when the Jews go there to weep. Men in long velvet robes, moving together in a sort of collective swaying, seen from the back, like so many bears in a cage, all facing the gigantic debris, beating their heads against the stones, muttering some trembling chant . . . Their robes are magnificent, black velvet,

226

blue velvet, violet or crimson velvet, lined with valuable furs. Their caps are all of black velvet, bordered with shaggy fur which casts a shadow over their knife-blade eyes . . . Their faces have the tint of unhealthy wax, and over each ear hang corkscrew curls recalling the "Anglaises" worn in 1830, and which complete their disturbing resemblance to ancient bearded ladies . . .

'There are also some children, fresh-looking like little sugar bonbons, already wearing ringlets, who sway and wail, Bible in hand, like their elders. Tonight, almost all are the Ashkenazi, Jews from Germany, weakened and pallid from centuries of trading and money-lending under northern skies, very different to the Sephardim, who are their brothers from Spain or Morocco, where one sees dark skins and the admirable faces of ancient prophets . . .'

Next Loti describes a visit to the Franciscans who were custodians of the *Trésor des Latins*. 'A mass of riches. From the middle ages, kings and emperors and nations have never ceased to send superb gifts. They showed us diamond crosses and candlesticks of enamel and gold. In a long line of cupboards, priestly costumes beyond price, rigid, sumptuous vestments. In what a strange fashion the Catholic and the Orthodox churches have interpreted that simplicity which Jesus came among us to give!'

After a month in the Holy City, Loti rode away heading east towards Damascus, following those desert wastes where God seemed nearer.

This journey through Palestine to Syria and the Lebanon is recorded in his book *La Galilée*, third of this Middle Eastern trilogy. It is dedicated to his companion, Léo Thémèze, and as they go deeper into the land, far from the pilgrims and hauntings of Jerusalem, a sense of release is apparent. Loti returns to his customary ways of travel, and there is no more repining. Loti the traveller had shed Loti the pilgrim and briefly travels light without those longings which had consumed him in Jerusalem.

He had not imagined Damascus to be as he found it. 'An Orient which is gay – a Moslem town so smiling and open,' he exults. *'Who can look on Damascus for the first time, and remain unmoved?'* It was Mohammed's paradise on earth – and so to be resisted. But Loti plunges into the bazaars and finds the marvellous Orient of the *Thousand and One Nights* in the house of Pasha Abdullah, and the rich souks. He sees everything under the resplendent spring sunlight, where doves and swallows wheel in the blue, the fountained courts offer repose, and palaces, funeral kiosques, hammams and celebrated libraries of learning all recall the great epoch of Moslem culture.

Leaving Damascus, and its delectable surroundings of green oasis gardens – the Gouta (said to be the Garden of Eden) – Loti and his companions turned homeward, by Baalbek, and the cedars of Lebanon. The Orient they cherished faded with each mile westward. Viewing Beirut and its harbour from the heights, they saw what appeared to be numbers of little grey fish strewn about the bay. 'European squadrons and fast liners – iron-clad visitors which arrive here, every day more numerous, to overthrow the old Orient in its decline . . .' Smoking a last narghile, Loti wrote: 'Tonight, our pilgrimage without hope or faith is over . . . and we can see clearly that lugubrious future lying ahead . . . dark ages that will begin after the destruction of all those great celestial dreams . . . appalling democratic tyrannies, where the desolate will no more realize what it was to pray.'

They returned by way of Turkey, and the few days spent in Broussa, the ancient capital of the Ottoman Empire, inspired one of his most evocative chapters, *La Mosquée Verte* being published as a postscript to *La Galilée*. In this halcyon scene Loti found a microcosm of all he most loved in Turkish life: serenity, dignity and beauty. This small, radiant town was set on the lower slopes of the Bythinian Mount Olympus; streams cascaded down through the groves of ancient cyprus and gigantic plane trees. The way of life was patriarchal, the people living as their ancestors had done, steaming themselves in the same hot-spring bath houses such as the one which the Emperor Justinian built for Theodora. By day, they tended their silk-worms, cultivated their crops, and at dusk congregated in little cafés like the one among the tombs and willow trees of Bounar Bachi where Loti came to idle among them enviously. 'A few hours' work each day earns enough for their moderate needs and desires. Then, as life draws to a close, there is Faith, to chase away the terrors of death.'

As if seeking some further revelation – if not of faith, at least of the serenity he saw around him at Broussa – he was drawn back again and again to the terrace of a small rather dilapidated café beside the

Green Mosque, much frequented by the imams, figures of piety, who gathered there in quiet contemplation of the lovely verdant plains spread out below. Each evening, Loti observed a group of men who remained a little apart from the imams, handsome creatures lolling nonchalantly on the low wall of the café, a silent band, who intrigued him. 'Tall, dark-eyed, superb,' he noted. They wore short red or blue jackets revealing narrow waists bound round with cashmere sashes. Their pantaloons were finely gathered and their sleeves, cut Tartar-fashion, hung free from their shoulders like wings. Loti thought they might be brigands, or perhaps soldiers, 'some of those true-believers, so brave under fire, who are the strength of the Turkish army . . . warrior-mystics, men who regard everything of this world as transitory; who believe in God, and pray; who have few needs, are seldom perturbed, and savour to the utmost all that is real beauty on earth: spring time, clear mornings and golden evenings'.

Next day, these martial figures were to be seen again, silently surveying the plain. Loti asked one of the imams what they were doing there – what they were waiting for. The imam seemed surprised at such a question, and with a sweeping gesture, indicated the beauty spread out before them.

'They are looking,' he replied: which seemed both natural and sufficient to Loti.

15

*The pang of all the partings gone
And partings yet to be.*

Francis Thompson

Loti's return to his mother's side was shadowed by the necessity of admitting what she could read in his eyes. Not all her prayers, nor his own, nor the Holy Land, had enabled him to regain his lost faith. To distract them both, he gave several splendid parties in her honour, elaborate affairs in the huge Renaissance hall where she, rather than Blanche, presided, greeting his Paris friends as well as the old Rochefort families. Not all of them had stood by her so long ago, when disaster struck the Viauds: but the old lady smiled happily on everyone, for she bore no rancour. Loti himself still nursed injured pride, and took particular pleasure to see his darling mother enthroned, himself a world-famous writer and the family honour vindicated.

As the years went by he became more and more restless; his desk work at the Préfecture de la Marine was monotonous; he hankered after the wide vistas of light and water surrounding both the *Javelot*, and the Bakhar Etchea; there were no more adventurous sorties with the smugglers, and the people of Rochefort compared poorly with the dashing Basques. A posting to some ship sailing for far seas would have calmed his nervous depressions and he longed to be once more surrounded by 'the great circle of blue', and the camaraderie of the fleet. But that could never be, as long as his mother lived.

For some while a plan had been germinating in his mind, and now he set about realizing it. If he could not return to Hendaye, there to share the life of the Basques, he could at least found a Basque family, his blood mingling with this splendid race, so that something of himself would be perpetuated among them. It was an echo, or continuation of that earlier craving for salvation through union with some primitive stock, which had haunted him ever since the Breton fisher-girl had refused him. A second, Basque, family could not bear his name, or be officially recognized, he knew; nevertheless such questions were brushed aside in a surge of enthusiasm which shook him out of his gloom. It was to his friend Doctor Durutty that he now confided the delicate mission of finding some suitable local girl of simple origins, and a great deal of guarded correspondence on this genetic question now passed between the doctor at Hendaye, and Loti at Rochefort. The doctor's letters are interspersed with prescriptions for concoctions of permanganate and walnut juice, calculated to restore Loti's greying moustache, a mark of age which belied his trim, athletic body.

A number of possible girls had backed out, the doctor wrote, dwelling on the exasperating obstinacy of some who, while agreeing to do their best to provide 'ce Monsieur V.' with children, flatly declined to take part in an elaborate charade calculated to hoodwink their families. It had been decided the candidate must appear to leave for domestic service in Paris or some other faraway town (domestic service being a respectable way of life, and one to which no parent would object); but in reality the girl would head for Rochefort, where Loti guaranteed a comfortable, though back-street establishment.

When Loti chose to settle this second ménage at Rochefort rather than anywhere else, where anonymity might be preserved, it told of his indifference to public opinion in his home town, and to the distress it would cause his wife – to say nothing of his mother, though perhaps, ostrich-like, he thought this new life could be concealed from her at least. What he wanted he usually obtained, and with fame and money he had become more autocratic, more able to ride roughshod over the conventions. Rochefort was his root, and there the second foyer must be planted. At last a suitable young girl was found who agreed to all the terms. She went by the charming name of Crucita – little Cross – and her brother worked as a carpenter down the lane beyond Bakhar Etchea. In September Crucita Gainza departed from her homeland to live in a modest house some way from the Rue Saint-Pierre.

It was a difficult, solitary life to which he had led her . . . Why did she go? It was no rape, nor had she been coerced. No large sums of money had bribed her brother to be compliant, nor had she known Loti earlier and been bemused by his fame, or the charm he could exercise. It is impossible to guess what made her accept the situation in which she was to remain for the rest of her life, accepting Loti's

231

comings and goings with docility, awaiting his return from afar, finding few friends, remaining remote from Hendaye, alone with the children he had wanted. Only once did Loti make a veiled reference to this second family, in a short passage in one of his books. His journals are more forthcoming, describing Crucita's sufferings when, standing beside her bed, he witnessed the butchery of doctor and midwife, till at last the Basque child he had determined on was obtained.

Whether Blanche was aware of this second home from the beginning is doubtful. She was certainly aware of it later, for Crucita was to provide Loti with three Basque sons, and when he set out on further travels in remote lands, Blanche promised to be responsible for them should he die. No husband could ask for more, and Loti's respect for her deepened.

Mother and mistress of the house, that was Blanche's rôle; it was one set apart from the two distinct categories by which Loti classified women – bodies or brains. The women with whom he shared the transports of the flesh were not expected to have intellects, or to make conversation. Their bodies communicated sufficiently. His taste had been formed forever by that first revelation of the senses in the woods of Roche-Courbon. Rarahu and Aziyadé, sensual and illiterate primitives, continued the line, which was maintained with varying degrees of abandon by Madame Chrysanthème, Pasquala Ivanovitch, the Bordeaux siren, Zohra the prostitute, numbers of savagely seductive Ouled Naïla and legions of lovely come-by-chance brown bodies encountered on his voyages. Such were the women Loti loved to love.

Then there were other women – those with brains, whom he admitted to have souls too; they were among his friends and confidantes, devoted friends like Madame Adam or the Duchesse de Richelieu. Many cultivated women responded to the subtle charm of this most complicated, hyper-sensitive writer who could seem a pathetic child genius needing their sympathy and understanding, and who yet showed an uncanny ability to read their innermost selves. Loti took care not to mix the two categories, it saved a lot of complications; though the divine Sarah's prodigious personality could not be contained in one or the other. Throughout her long life, she was to represent the world, the flesh and the devil, the intellect and the faithful friend.

232

Loti's restlessness was not stilled by the installation of Crucita Gainza at Rochefort, but it gave an illusion of being nearer to the Basque lands from which he, the eternal exile, now felt exiled. 'Wherever I am, I always miss something of myself that I have left elsewhere.' Crucita was in fact far more of an exile, alone on the outskirts of the town, among strangers, her only link with home this curious man who was a gentle master but who always vanished after an hour or two in her company. Most evenings, around ten o'clock, Loti visited her. 'She is a good little soul,' he notes, 'but still quite disorientated. Her Spanish piety, and remorse at what she has done, leads her to church incessantly, poor little daughter of the mountains.'

It is clear that Crucita and the Basque babies were a very small part of his established life, even more marginal figures than Blanche and her son . . . (*'Could I love them, Aziyadé, if your blood and mine did not mingle in their veins?'*) . . . Aziyadé's spell still held fast, as the Turkish mirage still beckoned.

All Loti's fantasies were now concentrated on perfecting his mosque. Day by day it grew in beauty. Fine Oriental rugs were laid traditionally, over straw matting. Gigantic brass candlesticks flanked the mihrab, or prayer niche, while chased silver mosque lamps, from which dangled the usual tasselled ostrich eggs, hung from an exquisite ceiling of carved cedar wood. Illuminated Koranic texts in flowing Arabic script were beside Kufic tiles; some of the faïences were of that rare tomato red from Iznik, some of Persian azure so that here, briefly, the escapist could reach some Islamic limbo-land.

Early in 1896 Loti was appointed for a second term of duty at Hendaye, once more to command the *Javelot*. Demanding as ever, he did not hesitate to shuttle his mother backwards and forwards between Rochefort and Hendaye, for he sensed their days together were numbered. Blanche and Samuel, the two ex-seamen Pierre and Lucien, both incorporated into the household as domestics, were also transferred to Hendaye; but cruelly, Crucita was left behind at Rochefort to await his rare returns there. He leased Bakhar Etchea once more, though it was anything but snug for his frail mother.

When la Tourmenta howled round, banging the shutters and whining under the doors, nothing warmed the place. Camelias and bamboos grew in the tangled garden but fires were needed most of the year, and dangerous little oil stoves smoked on each turn of the stairs leading to 'Mama Nadine's' room. Although she was lapped in love and had her faithful maid Mélanie to cosset her, it must have been a trial to her.

Loti resumed his old friendships among the people, smugglers, fisher folk and shepherds, and every evening went to the fronton to play pelota, generally accompanied by the adoring Madame Durutty: it had become a ritual, and she braved the gossip these innocent expeditions caused in the town. Obviously his mistress, wagged the local tongues, and both she and Loti wished it were so. But it was not: her religious convictions held fast and Loti railed at Catholic moralities. The Abbadies, now very old, were others who welcomed his return. They wished to bequeath him their magnificent château, but Loti refused it, so that they had to be content with presenting Samuel with a little donkey, on which he trotted over to visit the menagerie where the eagles and other fierce creatures were consistently amiable to him; something the child accepted unquestioningly, like the eccentricities of Madame Abbadie, even when she stuck small scraps of white paper, like large snowflakes, all over her face, a manoeuvre she believed would disguise a number of blemishes which had ruined her complexion.

In the autumn of the same year it was clear to Loti that his mother was failing fast and longed to return to Rochefort. He took her back there, settling her once more in her own armchair by the fire in her pretty blue room, where all was unchanged. On 12th November Nadine Viaud died; at the end she had opened her eyes and seen Marie and her Julien beside her, united in their tears, as she knew them never to be in life. 'Love one another, my children,' she said, and closed her eyes for ever. Loti had foreseen that terrible moment throughout his life. When it happened, he who had always poured out his sorrows and loves in letters, journals and books, remained mute. In the words of Walter Savage Landor, *there is a gloom in deep love, as in deep water; there is a silence in it* . . . Loti the Magician of Words had none for this loss. Only some months later could he write to Madame Adam: 'I have lost my mother.' Nothing more: but one page of his journal tells something of the agony of that parting, and the torture he suffered, by his doubts of any future reunion. 'When I arrived on Wednesday morning she clasped me close, half raising herself, her voice still strong, in the strange exaltation of farewell: "You believe, don't you? You do believe that we shall find each other again?" Who knows, O! God! perhaps! Without that hope, what an odious, cowardly deception our lives would be!'

At that time there were numbers of highly colourful persons who congregated in the Basque lands, between the chic of Biarritz, the arcaded calm of Bayonne, or the unspoiled coast from St Jean-de-Luz to Hendaye; and for all of them Loti was the magnet which drew them to Bakhar Etchea.

At Arnaga, the playwright Edmond Rostand had built, and was constantly enlarging, a small château with grandiose fountained gardens which came to be known as Le petit Versailles Basque. There he wrote *Chanticleer* and *La Derniere Nuit d'Amour de Don Juan*. The future President Poincaré was also an habitué of Arnaga. He had known Loti from the time when he had been Minister of Education, Fine Arts and Religion. Such an armful of Portfolios cannot have left much time for cultivating friendship, but he regarded the author of *Aziyadé* as a being apart, and kept up the friendship, arriving sometimes accompanied by Sarah Bernhardt. '*La Grande Vieille Amie*' was still exotic, in spite of motoring outfits and boots, as she embarked on golf, the latest craze. At the House of the Solitary Loti did not feel 'fossilized', as at Rochefort. Anatole France, with his Egeria, Madame Cavaillet and Reynaldo Hahn also brought the cultural life of Paris to the Basque coast, and Loti's house was always the first place of pilgrimage.

Reynaldo Hahn was then writing a musical score based on *Le Mariage de Loti*: his Peruvian blood responded to its tropic luxuriance and he and Loti were in constant consultation. 'If one can trace a little poetry in my modest talent,' he wrote to Loti, 'then I owe it to you . . . It is you who have charmed yet cast a vaporous melancholy over my whole adolescence.'

Francis Jammes the poet lived in a small house near St Jean-de-Luz. He describes Loti attending a gala evening: 'He had changed into a uniform so covered in decorations that he had the air of a Japanese warrior, one of those who resemble some kind of creature covered in a carapace of precious stones. His long nose was framed by painted cheeks, but his large dark eyes seemed to be looking into who knows what profound depths? They reflected such compassion, such dread too, that one forgot the make-up.'

Ex-Queen Natalie of Serbia was still living at Sashino, and further afield, in Madrid, there was a double distillation of majesty. The Queen Regent, Marie Christine of Spain, was a Hapsburg Arch-duchess by birth and a Bourbon Queen by her marriage; thus, doubly royal. She lived in the oppressive grandeur of the Escorial, where Loti visited her, for his sympathies were with the Spanish during their war with the United States, to retain their colonies of Cuba and Porto Rico. He voiced his indignation right and left . . . all the aggression and might of that huge, rapacious, English-speaking Goliath to be turned on the Spanish David! He seethed: it was more of that Imperialism he loathed! Rumour had it that, in his fury, he was planning to resign and join the Spanish Navy, or to man a ship with a crew of Basque mercenaries and head for the battle . . . Needless to say he did neither of these things, but he did endeavour to raise money to equip a hospital ship: and by his pen, if not his sword, was prepared to fight for the Queen's cause. In this mood of chivalry Loti was apt to overlook his position in the French Navy, one which forbade political or international involvements, so that, finally, ardent sympathy was all he was able to offer the Spanish Queen and her people.

On the sidelines of such exaltation there was his friend of many years past, of the days when Oirda introduced him to le beau monde, 'the delicious little Duchesse de Richelieu', Heine's great-niece, who, on the death of the Duke, had become Her Serene Highness the Princesse Alice of Monaco, bride of Prince Albert of oceanographic fame. ('And to think I could have married her,' Loti noted.) He sometimes visited her at the Palace, where Frank Harris records watching him turn backward somersaults with astonishing ease. At Rochefort, the 'Princess Alice's room' was always kept ready for her, and when, much later, the Princess reverted to the more Bohemian ways of her great-uncle, and scorning scandal turned her back on the Principality to take up with the musician Isidore de Lara, Loti remained faithful. Snob he may have been, but he was ever a faithful friend.

Then there was Madame Mounet-Sully, the famous actor's wife, who sighed for Loti with unconcealed passion. Madame Durutty sighed as longingly but with more discretion. Innumerable women appear to have lived for his presence, or the letters which he wrote in his flowing, elegant hand on the bright orange-coloured paper he had now adopted. Many of the missives he received from women both known and unknown offered their love, offered talismans, offered to elope, to bear his children, to be his unpaid secretaries, his slaves, or to accompany him on his travels. Did any of them ever suggest following him to sea as stowaways? It would have been in the romantic tradition by which Loti lived. Madame Adam, watching these embroilments with misgivings, cautioned him. 'I am the Commendator's statue, Don-Juan Loti! Beware.' But romance, in terms of passing adventures or perfervid correspondence, was part of Loti's life. All romantic missives were kept, tied in accumulating packets, and sometimes he re-read them, as if to reassure himself of his still potent attraction. 'His whole person radiated irresistible charm . . . Men and women alike were conquered by the singular, indefinable attraction of this man,' wrote Louis de Robert, at one time his secretary. No doubt a large number of the letters Loti kept so long were also from men who fell under his spell or with whom he was infatuated: but these are no more among his papers. They were either destroyed by him at the end of his life, or, after his death, by his son, thus that side of his life, so much of which roused criticism and gossip, remains conjecture.

From all over the world, readers wrote of the pleasure his books gave them. His fan mail, as it would be called today, was enormous. Then there were the innumerable appeals for help which he never neglected. To these he responded unquestioningly, giving of himself and his time as well as money, writing letters of recommendation to those in high places, letters of counsel, of comfort and encouragement. He was what is called a soft touch. Any hard-luck story moved him: an old salt fallen on bad times, a sailor's widow, victim of injustice or some crooked business venture, any struggling author could count on his aid. 'Such kindness, such warmth of heart – was there ever anyone more generous?' wrote one of his secretaries. Loti was now earning very large sums of money but nothing was ever banked, for he obstinately refused to open an account or make prudent investments (though, with his addiction to all things Turkish, it is surprising he was not tempted by some branch of the Ottoman Bank). Publishers and editors paid his royalties and dues direct, cash and bank notes lying about the house in careless heaps.

In vain did Blanche preach prudence, in vain did his secretary try to set things in order, in vain did Calmann-Lévy suggest he might be a little less open-handed with his royalties. Money was for spending, for giving, for sharing. One of his old uniform caps, stuffed with loose money, was always kept in the entrance to 141 Rue Saint-Pierre, and anyone who knocked on that door for help was told to take what he needed.

With all the accumulation of correspondence, invitations, business and personal letters which flooded into the house by every post, Loti presently found it necessary to have two secretaries. One, who had his entire confidence, was Gaston Mauberger, who had first joined him in 1880 and was to remain devotedly attached until Loti's death. At Rochefort he generally worked in a small, narrow room, known as the Salle des Momies, leading out of Gustave's study, which had, of course, been left untouched, a sacred shrine, and still housed his books and collections of tropicana. Gradually the Salle des Momies had been turned into a mixture of museum, portrait gallery, and wardrobe or theatrical dressing room. Here in glass-doored cupboards were ranged the exotic costumes Loti had collected – and wore. Japanese kimonos, Egyptian robes and winged Pharaonic head-dresses, ceremonial Breton costumes, necklaces of shells, fans, painted masks, Turkish pattens, or muslin pareos; all the exotic trimmings he loved were there, along with curious two-foot high starched lace caps of the Breton women, no doubt recalling his Breton love. There were also plaster casts of hands – Loti's among them. Here he had amassed elaborately framed signed photographs of royalty and lesser luminaries of the Almanach de Gotha. Well might this room be called the Salle des Momies when we see all these figures from another age, rigid, bejewelled, staring out, as if embalmed in majesty. Here are queens galore: the Queens of Spain and Serbia; Queen Alexandra beside Queen Pomaré of Papeete, and a sketch by Loti of Queen Vaé-Kéhu of Nuka Hiva; Queen Elizabeth of the Belgians; Queen Elizabeth of Romania; Crown Princess Marie of Romania; the Grand Duchess Vladimir of Russia. Great ladies, all of them expressing Loti's instinct for collecting. Not that the ladies had to be pursued. By the flowery.inscriptions scrawled across their portraits, Loti, or his books, had won them easily. Here, too, are statesmen, ambassadors, a famous matador, Egyptian and Persian princes, maharajas, musicians, writers, the divine Sarah, Réjane and

Duse, and a chill English beauty, illegibly inscribed and arrogant beneath her splendid tiara, perhaps some ambassadress encountered on a voyage. Among this shimmering galaxy the faithful Mauberger strove to keep abreast of the paper-work as it flooded in. On the frequent migrations to Hendaye, he would board the train with laundry baskets full of correspondence to be dealt with by degrees.

In April 1899 Loti was able to buy back the old house on the ISLAND – the Maison des Aïeulles at Saint-Pierre-d'Oléron, cradle of his race, where generations of ancestors had lived and died. He did not plan to live there – it was enough to possess it, to hold it, bastion of his mother's people against any defiling outside presence. Sometimes he visited it, taking the child Samuel with him, opening the barred green door in the high white wall and entering the courtyard with the reverence of one treading on holy ground, as indeed it was to him, for some of his Huguenot ancestors were buried there. Samuel enjoyed these outings and Loti was gratified that this fair-haired child, seemingly all Ferrière, was yet of the race of Renaudins and Texiers – like himself, a child of the ISLAND.

Loti was to remain at Hendaye in command of the *Javelot* for another two years, during which time he published *Ramuntcho* and a book of sketches, *Figures et Choses qui Passaient*, which like *Ramuntcho* reflects many aspects of Basque life. Both are low-keyed in mood, though as perfectly evocative of the genius loci as Loti's writings always were, whether he described the Spahis' Africa or Montenegrin mountains. But now it was as if some early frost had chilled him through; the youthful love of Ramuntcho and Gracieuse and her sustaining religion are seen remotely.

For all his sympathy with the people and the region, this is, to my mind, one of his books which can be skipped, unless read in a purely tourist spirit. There are no more of the passionate identifications of his earlier work though this did not diminish its popularity when it was published, in 1897. Love, loss and faith remain eternal themes, and a version was to be staged in Paris, thirteen years later, with music by Gabriel Pierné.

With the loss of his mother and the approach of his fiftieth year Loti felt himself an abandoned orphan, exiled for ever from both her side and his youth, and in March 1898, Fate dealt a further blow. Just three months after his command of the *Javelot* expired, while expecting to be posted for service on the high seas, something he could at last accept now that his mother was no more, the Ministère de la Marine informed him he was axed – placed on the retired list. This new measure, introduced to make way for a number of young officers, was for Loti a knife to the heart. To be deprived of that career which he placed above all else! That he, Julien Viaud, was no longer part of the Grand Corps de la Marine (the élite of the Service) which he had served with devotion – the navy that was his predestined and chosen life – was this to be yet another exile?

He had received the official decree in Paris, as he was setting out for the theatre, to attend the first night of Reynaldo Hahn's musical version of *Le Mariage de Loti*, now billed as *L'Ile du Rêve – idylle polynésienne en trois actes*. At the theatre he joined Queen Natalie in her box, beside Madame Adam and other friends, but he could hardly restrain his tears. The curtain rose on Act I, *A tropic scene, at the foot of the cascade of Fatahua*, where the vahinés sang in chorus, undulating round two young officers – operatic tenors representing himself and Joseph Bernard – and wearing that uniform which he must no longer wear. It was too much to bear, and he left the box, to wander miserably about the streets. But civility demanded his return: the Queen, the company, and the composer, all expected it of him. He took his place at the back of the box as the curtain rose on the last act.

'Loti! Loti!' called the soprano in the cardboard glades, and Loti heard again Rarahu calling to him across the years . . . 'Then I shut my eyes to see myself once more – oh! to see again – with what inexpressible sadness – the true scene . . . over there, across how many seas, far far away in the depth of time past . . . and it was as if under layer upon layer of ashes I found again the faces, the scents and that marvellous intoxication of my youth, in that vanished midnight, among the orange trees, under the southern stars . . .' It was his lost youth for which he wept, that youth he had passed at sea.

The sea! Was it possible that he was to be exiled from that other planet – that 'great circle of blue' he loved passionately? He had never set great store by advancement as such, forfeiting the rapid promotion which followed on a certain number of years at sea for those shore posts which kept him near his mother: but he was, nevertheless, a very experienced officer who had sailed across the world and doubled the Cape twice in those great three-masted sailing ships which were his early training: he knew his work thoroughly, and once at sea became, in his own words, his true self. It had seemed certain he would ultimately rise to Admiral's rank, an illustrious grey-headed figure whose writings set him a little apart, since they honoured the navy – 'la Royale' – and its men as no other French author had yet done. Now all was destroyed by an impersonal edict which stated he had not served the requisite number of years at sea! As with his Moslem life, his life afloat had been sacrificed to his mother: it was a bitter thought, made more bitter by the emptiness of life without her.

The decree was to come into force almost at once, and Lieutenant-Commander Viaud went about Rochefort raging, wearing his uniform to the last and taking a savage pleasure in receiving the salutes of every passing rating. He decided to appeal and take his case to the highest courts if necessary, and this he did, generously paying all the legal fees for a dozen fellow officers, also axed but unable to meet the costs of an appeal. Their battle was fought inch by inch, till it reached the Conseil d'Etat, where, in a labyrinth of naval administration and legal terms, it was proved that *le Sieur Viaud, dit Pierre Loti, Lieutenant de Vaisseau en retraite, membre de l'Académie Française, demeurant à Rochefort*, was, in view of certain rulings, and in consideration of this and that Code, together with his uncontested qualifications for service at sea, now entitled to demand reinstatement. Thus, in March 1890 the former decree was annulled for Loti, and his fellow officers too.

However, before that battle was won, there had been a year of premature retirement; for Loti a year of despair, fluctuating between Hendaye, Rochefort and Paris, where he harassed lawyers and influential persons in the Government to reverse the decree. His uniforms were stored away as precious relics, embalmed in moth balls, objects of fetish worship. All his longings for yesterday were lavished on reminders of his life at sea. If he played the piano, seated in the gallery above the lofty Renaissance hall, he nevertheless continued to play from those miniature scores of Bach or Chopin such as he had been accustomed to take to sea, where every inch of space counted. His publishers, aware of the publicity Loti's retirement had roused, now rushed out a second edition of *Matelot*, so that it seemed his supreme salute to that naval life which was no longer his.

16

Des villes, encore des villes: j'ai des souvenirs
des villes comme on a des souvenirs d'amour.

Valéry Larbaud

During Loti's traumatic period of retirement from the navy, he followed the classic pattern of all unhappy romantics and sought forgetfulness in travel; and like most romantics, he turned towards the sun. When Loti's friends in high places, disturbed by his melancholy, arranged that he should undertake a special mission to India, to present some Order of distinction to the Maharajah of Travancore, he accepted with alacrity. It tied in with his intention of visiting Persia, and it could also put to the test some nebulous notions he was then forming on the question of the Vedic teachings. For some while Blanche had been studying this subject, no doubt seeking the detachment it taught to help her in the turmoil of life beside Loti. At last this ill-assorted couple had found a point of common interest in theosophist doctrines, so that Loti decided to visit Mrs Annie Besant and her disciples, as well as other sages whose headquarters were spread about India. From these two journeys across India and Persia came his books *L'Inde sans les Anglais*, published in 1903, and *Vers Ispahan*, published a year later.

The Indian book emphasized Loti's dislike of England: *'India without the English'* was eloquent of his attitude to British Imperialism, something which so nettled him that he devised an ingenuously zig-zag route about the sub-continent, going from one native ruler to the next, avoiding territories most blatantly Anglicized by the civil or military administrators and their mem-sahibs. In a further flush of Anglophobia he was to dedicate his Indian book to President Kruger, for like many others, he saw the Boer War as an unpardonable example of British colonial aggression, and every Boer a hero, defending his homeland against overwhelming odds.

Loti's life as a traveller had now shifted permanently to another key. There was to be no more of the old loving, leaving and grieving. The Indian journey, the subsequent one across Persia, and a later pilgrimage to Angkor Vat which had beckoned him since childhood, were in the nature of sightseeing. He had planned to go first to Afghanistan, its almost unknown, wild beauty being the quintessential Central Asia; but there seemed no way of penetrating its cut-throat frontier gorges. The long record of fierce tribal opposition to the passage of foreigners, from the British Army, slaughtered to a man in 1842, to the more recent murder of Sir Louis Cavagnari and his Mission, discouraged visitors. Since any nation which repulsed attempts at colonization always won Loti's sympathy, he even turned to Cook's Travel Agency for aid: but Cook's were categoric. Quite impossible. Under no circumstances. For no money. Perhaps they had heard of the Afghan saying: *there is no arbiter but the Afghan knife.*

The journeys Loti made at this time were brief excursions by comparison to those made by certain Asian travellers. He was well aware of this, but held that the first impressions of an experienced traveller could have a real value. 'There are various ways of describing remote countries: first, profound and detailed studies such as those which are written by people who have lived long in the places they describe. Then there are rapid notes – shorthand impressions by a passing traveller, first impressions that fade quickly, that must be noted at once, because a little while later one doesn't note them. Certain aspects of countries new to one strike one at first sight, by contrast to others which, after several days one no longer remarks. Later still, it seems idle to speak of them at all. Which is why journeys at speed are not a bad thing. When one has already travelled about the world, one becomes used to forming a snap judgement of a whole land. A jumble of things seen in a few hours can produce an ensemble – a sketch traced in broad lines, but often exact.'

He set out in November 1899 with no precise date for his return. A return to what? To life as a retired naval officer, Blanche's husband, Samuel's father, and an Academician? As he wrote to Madame Adam: 'What does it matter, now, how long I stay away, since on my return I shall never again find Her awaiting me?' His mother was no more, nor his life in the navy, and it was in this mood of profound indifference that he sailed east.

He was to divide this journey into three sections: the India of palms and jungles; the India of famines and palaces, and the India of the sages. He landed in Ceylon, as guest of the Maharaja, first of those rulers who were to make his travels a privileged progress. At Travancore the gesture of hospitality which most delighted him was the Maharaja's invitation to visit his model college for noble young ladies. Education was dear to the Maharaja's heart – Western education for women a daring innovation which he was proud to show his distinguished visitor. To make the visit even more of an occasion he had ordered the little pupils to be adorned with the most magnificent jewels from the family coffers. All the treasures of their parents and ancestors were to be worn. Thus Loti entered a scintillating scene, where, before blackboards and maps the small pupils seated at their desks were like so many idols, bowed down by fabulous stomachers of rubies, cascades of diamonds and emeralds, their puny little arms emerging like matchsticks from massive bracelets.

Exploring the ancient palace of the Cochin rajas, long abandoned, he found frescoes of the most stupefying order . . . 'an art quite unique, exuberant, prodigious . . . A mass of nudity, rendered with minute regard for anatomy . . . yet with an exaggeration of Indian canons of beauty . . . waists too narrow, breasts too full . . . a multiple confusion of arms and heavy thighs; backs that bent, breasts that swelled, wrists and ankles braceleted, heads with tiaras, and throats with necklaces . . . Wild animals too, enlaced in this debauch of copper muscles . . . a nightmare of human and animal flesh . . . lascivious beyond measure; goddesses, men, animals, monkeys, bears, gazelles . . . all in voluptuous convulsions, delirious-eyed, enlaced and embracing in paroxysms of coupling'.

Today the erotica of India has become familiar, the camera recording every posture faithfully in those sumptuous editions with an intellectualized text which flood the market. But in Loti's day this was not so, and his descriptions of the frescoes came as a shock to many of his readers.

After a few days in the old French city of Pondicherry he turned north, making for Hyderabad, where once again a ruling prince, the Nizam, was to be his host. This was the second phase of his journey; the India of famine or luxury, of desert lands where the maharajas and raos still ruled from their fabulous marble palaces, in medieval splendour. The ebb and flow of the population was a constant

244

everchanging spectacle, 'Towards sunset', Loti noted, 'persons who seemed to belong to *The Thousand and One Nights* appeared about the streets; they were elegant figures, their eyes painted blue, their beards dyed vermilion, their robes of brocade or velvet shimmering with gold; all were hung with precious stones, and tame hawks were perched on their wrists.' These were the Nizam's courtiers, and very much to Loti's taste for this was Moslem India.

From Hyderabad he reached Rajputana (today known as Rajasthan). There it was as if colour and light reached an undreamed-of intensity, by which the rest of India seemed almost faded. Loti is at his most evocative in Rajput India, going from one kingdom to the next, wandering about the rose-red city of Jaipur, with its white oxen garlanded with marigolds, its jewel bazaar, and the extraordinary medieval observatory, with its strange instruments wrought in stone. Bundi, Amber, Gwalior, Ajmer . . . all enchantments were met in Rajput India.

Let us follow him to Udaipur, the quintessential Rajput kingdom, where famine was less in evidence. The ruler bore the title of Maharana, and took precedence over all the other Rajput kings, for he was held to descend from the Sun, no less, and was sometimes addressed as Sun of the Hindus. He too was Loti's host, placing his palace, servitors, horses and State barges at his guest's disposal. Loti was conducted about this loveliest of Indian cities, visiting the little white marble palaces, which emerge from the lake like delicious confectionery, or exploring the surrounding country, with its Brahmin and Jaïn temples. At sunset he was rowed across Lake Picchola, under clouds of green parakeets flying homeward to roost on the far shore where woods grew to the water's edge and troops of peacocks rustled in the dry undergrowth. This was the hour when the wild boar gathered round an abandoned hunting lodge to be fed maize, a royal tradition. One evening, three handsome young fakirs whom Loti had observed before were seated there in immobility. Now one broke his hieratical pose, produced a little mirror, white powder and a red pigment; he re-whitened his face, and carefully repainted the scarlet sign of Siva on his brow . . . 'But there is no-one here,' writes Loti, 'only the doves and the peacocks . . . In whose honour is this twilight toilette?'

At that moment there was the sound of horses approaching – a galloping cavalcade. 'It was the King. He passed with thirty or more personages of his Court; the beautiful horses were harnessed in a thousand colours, but the riders were in white, their long robes moulded to their slim bodies. Their beards and moustaches were brushed upwards, in the fashion of Udaipur, which gave a whiskered, cat-like air to their cameo-cut features of palest bronze, extremely delicate, yet very virile. And the king galloping at the head of his escort also had that cat-like retroussé beard, his whole allure one of perfect beauty and distinction.' The riders swept past and vanished among the shadowy trees like some fleeting apparition of medieval splendour, leaving Loti and the fakirs alone in the darkening twilight.

Loti left the brilliant Rajput Kingdoms for Madras, where he sought a circle of Hindu mystics, and lugubrious company he found them. For such a character as he, the impersonality of their doctrines was chilling. 'An anonymous Deity, a collective immortality without any personal soul, a purification without prayer . . . I had come here as my last hope, and that was all they offered me. "Prayer?" they said – "and who is there to hear it? Man stands alone in the face of his responsibilities . . . Man is born alone, lives alone, and dies alone. To whom do you pray, since you yourself are God?"

'A silence fell over the room, and it seemed as if I caught the almost imperceptible sound of something falling into the void . . . my last vague beliefs.'

Timidly, Loti asked to be directed to one of those transcendental fakirs who could work miracles. ' "Fakirs? There are no more of such," the Hindu replied coldly, and his condemnation destroyed my last hopes of some marvel left on earth. "But at Benares?" Loti persisted. "I had hoped . . . I had heard . . ."

"Fakirs, those begging fakirs, either drugged or contortionists; they are everywhere . . . you can find them without our aid," he was told. "The true fakirs, those with real powers, did exist once, but they are gone with the century that has just passed. The ancient fakir spirit of India is dead. We are a race which is declining on contact with the more materialistic races of the West – and they in turn will also decline . . . it is the law." '

As once before at the grim Trappist monastery, Loti found no solace. 'I need the continuation of my self, my being, integral, intense, aware and separate, capable of finding once more those I have loved to love them as before . . . Without that – à quoi bon?'

Loti's Indian journeys ended at Benares when he sought out a group of theosophists suggested by the sages of Madras. Mrs Annie Besant, the English mystic, occupied a considerable place among them, and Loti hoped that through another European he might come closer to understanding their precepts. He found her in a simple white-walled house surrounded by a small garden. Her companions were gravely benign figures, 'as if bronze, black-haired Christs', and Loti noted they appeared to be remote, already removed to another, astral plane. Mrs Besant was a charming white-haired woman without any pretension, bare-footed and dressed in white robes, living as frugally as a peasant and as austerely as an ascetic, but she welcomed him with understanding. Loti asked her to outline their dogmas.

'Our dogmas? But we don't have any,' she told him. 'Among the theosophists you will find Buddhists, Brahmins, Moslems, Protestants, Catholics and Orthodox, and people like yourself.' The essential oath which admitted him to this company was simple . . . *to consider all mankind as his brothers, and above all, to seek truth in the most anti-materialistic sense.* The theosophists believed that all human individuality was ephemeral, almost illusory. Mrs Besant read Loti clearly from the start. 'For someone as intensely individual as you,' she told him, 'this is a very difficult point. Do not blame us if we succeed in destroying those unconscious hopes by which, perhaps, in spite of yourself, you are still sustained.' Loti told her that he had no more hopes to lose; and so was invited to join them.

He studied diligently, he questioned, he listened, he meditated, but it was still a losing struggle.

All the while, beyond the little white house of renunciations, lay the extraordinary, magnetic spectacle of Benares, 'at once mystic and sensual, where a whole people think only of prayer and death; yet all around are the seductions of the senses, light, colour, half-naked women, languorous, yet ardent – O! those Indian eyes, so indescribably alluring.' Did he still seek some Hindu Aziyadé, or in the street of the harlots appraise the women there, hoping to recapture something of those raptures he had first known with the Tzigane?

All streets in Benares, sacred or profane, led to the Ganges, to those long flights of steps that plunged down to its holy waters where the débris of corpses flung from the burning ghats drifted down stream among the votive garlands, the flowers and the filth, and where the seekers after faith bathed, washing away their sins. That too was an expression of faith.

'How little wood is needed to burn a body,' Loti noted, standing among the funeral pyres that smoked and flamed around him. The body of a young and lovely woman was carried past, her transparent rose-coloured sari clinging to her body, and Loti felt it a profanation to see her there. He was still too aware of the flesh for the immaterial doctrines he pursued, and turned away; but later watched the flames finishing their work . . . only one foot remained, protruding grotesquely from the bier, silhouetted against the flames. Close by, a small boy's body burned fitfully, for there was too little wood on this pyre, and it was damp. 'Poor folk – they can't afford better,' Loti's boatman remarked. Loti saw no horror of death among these people, no scenes of grief. The ritual holocaust continued, and on the nearby pyre, the dead woman's charred foot fell at last into the ashes.

Soon Loti must leave the East, but although he had not found the spiritual path he had sought among the sages, something of their teachings had reached him. 'Everything is changing for me. Life and even death assume a new aspect. It seems that my being, my individuality begins to merge, in the great universal soul . . .' He ends his Indian book by telling his readers that what he has learned from the sages in the little house of renunciation is not for the telling – certainly not by such a novice as he.

Loti's all-seeing eyes were now to range over Persia, the Turquoise Kingdom – 'this debauch of blue' – where the gamut of turquoise, lapis and peacock reached its apotheosis in the decoration of mosque and palace. He had decided to return to France by land, across Persia, rather than by boat from an Indian port, and so, having crossed the Arabian Sea to Muscat, landed at Bendir-Bouchir (Bushire) on the Persian Gulf. There he set about engaging horses and pack mules and an escort for the long road to Isfahan. This fabled city was his main reason for undertaking the journey. His imagination had long been fired by earlier travellers' accounts of its beauty. Other cities and historic sites, Shiraz of the poets, Persepolis and its mighty ruins from where Cyrus ruled his vast empire, or most holy golden Qum, were of less account. Isfahan was his lodestar. All its poetry and his longings sound in the opening pages of his book *Vers Ispahan* and if I venture to quote it here, in translation, I am well aware how little of its music survives the change. Nevertheless, it is Loti the traveller at his most seducing. This is how he casts his spell.

'Who comes with me to Isfahan in the season of roses must ride by slow stages, as in olden days. Who comes with me to Isfahan at the season of roses must accept the perils of evil paths where horses stumble, must sleep in caravanserais, crouched in a niche of beaten earth, among the flies and vermin . . . Who comes with me towards some lost oasis in fields of white poppies and gardens of pink roses, will find an old town of ruins and mystery, its blue domes and minarets of changeless azure . . . Who comes with me to Isfahan under the radiant skies of May must brave long marches under burning suns, and the bitter winds of icy altitudes; must cross the vast plateaux of Asia, highest in all the world, once the cradle of humanity but desert now . . . Who follows me must know many days amid such solitudes . . .'

Who would not follow Loti there? In the hotels and bookshops of Iran, new editions of *Vers Ispahan* have always taken pride of place among the latest travel books and guides for the region. It is less personal than much of his writing, and there are few social interludes nor any spiritual yearnings, as in India. The sages of Benares had calmed him temporarily and none of the veiled women, cypher figures in their long dark chadors and white eye-holed masks, aroused more than his passing curiosity. A certain note of disillusion sounds, even a curious lack of involvement. Everywhere, he was conquered by Persia's beauty, but was that enough? *'Never yet in the House of Islam have I felt myself so much a stranger, so much alone,'* he wrote. Persians are a complicated people, even the simplest have a sophisticated or convoluted approach; there was none of that outgoing warmth found among other Moslem races.

Loti travelled in style with a cook, servants, armed guards and pack mules in the practical style of a seasoned traveller prepared to face the roughest tracks. They followed the immemorial rhythm of the road, and each torrid noon found them sheltering in some scant grove of trees or the narrow shade of a rock gully. Then carpets were spread, the kalyan (or Persian water-pipe) passed round with little glasses of very sweet tea, the customary refreshment. So they made their way, going ever higher, to the vast plateaux surrounding Shiraz.

'Shiraz, the country of Saadi and roses! We entered it at night, no sounds, no lights, no passers-by.'

Loti installed himself in one of the ramshackle old houses, once elegant but now decayed, which were let as lodgings for passing travellers. Such houses were completely bare, the travellers bringing all they needed with them. Loti's servants unloaded the pack mules and furnished it within minutes. Rugs were spread, hangings nailed to the walls, which were further embellished by the splendid old weapons Loti had collected en route. A brazier glowed, the kalyan bubbled. 'I told myself "I am at Shiraz!"' and there was magic in repeating those words. But when the servants left – Loti heard them turning the huge locks behind them – an uneasy silence closed round him oppressively. He was aware of some menace in the air. 'I felt myself among desolate ruins rather than in a town of sixty-thousand inhabitants . . .' Suddenly Loti the life-long traveller knew something akin to panic, something he had never experienced elsewhere.

'May 12. At last almost in sight of Isfahan.' Loti had left Shiraz ten days earlier, and ridden northwards again crossing the high plateaux, their harshness only softened occasionally by villages where a line of poplars marked a small stream. Now they were within reach of the turquoise opulence that had been Shah Abbas' capital. 'Another hour crossing a sinister little desert of brownish clay . . . and then, with the effect of a curtain rising on a scene at the theatre, two bare hills opened before us, slowly revealing an Eden, lying beyond. First, fields of large white flowers, which after the arid desert, dazzled like snow. Next, a mass of trees, poplars, willows, cyprus and plantains, from which emerged all the blue domes and minarets of Isfahan! . . . It was as entrancing as some ancient Oriental tale.

'Roses everywhere. The little merchants of tea or cakes had roses adorning their wares, or pinned to their belts; each flea-bitten beggar crouched under the arches was fingering and tormenting a rose.' The roads were bordered by roses blooming exuberantly, their petals shed over the ground, so that Loti seemed to move in a rosy dream. But on reaching the centre of the town, the rosy dream faded, for no lodgings could be found. Wherever they knocked the doors remained fast, and even the caravanserais proved inhospitable. At last a foxy-looking individual whispered furtively that he knew of a gentleman who was in pecuniary difficulties, and prepared to let his house – at a price. Loti was led through ruined quarters till they reached a worm-eaten doorway that had an air of opening on to a cemetery – but which revealed a paradise.

'O! perfect dwelling!' Loti gloats. 'A garden, or rather, a nest of roses climbing everywhere, as tall as trees. At one end, a little palace from *The Thousand and One Nights*, with its row of delicate columns in the ancient Persian style inspired by Achemenian architecture. The interior is pure Orient; a faded ivory picked out with tarnished gilding, the ceilings, a mosaic of mirror fragments, give a subdued glitter: beside those ornaments customary in every Persian palace, clusters of mirrored stalactites massed like honey-combs. Divans covered in silk patterned with rose-coloured flames, cushions and carpets from Kerman or Shiraz . . . beyond, arches giving on to shadowy depths . . . And all of it steeped in the charm of antiquity, mystery and adventure . . . Over all, the scent of roses merged with an indefinable essence as from some harem, with which the hangings are impregnated.' All Loti's romantic visions of Isfahan were realized here. O rapture! O rare and vanished beauty! O reader! (and this is the moment to catch his exclamatory style) I too have known such old houses in Iran . . . where are they now?

Loti lived a brief interlude of European comfort in an Oriental framework while staying with Prince Dabidja, the Russian Consul in Isfahan. The population, his host told him, were hostile to strangers. Although he was under the protection of the Russian flag (then of enormous power and prestige in Persia) it was advisable that wherever he went, he should be accompanied by an escort. Thus he explored the Turquoise city pompously. 'Two armed soldiers led the way, and behind, a gold-braided Cossack, in the Prince's livery.' It was reassuring, but not something be enjoyed. When as usual he joined the people, sitting in their *tchai-khanas* under the trees, his guard of honour was an embarrassment. 'I was served my tea scornfully, and the kalyan was refused me . . . Nothing for it but to walk on, since the delicious idling of the Mussulmen was denied me here. Never in the House of Islam have I felt myself so much a stranger . . .'

Loti's last evocation of Isfahan describes a strange ceremony, the Nagareh-Khaneh or custom of saluting the rising and setting sun (something now only continued at the holy city of Mashad). He took up his position in the Maidan, a vast open space before the royal mosque. 'At the moment when the Mosque of the Shah, so blue by day, became for one magic moment an intense violet under the last rays of the setting sun, an orchestra appeared on a loggia above the big doors beside the Sheik Lotfollah mosque. There were monstrous drums and long trumpets for this thousand-year-old salutation which is still offered to the sun at the precise moment that it dies. As its rays vanish the music bursts out, sudden and savage, great cavernous roarings, which thunder across the Maïdan, now almost deserted, except for a few crouched camel caravans. Then the trumpets sound, like the bellowing of some wild creature baying at the fading daylight . . . And tomorrow morning the musicians will climb to the same loggia, to sound their terrible salutation to the rising sun.'

On his last night in Isfahan Loti went once again to marvel at the great mosque of the Shah. Starlight glittered over its turquoise and lapis inlays 'which continued to remain blue, when all other colours on earth were dimmed'. It was his last sight of that 'debauch of blueness' which was his summing up of Isfahan.

He reached Teheran, the unlovely Qadjar capital, by way of Qum, whose golden domes seemed faded, for all was an anticlimax after Isfahan. Teheran was then still a come-by-chance city of mud walls and unpaved ways, and he left it without regrets. From a Caspian port he reached Baku, and crossed the Caucasus to reach Tiflis and Europe. Alas! he tells us nothing of his brief Caucasian journey, or his impressions of Russian ports. He had gone towards Isfahan; he had reached it, and all the rest was mere mileage to him.

17

*I have seen the evening star rise over the
mysterious ruins of Angkor . . . The cycle of
my life closes.*

Pierre Loti

Loti arrived home early in July, and after the Persian *débauche de bleu*
it seemed a sepia scene. The old house remained an empty shell
without his mother's presence, and domesticity was as stultifying as
ever. Not that he had long to fret, for barely a month later the
pendulum pattern of life – now east, now west – swung him again to
far horizons. This time it was to China. By the decision of the Conseil
d'Etat, he was reinstated and appointed first aide-de-camp to Vice-
Admiral Pottier, which might be seen as the Admiralty's *amende
honorable* for the premature axing Loti had fought so tenaciously.
Admiral Pottier was then commanding the French fleet in the gulf of
Pechili, in the China Seas, and bombarding the forts at Taku,
preparatory to landings of a huge international force converging
there to crush the Boxer rebellion. Loti was overjoyed. To be once
more among his comrades! To serve at sea! 'I have become twenty
years younger,' he told Madame Adam, writing to thank her for
having been on the quay to wave him god-speed when he sailed east
on the *Redoutable*. His journals make no mention of Blanche at this
rapturous moment of departure.

For some months the Boxer rebellion had spread terror about the
Chinese provinces, and now had taken hold in the Imperial City,
where the European colony and numbers of native Christian con-
verts were under siege in the Legation quarter. It was to rescue them
from the unspeakable horrors which would befall them at the hands
of the Boxers, and no doubt also to safeguard commercial interests,
that the allied European forces had decided on concerted action.
When Loti sailed east he knew something of the Boxer menace; for
all Europe was aware of the drama being played out in Peking, and
the newspapers were dwelling in blood-curdling detail on the
massacres, looting, rape and tortures practised by the Boxers, but

throughout the long slow voyage out, he knew nothing of what was actually happening in China; it was only on entering the Yellow Sea that he learned Peking had fallen. Overnight, the jealously guarded, impenetrable places of this most exquisite, wealthy and civilized of ancient cities, lay open to the conquerors. Their flags floated above the curved and painted eaves of lacquered temples, now turned depots for supplies or shelter for men and horses. All around, blackened ruins; over all, the pestiferous odour of still unburied bodies and the decaying carcases of animals. Even so, there were still some strangely pleasant sounds which remained, sounds eternally Chinese, of gongs and bells and the tinkling of little cascades of glass still stirring frivolously.

Such was the scene which awaited Loti when he left Taku in early September and headed north, carrying despatches for the French Minister in Peking, with orders to report on the situation en route. Could any writer ask for a more fabulous assignment? He set about noting his own impressions apart from the official reports, and it is his unofficial notes which make up one of his best, least-known books, *Les Derniers Jours de Pékin*. Here straight reporting overcomes his tendency to sentimentalize or place a romantic vision of himself in the foreground; and there is no Chinese Madame Butterfly.

Loti reached Peking on horseback, by an interminable dusty track. Crossing a low dune, he suddenly saw, rising before him, a terrifying wall of superhuman proportions . . . 'the walls of Peking crushed us. This densely dark mass appeared Babylonian in the gloomy, glacial autumn light.' As they entered the ruined Celestial City all Loti's preconceived dreams of its beauties fell around him. Everywhere, desolation and hostility. In the sacked city, temples, palaces, alleyways, gardens, tombs and more palaces were all deserted. The Chinese City, the Tartar City, the Yellow or Imperial City, with its Great Within containing the Violet City, were each a mysterious complex enclosing another: outer, inner, and forbidden city, box within box, park enclosing park, a vast Chinese puzzle. Over all, dust clouds swirled ceaselessly, blown in from the Mongolian deserts on demoniacal winds against which even the great ramparts were no protection. On all sides, Loti heard first-hand accounts of the horrors the Europeans had known, decapitations at every street corner, the shrieks of victims disembowelled by the hideously grinning Boxers, plague, and at last the terrors of a Chinese army and mob closing in for the kill. Boxer bandits still infested the surrounding countryside, and sporadic fighting continued, while the occupying European forces had, in the classic manner, been given over to a period of reprisals and looting, before an uneasy order was established.

In recognition of his distinction as both the Admiral's emissary and a leading French writer, Loti was given quarters in the Summer Palace, on the hillside of the Ten Thousand Ancients. This unexpected good fortune intoxicated him. Everywhere, he saw unimaginable luxury: but these halls of splendour were unheated. Seated at a superbly carved ebony table Loti and his companion and guide, a French army officer, turned up the collars of their greatcoats, and served by shivering orderlies, ate army rations off a priceless service of yellow Imperial porcelain, marked with the *chiffre* of an Emperor who was the contemporary of Louis XIV – 'but our ration of wine was stoppered by a chunk of raw potato, the room lit only by a half-burned candle found among the débris of some ancestor's altar.' Loti shivered through the night in a huge Imperial bed of sculptured ebony, 'my mattress and pillows of precious silks woven with gold. No sheets, my only covering a grey army blanket.'

In part of the palace reserved for the Dowager Empress, Loti was astonished to find a Gothic-styled church with a granite belfry, presbytery and school attached. This unlikely complex had been originally built by the Jesuits, but was now a store-house where Her Majesty had amassed a vast accumulation of treasures. This agglomeration of ivories, porcelains, furniture, paintings and State offerings was now in process of being unpacked and catalogued by the allied armies, who no doubt were able to help themselves discreetly. The German command openly took away the massive bronze astronomical instruments of the oldest observatory in the world, founded by Kublai Khan, and installed them at Potsdam, though later they were obliged to return them. Loti was less ambitious but acquired some splendid Imperial treasures which were to adorn his Chinese pavilion at Rochefort.

It took a number of authorisations, countersigned and countersigned again, before Loti overcame the cunning and reluctance of the remaining Imperial eunuchs who, as guardians, still occupied the secret heart of the palace labyrinth which he was determined to visit. '. . . Room after room in this remote, colossal Versailles, was now invaded by rank cemetery weeds, and all was silent save for the croaking of crows. In the golden throne rooms, the sumptuous carpets were covered with bird droppings.' At last, beyond these gloomy *enfilades*, led by trotting eunuchs, Loti reached his objective and, sacrilege of sacrileges, set foot in the apartments of the Son of Heaven, 'small, shadowy rooms made darker by the ebony furniture. There was a piano which the young Emperor had learned to play, in spite of his long fragile nails, and a musical box that ground out popular Chinese tunes . . . His bedroom was as narrow and low-ceilinged as a ship's cabin, and still smelt faintly of dried roses and tea . . . The alcoved bed with its dark, night-blue coverings still bore the imprint of its owner, this Son of Heaven who had fled from his triple-walled, most secret retreat, where generations of ancestors had lived inaccessibly.'

Unlike Loti's other sojourns in remote lands, he did not strike up any friendships among the Chinese during his year in the country. He was not drawn to the yellow races and he seems to have felt a real repugnance here, though no doubt the moment was not propitious to communication. He foresaw the Yellow Peril clearly: 'My God! The day that China, in place of all these little regiments of mercenaries or bandits, rises en masse for a supreme revolt, all these myriad young peasants such as I have seen, sober and lean and muscled . . . what a terrifying force will be there if our modern methods of destruction fall into their hands.'

On almost his last night in the Celestial City Loti attended the celebrated ball given by the French and organized by Colonel Marchand (of the Fashoda Incident, which, three years earlier, had provoked grave international tension between France, England and Egypt). The ball was held in the Great Within, its purpose being to stress the return to order and the reinstatement of the Imperial fugitives and their Ministers. The entire European colony, survivors of the siege, the Allied officers and two Jesuit priests in violet robes were present, as were the Imperial princes and highest Chinese dignitaries, in full splendour. It must have been an ordeal for them, mixing with their barbarian invaders in this sacrosanct setting: 'One of the most singular incoherencies of our time', Loti describes the evening. In his speech Colonel Marchand dwelt on the pacific rôle of the occupying armies, who had only come there 'to liberate Peking from Boxer persecutions'. Trading concessions were not mentioned: it saved everyone's face. The Emperor's Representative Extraordinary returned the ball with supple Asiatic ease. He was known to have been a fervent supporter of the Boxers but now bowed suavely, his face inscrutable, as he thanked the Europeans for coming to the aid of his Government in what he described as the gravest crisis his country had ever known.

After a number of toasts were drunk in champagne or rice wine, this phantasmagoric celebration continued around the deserted pagodas and kiosks of the Summer Palace, which that night were lit by a thousand lanterns. The Chinese dignitaries had discreetly withdrawn, but the European guests danced or were rowed about the ornamental waters of the lake in barques belonging to the Empress and her ladies. Loti watched them gliding across those same waters where in winter he had so often seen mutilated bodies floating among the water-lilies. 'They were still there, but they had, by now, achieved their slow descent into the mud,' he noted. In the small hours, Loti and the Colonel walked back to their quarters together. They spoke little. Each knew that the ball had, in essence, marked the irrevocable disappearance of a whole world. Whatever would follow, the legendary Celestial Court would never be the same, 'its prestige gone, its mystery unveiled. This Imperial City represented a last refuge of the unknown and the marvellous; it was one of the remaining bastions of ancient humanity, as incomprehensible to us as it was fabulous.'

When Loti rejoined the *Redoutable* at Taku it was to find the French fleet on the move. They had been in Chinese waters for over a year, and the climate was telling on the men; they sailed for a restorative period in Japanese waters, anchoring at Nagasaki. Loti found it as petty as before, but soothing. Indeed it hardly seemed Asiatic after the harshness of China. He revisited his old haunts, finding again many of his old friends, and from this excursion into the past which did not revive well, came *Japoneries d'Automne* and *La troisième jeunesse de Madame Prune*. Both these books have a fragile charm for the reader who is prepared to saunter beside Loti as he evokes a vanished Japan, but he was soon satiated with those autumnal evocations, and applied for leave to visit Angkor Vat. The mysterious temples deep in their jungles had fired his imagination since he first read of them as a child. Angkor Vat! Angkor Thom! Even then he had known, by that strange prescience which never misled him, that one day he would reach the mysterious Khmer ruins tangled in steamy forests. For the child, those pictures of strangely shaped towers, of mythological gods and beasts rising above seas of tropic vegetation, had represented the quintessential '*ailleurs*'. This was the final goal to which, one day, his travels would lead him. How, the child did not know, but certainty lay in those yellowing pages over which he pored.

Forty years later in November 1901 the man set out from Saïgon, making for Phnom-Penh, the Cambodian capital of what was then French Indo-China. The Governor General, Paul Doumer, was an old friend and smoothed his path. And so the longing child who still stirred in the world-weary man of letters, the Academician, traveller, and ADC to the Admiral, at last realized this cherished dream. The marvellous stone tiara-towers which rose from the devouring jungle seemed familiar . . . 'At last, then, I behold it, this mysterious Angkor; yet I am scarcely moved. It has come too late in my life, and then, I have known so many historic remains. Too many temples, too many palaces, too many ruins . . . Angkor Vat! Here is the sanctuary which obsessed my childish imagination, the sanctuary which I have reached after so many wanderings, as night begins to fall over my vagrant life. Angkor Vat! And it can only offer a dismal welcome. Torrents of rain, and an enforced refuge among spiders' webs, and the excrement of innumerable bats, which foul the statues of phantom gods . . .'

In spite of his disillusionment he explored the fabled site conscientiously, and his descriptions, published as *Un Pèlerin d'Angkor*, are scrupulously unbiased. On leaving, as he plunged into the surrounding forests he turned to take a last look. 'This pilgrimage which I had promised myself in my childhood was at last realized. Already it belongs to the past . . . Never again shall I see those strange towers rising into the sky. Even as I look back the forest hides them from me.' Illusion, reality, and disillusion; an elegiac melancholy pervades *Un Pèlerin d'Angkor*. It is Loti's farewell to the Far East, and his last desires . . . 'I have seen the evening star rise over the mysterious ruins of Angkor . . . The cycle of my life closes . . .'

18

*Un charme dont je ne me défendrai jamais
m'a été jeté par Islam.*

Pierre Loti

Now east, now west. Once more the pendulum pulse swung Loti
back to base at Rochefort and a post at the Préfecture de la Marine.
His duties were tedious, but kept him in touch with naval life. 'I
could have had no other,' he would reiterate. For the next eighteen
months he was also preparing the books he was to publish on his Far
Eastern travels, as well as devising a Chinese salon and pagoda, all
scarlet lacquer, porcelains and treasures brought back from the Far
East, while acclimatizing several corpulent Japanese toads to life in
the garden, beside the cats and Suliëma the tortoise, now doyenne of
the menagerie. After Gaspard, the mongrel dog he had loved and lost
in childhood, there were no more dogs. Loti had small feeling for
them beside his passion for the cats: the latest, a stray from the Great
Within.

There was little to record in the journals of this moment; only a
slow seeping of time, and the steady monotony of his days, between
domestic life and routine occupations at the Préfecture Maritime.
Rarely he appeared in Paris, for his routine attendance at the
Académie or some exceptional gathering, such as a poetry reading
by Robert de Montesquiou, though Loti disliked poetry as much as
Paris life. *'I am again in your horrifying Paris,'* he wrote to Madame
Adam, then absent from the capital in her château at Gif, from where
she still reigned over a recherché circle of politicians and men of
letters. But Loti wanted none of the capital: however provincial
Rochefort might be, it was his homeland, with the mosque to recall
the Oriental dream. It had now attained perfection by a gradual
accumulation of treasures and that subtle ambiance which four
walls, whether lowly or grandiose, can contain when they are loved.
And Loti had poured his love – both sacred and profane – for Islam
and Aziyadé – into these walls.

259

Many years later when he was asked which was the loveliest of all the mosques he had known, he replied simply – 'my own'. And it is of the greatest beauty, with its glowing red porphyry pillars, its tall graceful Moorish arches, and the fine tracery of stone-work.

Loti now wrote, and slept, and, indeed, lived almost entirely on the far side of the house from the entrance. A fretted mouchrabiyeh screened a small door in the mosque, which opened discreetly into his bedroom, where he also wrote. He had transformed one of the smallest rooms facing across the courtyard, into something as stark and spartan as a ship's cabin – though not the sort of cabin he used to embellish when at sea. In those, in a spirit of contradiction, he had always flaunted his taste for exotic luxury, imposing silk hangings, ancient gilt mirrors and *objets de vertu*: now, ashore, he was at pains to recreate the austerity of a typical cabin with white walls, a brass-bound seaman's trunk, a narrow iron cot, and little else. But one step beyond, on either side, lay all his Turkish and Arab fantasies – the East, gathered round as a bulwark against the West.

Emerging from such retreats must have made daily life seem even more exasperating. When the heavy kelim door-hangings fell behind him and he had turned the key, Europe rose round him again: Europe, domesticity, the family Protestantism, middle age, and a thousand and one tiresome obligations, though Blanche took many of these off his shoulders. Shoals of letters continued to pour in, more each year, from ecstatic readers all over the world; love letters, equally ecstatic; letters from publishers; begging letters, to which his compassion always responded; and threatening letters too. His fame and fortune laid him open to mysterious blackmailers, probably connected with some forgotten episode of his youth. At last a lawyer had to be retained to deal exclusively with these.

Although Loti's generosity was unbounded, he was becoming increasingly impatient of the continued demands on his money and time made by hangers-on and old family friends, more leech-like than ever. He was now living in considerable style: Pierre and Lucien wore smart dark blue, gold-buttoned liveries, while for special occasions they were assisted by white-gloved flunkeys in knee breeches. A series of elaborate receptions kept Rochefort agog, while Loti's passion for authenticity recalled the first medieval junket. There was the Carthaginian evening, *à la Salammbô*, and the Chinese fête, celebrating the completion of the new Pagoda room with the ex-Queen Natalie of Serbia and Madame Adam taking turns to be seated on an ebony throne from the Empress Tzu Hsi's apartments in the Great Within. Loti's superb costume and mandarin make-up, the guests' similar splendours, a chopstick banquet, and a special dim, cushioned salon for opium smokers (which unfortunately became more of a vomitorium, for some beginners) was the talk of *le tout Paris*, who had thronged there to exclaim.

All these extravagances were the envy of Ninette, who aspired to live on the same scale. She generally looked to her indulgent uncle to settle her debts when she was in financial straits, which he did. She basked in the reflected glory of being Loti's niece, but gradually, her demands began to exasperate him. 'Yes,' he had written, after some particularly heavy charge, 'I could give you the money, at the cost of renouncing my next journey. But why should I?'

Nevertheless when, some years later, her husband was sinking into an apathetic colonial exile (alcohol and the climate taking its toll), it was once again Loti who came to the rescue and until he died, in Senegal, was to make him an allowance. Notwithstanding all Loti's endless generosity, there was litigation between uncle and niece, when Ninette sued him over the value of a picture, a Madonna, said to be by Raphael. It was a family inheritance from a distant relative; Loti wanted the picture, and after sordid squabbles Ninette waived her claim in exchange for hard cash. Loti found himself the poorer, for the picture was pronounced a copy, but Ninette had the cash. Such were some of the exasperations and disillusionments which his hard-won fortune brought him. 'Only youth and the sun are worth having,' he would sigh.

Further annoyances came from the nearness of his sister, Marie Bon, and her husband Armand, to whom he had given a house adjoining his own. He had rashly removed an old wall and run the two gardens together, adding a ruined Gothic cloister: but the solemn lichen-covered arches and gargoyle trimmings clashed with the innocent charm of the little provincial garden of his childhood, where Aunt Claire's roses and Gustave's grotto remained. Marie was bigoted and possessive, Loti increasingly overbearing, and their quarrels grew more and more violent, often arising from the most trivial issues. Over the convulsive political scandal caused by the Dreyfus case, which had split the French nation, and many households too, they were irreconcilable. When the whole ugly business was revived, and Dreyfus the Jewish scapegoat brought back from Devil's Isle for retrial, and again unjustly condemned, brother and sister came to blows.

Marie was passionately pro-Dreyfus, Loti passionately anti. In his case, it was not a question of that anti-Jewish prejudice then so prevalent in France; nor was it due to his Islamic sympathies, for many Jews were numbered among his friends; rather he was simply remaining true to his caste. In France, the upper ranks of both army and navy were a closed world. In the navy, the officers of the Grand Cadre de la Marine, the élite to which Loti belonged (as opposed to naval personnel such as doctors, accountants, those who did clerical work or were responsible for supplies) joined forces with the army over the Dreyfus Affair. Patriotism demanded blind loyalty. Had a high-ranking officer really been guilty of selling secrets to Germany? Then better to stifle the scandal and let some scapegoat perish. Such was the view generally held by both Services, though there were dissenters. At Rochefort, furious recriminations between Loti and his sister continued, clouding the last traces of a relationship which had once been so close, and Loti's wife and son, of calmer blood, watched this intemperate pair raging across the dinner table or under the Gothic arches.

Next, Blanche took issue against her husband, for Samuel's education had become a tug of war between them. The boy was no sooner settled with a tutor at Hendaye than he was packed off to school in Switzerland, or brought back and enrolled at a college in Normandy, only to be uprooted and sent to a lycée in Paris. He was to spend his holidays with his mother's family. Certainly not, said Loti. But Blanche, usually so effacing and docile, began to show a most unwelcome obstinacy where anything to do with her son was concerned. The boy adored his mother, who tried to give him the loving warmth he lacked from Loti. Nevertheless Samuel adored his father too. With a sort of timid hero worship he tried to please this unresponsive and remote father, and his loyalties were torn between such ill-assorted parents whose chill lack of intimacy was apparent even to the child, though Loti always showed the greatest courtesy towards Blanche, setting her in the authoritative place once held in the household by his mother. Was she not the wife his mother had chosen for him? Was not his whole married life a living sacrifice laid on the altar of mother-love? Though that was hardly a base on which to build a happy marriage.

Blanche did her best to be conciliatory in most matters, and over questions of her wardrobe, which Loti still liked to supervise, she was obedient, eschewing furs and feathers, the muffs and boas, aigrettes and bird of paradise plumes then à la mode. Loti was opposed to all such adornments on humanitarian grounds. The horrors of the abattoir haunted him, and in *Le Livre de la Pitié et de la Mort*, in a short piece entitled *Viande de Boucherie* – Butcher's Meat – he expressed his horror of man's treatment of animals. He came to live almost entirely on fruit and sour milk concoctions such as yoghourt which recalled the Turkish cuisine. He would have liked to outlaw the organized massacres we know as 'a shoot', the circus of performing animals listed as entertainment, the slaughter-houses that supply our tables, the big-game hunting called sport, and the vivisection we are told is necessary to the development of scientific research. But Loti had no reformer's zeal: he could pity but he could not lead a revolt. For him, sorrow or suffering was something to which he abandoned himself passively.

Apart from the pressures and tedium of family life, there was that second, Basque, family tucked away in the small house at the other end of the town, where Crucita Gainza and Loti's sons by her lived apart, unrecognized by the scandalized citizens of Rochefort. Loti visited them most evenings, and was meticulous in attending to all their financial needs. They were undemanding and scarcely caused a ripple on the surface of his life. But they were Basques – his link with that splendid race, and he mourned the death of the youngest, who had died while still a baby. Blanche had long been aware of their existence and, it will be recalled, had promised her husband that were he to die on one of his faraway journeys she would be responsible for their future. His sister Marie was less accommodating. She could not overlook the fact that Crucita was bringing up the little Gainzas in the Roman Catholic faith. 'Papists! Papist bastards,' she would hiss, rounding on her brother for his indifference: but then he always maintained any faith was better than none, and continued to envy those 'delicious illusions' of Christianity which he could not share.

Blanche had never acquired a carapace of cynicism, such as life married to Loti might have induced, though she had developed an imperturbable dignity, while retaining her earlier simplicity and outward calm. What did she really think of this man, her husband, whom she still loved? What was her life, always remaining on the side? What did she think of his frequent absences, no sooner home than gone away or gone to earth in his mosque, where no-one, except Léo, was ever allowed to enter? How did she view the handsome sailors he frequented, or the women who became his mistresses? Flamboyant sirens such as Madame Catulle Mendés must have grated. She was a particularly striking figure among the more bizarre personalities of literary Paris, wife of the poet, an opulent Jewish beauty with dark, heavily painted eyes, who also emphasized her flaring nostrils by touches of rouge, rather in the manner war horses used to be depicted in scenes of battle. It was a fad of the moment; Sarah Bernhardt too was up to such tricks, and was remarked to flare her nostrils when denoting high passions. The nose was much admired then, and if well shaped, as was Loti's, size was no disadvantage. It was an ample age – large features, bushy eyebrows and heavy moustaches balanced large noses, which did not seem disproportionate when so surrounded.

One way and another, Madame Catulle Mendès caused Loti a lot of trouble. There were those 'furtive' rendezvous, or so she described them, claiming both the conventions and a jealous husband to heighten the drama. Intriguing by nature, she persuaded Loti to leave his original publisher, Calmann-Lévy, for Flammarion (by whom, it was said, she was to be well rewarded for her persuasions). Woolly-headed Loti appears to have overlooked the fact that he was not only bound to Calmann-Lévy by a lifetime of friendship and loyalty, but also by contracts. Why did he even contemplate such a move? No doubt in pique, for he always claimed Calmann-Lévy had exploited him as a young unknown author, and driven very hard bargains: which in fact was true, Tense dramas followed Loti's break, and only the intervention of a devoted naval friend, Commandant Emile Védel, who, like Jousselin-Plumkett of earlier days, took both a literary and personal interest in Loti, saved him from the disaster of a lawsuit he would certainly have lost.

Emile Védel was a striking personality, very tall and handsome, extremely cultivated and one of Loti's intimates, their friendship dating from early voyages together. He shared Loti's liking for the picturesque, and would sometimes appear wearing a flowing cloak, lined with violet silk.

For some while, Védel and Loti had been working together on a translation of *King Lear*, for they considered Shakespeare had not been fairly represented in the French theatre. Their venture interested the producer Antoine, and in January 1903 he arrived at Rochefort for a reading. He has left an account of his visit, and the extraordinary contrasts the old house provided. Two superb menservants in velvet knee-breeches and gold-laced jackets 'which would have done justice to some royal carriage' bowed him into the modest little Louis-Philippe parlour, which remained as it was when the *chères vieilles* knew it. Antoine noted Loti's mocking smile, observing his guest's undisguised astonishment. There were further amusements: the sequence of Chinese, Arab, Louis XVI and Renaissance rooms: and then, the mosque, its haunting beauty dominated by Aziyadé's stele. After a ceremonious dinner in the Renaissance hall, at which Loti only nibbled a few hothouse fruits, they repaired to the Turkish room for Védel's reading of the play. Antoine was at once enthusiastic, and plans for production went ahead, with Debussy promising to compose the music (though later he was regretfully to withdraw his promise). In December 1904, this version of *King Lear* was produced at the Odéon, with many elaborate scenic innovations, and won considerable acclaim, though by that time neither Védel nor Loti was able to be present, Védel being at sea and Loti once more in Turkey.

A feminine streak in Loti's nature always made him crave a confidant to whom he could pour out his problems, hopes and griefs. There were many: Oirda, Madame Adam, Daudet, Jousselin, Louis Barthou, Emile Védel, and a fellow writer, Emile Pouvillon were among those who acted as catalysts for his emotions. In a fit of self-pity he confided to Pouvillon that for some years he had felt dead, that life held nothing more for him. Now a note of resignation crept in, resembling the closing lines of *Un Pélerin d'Angkor* . . . Had he really come to believe the cycle of his life was closing? Pouvillon had said: 'I cannot easily imagine you would be able to live without the intensity of sensations which love alone can give.' But as the years passed Loti felt himself each day more of a faded puppet – he, who had been the demon lover! Where, now, was that pulsating intensity to be found? Who now could give him back his youth? No-one, no-one; the mournful echoes sounded around him, alone in his mosque.

It was to be a cut and dried order from the Ministère de la Marine which gave him three more years of romantic living along the shores of the Bosphorus. He was appointed Naval Attaché to the French Embassy (then situated in Constantinople) and also given command of the *Vautour*, a warship permanently stationed in Turkish waters. Stamboul once more! The Turkish people and that way of life he loved so profoundly! That was a life worth living, romance or no. He left Rochefort without a backward glance. At that moment, international tension centred on the Balkans, a melting pot of small nations still under Turkish rule, their growing agitation for autonomy fomented by the European Powers who wished to see the Sultan's extensive possessions reduced. These spread across North Africa, Egypt, Syria, much of Greece, the Balkans, Bulgaria and Serbia, and had once reached as far as Vienna. Germany had lately been making marked overtures to the Sultan, which prodded France into improving their relations at the Sublime Porte. Thus Loti's stature as a world-renowned writer of strongly pro-Turkish sympathies made him the perfect choice: he would be an unofficial ambassador, having the entrée to all classes of Turks.

The Sultan Abdul Hamid enjoyed setting one foreign power against another as they jockeyed round his throne, and was aware that the pro-French sympathies which Loti's presence in Constantinople would rouse in both harems and Ministries would greatly agitate the Kaiser's ministers. He foresaw some agreeable political intrigues ahead, and instructed that silent army of secret police and informers which he controlled to be at once vigilant and indulgent concerning Loti's official and private life. He was to be persona grata.

Lieutenant-Commander Viaud reached Constantinople to take over his ship in October 1903, and, at once, the salons and boudoirs of European Pera were in a ferment. Pierre Loti, the author of *Aziyadé* and *Fantôme d'Orient*, was in their midst! They would see the great seducer in the flesh – would meet the Enchanter at diplomatic dinner parties . . . they grew dizzy at the prospect. Quite as much emotion agitated the aristocratic Turkish ladies, for although sequestered in their harems, they all knew French and were nourished on Loti's daring descriptions of his stolen idyll. Had he really so loved one of them? . . . Had he . . . ? Had Aziyadé really . . . ? Of course, they wept over her fate, and pined to encounter such a Roumi lover themselves, who would free them from their bondage, and lift their veils. But none of them ever hoped to encounter Loti, for in spite of the growing influence of a European education, they never came face to face with any men beyond their fathers, brothers or husbands.

Presently it was discovered that Loti was living a very retired life, remaining chiefly on board or making solitary excursions along the Asiatic shore, rather than appearing in the drawing rooms that waited to lionize him. Sometimes, as before, he chose to vanish, spending whole days in the labyrinths of Stamboul, wearing a fez and passing for a Turk. Encountering by chance some of his officers, he would glower and turn away, and it became understood that when he was in Turkish clothes he must remain invisible to them. But every move it was possible to follow was followed by the ladies of Constantinople. Every detail of his uniforms and medals or civilian suits was known; the European ladies outside the harems' bars reported back to their friends who languished within. He had been seen at the book shop by the Tunnel, at Galata, the only European book shop then, and doing a brisk trade in all Loti's writings. He was wearing a grey suit and a panama hat . . . he had lunched at the German Embassy and worn a chestnut-coloured tweed: the harems devoured such details. The wife of the First Secretary of the Italian Embassy – or perhaps it was the Spanish? – had reported on his 'wonderful dark sorrow-drenched eyes'. Once again, Loti's reputation as *le grand séducteur* had taken over from the self-consciously middle-aged man who now preferred solitude or the company of his cats, for he had brought several on board.

Not that he appeared old or faded. He was a spare figure and thought nothing of walking twenty or more miles about the old city. His hair was still dark – dyes took care of that – and he could, by the charm of his childish outburst of laughter, his excellent teeth and athletic body, still appear nearer thirty than fifty. He saw the decrepitude of old age as a disgrace, and fought it with horror, with artifices, and the discipline of exercise and sober living . . . Had he been alive today, he would no doubt have welcomed the rejuvenating treatments to which many men, not only film stars, but public figures and others, as well as women, now turn.

He had quickly become reabsorbed into the stream of Turkish life, and although there were now more and more signs of that progress he abhorred, factories and railways, the influence of the Young Turk party, and big business, the old, dignified, traditional ways were still there. But if Loti had lost the life he had once known, he now tasted pleasures undreamed of by the impoverished impostor Arik Ussim Effendi. Now he kept his own caïque in which to skim across the Bosphorus, or glide down the inlet known as The Sweet Waters of Asia. This was the elegant thing to do, and the veiled inmates of the harems made it their afternoon promenade, rowed up and down, gloved hands holding parasols, eyeing and being eyed across their tantalizing yashmaks.

The élite kept caïques which were splendid in the extreme. Silken carpets trailed in their wake; often fine gilt chains to which golden fish were attached bobbed and frisked in the froth of water round them. The boatmen (two pairs of oars were *de rigueur*) wore elaborate costumes. Loti's white and gold caïque was sumptuous, and his oarsmen wore liveries of turquoise blue velvet, their shirts of creamy silk gauze, their caps the customary scarlet. Even the Persian Ambassador's emerald green velvets took second place, his daughter told me, for Loti was Loti, and to see him pass was to crown the day. Did he, when idling along those silky waters, recall Aziyadé's barque, that 'floating bed', where the same kiss, 'began at night, lasted until morning'? It may have accounted for that proud, withdrawn expression the ladies found irresistible.

Lieutenant-Commander Viaud had arrived in Constantinople with his customary large amount of baggage; he was never one to travel light, and the Sultan's secret police were not long in suspecting that one massive packing case contained a tombstone. Was this Aziyadé's stele, copy or original, now shipped from Rochefort back to the land of its origin to be beside Loti during his term of service in Turkish waters? The Porte had long been aware of Loti's involvement with this, and no awkward questions arose. However, it may be imagined what curiosity it aroused on board. Loti never offered any explanations and soon all his eccentricities were accepted; he was unlike anyone else, in or out of the Service and, withal, a commander who always gained the loyalty and respect of his crew. When those few guests whom he invited aboard were confronted by the marble tombstone with its green and gold

Arabic inscription, they remained silent – nonplussed, we may suppose.

The *Vautour* was a small ship, and even the Captain's quarters were cramped, so that the grand piano Loti installed there took up most of his quarters which opened on to a small balcony on the poop. The officers' cabins were only separated by thin partitioning, and it was soon known that their Commander's preference was for Chopin, with an occasional switch to Beethoven, or César Franck. 'It is his Chorale which comforts me most in my hours of anguish,' wrote Loti, for such hours accompanied him, even here, where he was once again in the land of his predilection, famous, rich, and among friends.

Apart from the crew of the *Vautour,* Loti added an extra, or shore, staff, to wait on his whims. These Turkish servitors accompanied him on some of his nocturnal expeditions about the countryside, ran errands for him, and were treated confidentially. They were headed by Choukri, a handsome colossus, who acted as dragoman, and wore the most picturesque gold-laced costumes. Hamdi and Djemil were more rustic figures, originally shepherds of some remote Anatolian region. Loti enjoyed airing his Turkish on them, and listening to the legends they recounted, or sung, to the accompaniment of Hamdi's flute.

Although the Sultan continued to show Loti innumerable marks of esteem, thus fulfilling the French Government's hopes that his rôle would be that of unofficial ambassador, he remained elusive, shunning European social life and shrouding himself in mystery. Among the few Europeans with whom he was on terms of close friendship were his compatriots Count and Countess Ostrorog. They lived in a crimson-walled yali, one of those lovely old wooden houses overhanging the waters of the Bosphorus, whose upper storeys project even further to form a sort of latticed gazebo where the ladies of the harem were used to pass their days, lolling on cushioned divans, observing, unobserved, through the lattices, all that passed along the great water-way below. Loti was a frequent visitor to the yali at Kandili, and enjoyed the Ostrorogs' exceptional knowledge of Turkish tradition and culture. Sometimes he would retreat to a dim, divan-lined room, there to smoke opium. The room is still there, still dim and divan-lined, and the late Count Jean Ostrorog, who as a child, had known Loti, told me many stories of his life at the yali. One anecdote was particularly revealing of the emotion all things

269

Turkish aroused in Loti. He had been sitting by the overhanging window, peeping through the latticed grille to watch, by stealth, the arrival of a Turkish princess who had come to visit the Countess. Her splendid caïque slid up to the marble landing stage and as she stepped ashore, her yashmak slipped aside for one brief moment, and Loti glimpsed her pallid, tragic beauty. She was doomed by some incurable malady and he found her an infinitely romantic figure, representing all the beauty, elegance and mystery of the great harems. During her visit, she had swooned away – how perfectly in keeping – and was carried to the nearest bedroom, which happened to be Loti's. On recovering, they told her on whose bed she lay, and she spoke of the joy his writings gave her. But Loti, denied the joy of meeting this *Princesse Lointaine*, insisted that no-one should change the pillow upon which her lovely head had rested. This too, was perfectly in keeping.

When Loti entertained aboard, which was seldom, for he was said to be less accessible than the Sultan himself, it was always in a very personal manner which emphasized his Oriental affinities. His menus were a subtle mixture of French dishes and local foods. He kept an excellent table, though he himself took no interest in food or wines.

He was always on good terms with his officers and crew. 'Aboard the *Vautour*, I was a king, but not a tyrant,' he was to recall. His men respected his meticulous running of their ship; his seamanship too, for when the *Vautour* put to sea, cruising about the Black Sea or the Adriatic, it sometimes ran into treacherous waters and violent storms. One and all loved him for his humanity, his understanding of each man's problems. He never invited his officers to dine with him en bloc, nor did he frequent their mess, preferring to ask each one to his table separately: thus he came to know them better, just as he would often choose one or another to accompany him on his long expeditions about the less frequented quarters of the old city, a chance which some, like Claude Farrère, could appreciate fully. Farrère shared Loti's love of all things Turkish. He too was a writer and one of his novels was to win the Prix Goncourt; in time he became one of Loti's most devoted friends, their shared Turcophil sympathies lessening the gap between Captain and junior officer which etiquette imposed. Farrère has left illuminating memoirs of Loti as he knew him both aboard and ashore.

Everything Loti did or said was circulated round the salons of international Pera. A childish ceremony, the christening of his cat Belkis, did not improve his image among the Diplomatic Corps, and there were even repercussions in Paris. It had not been his idea: it was a prank thought up by his younger officers, who enjoyed it as an excuse for a giddy party aboard: unfortunately, Loti did nothing to stop them: he was amused by the parody of font, tapers, cortège and a high priest reciting prayers to some great god of cats. But the international press fastened on it as an insult to Christian ritual, while the French colony, largely Roman Catholics, held Loti's Huguenot background responsible for such irreverence. How the Turks viewed the affair is not known. They shared Loti's affection for cats, and possibly thought it a sympathetic aspect of Infidel dogma. However, since Loti was held in real esteem by all Constantinople, the scandal soon subsided; though Loti himself continued to regret that he had unwittingly caused offence on religious grounds, for he held any creed in respect.

The French Ambassador did not always find the commander of the *Vautour's* extravagances to his liking. He particularly deplored the refulgence of the Oriental costumes which Loti chose for his Turkish domestics and boatmen. Although the two men were on excellent terms, Loti could never resist baiting Embassy conventions and in his turn deplored the Ambassador's lack of aesthetic sensibility.

In April 1904, six months after Loti had established this agreeable way of life in Turkish waters and ashore, he received a letter which was to destroy his calm and finally embroil him in the saddest, silliest, most ignoble hoax. He was to be the dupe of three unscrupulous women who became known to the world as *Les Désenchantées*, this being the title of the celebrated book Loti was to write concerning the tragedies of harem life as lived by the disenchanted women they purported to represent.

Two of them were the daughters of Nouri Bey, a high official of the Sublime Porte already known to Loti. His father had been a Frenchman, the Comte de Châteauneuf, converted to Islam under the name of Rachid Bey. On their mother's side, Nouri Bey's daughters Zennour and Nouryié had Circassian blood. The third intriguer was a French woman, Madame Léra, a journalist who wrote under the name of Marc Hélys. She knew Turkey well and had interested herself in the question of Turkish women's continued sequestration in the harem. Zennour and Nouryié longed for something to change the monotony of their lives and, abetted by Madame Léra, decided to write to Loti and solicit a meeting – an insane notion, since for them there could be no meetings with men, let alone foreigners. Although Nouri Bey was of the more liberal Europeanized Turks, custom held fast. He had taken pride in giving his daughters an excellent education, modern languages, literature, music, the arts; but now expected them to forget those wide horizons and retreat into the restricted life decreed for all Turkish women. That they would be rebellious and infinitely more bored than their illiterate mothers or grandmothers had not occurred to Nouri Bey. Therefore, stifled in the modern European-styled rooms they had demanded from their uncomprehending father, they planned an elaborate diversion.

It was decided that since Zennour had already written to Loti a few years earlier, describing the emotions his book *Aziyadé* had aroused in her, she should now write reminding him of this by way of introduction. 'Today,' she wrote, 'that same young Turkish girl, grown ambitious, asks to see you, to know the author, loved and re-read a hundred times, each time with more emotion . . .' A daring rendezvous was suggested, at a deserted stretch along the Bosphorus near Thérapia. She would come with two friends, all of them heavily veiled of course. They would arrive in a carriage, which they then would leave, and Loti was to follow them, and wait for them to speak . . . a dozen precautions followed . . . 'You know our country: you know the risks we run . . . though we know you for a chivalrous gentleman, and count on your discretion . . . But perhaps you have forgotten Aziyadé? Perhaps her sisters no longer interest you? Nevertheless, if you would know something of the soul of an Aziyadé of today, send me your answer . . .'

Loti rose to the bait: although suspicious he was enthralled. They had not used Aziyadé's name in vain, although he was reluctant to become involved in some cheap adventure. His reply was cold, but he agreed to meet them *'if the weather is fine'*. He would wait there for one hour, 'so as not to disappoint you, if you are really serious'. It was only signed L. Piqued. The impudent trio decided to amuse themselves at his expense. When they started out, they were darkly bundled up in their tcharchafs, but before reaching the rendezvous they added elegant slippers, white kid gloves and bunches of violets, to whet the great seducer's appetite. It had not been difficult to obtain Nouri Bey's permission for the expedition. On the pretext of a picnic in the gardens of a summer house he owned at Thérapia they even succeeded in setting out without the traditional encumbrance of an accompanying slave or eunuch. Nouri Bey was progressive. Thus far liberty; nevertheless curfew was at sundown.

Loti was awaiting them, seated by a café. At first they found 'the Enchanter' a disappointment. They had imagined a more dashing figure. He was timid, silent, awkward even, and he seemed to plead, as if begging their forgiveness for being so staid, middle-aged – and *small* – the eternal regret. But gradually, they fell under his spell and ceased to mock. For Loti, these veiled women represented all romantic promise. He begged them to lift their veils – how could he talk with faceless cyphers? But they remained adamant, and he never again insisted. After all, there was a charm in mystery. They led him on to speak of his loves – his heart: according to his writings he had left fragments of it all over the world . . . There could not be much left, suggested the French woman, who posed as another Turk, Leyla by name. Loti protested: he had left nothing in Japan, very little in Tahiti, and most of it had remained in Turkey. The ladies found him uncommunicative, monosyllabic even, yet when the time came to separate, they saw him flush, and his hands trembled: his eyes seemed to ask for another meeting, but he remained silent. The ladies, asking for autographed copies of his books, hinted that further rendezvous might be possible . . .

On reaching home they could talk of nothing else. Letters were to be received post restante, and now they launched into all kinds of coquetries to hold his interest, such as flowers, warm from their corsages, to which Loti replied with circumspection. He felt himself middle-aged, and was not to be drawn into any undignified pseudo-romantic situations. But his '*petits fantômes noirs*,' as they archly described themselves, had succeeded in attracting him to their side, and now were determined to keep him there. He was an elusive but thrilling antidote to boredom, and they regretted they could not disclose their secret to friends who dreamed of him in other, more restricted, harems.

Now began this tragi-comedy, this imbroglio of lies which was to cost Loti dear. There were further stealthy encounters, one at

Eyoub, beside the most sacred mosque of Ansari, but it was of Aziyadé and that vanished house for lovers' meetings that they were all thinking. Loti's *'petits fantômes noirs'* were in ecstasies. Could it be true? Presently they suggesed they might be able to look after Aziyadé's grave – they too had Circassian blood; it made a link. Emboldened by Loti's tentative agreement and their ripening friendship they achieved a far more secretive place of meeting, in the house of an obliging friend, who, poor, and nursing an invalid husband, agreed to loan them an empty room. This they furnished with all the Turkish trimmings they could obtain: their father's house had been much Europeanized to please them, and now they regretted the vanished treasures which would have charmed Loti. However, Loti accepted it all as genuine, and there they passed strangely innocent yet dangerous hours. The phantoms remained obstinately veiled, but all of them, Loti too, by degrees exchanged confidences of a personal nature: the *désenchantées* dwelled on their boredom and the tragic lot of their sisters, tyrannized, sequestered, and terrified . . . so many little birds, beating their wings against the bars . . . Mystery, secrecy, spying everywhere . . . Surely Loti's great heart bled for them?

But Loti was not to be drawn. An arch-conservative at heart and blindly devoted to every facet of traditional life, he seemed unable to commiserate with their sequestered lot as they would have wished. It was not that he seemed disbelieving or cynical, but he had known something of the loopholes and corruption of harem life at first hand, and for him, it was those very elements of stealth, danger and tradition which had been the essence of his adventure with Aziyadé. His reactions were instinctively masculine: the veil was a fascinating institution. The *désenchantées* were really rather shallow little creatures, like their sisters of other harems. Their chief amusement was dreaming of chic life in Paris derived from the latest periodicals. They read novels and novelettes indiscriminately, by de Maupassant or Gyp, or got into deep waters with Nietzsche, and other *fin de siècle* philosophers. They followed fashion avidly, adopting each new European craze with doll-like docility, and like all Eastern women of their class, being surrounded by slaves, were in consequence, bone idle. Although their aura of mystery enchanted Loti, they were aware that to hold his interest they would have to contrive some lofty aims, some pathos . . . drama, even.

Meanwhile there were further risky meetings – risky for all of them: for the ladies it was unthinkable that they could risk a rendezvous with any man, let alone a foreigner: as for Loti, *persona grata* at the Sublime Porte or no, it was still highly inprudent to trifle with Turkish prejudice where the sacred institution of the harem was concerned. Nevertheless, there was a visit to the *Vautour*, which proved an anti-climax, for the ladies were disillusioned by the bleak cabin in which he received them. They had expected some *Arabian Nights* setting full of exotic souvenirs; but Loti had become used to the locust-like visitations of admirers, and prudently removed everything except the piano and Aziyadé's tombstone. The phantoms were overcome with emotion on reading the stele's inscription giving her real name, Hakidjé Khalkhassé, and Loti played one of Chopin's nocturnes for them: 'not much technique, but great feeling' was their verdict. Gradually, these stolen meetings had become a heady drug for all of them. An outing to Aziyadé's grave now took place, with the ladies in one carriage, and Loti in another, for etiquette forbade any man to drive in the same carriage as a woman – even one of his household. Loti in a fez, fingering his tespeyh beads, led them to the grave playing the Bey, followed by his harem. It appeared all calm decorum to the cemetery guardian: but emotions sizzled round this group, who were nourished by such. '*To stand by Aziyadé's grave with Loti* – what a moment!' *Les petits fantômes noirs* felt their cup overflowing, and tears filled Loti's eyes, as he wondered if, somehow, Aziyadé's spirit was aware of this pious pilgrimage, her ever faithful lover and her little sisters under the veil.

Loti was always fascinated by disguises and masks such as he himself adopted, and a veiled woman became automatically desirable. He had come to identify himself with so many aspects of Turkish life that he now saw the mystique of the veil – the *feredjé*, *yashmak* or *tcharchaf* and its sexual connotations – with both an Eastern and Western eye. Vibrating with emotion – exasperation too – he stood before this flimsy, yet impenetrable barrier that his phantoms wore but which he would not destroy. By tradition, the veil signifies *harem* – sanctuary – it is an all-powerful taboo still in evidence in many places, 'progress' or no. Many Eastern women would sooner stand naked in the market place than uncover their faces. I am reminded of that lively passage in *Vathek*, where the Caliph's harem are caught by a forest fire and pitched from their litters in disarray. 'Better be eaten by tigers – we are undone!' the

275

ladies cry . . . 'Not a porter nor a carrier of camels but hath seen some part of our bodies, *and what is worse*, our very faces!' So the *petits fantômes noirs* remained veiled, and Loti savoured his delicious torments to the full.

With such intrigues afoot it can be imagined that Loti's social life among the Europeans grew more and more neglected, though when Sarah Bernhardt arrived there were numbers of Embassy junkets. Loti gratified her wish to see the Whirling Dervishes, whose tekké was at Pera, Sarah slashing her way through the crowd of spectators with her parasol.

Blanche and Samuel came out for a spell of tourism, but did not stay long. Blanche was aware of the *désenchantées*, and took an interest in their problem. Her life, too, might have been described as one of subjection, behind the bars of her husband's indifference.

According to Madame Léra, who as Marc Hélys was to rush into print after Loti's death with a book entitled *Le Secret des Désenchantées*, which purported to tell the whole story behind Loti's own book, *Les Désenchantées*, the whole affair derived solely from their wish that he should speak for the legion of oppressed women in the harems. Were he to live yet one more romance in Turkey, he might be inspired to write a worthy sequel to *Aziyadé*. Then, public opinion everywhere might be roused. With abominable cynicism they engineered an elaborate charade whereby Leyla (or Madame Léra) must appear unhappily married and falling deeply in love with Loti. Since Madame Léra was obliged to return to France for some journalistic commitments, her departure was transposed to further drama. Leyla's family were becoming suspicious . . . As a victim of their tyranny she was now languishing in the harem of her husband's country house at Smyrna. The young Bey possessed her body, but O! her soul was Loti's! All this farrago was believed by Loti and his interest was kept simmering by Leyla's letters, outpourings of love, with heartbreaking accounts of her enslaved life in the harem beside her rival, the new favourite. These letters were smuggled out to Loti from behind the harem grilles – or so he believed. In fact, they were written in Paris and sent to be posted by a go-between in Smyrna. Copies were sent to the two remaining phantoms in Constantinople, who sometimes advised a more passionate tone or invented further tragic details to spur Madame Léra's pen. Loti treasured Leyla's letters, not only for the love they expressed but as some strange, ghostly echoes of that other earlier love; this, he believed, was how Aziyadé, a more literate Aziyadé, would have written . . . Phantoms everywhere.

Presently, his growing concern as to Leyla's fate, and the rash project of visiting Smyrna (another abduction from the Seraglio?), alarmed Zennour and Nouryié and they decided to end the affair. But to confess all would have been too cruel, would have destroyed any hope of further meetings, or of Loti writing the book they envisaged. Therefore it was decided that Leyla must be killed off, a victim of love. Presently, Loti received a farewell letter from her, written, it said, after she had swallowed poison, and was drifting towards the eternal darkness while gazing at Loti's photograph and imagining herself in his arms. It was a beautiful and harrowing letter, and Loti was, of course, harrowed. This cruel trick went even further, for to make it more convincing the schemers sent him a notice of the funeral which they had printed especially. Cynicism could go no further. But the ruse had worked. Middle-aged Loti saw himself once more as *l'amant fatal*, sowing tragedy around him, and the book he was to write followed faithfully this dramatic theme, and quoted Leyla's correspondence extensively.

When Loti's command of the *Vautour* ended in March 1905 and he was appointed to take charge of the naval depot at Rochefort, he might have imagined the episode of *les petits fantômes noirs* was over, with his Turkish days. But while Leyla had to remain dead, the other two intriguers were to reappear. In a further climate of drama, they arrived in France, having fled the harem, an event out of which they made much capital in the press. Since they knew no-one in Paris and had no means of support, they turned to Loti, arriving at Rochefort expecting to be sheltered. Loti felt obliged to accept this charge, for, they insisted, it was he who had really encouraged them to become so daringly independent and to flee the cage. Gradually, their octopus tentacles spread over the whole house. Lodged, fed, included in the household, imposing on Blanche's kindness, they demanded luxury, were sluttish, lazy and mischief-making – in short, unbearable. After some time, they were tactfully edged off to

277

Paris and installed there at Loti's expense, although they soon found ways to impose on others too.

Loti was finding life in Rochefort particularly depressing after Constantinople's beauty and emotions, and he set about reliving those days by writing *Les Désenchantées*. This over-romanticized tale does not stand up to the passing years, as Loti's earlier novels or travel pieces do. In spite of admirable descriptions of Stamboul, and intriguing details of harem life and its protocol, culled from the phantoms, there is an overall falsity, and a great deal of wishful thinking. Loti is thinly disguised as the hero, André Léhry: a world-weary, world-famous writer (handsome and fascinating to women) who returns to the scene of a youthful love affair (Aziyadé is here called Nejibé). The heroine of this book (Madame Léra or Leyla) becomes Djénane, and both incidents and letters follow the real Turkish imbroglio, culminating in the fatal letter. But in the book, Loti's wishful thinking develops the emotions that were, in life, beginning to entangle him with the real-life Leyla, before she vanished so mysteriously. Their unavowed love is brought to a climax by that scene where she yields to his pleadings and for one traumatic moment lifts her veil.

Apart from that passage, clearly expressing all Loti's longings, the book lacks spontaneity – conviction, even. It is as if Loti had laboured to discharge a debt he believed he owed to both Aziyadé and Leyla, both victims of the harem, both Circassians, and both dead for love of him – *l'amant fatal*. It does not work. For all Loti's art it seems forced, as if dictated: as indeed, much of it was, for the meddling phantoms insisted they must go over each chapter, to look for any errors regarding life in the harems, details only they could know. By now they were proving even more unbearable to Loti, the professional writer, for as the pages were sent to them in Paris, they dawdled over them, mislaid them, or sent them back covered in illegibly scrawled suggestions. When at last the book reached proof form the printers were again delayed by such incompetence, till Loti was at the end of his patience. The phantoms had now begun writing articles themselves, and expected him to edit and polish their amateur efforts, which Loti patiently did. After all, they were Circassians – Aziyadé's sisters in misfortune – a sacred charge.

When at last *Les Désenchantées* was published, it was enormously popular, running, ultimately, into over 400 editions, but while acclaimed by a wide international public, more discerning readers thought it far from Loti's best. Robert de Montesquiou wrote: 'If *Rarahu (Le Mariage de Loti)* and *Bérénice* had not opened the career of both Loti and Barrès, their respective careers would probably have been less brilliant . . . Suppose Loti had made his début with *Les Désenchantées* . . . ?' Nevertheless, its popularity and the large sums it was earning, incited his insufferable protégées to make further demands. Were a stage version to be made, as seemed likely, then they wanted half the proceeds, for was it not basically *their* book? *They* had first suggested it, inspired it, and aided him to write it, said the *Désenchantées*. Loti was now the true *désenchanté*, but he still refused to believe he had been duped . . . Leyla-Djénane's death haunted him. 'You would not play such an odious trick on me?' he asked them, and they kept up the deception with particular care, for he represented their only means of support, and no return to Turkey was possible after their flight. When, some years later, Loti spoke at a meeting which was designed to arouse public sympathy for the harem women's lot – a precursor of Woman's Lib, perhaps – much was made of his book, and Leyla-Djénane's poignant farewell letter was read out, at which Loti was seen to bury his face in his hands. Had he, by then, lost his last illusion and did he know himself to have been the dupe of three unscrupulous adventuresses? But incurable romantics cling to their illusions, and the farewell letter was to remain beside Aziyadé's tombstone till he died.

19

*Ne pouvons-nous jamais, sur l'océan des âges
Jeter l'ancre un seul jour?*

Lamartine, *Le Lac*

Brooding over his lost Islamic life had become a whole way of life for Loti. It was a secret world into which he retreated each night, on leaving the Dépôt Maritime. Home life in its conventional sense was no more. Those faded rooms he preserved in memory of the *chères vieilles* were a cult representing another life, lived by another self. With the impatient step of a lover he would mount the grandiose stone stairway of the Renaissance Salon, gain a further, steep stair and reach a curtained doorway leading to the mosque and Aziyadé's stele. By now his mystical cravings for Islam had become inextricably interwoven with the mystique of Aziyadé. The secret of his love for Islam was contained in her tombstone. Beside it he spent hours of dreamy immobility that were at odd variance with the violent activities of fencing, pelota or boxing which his athletic body still demanded.

To him, Islam remained 'a garden in the desert of civilization', 'an island of reveries and calm, against which western waves lash threateningly'. To live becalmed within that dream was yet another escape route which, like his travels, removed him from the pin-pricks and turmoil of daily life – ashore, that is – for once at sea even the mosque was scarcely missed. 'The great circle of blue' enclosed him, shutting out all else. But alas! he was not at sea: the Ministère de la Marine had become used to his applying for shore posts (to be near his mother) and still thought him suitably placed commanding the Dépôt Maritime at Rochefort. Besides, they said, it gave him plenty of time to write more of those books which, by now, even the crustiest Admirals admitted shed lustre on the navy. Moreover, it seemed they had influenced large numbers of young men to join the navy.

Thus, landlocked in the fossil port of his ancestors, Loti watched from afar the Eastern traditions he cherished becoming engulfed by the West. Longingly, his journal notes: 'The moral of the Orient is immobility, and if one's aim is to go through life with the minimum of unhappiness, eschewing all vain agitations, to die anaesthetized by serene faith, then the Orient is truly wise . . . But those dreams are no longer possible, now that other nations close in on all sides, like birds of prey.' Such encroachments strengthened his determination to preserve his own Islamic island, and some of his sailors from the port were now coached to perform the rituals of Moslem worship, while one who possessed a melting tenor was rehearsed to perfect the muezzin's call to prayer.

Loti had created a house for dreams, rooms of reverie and regret. He could no longer be said to *live* at 141 Rue Saint-Pierre: it was there he dreamed. There have been many examples, especially in nineteenth-century France, of writers who gave free rein to their imaginations in their dwellings; but never a more fantastic imagining than Loti's mosque, the concrete expression of all his loneliness and longings.

Sometimes, enmeshed in melancholy, even the solace of the mosque failed him, and in spite of all his loving attention to details of Arab dress and prayers, he knew himself an exile there too – an exile from Islam. Had it become, even to him, a sort of theatrical, pseudo-mystical chimera, as some cynics saw it? Robert de Montesquiou described Loti's Turqueries as so many funeral wreaths repainted to look fresh. He had been one of the chosen few invited to the mosque; but after the ritual hour of prayer, his cynicism fell away.

Since there was now no longer any façade of married life to be maintained, Blanche too had retreated into her own withdrawn world, Berternet, a large family estate she had inherited in the Dordogne. The parting was amiable, with no dramatics. No more was she obliged to shuttle between Rochefort and Hendaye, both houses being singularly uncomfortable; no longer was she obliged to pack and unpack, according to Loti's nomadic whim, or be obliged, suddenly to play hostess at some Tzigane fête or walk beside him at a Breton penitential procession, feeling self-conscious in Breton costume. Above all, she was no longer entrusted with peculiar and tormenting missions which, while proving Loti's trust in her obedience and discretion, cast mysterious shadows over any confidence she still had in him as head of the household and father of her child. What dark secrets might those sealed boxes he entrusted to her contain? As long ago as his departure for Morocco, immediately after their son's birth, he had plagued her with minute instructions for destroying various packets of letters, in case of fire – 'Léo has the keys,' he had written, dotting the i's on the privileged place Léo occupied. Now she was tired of Pandora's role, tempted (but not succumbing, I have been told) by all the papers she might handle, but must never read. Here is a fair sample of the sort of demands Loti made, and the chill terms in which he wrote to her. The letter is undated. Perhaps he was in Paris, or the House of the Solitary at Hendaye, when he wrote as follows:

My dear Blanche,
    I am confiding to you a mission of the strictest confidence – I do not have to tell you that I have absolute confidence in your discretion . . . [He warns her to handle everything with the greatest care, leaving no disorder, when opening various sealed boxes.] There are letters from Samuel Greusiller [his particularly favoured sailor friend]. In my will I have already stated that such papers may not be opened for thirty years after my death . . . Therefore, you must collect them, *without reading them*. [The journals of this moment were, he told her, divided into little packets, a month at a time, tied by ribbons . . .] You must find Dec. 1900, Jan., Feb., March, April, July, Oct., Nov. 1901. Eight months in all. Pack them in a strong wooden box, nailed up and sealed with wax, to be posted to me. (Declare value at 500 francs.) You will find everything in the middle shelf of the cupboard in my dressing room. The keys are labelled. After which you must at once lock up everything and return the keys to their proper place.

Julien

Enough was enough. Blanche had done with Pandora missions and Loti's exigencies. As châtelaine of her new home she lived on her own terms, occupied with her lands, her garden and a house stocked with Ferrière furniture, silver and linen, in the finest French family tradition. As if to cast off memories of the elaborate, richly coloured velvets and silks Loti selected for her so high-handedly, she now adopted simple white garments, and became absorbed in theosophic studies; not that higher thought prevented her living in considerable comfort, with four servants and a companion at her beck and call. Samuel, the loving and dutiful son, was studying art in Paris, happy among the students of the Quartier Latin, but he was ever-obedient, hurrying between the two parental households, satisfying the demands of this exigent pair. Presently he found himself more at home with his remote father than his increasingly despotic mother. That wilful streak which Blanche had seldom displayed as Loti's wife was now concentrated on her son. She wished to control his every movement, read his letters, dictate his replies, and regulate his friendships, demanding unquestioning obedience. All her past wifely subservience was now reversed and she became a masterful matriarch. But Samuel bore with her, as if trying to make up for all the years he had seen her crushed. Thus he accepted her tyrannies as he had always accepted those of his father; his was a generous and sweet temper, tried but never found wanting in this triangular tug of war and love – for such it was, since Loti was slowly beginning to return his son's devotion with a genuine affection. Devotion was not something Loti ever again showed after the death of his mother.

It was in the autumn of 1906 that Loti first met Louis Barthou, who was to become one of his most intimate friends. Yet in Barthou's words, there was, at the beginning, a terrible obstacle between them. Barthou was then a high-ranking Minister, and Loti detested all Ministers on principle. He had fallen foul of the Government on several occasions, scorning them from that day, far back in 1880, when the President and the Government had visited the fleet at Cherbourg and had compared unfavourably with the sailors. ('Sickening ceremony, salvoes, flags . . . it is this collection of commercial travellers, a thoroughly ugly, trashy lot, who govern us.') Louis Barthou was not at all the kind of petty Government official Loti had scorned then: he held many high offices, was cultivated, musical, a member of l'Académie Française, and widely travelled. Nevertheless, it was only with great difficulty he finally overcame Loti's reserve, and their friendship took root. 'I count it one of the greatest honours of my life to have known him,' wrote Barthou, after Loti's death.

Madame Barthou revelled in Loti's exoticisms and was an exotic figure herself, a tall, commanding beauty, always elaborately dressed, and much given to turbans and aigrettes. Her life-style was luxuriously complicated. Sometimes she would arrive at Hendaye accompanied by her maid and quantities of luggage which overwhelmed the modest little house, so that at last Loti struck. 'My son and my secretary are crowded out when she is here, and she upsets the servants. She must go.' She was only persuaded to accept the Duruttys' hospitality, at Loti's instance, with some difficulty. It was an arrangement which pleased neither Madame Barthou nor the devoted Berthe Durutty, who endured her exigencies for Loti's sake, as she would have endured hell fire had he asked her. But she remained in the background at Hendaye, and for all Loti's love, never visited Rochefort or received the longed-for mark of intimacy he once accorded Madame Barthou, who was admitted to the mosque (veiled by the traditional *haïk*), there to share with 'the Magician' the ritual hour of prayer.

It was a twilight hour charged with emotion which Alice Barthou was later to describe and publish, in bemused detail. Responding to a wave of his wand, the muezzin chanted, and a line of phantom-like figures (Loti's sailors) filed in and prostrated themselves in prayer. The Magician himself was of course wearing white robes and burnous, and fingering an amber tespeyh. But once again, in his own words, whether he wore Arab robes, the rating's blue, or a Turkish fez, *'Je suis toujours un déclassé jouant une comédie.'*

In January 1907 Loti took four months' leave to turn eastward once more, now to the radiant skies of Egypt, where he was the guest of the Khedive Abbas Hilmi, and Mustafa Kemal, the fiery nationalist who had often visited him at Hendaye.

In *La Mort de Philae* he records his slow progress up the Nile on a dahabiyeh, one of those traditional sailing boats, placed at his disposal by the Khedive, who knew his guest's horror of any alternative steam-boat. But in spite of warm friendships, and Egypt's incomparable beauty, a sour note sounds throughout *La Mort de Philae*; it is as if Loti *cannot* stomach the alien presence not only of a British occupation, but those tourist hordes he loathed and despised, and whom he allowed to poison his every hour. His first Egyptian days were spent in Cairo, the city of three thousand mosques, of lace-like minarets and houses striped horizontally in cream and faded crimson, the ancient city of *The Thousand and One Nights*, and it enchanted him, till he recognized it was invaded on all sides by the abhorred 'Cookis and Cookesses'. On the walls of Mehemet Ali's fortress, on the very spot where the Mamelukes had ruled in splendour, only to be cut down treacherously, Loti found further treachery – a guard-post of British soldiers, 'the red coats and pale faces of the North'. His resentment was fomented whenever he left the labyrinthine ways of the old city, with its covered souks and street markets, to reach the smart Europeanized quarters of international life centred round the terrace of Shepheard's Hotel.

At the Al-Azhar mosque and university, heart and centre of Islamic learning, where strangers seldom penetrated, Loti was received by the Rector himself, a signal honour.

Throughout this Egyptian visit Loti was showered with rare privileges. Cairo's Museum of Egyptology was kept open for him – for him alone – at night, so that he might wander through the musty *enfilades* of mummies undistracted by chattering crowds. He thought the glare of electricity was a profanation, thus it was by candle light that he chose to go between sarcophagi and showcases; but Loti was not only indulging his sense of drama and necrophilic tendencies: he was also searching for his mummified self.

In Cairo he had become aware of some hallucinatory sense of *déjà vu*, of some strong affinity linking him with the vanished Pharaonic world. If this land preserved its dead, and he had once been of that past, as he held, then traces of himself must still be somewhere, and he might discover them. It does not seem to have occurred to him that he might have been some humble fellahin, buried in the common plot. No: he must have been of princely origin and embalmed with all the sacred rituals. Thus persuaded that this earlier self lay among the Pharaonic relics and that the two selves would inevitably recognize one another, he continued his search for several hours, until, having almost given up hope of establishing this strange confrontation, he was stopped in his tracks. In the last gallery, a wizened dark face stared up at him with insistence. 'The two selves, the living me and the dead me had come face to face! The one that stood there, and the one that lay there . . . I had found myself again!'

His mummified self had been no other than Rameses II, he was to tell questioners later, though there was a confusing moment when he discovered an extraordinary likeness between himself and Sesostris. His beaked nose had often been called Pharaonic: and he had the two profiles photographed side by side, sending this double likeness to friends, 'not yet mummified' scrawled across his own head.

As he sailed up the Nile, the lovely scenes of Upper Egypt slid past, in a dream-like repetition of palm groves, blue-washed houses and naked children splashing in the shallows beside the wallowing black water-buffaloes. The days too, slid past . . . Assiut, Abydos, Denderah, with its majestic temple to Hathor, goddess of love and joy . . . Kom Ombo, the crocodiles' sanctuary, and the Valley of the Kings, where the tombs lie hidden deep between lion-coloured mountains. Then the horror of these Hades-like vaults and passages surrounding the royal tombs clutched him, and he fled, making for the sun – 'the sun of the living, the air – the air that is still ours, for our remaining, numbered days'.

On reaching Aswan, his dahabiyeh anchored before the first cataract, and Loti's rather heavy humour was employed describing the smart hotel, 'its lawns and trim flower beds recalling Kensington Gardens – so reassuring, beside the infinite deserts beyond, or those huge granite blocks, now marked and catalogued, each Pharaonic inscription translated in the most discreet terms'. Again, there sounds the petulant, spoilt child whose favourite plaything has been taken away.

And then, passing the first cataract, reaching the still waters surrounding the almost submerged island of Philae, all such jibes were forgotten and he was overcome by the sombre beauty of this great, tragic decor, where the drowning sanctuary of Isis still seemed to reign, and at certain hours could be seen half emerging from the rising waters that would presently engulf it for ever. In the limpid twilight Loti's barque approached the Temple of Philae to glide silently beneath the ancient, sumptuous ruins. 'Strange, melancholy port without a name . . . Between the double row of columns the water lifts us to the height of the lofty capitals . . . It seems some promenade to the end of time.'

After the distinctly morbid flavour of Loti's Egyptian journey, it is not surprising that on his return he showed a revived interest in the matter of his own grave. Burial places had always exercised an attraction, and over the years he purchased several new concessions in the Rochefort cemetery, each in turn designed to be his last resting place. He was prone to conducting favoured friends to view each new choice, presenting them with a souvenir sprig of laurel or myrtle which he had already planted. He had shown a curiously illogical streak over the graves of his family, sometimes separating Viauds from Texiers. It may be remembered that when Loti's father had died in tragic circumstances there had not been enough money to buy a gravestone. Later, Loti erected a handsome granite obelisk where the names of his grandfather Viaud, who fought at Trafalgar, his father, his young uncle, the cabin boy who had perished on the raft of the *Méduse*, his brother Gustave, who had died at sea, and the baby Samuel who had died at birth were all inscribed: a strictly masculine memorial.

Some way off, against a wall, was another tomb, or family vault. Here lay the *chères vieilles*, his Viaud and Texier grandmothers, his mother, and Aunt Claire (though not Great-aunt Berthe, who, having become a Roman Catholic, was, as it were, sent to Coventry, and buried apart). The journal contains a grisly account of digging up certain remains and placing them in a new family sepulchre.

The grave was to remain a perpetual dread from which Loti was never altogether freed and the question of his own grave remained an obsession until he finally settled to be buried on the ISLAND. While the whole family, or clan of Viauds, were in death, as in life, close-knit, it is strange that Loti persisted in remaining aloof rather than choosing to be beside his mother. But so it was.

Graves and funeral rites were all part of his cult, and photographs of his loved ones on their death bed, framed in palms and wide black-ribboned wreaths accumulated, for he carried mourning celebrations to the point of self-indulgence. His animals, too, were interred with loving ceremony. From the time when, as a small child, he had prepared – well in advance of a pet finch's death – a little coffin-box lined with velvet, and shroud (one of Aunt Claire's best handkerchiefs), he had shown an excessive preoccupation with such rites. As time went by the narrow garden had became an extensive pets' cemetery, following the tradition of that Renaudin ancestor who had buried his favourite horse under the flagstones of the courtyard.

It was Loti's fate to have been born the youngest of a much, much older family who, one by one, died, leaving him stranded, with memories no-one else could share. In 1908 his last link with childhood was severed by the sudden death of his sister, after a particularly violent dispute had flared up between them. Her death added fuel to the fires of regret which scorched Loti ceaselessly – generally without reason, it might be remarked; but regrets were all part of that meloncholy upon which his neurosis was nourished. It was only slowly that he could bear to recall the closeness he and Marie had once known, only some years later write of those early days and what she had once meant to him. This memoir was published in 1919 as *Prime Jeunesse*, and dedicated to her memory. He described it as 'a long epitaph on some deeply revered gravestones'.

Tombs everywhere: another *ailleurs* where the loved and lost awaited him, as in a forbidden paradise he could not reach: then he would go restlessly between Rochefort and Hendaye, between his duties at the Port and Bakhar Etchea, the House of the Solitary, its name belied by the numbers of old friends and the adoring Madame Durutty who tried to console him. But Marie's death and his mother's last words haunted him. 'Love one another,' she had said, and he had not obeyed her.

Inconsolable, he was no sooner at Hendaye than he rushed back to Rochefort, to the attics filled with memories. Madame Durutty wrote pleading letters of love and sympathy. How could she help him, her adored, her Maïté Maïtia, beloved above all others? She implores him not to despair . . . It is terrible, *terrible* to see him in this state, and to be able to do nothing . . . If he decides to go abroad, can they not meet once more – just once more? Does he really mean that he will never return to Hendaye? She is in torment. But Loti, who, in his fashion, adored his *petite Madame*, seldom answered her outpourings, being too occupied with his own miseries: occasionally he, or a secretary, sent her a few lines of cold comfort, which she treasured.

It was during Loti's frequent returns to the Basque country that the cruel drama of the bull-ring claimed him – he who had written *Le Livre de la Pitié et de la Mort*, and who overflowed with anguish for all animals suffering, could now sit through the spectacle of mangled horses and tortured bulls, fascinated, apparently, by the colour and dramatic tension. There is no explanation for this, unless we belittle him further and accept that it was his weakness for royalty – for the Spanish Queen, who sometimes invited him to her box – which blinded him to the ghastly rituals beloved by Spaniards. In any case, he was frequently seen at the corridas of San Sebastian and none of his friends save old Madame Abbadie chided him, or thought it out of character. In that part of the world it was the thing to do, and for Loti anything was better, at that moment, than watching twilight creep over the Bidassoa towards the Solitary House. Thus he plunged into the gaieties of Biarritz, where there were a number of Parisian sirens, still headed by Madame Catulle Mendès who offered consolations of a more positive kind than his loving, timid

Berthe Durutty could supply, however much he urged her, and however deeply she mistrusted Madame Catulle Mendès' influence. Princesse Alice of Monaco was equally uneasy. '*Do not* marry her,' she wrote, anxiously. But Loti was still married, in name, to Blanche, and seems never to have contemplated risking the vulnerability of being a divorced man.

Seen from today, what an odd pair Loti and Madame Catulle Mendès appear. We imagine these mature charmers on the marble terrace of some chic *salon de thé*, yesterday's equivalent of the bar. The lady's serpentine curves are swathed in satin; in the shadow of an enormous hat heavy with trimming she toys with an éclair. Loti also wears a hat, a wide-brimmed, swaggering panama which balances his Pharaonic nose. His tie-pin is a royal crown, souvenir of the Romanian Queen Carmen Sylva; his fingers are 'gloved in rings', according to one observer. He smokes a scented cigarette, wafts of amber or Latikiyeh wreathe from beneath his moustaches, those jetty and luxuriant appendages of which he is so proud. No man should be clean-shaven, he maintained – it denoted a lack of virility.

Yet with all his poses, high heels and artifices, he could still overcome the prejudices these aroused. Here is a recollection of him, as he appeared to Frédéric Chassériau, whom he was awaiting on the station at Biarritz. 'He had a solitary air – absolutely alone, lost, among the crowds. His huge sad eyes which seemed to watch for the train's arrival saw, instead, that cemetery where Aziyadé sleeps, saw the desert, the great melancholy wastes of Bora-Bora, and the passing of time . . . but not myself, who was obliged to make myself known.'

Some childish and poignant appeal remained below all the extravagant poses, and it was something to which people responded unquestioningly. He still dressed appallingly; when out of uniform he would ask advice with pathetic earnestness. There is a photograph of him on his horse Tamboul, taken about this time, when sartorial indecision reaches comic proportions. He wears a flowing cravat, the skin-tight breeches of a circus rider and a Basque beret crammed down over his ears. When a loyal friend ventured to say the effect was not classical he replied . . . 'So much the better – I don't want to be mistaken for an Englishman!'

Loti's dislike of England and all things English remained unchanged, until in 1909 he was persuaded by Lord Redesdale to visit

London: 'The city I had vowed I would never visit!' Redesdale, as a diplomat, had been en poste in the Far East, and was a great admirer of Loti's Far Eastern books. His son had been sent to Rochefort to improve his French, and this chance brought Loti and the Englishman together. But it needed all the persuasive powers of the diplomat and aristocrat to persuade Loti to put aside his Anglophobe prejudices. As usual on his later travels, it was among the most influential and interesting section of society that he moved. July was the height of the London season, and at a ball at the French Embassy he observed a beautiful and elegant woman standing watching the dancers and smiling. It was Queen Alexandra, to whom he was presented and under whose charm he immediately fell. She looked so amazingly young – and *she was a Queen*! She wore a small diamond circlet – but it was that *closed* circle, the *couronne fermée* which only a Queen may wear, a detail Loti's royalist eye did not overlook. At that moment King Edward, portly and affable, emerged from the card room. 'Ah!' he said, smiling and holding out his hand, 'so this is the Anglophobe!' . . . 'Sire, I am already less so,' replied Loti, and such delicate diplomacy won him an invitation to Buckingham Palace, where the Queen received him in private audience and at once began talking about his books, which made Loti uneasy. Had she read *L'Inde sans les Anglais* with its dedication to Kruger the Boer, he wondered. 'But all that is over now, isn't it?' said the Queen, with an engaging air of confidence, and Loti, the hardened Anglophobe, bowed his acquiescence.

He was only in London for a week, but it was long enough for him to change some of his preconceived notions; he admired the open, countrified parks at its heart, the window boxes 'like florists' shops' and the general air of security and quiet luxury. 'The crowds here gather to watch their King and Queen go past with the respectful enthusiasm which in France is reserved for the passing of the Holy Sacrament . . . the monarch still represents the *soul* of England.'

He was less appreciative of New York when in 1912 his play *La Fille du Ciel* (*The Daughter of Heaven* on Broadway) was in rehearsal; its theme, the thwarted love of a Chinese princess and a Tartar emperor. Loti had collaborated with Judith Gautier, daughter of Théophile, herself a poet and orientalist of distinction. Even so, the play was not much better than another of Loti's theatrical ventures, *Judith Renaudin*. At first Sarah Bernhardt had been intrigued by its exotic theme, and planned to play the title role: but there were problems. She had no intention of hiding her fuzz of carroty hair under the sleek black wig suitable to a Chinese princess. When Loti was firm on that point, Sarah turned her attention elsewhere.

From the beginning he disliked New York, dubbing it a parvenu city. How could it seem otherwise to this man whose love and admiration was all for the traditions and cultures of ancient lands? On sighting the Statue of Liberty, his reaction was not enthusiastic. 'She seemed to be calling the whole world – here is the door! Enter, all of you, into the furnace! Throw yourselves head first into the abyss of business, uproar, turmoil and gold!' Then, the sky-scrapers: 'one might describe them as houses pushed up beyond all measure, like asparagus in April.' He found them alien, like 'the blazing rule of electricity' . . . Everywhere its glare: blinding electric signs, tangles of wires, overhead railway lines (the old elevated railway of Third Avenue), everywhere, too many things hiding the skies from this 'old Oriental Savage' as he describes himself.

New York welcomed Loti royally, and he was submitted to the usual barrage of press photographers and publicity, patiently replying to questions regarding his views on American women, hygiene, castration for criminals, rhinoceros hunting and religion . . . He attended the rehearsals of his play, finding the lavish production excellent, and was struck to see numbers of Chinese playing small parts. They were university students who had left their own country after the fall of the Manchus, and enjoyed being part of a reconstitution of their Celestial ancestry. The rise of a new China had roused American public interest in all things Chinese, which should have augured well for Loti's play: but by now he must have realized what the audience were to discover on the first night: the play simply was not good enough. Author and leading lady took several curtain calls in response to polite applause, but one critic called it 'the year's most colossal failure'.

Loti appears to have been quite indifferent. Nothing touched him in New York: it was as if he was there, bodily, but not in spirit: and indeed in spirit he was beside the Turkish people, then fighting a losing battle against Christian Europe's depredations. Before sailing for home he went about the monstrous city, amazed and appalled by its materialism. Only the impudent little squirrels of Central Park charmed him, as he wandered, a solitary figure among the falling leaves of an autumn twilight. Always, his thoughts turned back to Turkey, and the fate of all he loved there. American newspapers seemed curiously uninterested in what was happening in the Balkans;

theirs was a *here* and *now* style of reporting; and the Atlantic was still an isolating force. Loti was invited to meet President Taft, and was entertained at numbers of clubs, but this 'backward Oriental', as he termed himself could not accept the giddy speed that was America's key-note. 'In all this luxury, something is lacking . . . an indefinable something, which perhaps is simply the soul of a past.'

How charming the small, two-storeyed houses of Rochefort seemed on his return; how pleasant the wide expanse of sky they revealed. Thus Loti savouring all his old haunts – the Porte Martrou, or the Place Colbert, or lingering in the attics charged with memories. In the mosque, a light burned before Aziyadé's tombstone, for the faithful Pierre and Lucien had observed all their master's fetishes, placing fresh flowers in Aunt Claire's room, and dusting the intricacies of his childhood's museum. New York had, at least, served to sharpen Loti's abiding veneration for all things of the past, and now he began another battle – to preserve France's countryside. Ancient trees and historic buildings found in him a defender – forerunner of those who today are concerned with environmental issues. In his book *Le Château de la Belle au Bois Dormant*, Loti describes his efforts to save the lovely château of La Roche-Courbon, in the Saintonge countryside, not far from Rochefort. It stood there, threatened, becalmed in its doomed forests. This was the enchanted domain Loti had explored as a boy, and where, in the green depths of its ravines, he had lain with the gypsy.

For once putting aside the temptation to indulge in reveries of a personal nature, he set about appealing for funds to preserve it from destruction. In the columns of *Figaro* he evoked this legacy from the past with such persuasion that he rescued La Roche-Courbon from annihilation. 'In our country, all of the rich are not yet those vulgar, grasping business men who fell ancient forests to feed their mechanical saws or paper mills,' he wrote, with gratitude. Restored by Monsieur Chenereau, the château now stands as he wished it to be, revivified and inhabited, its proud halls and stairways, and formal parterres, like the great trees and green glades he knew, free to those who wish to wander there.

20

I've lived to bury my desires
And see my dreams corrode with rust
Now all that's left are fruitless fires
That burn my empty heart to dust.

Alexander Pushkin
trans. Maurice Baring

It was two years earlier, in 1910, that Loti's naval life had ended after
42 years, 3 months and 13 days of service. The void in which he found
himself was yet another kind of exile, shut away from the camaraderie and routine that had been his chosen life. The sea's 'great
circle of infinity' was still there, but he was no longer *of* it. Restlessness and nostalgia remained: inevitably he turned eastward to
Turkey. Turkey was at once solace and torment, and from this
melancholy *recherche du temps perdu* came *Suprêmes Visions d'Orient*, the
third of his autobiographical Turkish books. (I set the largely
fictionalized *Désenchantées* apart from this trilogy.) He thought this
return would be his last, though in fact it was not, and every page
reads like some long-drawn-out sigh for all that was gone. But
sighing is not moaning: Loti's Turkish melancholies are poetic
reveries, long, musical refrains, nostalgic, but not self-pitying
whines, and *Suprêmes Visions d'Orient* is one of the loveliest of all his
evocations of Stamboul. Even in the seven years since he had taken
command of the *Vautour*, Constantinople had changed drastically,
causing that earlier time to seem, in retrospect, as remote as those
first intoxicating days of adventure. The 'Red Sultan' Abdul Hamid
had been deposed, and succeeded by his younger brother, the dim
Mahomet V; new industries were changing the countryside, and the
glare of electric street lighting revealed some daringly advanced
ladies going about *unveiled*. The picturesque national costume of the
people was slowly giving place to those Western suits Loti abhorred,
but he himself still sometimes escaped into the old disguises, and
always wore the fez. Sitting once more in a café under the giant plane
trees, where the glou-glou of the narghiles and the rattle of tric-trac
counters were all that broke the tranquillity, the exile had returned.
Naturally there had been the ritual visit to the Field of the Dead,

where Aziyadé's grave seemed to await him. There were also some more abortive attempts to pierce the mystery surrounding the death or disappearance of *l'Autre* – that Other (Djénane of *Les Désenchantées*), whom he preferred to believe had really been of Circassian blood, like Aziyadé, and also died for love of him. By now she had become a sort of lesser Loved and Lost, and he had resolutely put aside any doubts as to her reality. 'If you only knew how *impenetrable* are the secrets which surround those sorts of matters in our country,' he was told. 'Thus, she, *l'Autre* – who in a lesser fashion had held and haunted my imagination, she too had vanished forever, into the mystery of sequestration and death.'

Throughout Loti's years of wandering he had dreamed of living entirely in the Turkish manner, as he had done at Eyoub, and to that end he leased a small house in the heart of old Stamboul, at Eski-Ali-Djiami. Osman, a favoured French protégé, had again accompanied him, and now the household was completed by Hamdi and Djemil, who had served him in the *Vautour* days. They were happy to be once again with this foreigner, this *ferenghi* who loved their country and spoke their language, and still mourned at the grave of their countrywoman. Loti was determined that nothing Western should break the spell of this Turkish interlude, and the few household goods that were needed came from the bazaar; cushioned *takhts* instead of chairs, and huge round scarlet trays painted with flowers, which served as tables for the simple dishes Hamdi served. Loti's first preoccupation was to buy some of those Koranic texts, prayers, or the words of the Prophet, which the calligraphers' art transformed into exquisite arabesques, objects of decoration found in mosques, markets and houses alike. At dusk, when all the purchases were amassed, and he could indulge in his passion for arranging whatever house, room or cabin he inhabited, Osman reminded him that there were still a number of necessities lacking. Loti was sharp. '*Nothing* is more urgent than the décor,' he said; 'one can always do without the necessities.' However, there was nothing with which to cook, no crockery, nor jugs and basins for washing, so Loti gave in. Hamdi rushed off, returning proudly with frightful examples of the latest Western import – cheap white enamel ware from Germany – and Loti sighed, recalling the graceful copper vessels of other days. However, the house soon became passably authentic and Loti enjoyed receiving his Turkish friends there.

Lying on the quilted *yatak* that replaced a bed, he woke to the immemorial chant, *It is better to pray than sleep.* The muezzin's call to the Faithful told the hours which drifted past to the plaintive sound of Hamdi's flute, and at dusk, in the luminous half-light, all of it was balm. But not for long. Watching the moonlight falling across his grilled windows, which had once been those of the harem, he felt a sudden twinge of Lovelace exasperation. Bars – for this empty room? A room once holding veiled charmers, perhaps those Circassian slaves chosen for their blonde beauty – and he, alone in the emptiness? What irony! He might have echoed Browning's lines:

> Dear dead women, with such hair, too.
> What's become of all the gold
> Used to hang and brush their bosoms?
> I feel chilly and grown old.

It is to be wondered, why, at this point in his life, Loti did not settle in Turkey permanently. There was no longer anything to keep him in France. His seafaring days were over, like his marriage: his son was grown up, the second, Basque, family too, and well provided for. He detested Paris life, where many of his friends had now died. The fortune his writings earned was largely used for the needs of the many people to whom he was so generous, and there was still enough left for him to travel or live as he chose elsewhere. Why, then, during this time in Constantinople was he constantly harping on his imminent departure? Was his addiction to unhappiness now so strong that he could not allow himself to look for any further happiness? Now that all the obstacles were removed it seemed too late to do what he had longed to do, when Achmet and Aziyadé had implored him to stay among them.

The new Sultan had not overlooked Loti's return, and like all the Ottoman princes, shared his predecessor's interest in the famous French writer who expressed such affection for everything Turkish. Loti was bidden to an audience at the palace of Dolma Bagtché, which gave Loti occasion to recall the more inaccessible palace of Yildiz, where, nevertheless, the Sultan Rouge had received him and shown him so many marks of esteem. 'He, the master of terror, whose eagle glance could, nevertheless, charm, when he was touched by pity . . . He was a great sovereign, in the mould of other days.' Thus Loti, saluting his shade.

Mahomet V was of softer clay. He wore a grey suit and but for the fez would have passed for any bourgeois Frenchman, Loti noted regretfully. But he was all cordiality, and the traditional extravaganzas of Oriental taste were still in evidence, like a four-ton crystal chandelier. While awaiting his audience Loti was served coffee, 'that exquisite blond coffee, the colour of tea, such as one drinks only in the Palace, offered on a gold tray, in a small cup mounted in gold and encrusted with diamonds. Following the etiquette of the court, it was covered by a drapery of gold-embroidered crimson velvet, thrown in the form of a cloak, to cover not only the delicate brew, but the arm and shoulder of the servitor who presented it.'

Towards the end of this time of hallowed memories, Loti's son joined him for a short holiday before beginning his military service. His boat docked early in the morning, and he was met by Hamdi and Osman, who quickly clapped a fez on his head and exchanged his boots for slippers. Loti's orders were categoric. It was a Turkish household, and the boy must not arrive looking Western. Samuel was delighted with all he saw around him, and spellbound by his father's accounts of that far-away adventure lived at Eyoub. Sightseeing with this marvellous paternal guide was interwoven with high romance, and there was a ceremonial visit to Aziyadé's grave. Loti was particularly anxious for his son to visit this spot at least once in his lifetime . . . for who knew if the boy would ever return to Turkey? Loti was beginning to burn with a fever which presently necessitated entering the French hospital. He therefore pushed forward Samuel's visit, though trembling and dizzy with fever, as well as emotion. 'To take my son there may seem rather strange,' he confides to his journal, 'but over the years my memories of her have become purified – as it were immaterialized.' This stilled a curiously puritan streak that was gradually to emerge, and bring him to say he thought all his earlier books unhealthy – immoral, even.

After two weeks in the hospital, where he dictated his last wishes to the alarmed Samuel, he rallied sufficiently to accept the French Consul-General's hospitality at his country house above Ortakeui, on the European shores of the Bosphorus. Autumn came early that year and muffled in overcoats and rugs the convalescent Loti sat in the garden among the yellowing leaves and wilting asters, watching the passage of shipping up and down the ruffled waters below. There were few caïques to be seen, and the fishermen's gaily painted sailing boats were giving place to steamboats and noisy engines. The reforms of the Young Turks were never to his liking; he clung to the beauty of the past . . . 'It is still the Orient – but the Orient of autumn, of evening, of decline and death.' Sadness fell round him like a fine rain. Uneasiness was in the air. Already he could sense the coming horrors of the Balkan wars where, by the rapacity of Turkey's traditional Western enemies, the Ottoman Empire was to be dismembered, never again to regain its former power or the old tranquil ways Loti revered.

Those horrors were not long in coming. In September 1911 Italy seized Tripoli and the final downfall of the Ottoman Empire was begun. Tripoli, like Tunis, had for centuries been a Turkish dominion, its population entirely Moslem. Yet no voice was raised internationally against this rape. Loti sprang to Turkey's defence, and denounced Italy's infamy in a polemic published by *Figaro*, where he remarked with bitterness that, in the climate of international politics, Moslem countries seemed to have become fair game, to be hunted at any season. The Italians justified their seizure of Tripoli as an act of commendable enterprise, bringing civilization to a backward race; and no-one contradicted this statement.

In October of the same year, Serbia, Bulgaria and Montenegro declared war on Turkey. These predominantly Christian peoples were religious minorities in the vast Ottoman Empire which overshadowed them, and now, encouraged by the way the wind of sympathy was blowing from the West, they determined to become independent states.

For Turkey things went badly from the start. Its forces were spread across vast distances of Asia Minor and the Levant, and could not be deployed quickly to fight on the Balkan front, for railroads were still few. There was disastrous incompetence and corruption at Staff Headquarters, where chaos reigned; by the end of October, the Turks were finally routed.

The Great Powers had always seen Turkey as a pawn to be manoeuvred to each player's advantage, and now a series of conferences were hurriedly called, to decide Turkey's future standing. While these conferences continued, the massacres and atrocities for which the Balkan wars are chiefly remembered, raged unchecked and acts of unimaginable barbarism were perpetrated by Christian and Moslem alike. Whole villages were encircled and set alight; mosques were defiled, wells choked with dismembered bodies. Rape, pillage, torture . . . the horrors continued unabated.

Loti felt Turkey's anguish as his own, and was lacerated, humiliated, and helpless. He was past sixty now, no longer a fighting man able to take up arms for his second country. Once, as Aziyadé's lover, he had been tempted to enlist under the Sultan's banners: but then, his loyalties as a French officer had held him back. Now, in Turgenev's tragic phrase, he was tied to the pier of old age.

But was he? All his old fighting instincts rose up: he could still do battle by the pen. He flung himself into the struggle, entering the lists as journalist, fighting the prejudices of editors and government figures, battering every influential door open by the weight of his name, harassing, persuading, pleading on behalf of the Turkish nation, as it stood at bay.

It should not be imagined that his impassioned partisanship was due solely to his memories of a romantic past lived in the City of the Sultans. He was generally subjective in his views, rarely political, but among the Turks of all degrees he had found the best life had to offer and he would defend them to the end. Thus he persisted in putting forward the most disconcerting arguments in their favour. French Sisters of Mercy, doctors and teachers who had lived and worked for many years among the Turks, now joined Loti in his defence, and some of their fervent depositions are to be found in his book *Turquie Agonisante*.

This was published in 1913, an age we look back on as sheltered – which it was for certain people. But the public in general had not then experienced two world wars, nor become hardened to the sight of horrors such as we are fed daily by reporters, cameras and television. Thus, when *Turquie Agonisante* appeared, bearing on the cover one of the most appalling photographs imaginable, it did something to rouse public opinion, as Loti had hoped. No-one could ignore this picture of a Turkish soldier – a grinning mask of hideous hilarity, which had once been a human face. Mutilated by the enemy, the nose sliced off, the whole mouth and jaw slashed wide, the teeth remained in the middle of a gaping wound.

Loti was not to be turned aside by any appeals for discretion, but his zeal was beginning to embarrass and exasperate the French Government, balancing on the tightrope of neutrality. Loti was too involved, they said, and his imprudently worded diatribes were becoming unprintable. Old friends such as Poincaré, then Prime Minister, or Louis Barthou, as well as the editors of influential papers, *Figaro* or *l'Humanité*, warned him to stay outside the political arena, and presently the press began to find they had no space for his appeals, which they regarded as so many rodomontades, while hostesses of the salons which had once courted him shrugged off his frantic speeches. But Loti was seeing far ahead. In France's singular hostility towards Turkey he foresaw, not only the further decline of the Ottoman Empire, but the decline of French interests in their former spheres of influence about the Near and Middle East. For once he showed real political acumen, and the letters and articles which he wrote at this time were published later, in 1920, entitled *La Mort de Notre Chère France en Orient*.

The invective Loti employed against Turkey's enemies individually or as a group was violent and continued to exasperate the French authorities. After exposing some of the more hideous atrocities of the Bulgarian troops, sanctioned by their Coburg-born princeling Tsar Ferdinand, he described that monarch as having 'the profile of a vulture, the tiny glinting eyes of a tapir, gimlet-like under hanging folds of flesh'.

The portrait was wounding in its veracity, and had infuriated a young Armenian, Lieutenant Torcom, then serving with the Bulgarian army. He was further inflamed by the articles Loti had been publishing stressing his growing hostility to Turkey's Armenian population, and he challenged '*the ex-sailor*' to a duel. He would come to Paris and force a retraction of the odious statements (published in *Turquie Agonisante*) where Loti attributed part of recent Turkish defeats to Armenian lassitude in battle (some Armenians having been absorbed into the Turkish ranks). The duel was to be held outside Paris, and Loti had chosen Briettmayer, the French foils champion, as his second, before anxious friends manoeuvred him out of the conflict, and the challenge was taken up by Briettmayer. A violent combat followed, and when the opponents were separated, neither considered honour had been satisfied. Loti had to be persuaded to retract or soften some of his more offensive anti-Armenian statements before the matter was closed.

Presently, Turkey's enemies began fighting among themselves, savage for gains. Greeks and Bulgarians haggled over Macedonia, Bulgaria and Romania disputed frontiers and railways lines, and Montenegro looked to Russia to support its claims. While they were at each other's throats, the Great Powers began dismembering the Ottoman Empire as they thought fit. When Turkey was being loudly condemned for the Armenian massacres, single-minded Loti dismissed the charges with airy nonchalance. 'My poor Turks! I must admit they did make a regrettable show of vivacity regarding the Armenians.' It was useless to argue with him – Turkey was always to be justified, and neither Loti nor the Turks ever admitted the charge of genocide. Loti continued to go between Rochefort and Paris, alienating more and more friends in high places, until at last he realized it was wiser to desist, and skulked, alone in his mosque. Madame Adam feared these moods of bitter withdrawal alternating with political fulminations would be at the cost of his writing, and she urged him to return to work – to his old vein. 'I am not like you and George Sand,' he replied. 'I cannot *always* write.'

At Rochefort Loti had never been popular, in spite of Viaud roots, his aura of fame, and the affection with which his mother was remembered. There too, he now found blind, political prejudice against the Moslems. He was one himself, said the townspeople, not unnaturally, for the presence of the mosque, although invisible, seemed conclusive. He might be a world-famous author, Rochefort's most distinguished citizen, but to them he was a bizarre figure, a bad father and a worse husband, while Blanche had left behind her an aura of martyred saintliness. And then there was the deplorable business of that other family – those Basques he visited so openly, even having Raymond (Raimuntcho) and Edmond Gainza photographed with Samuel, saying that as he had three sons he was not going to be hypocritical about it. Some of the lesser officers at the Préfecture de la Marine frowned too. They were not of the Grand Cadre, the upper ranks of the Service, as Loti had been, and they resented his rank and fortune. There were few friends left from the old days, such as the Duplais, who had known and loved their Julien before all the poses and scandals had clouded his image. Rochefort was now a ghost town, his house an abode of shadows, the mosque a sounding-board for Turkish lamentations.

Samuel was still away, doing his military service, and with a sense of surprise Loti admitted that he had come to miss him – this son he had desired but had not loved. The time they spent together in Turkey had brought them together. Samuel had been wonderfully understanding about Aziyadé's grave. Dimly, Loti began to realize that Samuel was another of those who loved him unreservedly, however defensive he knew the boy to be where his mother was concerned. Alone, under the shadowy arches of the mosque, he sought consolation beside Aziyadé's stele. It was as if she knew and shared his torments over the disasters of the war: as if she knew, too, how passionately he regretted that he had not fought for Turkey so long ago; as if she knew the depths of his present unhappiness . . . *Allah selamit versen Loti* . . . May Allah protect Loti, she had said in her soft voice, and still the echo sounded.

21

The darkness thickened
Upon him creeping.
In the heart of age
A child lay weeping

A. E. Housman, *The Lonely*

Loti was to return to Turkey once more, in 1913, three years after what he had thought was his final visit, last of the last of those lacerating farewells to all he loved, which he has described in *Suprêmes Visions d'Orient*. This ultimate vision, published as a postscript to the first two books is the apotheosis of his whole Turkish life. In August 1913 Turkey was living the crucial hours when its fate was being finally decided by the Great Powers. The manner in which his Turkish books were, first of all, love poems to that land, the international prestige of his *Vautour* days, and now, his passionate championship of Turkey at war, had made him all theirs, and people in every walk of life wanted to show their gratitude to this 'friend of the dark days,' as they called him. Aziyadé's lover was returning as a national hero. Yet in spite of the official invitation extended to him he seems to have been unaware of the depths of gratitude and the welcome awaiting him. Loti was genuinely modest.

When his ship anchored off Galata 'in the pale rosy light of early morning' he saw an enormous crowd on the quay, flags, massed flowers, red carpets, bands playing and troops standing to attention . . . For whom could all this be, he wondered. 'For you, mon Commandant,' said Osman, who with Samuel had once more accompanied him. Only when the various delegations, the generals representing the Sultan and the princes, the representatives of all the corporations, the imams, the dervishes, and numerous high personages had come aboard and were surrounding him did Loti know it was indeed himself they honoured.

'I had never imagined such a welcome! As I stepped ashore to where a Court carriage awaited me, the crowds cheered and waved banners, and all the way to Top Hané, where one of the Sultan's own launches awaited me, I passed through hedges of soldiers at the salute, and backed by cheering crowds. There was even a confederation of street porters who had gathered with inscribed banners, their horny hands thundering applause. Here, from this unchanged quay where long ago I had so often embarked as an obscure young officer, I now embarked in triumph on the Imperial launch, amid military salutes.' It was roses, roses, all the way.

Next day, there were visits to the Imperial Princes Yusseff-Izeddin and Abd-ul-Mejed, his old friends; and on returning to the Ostrorogs' yali at Kandili, he found the faithful Djemil awaiting him; an emotional meeting. Djemil was a careworn, grizzled figure, in a soldier's tattered uniform. He had survived the bitter defeats, but broke down describing them. 'During the day,' writes Loti, 'I had regained confidence in the eternal Orient and Islam . . . But tonight when we were sitting on the little marble landing stage outside the yali, watching a sombre mass of storm clouds lowering over the European shore, the latest news brought us was terrifying . . . The dismemberment of Turkey now seems irrevocably decided by Christian Europe.'

There were a series of further official ceremonies to honour Loti, some of a national character, such as one at the theatre, with Loti in the Imperial box, responding to a frantically cheering audience. The Grand Vizier put his State Caïque with its scarlet and gold-laced oarsmen at Loti's disposal. The Sultan, like the Cheik-ul-Islam and the chief of the Dervishes, all vied to express their recognition of Loti's loyalty. The villagers of Kandili (where he was regarded as their special friend, since he frequently stayed at the Ostrorogs' yali there) prepared their own celebration. From a barque hung with flowers, with eight standing oarsmen in the old manner and dressed in their traditional garments, Loti was hailed, and invited to take his place aboard. Reclining on fine rugs and cushions, like a pacha, he smoked the narghile of honour, while listening to songs composed for the occasion.

The secret of Loti's love story with Aziyadé had been long accepted by the Turks, and he was considerably comforted to know that when he must leave Constantinople, the cherished grave would be maintained as he would have wished. It was no less a personage than his friend Tewfik Bey, an all-powerful figure in the military hierarchy, who undertook to be responsible for this, a charge which he, and, after his death, other of Loti's Turkish friends, faithfully fulfilled.

The Turks, who had come to know their Loti as well as he knew them, devised many ways to give him pleasure, and at the Sultan's suggestion he was commanded to a dinner to be held in the inviolate precincts of Top Kapou Seraglio, a dinner to be conducted entirely in the ancient, ceremonial manner, with all the fabled luxuries still hidden behind those menacing walls. Nothing could have delighted Loti more, for the palace remained, in its abandonment, as inviolate and mysterious as when the mighty Sultans lived there, surrounded by their Court, their guards, pages, musicians, cup bearers, astrologers, and eunuchs, black or white, who guarded the whole hierarchy of the harem. The Seraglio had already passed into legend when Loti first knew Turkey; and forty years later, it still stood as inviolate as ever, but now it was the haunt of sinister shadows, all its richness tarnished and crumbling, the shelter of a few aged kadines and eunuchs, who lingered on there, in dark, hidden quarters where the bats circled.

Present-day Turkish enterprise has made this fabulous palace the first tourist attraction of the whole city, but Loti saw it under extraordinary circumstances of privilege. He has described its puissant mixture of oppression, terror, silence, and almost barbaric luxury. The dinner was held in one of those small, box-like rooms favoured as retreats by the Ottoman Sultans. Eight distinguished persons welcomed him, and were seated round a low table of solid silver, spread with a service beyond price. 'The dinner, served in such splendour was without wines, naturally, but presented by solemn men in long silken robes of an ancient cut.' As darkness fell, they repaired to another small, secretive room to smoke the customary tchibouque. 'They brought, to each of us, a pipe heavy with historic diamonds, each worth a fortune, where the pipe-stems of scented jasmin wood were so long that the smokers were unable to light them; a question of etiquette, this, obliging a servitor in his silken robe, to kneel beside each smoker to keep the tchibouque glowing . . .'

Loti, who was in a daze of pleasure, learned that the Sultan had originally wished to lodge him there, at the very heart of Ottoman splendour – an honour never before accorded to any foreigner. But he was dissuaded: 'too many phantoms here, at night,' said Loti's hosts, and he tried to hide his disappointment.

'*16 August.* The Sultan received me in a lengthy audience at Yildiz. Just as I was leaving he took off his watch, with its massive gold chain and his monogram in diamonds and thrust it, almost by force, into my waistcoat.' This resplendent souvenir was to take its place among all the other brilliant orders and decorations bestowed on Loti during his long life. In the bank vaults, where, together with his daughter-in-law, Madame Samuel Loti-Viaud, I was examining the glittering remains of his honoured days, I came on a small cardboard box containing a heavy gold ring with a Turkish inscription – Aziyadé's ring – more dear to him than all the rest.

During this brief, golden afterglow, Loti lived in a house his friends had prepared specially for him, furnished entirely in Turkish style. It was in the ancient quarter of the Fatih mosque, the quarter where once Aziyadé had pined for him, and every shadowy cobbled street recalled that past. On his last visit to Constantinople, in 1910, he had bought the few modest furnishings he required from the Bazaar; now he found an establishment of sumptuous luxury awaiting him. The servants and guards, like the Court carriage and splendid horses, were all sent from the Sultan's own household, as were the priceless carpets and porcelain. That such splendour was only revealed, almost furtively, after passing narrow sinister labyrinthine ways was in the Oriental tradition of secrecy, and much to Loti's taste. He describes the luxuries in voluptuous detail. 'Only Turkish food is prepared. My dinner table was once that of the Sultan Abdul Aziz. Koranic inscriptions and gold ewers are marked with the cypher of some long dead Sultan. In the bedroom there are silken mattresses on the floor, and dressing gowns of Damascus brocade, the bed linen embroidered magnificently in gold and silver thread.' Perhaps, above all else, Loti enjoyed the muezzin's chant sounding from the minaret of a little mosque close by. 'To give me special pleasure, the Turks sent muezzins chosen for the beauty of their voice.' It was thus, in such imaginative ways, that the Turks expressed their gratitude to their 'friend of the dark days'.

Loti left Constantinople and the glow of his welcome after only five weeks of basking and once again we wonder why he tore himself away so soon. Among the Turkish people who loved him he might have come at last to be buried, under the cypress trees of some calm field of the dead – perhaps even that one where Aziyadé lay. It

304

would have been in the supreme romantic tradition. But once again, Janus-headed Loti, ever looking east, turned west.

At Rochefort, he felt old age falling on him like a dusty cloak. He was sixty-three, in no way infirm, but all that was not youth was inadmissible. Old age was the negation of all that life stood for; of what use was money, when one no longer had the youth to enjoy it? Such were his thoughts as winter drew on, soft and grey and muffled in Rochefort, blustering and sharp at Hendaye, as he moved between the two, restless as ever. Only the sea had ever been able to stay him, 'that great infinity that blotted out all memories and sorrows'. Early in 1914 President Poincaré came to Hendaye, and visited Bakhar Etchea. His views of the political horizon were not reassuring. The hideous face of war began to form again. Loti was still haunted by the horrors of the Balkan wars, and now knew that were such horrors, and more, to reappear nearer home, his own son would be drawn into the maelstrom. And he – where would war find him? He had always said that death in battle was 'the only death that is not lugubrious, that one does not fear', but he was no longer listed for active service.

On August 2nd the German armies invaded Luxembourg. Samuel was with his mother, but in answer to Loti's telegram, returned to his father's side. Together, father and son heard the declaration of war. There was nothing to say. In silence each looked out his uniforms. Samuel's had been laid away since his days of military service; Loti's had been embalmed in tissue paper and camphor, preserved as yet another sacred relic, never, he imagined, to be worn again. To Loti it represented something akin to the *tricolor*, and he regarded both with an almost fetish worship. For all his railings at Western ways, and his cravings to be one with the East, he was, fundamentally, instinctively, devoted to the ideals of honour and the motherland and his uniform was the symbol of all that was finest in France. Therefore, on that torrid August 3rd when he put on a white tropical uniform, 'the kind in which I always felt most myself', he knew a sense of elation. At the Préfecture, he signed on for service, as he used to do before embarking on a voyage. He was on the reserve list, but believed he would be able to serve his country once more. It was a disappointment to find himself brushed aside in the tumult, and only allotted an insignificant post at the Arsenal; yet the cult of the motherland was very strong, and he refused to be discouraged or humiliated when his requests, his pleadings even, for some more active and responsible assignment went unanswered.

Meanwhile, any personal frustrations were dimmed, as he watched the continuing Governmental blunders vis à vis Turkey. Long ago he had warned those in authority of the dangers they risked, if they continued to alienate so valuable a potential ally. And now, at this crucial hour, there were still no moves to win over the Sublime Porte. This was an aspect of the conflict where Loti believed his influence could be valuable. On September 6th, through the columns of *Figaro*, he addressed an open letter to Enver Pacha. The Pacha had always been pro-German, but he had also been appreciative of Loti's bold support during both the Tripolitanian and Balkan wars, and Loti, and no doubt the French Government, too, now hoped there would be a response to this overture. There was none. Loti had written of the anguish he would feel, even at the inevitable hour of victory over Germany, if Turkey, his second country, lay crushed beneath the ruins of the hideous Prussian empire . . . In October, Loti wrote another open letter, probably with the connivance of the French Government where he had many friends who now belatedly realized the strategic importance of a Turkish alliance. This second letter was addressed to Loti's old friend Prince Yusseff Izeddin, heir to the Ottoman throne and ever a staunch supporter of French interests in Turkish territories. Again, there was no reply to 'the friend of dark days'. Soon it was known why. On August 2nd Turkey had signed a secret pact with Germany, and on November 1st entered the war beside the German army. Loti had the bitterness of knowing his second country was now the enemy.

He asked to be sent to the front lines – in any capacity. 'I shall find ways to make myself useful, I assure you,' he wrote. There is something pathetic in this ageing, disillusioned and distinguished man begging for any place in which to serve, however far beneath the position his captain's five gold stripes or his lustre as a writer merited. His appeal to the Admiralty was passed over. He had been on the reserve list since 1910, and red tape now blocked his request for service afloat. But while Loti insisted on his right to serve with the navy in one capacity or another, it was to be the army which rescued him from stagnation. General Gallieni, then military governor of Paris, appointed him liaison officer at his headquarters, and it was thus that Commander Viaud, this highly decorated officer from the Grand Cadre de la Marine, found himself attached to the land forces.

By the end of 1914 he was again trying to use his personal influence with certain powerful Turkish figures, and so began a series of secret negotiations on the highest level. Loti's biographers have generally remained silent over these, for little is known with exactitude. Prince Saba Eddine, a nephew of the Sultan who was opposed to Enver Pacha's policies, was one of those with whom Loti had continued to be in close touch and this enabled him to furnish the French authorities with a confidential report on Turkey at war; also, to denounce the folly of a projected campaign in the Dardanelles – advice that was not heeded. There were further secret negotiations in which Loti played a significant rôle. In May 1915, when it was known that the Young Turk party was in favour of negotiating a separate peace with France, Loti believed that his efforts as an intermediary would be crowned. But the French, very properly, would not consider any separate peace apart from their British and Russian allies, and matters hung fire. Presently, secret meetings at the Turkish Consulate in Geneva were planned. The British and Russians were in agreement, and Loti expected to meet Talaat Pacha, Minister of the Interior. Abruptly, Talaat Pacha sent word he could not leave the Porte, and one of his government, Djavid Bey, would represent him: next, a message from Djavid Bey stated he was detained on the orders of Talaat Pacha. The French could make no sense of this Oriental imbroglio; Loti's frantic messages seem to have fallen on deaf ears, or into the wrong hands. On June 8th Poincaré noted: 'No news of Loti and his Turks.' On the 15th: 'The Russian setbacks and our impotence in the Dardanelles do not favour Loti's Turkish initiatives.'

When, later, another Turkish representative was to be sent to Geneva, the French Government inexplicably refused Loti the right to meet any envoy from Constantinople. Further, they appointed someone else to act as go-between, and it was through this third person that Loti was obliged to communicate with the nation which he held so dear. Forced to stand aside, he watched these vital negotiations drag on and at last peter out. Would they have done so had he been allowed direct contact – who now knows? Turkey was probably too deeply involved with the German war machine to break away.

Disillusioned, Loti found himself allotted a number of less vital missions, polite diplomatic encounters where his reputation as a man of letters counted, but his Turkish links rusted: to the King and Queen of the Belgians, in the ruins of Reims and Ypres; in 1916, to Madrid, to solicit the aid of neutral Spain (where he met with a rebuff); in 1917, to the Headquarters of the Italian army, then fighting the Austrians in the Dolomites. In Venice, among the Italian High Command, he was lodged at Danieli's and given the rooms once occupied by George Sand and Alfred de Musset, a graceful tribute to the writer.

Loti did not want to be received as a famous writer: he wanted to be in the thick of battle, plunged into some violent struggle that would wipe out his humiliating uselessness. Set aside from the Turkish negotiations, it was as if his whole life's blood and all hope had seeped from him, leaving only a phantom figure grown skeletal thin and old overnight. He was further saddened by the death of General Gallieni, followed by that of Yusseff-Izeddin, that prince whom he had counted on as an ally. The prince had not met with a natural death: pro-German elements saw to it that he did not live to oppose their designs. Loti wrote a valedictory piece on this friend of France, which was published later in *Quelques aspects du vertige mondial*. 'Think of him with regret,' Loti wrote, 'not only because he would have been a great and benevolent sovereign, but because he loved our country . . . His dream' (and Loti's too) 'was a vast Oriental empire, powerful by the unity of the Arab peoples, and the friendship of France. The Prince paid with his life for his clairvoyant horror of Germany.'

Between diplomatic missions Loti at last contrived to be sent to certain battle areas, which enabled him to write firsthand of all he saw around him, in the trenches, at the ambulance posts or the base hospitals, terrible scenes, where men were coughing out their lungs from poison gas attacks, then the latest invention of destruction. On the Somme, in Alsace and in Flanders mud or shattered towns, writing of the then new air warfare, Loti went anywhere that his pen might record, or serve as propaganda. Sometimes he returned briefly to Paris, holding conferences, raising funds or writing those bitter tirades later published as *La Hyène Enragée* and *L'Horreur Allemande*. These books are an almost hysterical denunciation of all things German. Wagner's music, in spite of *Parsifal*, which had once moved him profoundly, was now repulsive, the Kaiser 'a barbarous cretin with no soul, only blood-sucking tentacles, overlord of the abattoir and charnel house'.

But in an address made at the Comédie Française his key changed. There was no more ranting. The Minister of the Marine had asked him to speak of the sailors, 'and speak with all your heart,' he added. 'Speak of our sailors? But I have done that all my life,' was Loti's reply, and his address is an infinitely moving tribute. 'If there is anything of worth in my writings, it has been inspired by them . . . for half a century I have been among them . . . It is they whom I have had the honour to command,' he said, recalling the old Admiral's words to him, as a cadet, on the *Borda*. Loti came to consider the sailors as the nation's élite, a race apart, from father to son bred by the salt air of the coastal villages, and from childhood destined for the sea . . . 'that great teacher, terrible and splendid, from whom they learned a mutual devotion and true fraternity . . .' Such were the men whom he now evoked for the Parisian audience before him in words which can be read in *Quelques aspects du vertige mondial*: there is none of the loud-pedalling, nor tremolos which deform some of his political polemics.

The war had settled into its terrible stride. Losses were appalling. All over France, private houses, on no matter what scale, were being turned into hospitals or convalescent homes, and Loti was not to be found wanting. In a dash back from the front he gave instructions for a number of wounded soldiers to be taken into the old house at Rochefort; presently fifteen casualties were bedded down, rather uncomfortably, in the narrow rooms overlooking the courtyard, their truckle beds overflowing into the Chinese Room among the scarlet lacquer and grimacing porcelain figures. It was not a practical arrangement, for with all the sumptuous fantasies Loti had imposed there was still no electricity nor yet a bathroom, and the servants struggled to cook and serve relays of invalid meals from the small dark kitchen which had remained unchanged since Great-aunt Berthe had presided there.

Loti did not linger long among the wounded, allowing himself barely time to visit the mosque and Aziyadé's stele. Nostalgia must wait. He returned to the battles in which he might take no part: but it was remarked that he always seized the opportunity to press forward, to be under fire, as if he sought death, said those who saw him. And a lamentable figure he cut, for the conditions in which he lived, in the wet and cold of northern France, were undermining his last strength. He is described as being so small and frail that he was entirely lost beneath a heavy army overcoat. 'All that was to be seen was a hooked nose, a short-clipped white beard, faintly tinted, and boots so small they seemed fit for a Chinese doll.'

It was this ghost of his former self that struggled on, a lonely figure, among the vigorous, unthinking young officers who mocked this out-of-date ex-naval officer, so oddly placed among them, who seemed to have no specific job, but wore uniform, was a stickler for etiquette, and forever scribbling . . . There were few like Maréchal Franchet d'Esperey who knew Loti's true worth and realized how much he was suffering. The General found him in a wretched billet, shivering in a naval greatcoat, crouched by a smoking fire of green wood, his face haggard, his eyes brilliant with fever. He was sent home on sick leave for the second time in November 1917, when accumulated fatigue and frustration overcame him. At Hendaye he developed congestion of the lungs and his state became critical, so that his alarmed friends rallied round. Madame Barthou, who had been running various Red Cross organizations in Paris now descended, unbidden, on Bakhar Etchea, where she took command. Gone were the exotic turbans and paradise plumes she favoured: she now wore nurse's uniform with equal authority and crackled about in a starched cap and apron, conferring with the doctor and creating a clinical atmosphere. The Magician must not die! France needed him! *She* needed him! She set about her ministrations with energetic devotion, ordering gruels and tisanes, issuing bulletins and forbidding any visitors, which upset poor timid adoring Madame Durutty, waiting anxiously in her house nearby. But Madame Barthou was in possession, and perhaps it was due to her intensive care that Loti recovered, he later admitted, rather grudgingly. He was also to recall that his saviour had not been entirely disinterested, for she had seized this unique occasion to read the journals. There were secrets she hoped to discover: the exact relationship between Loti and Berthe Durutty being one of them.

Loti was barely convalescent when he brushed aside any further cossetting and returned to the front, though he was still alarmingly weak. However much make-up he plastered over his pallor (something which made him the butt of innumerable sarcasms in the mess, like his bewildering change of costumes – a képi with naval uniform, a bearskin cape over cavalry khaki, and such) he knew there was no chance of appearing fit enough to be sent anywhere near the front. Humbly, he continued to make himself useful where and how he could. 'It was not easy to make use of this shore sailor,' Maréchal Franchet d'Esperey was to recall; but Loti's solid naval training did enable him to produce a number of technical reports on the use of explosives for land mines, as well as valuable meteorological observations pertaining to the conduct of aerial warfare. Samuel had at last succeeded in being transferred to an advanced artillery post, and Loti fretted for news. All around, the children of his friends were dying . . . the Barthous had lost their son, Madame Adam her son-in-law . . . Why should Samuel be spared? In the remorseless chill of northern France he remained stoic, refusing any suggestion that he should try to regain his health somewhere in the south. This he saw as desertion, and with all his accustomed obstinacy refused to quit. But during the last great spring offensive of 1918, it was clear he would soon be forced to give up, and with that in mind, he took a decisive step; breaking the habit of a whole lifetime, he closed his journal forever. '20 April 1918. Today in anticipation of my death, I am finally closing the Journal of my life, which I began about forty-five years ago. It is of no further interest to me, and will be of no interest to anyone else. Pierre Loti.'

The renunciation of his journal deepened his sense of loneliness. Since childhood it had been his confidant and company. Since those early days of Fédin's hieroglyphics it had become a second self, and for Loti, who always imbued each of his belongings, and all those inanimate objects around him with a personality, the severance must have seemed a betrayal, something to haunt him with a sense of reproach. Yet he did not go back on his decision and there followed some wearisome months of fluctuating health and loneliness, surrounded by all the ugliness and suffering of war. By summer, he was forced to give up, and returned to Rochefort, death in his heart, humiliated by his weakness and general sense of uselessness.

In the silent house he waited for release from a life where he no longer had a place. However in November 1918, on the signing of the Armistice, his spirits revived. With the cease-fire he was officially demobilized, to use an official term for his irregular position in the army. The nightmare was over. Samuel had been spared, and he, Loti, had managed to stay the course and serve his country once again. Here are the terms of a citation he received from the War Office, something he valued more than all the eulogies or decorations of his younger days.

'. . . although dispensed by age from any military obligations, has served since the beginning of the war, setting a fine example of devotion and patriotism. Has fulfilled numerous missions under enemy fire, notably at Béhouille and the Fort of Manonvillers, the said missions being acquitted to the entire satisfaction of his commanding officers.

Has taken part in five campaigns as well as the Great War.'

As always with Loti, joy was short-lived; he had foreseen the Allied terms imposed on a defeated Turkey would be very harsh, and they were even more severe than he had believed. The Ottoman Empire was finally dismembered. Allied warships rode at anchor in the Bosphorus, and victorious troops were everywhere about the City of the Sultans, their guard-posts stationed at each end of the Galata bridge, controlling the comings and goings of the unhappy Turks whose impoverishment was aggravated by the numbers of refugees, Russian, Persian, Armenian and Caucasian, who poured in, fleeing from the Bolshevik offensives in southern Russia. Loti realized that now, as never before, he must find the force to re-open his campaign for clemency to be shown towards his second country. The old losing battle stretched before him anew, but now there seemed so little time or strength left to plead his cause – Turkey's cause. 'I am convinced it will be not only iniquitous but disastrous to annihilate this loyal, contemplative and pious people whose characteristics counter-balance our own,' he wrote to the President of the Commission of War Reparations: but no-one heeded him. More and more slices of the Ottoman Empire were parcelled out among the rapacious Balkan nations, the problem of minorities now being reversed. Meanwhile, the Turkish nation was to struggle through an uneasy Califate, awaiting the regenerative rule of Ataturk, but paying the price for his ruthless modernization by the destruction of all those age-old traditions which Loti valued.

The war was over, but for Loti there was no peace. He was facing that spectre of final annihilation which had dogged him since childhood. It had drawn very close. How much time remained in which to ensure that all those cherished, inanimate objects that he had endowed with a spirit, a life of their own, should not fall into indifferent hands? He wished to place them in safe keeping almost as if they were household pets. Above all there were his journals; a stack of cardboard boxes contained more than two hundred packets, the day to day records of his past, the loose sheets tied into sections, dated and sealed. All the fire and smoke of his life, and many secrets lay there . . . 'all that I was, all that I loved, and all that I wept for'. To go through them would be a painful process, the resurrection of a phantom self, but he had always believed that by committing himself to paper he was ensuring that something of himself would remain, a voice from the tomb which still sounded.

In view of posthumous publication there were certain passages that he believed should be destroyed, but his remaining strength was ebbing fast and he faltered before the two hundred packets. A raging sense of impotence still overcame him; Turkey's ruin gnawed at his entrails, while he persisted in spending himself on (often) unpublishable polemics. 'I am terribly, dangerously exhausted,' he wrote to Madame Adam. 'I have suffered too much these last months, seeing the infamous machinations against my beloved Turkey . . . Nothing exhausts or destroys like indignation.'

The old house, so silent and empty, closed round him as he drifted from room to room, a spectre among the souvenirs. There was the vaporous reva-reva headdress once worn by the vahinés, which seemed to mock him who had once been the amorous Julien Viaud, and was first named Loti on those seductive shores. There was the Turkish costume he had worn as Ussim Effendi, and another, of the Persian archer which had electrified le tout Paris at Madame Adam's costume ball. Beside the funereal wreaths with their inscribed violet silk ribbons which remained in his mother's room, there was another poignant reminder – his seaman's cap with its red pom-pon and gold printed ribbon – l'Entreprenant – the ship on which he had sailed to join Bernard in Senegal . . . the same seaman's cap that he, the young officer, had worn when he donned rating's blue and white, to sport about the bals calicots, or attain that black satin hung bedroom where Sarah Bernhardt and the skeleton awaited Pierre le Fou . . . There – O! anguish! was the china bear that had once consoled by the sweets hidden in its belly . . . All, all must be saved from the future's forgetfulness. All must be part of that stand against oblivion.

He set about re-drafting his will, with a sense of desperate urgency.

Next, Samuel was recalled from Paris, there again studying at the Beaux Arts. Before the war he had hoped that painting would be his future, but he had done very well in the army, won the Croix de Guerre, and decided to remain in the Service. However, his father would not hear of this. Had it been a question of remaining in the navy – of following in his own footsteps – he might have agreed – but the army? Certainly not. In any case, the boy was now needed urgently to work with him on the journals. He must return at once. So Samuel, loth but ever-loving, left the Beaux Arts and returned to Rochefort. His new life, he discovered, was to be his father's close companion and collaborator on future literary projects. It was a sombre life the two men led, shut away in the small dark rooms, sorting the avalanche of papers, old letters, even rolls of old wall paper (labelled in Loti's delicate hand *From Maman's bedroom . . . my first study*) were preserved, bills or note books of household accounts, meticulously inscribed by Théodore Viaud, which itemized the modest expenditure of those vanished days for which Loti still ached . . . tallow candles, subscriptions to the Missionary Fund, two yards of muslin for caps, a toy for Julien . . . Ah! Julien . . . a toy, to them, a toy wound up to weep . . . Turning everything over, he sometimes destroyed things without explanation, sometimes fell into a reverie recalling events of which Samuel knew nothing and was petulant if questioned.

Whenever Blanche's name occurred, a barrier was raised between the two men. Samuel flatly refused to have his mother's name even pronounced by the father he considered had behaved ill to her. His loyalties remained painfully divided. However, Loti's married life scarcely had a place in the whole romantic tapestry of distant lands and loves. He wanted, above all, to amass those parts of the journal which told of his last days in Stamboul, to make a kind of post-script to the earlier Turkish books. This project took shape as the beautiful *Suprême Vision d'Orient, fragments du Journal Intime*. It was signed *Pierre Loti et son fils Samuel Viaud*. Its matter has been described earlier, for it deals with that moment when Loti and his son were together in the City of the Sultans in 1910. Loti also planned to publish some earlier parts of his journal concerning his life as a young lieutenant and on these Samuel was to work both during his father's life and after his death. *Un Jeune Officier Pauvre* appeared in 1923, and two more volumes, *Journal Intime 1878–81* and *1882–85*, were not published till 1929, six years after Loti's death.

To Samuel, cooped up at Rochefort in those post-war years it seemed that the whole town was populated by crêpe-hung widows and bereaved families, with little youthful society to be had. Loti's two sons by Crucita Gainza had remained beyond the Viaud family perimeter, though Loti never denied them and they occasionally visited him. Raymond had chosen the merchant navy as his future, while Edmond, all Basque and very handsome, had chosen the army. Both enjoyed a freedom unknown to Samuel, but they lived in the shadow of their bastard birth, for Rochefort frowned on them; which irritated Loti though there was nothing to be done about provincial strictures. He had known that all his life. The question of what provision should be made for them, and their mother, the future of Lucien and Pierre and their families (Pierre's wife was the cook) was exercising him greatly. His seamens' families had come to be regarded as part of his own, so that houses were given them, the sanatorium charges for a tubercular sister met, like all their growing exigencies, to say nothing of the more immediate pressures of the Bon and Duvigneau contingent. ('Couldn't you be a little less generous?' his publisher and friends still urged, to no avail.)

His will was something which Loti had frequently changed, but now time pressed, and he drafted yet another in a fever of impatience. So little time left. So much to set in order. The manner in which he decided his burial seems, at first sight, a denial of his whole life and character, for he neither chose the romanticism of Turkish soil, nor burial at sea, sailor-fashion, nor yet a grave beside his adored mother. Instead, he chose to lie alone – quite alone – on the ISLAND in the garden of the Maison des Aïeulles, where the ancestral roots still twined, and the sea still sounded, as it had done, when, as a boy, he had stolen out, going towards that first fatidic encounter. Perhaps that was the real reason he had acquired the house in 1899, since he never lived in it. He selected the precise spot, stipulating a very deep grave (though I have been unable to ascertain if, as was said, he also directed he should lie facing Mecca). There was to be no elaborate tombstone – only a small granite slab, bearing his name. Two of his most cherished possessions were to be buried with him. They were a small trowel Aunt Claire had given him to encourage the infant gardener, and an embroidered muslin head scarf – Aziyadé's. They represented what he held most dear – Nature and Love. Finally, no

315

mourners or public must be allowed to pass the high wall that surrounded the house, except once a year, when ten persons might be admitted, briefly, at the discretion of the guardian.

Thus Loti's last wishes; thus the legion of detailed instructions with which he smothered Samuel. Day by day Loti was reviewing the whole house, room by room, giving meticulous instructions for the preservation, destruction, or sale of everything. Some things were to be burned rather than profaned by other hands, some things left him oddly unmoved. In the Louis XVI salon, once Blanche's domain, nothing counted, except a portrait of Lucette Duplais, his first love. The splendour of the Renaissance hall had come to mean little – for all its grandeur. The piano of his childhood was to be saved, while a little devil figure, placed inside the instrument, was to be burnt at once, like two wooden divans in the Turkish room. Strange commands: what secrets did they hide? Nothing was overlooked; Samuel and Mauberger assured him his wishes would be faithfully obeyed. The massive family Bible, dating from that first Protestant exodus, was holy of all holies, like the family portraits in the red parlour. Most of these had been painted by Marie; but portraits of Loti himself, by other hands, were of no account. Oddly, his mosque now seemed of less consequence than any trivial object linked with the family roots. 'In my mosque, I value nothing except the marble stele from Aziyadé's grave, and two primitive water colours, above the divan, one of the Green Mosque (at Broussa), and another of a winged horse with a woman's head (el Borak), on which the Prophet ascends to Heaven.

The valuable contents of the Pagoda room, Chinese and Japanese lacquer and porcelain, also meant nothing to him – they could be sold outright. But an Etruscan vase 'painted by myself when a young lieutenant' was to be treasured, like his sketch books, paintings and drawings. All of his childhood's museum was precious – must never fall into careless hands; while his toys, and the little model theatre of *Peau-d'Ane* were inexpressibly dear: they were as much part of himself as the journals, all part of his stand against oblivion.

Then there were his animals, the cats and the tortoises. It is his solicitude for them, and certain cherished plants too, which make this neurotic and autocratic man so touching, though no doubt he was very trying to those around him. To Mauberger, were Samuel to be absent, he entrusted 'the poor creatures who have lived here so many years'; the cats, of course, and then, the septuagenarian tor-

316

toise – 'faithful companions, and I ask they are not abandoned'. There followed precise instructions for their diet. Then it was the turn of the plants. A nenuphar, floating in the pool, had been brought from La Roche-Courbon, fifty years before (no doubt at the moment of his romantic encounter with the gypsy). There were even instructions for a dielytra, or *coeur de Jeannette rose*, planted by Aunt Claire, 'nearly seventy years old, and still flowering . . . it needs fresh earth each spring, and must be protected by iron stakes when it begins to grow. I also ask that cuttings are taken to Oléron, and planted beside my grave.'

Gravestones, last wishes, the dear dead days beyond recall – such was the life of Samuel and Mauberger beside this melancholy tyrant who anticipated his end with such precision.

Few old friends now came to lighten the gloom, and Loti made no more efforts to face life in the capital, although Sarah Bernhardt, one leg the less, still reigned there and sometimes suggested he should not remain so remote. At eighty-four, Madame Adam had withdrawn to Gif, and found consolation in a return to religion, writing often to her adopted son urging him to do likewise. He had always maintained he did not read, and none of the new books that reached him – authors' copies inscribed in flowery terms – interested him. He merely tore out the inscriptions, and had the books sent to the local hospital. So much for many genuine expressions of affection and admiration, such as Apollinaire's *'Au plus pur, au plus touchant des écrivains vivants . . .'*, Anna de Noailles' *'au plus grand poète dont l'oeuvre de génie a enchanté toute ma vie'*, or Verlaine's *'hommage bien confraternel'*.

At Rochefort a young girl who, as Odette Valence, was later to write of Loti with great understanding had now attached herself to him. She addressed him as *Mon Prince* (Loti much disliked being called *Cher Maître* – 'only my cats or horses call me that, he said) and this oddly assorted pair were often to be seen, walking slowly about the town, thus providing Samuel with a few hours off duty. Visits from Loti's former shipmates revived him briefly: then, forgetting the sad present he talked of past voyages with something of his old verve.

At the Préfecture de la Marine Loti had lately found links with the navy in the person of the Préfet, Vice-Admiral Louis Charlier, a genial figure whose wife was a devoted admirer of Loti's writings.

317

The Charliers and their two young daughters brought a sense of warmth and liveliness not only to their post at Rochefort, but to the gloomy household in the Rue Saint-Pierre, and before long Loti approached Madame Charlier with the suggestion that her eldest daughter, Elise, might be a suitable wife for his son. Samuel was unaware of this manoeuvre, but when he was told was enchanted with the idea. He had met Mademoiselle Charlier at dances the Admiral had given in the hope of livening the old port at a time when the country had barely emerged from national mourning. It was through this same Mademoiselle Charlier, whom, as Samuel's widow, I had the happiness of knowing some fifty years later, that I learned something of Loti at that time. Naturally, he was a legendary figure in the town, but rather forbidding to the young, when he visited her parents in the beautiful eighteenth-century Préfecture de la Marine. On the occasion of a ball there, she recalled, he had actually been persuaded to dance one of the traditional quadrilles, going through the intricate figures with lofty elegance, and she, Elise, had been one of his partners. At that same ball, she had remarked a very handsome stranger, but was advised not to dance with him – he was one of the Gainzas, still not admitted by Rochefort society in general.

When Samuel proposed he was accepted: he was an appealing, shy young man with exquisite manners and Elise was touched, for she realized how badly he needed to escape from the lugubrious atmosphere of the Rue Saint-Pierre and parental domination. She had not realized that neither Samuel nor Loti envisaged any other way of life. The Admiral was as enthusiastic at the idea of his daughter marrying into the great writer's family as Loti was to know his son's fiancée was an Admiral's daughter. To each, their concept of glory. Among the Charliers Samuel found a cheerful, uncomplicated, carefree life, in violent contrast to his own. With them he played tennis, sailed, and went on picnics. They teased the rather solemn young man, and suddenly Samuel became Sam, an abbreviation which his father deplored. However, he approved of his future daughter-in-law on all other counts. Protestant, an Admiral's daughter, healthy, pretty, of good stock – she would certainly give him a grandson – a Viaud descendant. He wanted that before the end.

As soon as the engagement was announced, he arranged that the young couple should visit Sarah Bernhardt for her blessing. It was a

318

visit of which the petrified Elise could only recall Sarah's marked affection for Samuel, and her manner of throwing scraps of food off her plate onto the carpet where numerous pets scuffled for them. A visit to Blanche at Berternet was scarcely less alarming. Blanche had become very remote, but though steeped in theosophy still displayed a matriarchal hold over Sam, which irked his fiancée. She was not yet conscious of the degree of filial devotion which kept Samuel torn between the two parental poles.

It was decided that the newly-weds should live at the Rue Saint-Pierre, beside Loti. There was no question of Samuel detaching from the roots. But at this point he suddenly issued an ultimatum to his astonished father. No marriage unless a proper modern bathroom and lavatory were added to the old house. Loti was thunderstruck. What was wrong with the old ways? But Samuel, now modernized, liberated as Sam, stood firm. He would not dream of asking his fiancée to accept such antiquated discomfort, he said. Lamps and candles too, should be changed for electricity. That was going too far. Loti ceded, grudgingly, over the plumbing, but electric light he thought very dangerous; all those cables could undermine the old walls. Besides, electricity was bad for the eyes; he had always written by candle or lamplight and still did not need spectacles. Now it was Sam's turn to yield.

The marriage was celebrated in Paris, in May 1920, and aroused almost as much interest as Loti's own marriage had done, for Loti (still seen by many readers as Aziyadé's lover, the hero of all those romantic episodes) continued to provide good copy for the press. Photographs of the ceremony show a grey-bearded Loti sitting hunched in his chair, seemingly as aloof and tormented as at his own wedding. He loathed all such ceremonial and particularly detested appearing before the public as the old man he had become; but it had to be faced, if there were to be the descendants he desired. That too was a way of ensuring a kind of immortality.

For the young couple there was only a brief honeymoon at Hendaye, because Samuel realized how urgent it was for his father to continue their work on the journals and other projects for future publications. Elise found work enough, pitting her inexperience as mistress of the house against the old domestics who had run the house their own way ever since Blanche's departure. They had the keys of the cellar, the linen cupboards were upside down, the shutters were seldom opened, the meals uninteresting and badly served.

319

Loti had become quite indifferent to all, except his approaching end. When Elise began organizing delicious menus, he remarked that meat and a vegetable were all that was required. Elise was firm. 'At home we had a different menu every day,' she said, 'and Sam enjoys all kinds of puddings, so he shall have them.' Loti retreated to the mosque, and Samuel trembled. But Elise had early discovered she must make a stand, if there was to be any life for herself and Sam. Loti seldom came downstairs except for meals, where he was a brooding presence, and glacial silence reigned, however much the young people tried to draw him out. 'The Commander,' as he was known to the household, remained aloof, sealed away in some doleful vale of memories. Did he never recall happy times, Elise wondered, watching the man who had achieved everything in his life, money, love, far travels, adventure, fame, and yet seemed sunk in gloom.

Elise saw Loti through other eyes than most. To her, he was, first, a crushingly selfish father who monopolized her husband as a second secretary, and was an unapproachable presence who chilled her. 'Why do you call your father-in-law the Commander?' asked Madame Barthou, to whom Loti remained 'the Magician'. 'Can't you invent some special pet name for him?' she persisted: but Loti remained the Commander to his daughter-in-law as to the rest of the household. It is difficult, in retrospect, to reconcile this close, firsthand image, with that of Loti, the sensitive, compassionate, and at times enchantingly gay companion of whom many others have left loving accounts. Elise only knew him at the end of his life, and we must accept that little was left of the Loti others had cherished.

In April 1921 Loti suffered a stroke, and his distracted son hung over him trying to decipher the blurred words. After a while he rallied partially, but remained much weakened, his speech impaired, though his brain remained clear, and his eyes spoke for the frustration he now endured. For a year his state varied, and sometimes his proud spirit forced him to his feet, only to stumble ignominiously. Lucien and Pierre looked after their Commander devotedly, but all outside visitors were kept away from this pathetic spectacle. An unlooked-for improvement allowed him to continue working sometimes, but for the most part he sat stonily by the fire in that small austere bedroom where all recalled a ship's cabin, and the window overlooking the courtyard let in little sunlight – too little for the man who all his life had worshipped Baal with pagan joy.

Whenever the weather was fine there was a ritual afternoon drive round the fossil town in a stuffy hired cab; propped up beside Samuel, Loti stared listlessly through the fly-blown windows at the familiar scenes of his youth, the charmingly named Chemin de la belle Judith, the Porte Martrou, where the sailors still racketed, and Colbert's noble grey façade of the Arsenal. For Loti this was a time of waiting – for the birth of Samuel's child, and his own death . . . He had lived too long; he had always seen old age as the negation of all life stood for, and he must have thought, bitterly, of his closing lines in *Pêcheur d'Islande*: 'It should be possible to break off the tale of a lifetime with the same deliberation one applies when writing a book.'

Sometimes an old pianist who lived near came to play for him, and shuffling down to the Renaissance Hall he listened to Chopin or Bach – the pieces he had once played, with that special 'singing touch' which was always remarked, and which had charmed the serpent, in Senegal.

In August 1921, with the birth of his grandson, Loti's wish was fulfilled. The baby was named Pierre, and embodied that continuity which he sought with such desperation. Holding the little creature precariously, he looked at it long and silently: then, 'he has the best of me – my eyes,' he said, and turned away, to hide his tears. For him, every newcomer on this earth was predestined to sorrow. Sarah Bernhardt's telegram was more uplifting: 'May this new little Pierre be worthy of the great, illustrious and beloved friend of Sarah Bernhardt,' she wired. Blanche wished to come to see the baby, and Samuel was in some trepidation, fearing his father might refuse. Maintaining his usual practice of never mentioning his mother to his father, he delegated this delicate request to Elise. But Loti raised no difficulties; Blanche arrived to stay in the house where she had passed so many wretched years, and the visit went off very well.

Before the darkness deepened further Loti was to receive a valedictory gesture from the navy which had been his whole life. There was a small but solemn ceremony at which Admiral Lacaze, a companion of early days, invested him with the insignia of the Grande Croix de la Légion d'Honneur. Loti had himself dressed in full uniform, his sword at his side, and standing to attention, supported by his son, contrived to salute, as a contingent of sailors presented arms. This was the last time he was seen in public: his pride forbade him to parade his infirmities, which now worsened rapidly. But one day, when his speech seemed rather more distinct, he suddenly ordered them to take him to La Roche-Courbon; to the Château de la Belle au Bois Dormant, they supposed, but it was to the surrounding woods where he had first lain in love with the Tzigane that he wished to return. They carried his wheeled chair through the green twilight, to the grottos in the ravine beside the stream, and there he asked to be left for a while. There, in his own words, he had first learned 'the great secret of life and love'. It was fitting he should make this last pilgrimage, as to a tomb.

Many years later, one of his admiring readers heard of this, and caused Loti's name to be graven on the face of a nearby rock. And there it remains, a memorial that Loti would have surely found to his liking.

The Turkish nation had never forgotten their own 'friend of the dark days'. Late in December 1921 a small Governmental delegation arrived from Ankara and announced they wished to present Loti with a carpet specially woven for him by the children whose fathers – and mothers too – had been massacred by the Greeks during the time Loti had stood so staunchly beside Turkey. It happened that this visit fell at one of the rare moments when Samuel and Elise were absent, and Mauberger called on Loti's friend and former officer aboard the *Vautour*, Claude Farrère, also an ardent Turcophil, to act as host, since Loti was in no state for formal occasions. Farrère, who venerated Loti, arrived at once, and it is to his account, published in his book on Loti, that I owe the following details.

Loti wished to receive the Turks in fitting style, in his mosque, and on that winter night it was a chill, sombre scene, lit only by two tall candles beside the catafalques, and the lamp flickering before Aziyadé's stele. Loti was a ghostly figure, muffled in a dark cloak, his eyes blazing out from his livid face. One of the diplomats was accompanied by his wife, the Hanum Fered Bey. She was a typically soft and graceful young Turkish woman, who did her best to draw Loti out when, later, tea was served in the Turkish room. Loti struggled painfully to form the simplest sentences, and conversation dragged. Presently he indicated to Farrère that he wanted a candle held close to his charming guest, the better to see, once more, the face of a Turkish woman. The Hanum Fered Bey had not kept to the old-fashioned *tcharchaf* and was unveiled. As the candlelight fell over her, Loti gazed hungrily, as if trying to trace some likeness to his long-gone love. Aziyadé's portrait in its golden frame still occupied the place of honour, and the Hanum asked casually who it represented . . . 'But perhaps you don't remember her name by now?' she suggested, for Loti seemed to hesitate. Then he spoke, an unexpected force sounding through his stumbling reply. 'Remember? Ah yes! That I shall remember till the hour of my death.'

The Turkish visit had drained his last strength, for he had insisted on descending the steep stairs, accompanying his guests to the door, a puppet figure supported on each side by Lucien and Pierre. Later, the Hanum Fered Bey was on the point of catching the night train to Paris when she received Loti's plea to see her once more and agreed to return. He again received her in the mosque. From below, in the silence of the quiet house, Farrère heard voices – a man and a woman talking together – talking in Turkish! Some timbre in the Hanum's voice had recalled that of Aziyadé, and with those loved Turkish syllables Loti's speech returned to him.

The months dragged by, and although he now spoke with more ease, he was too weak to talk much or hold a pen. Sarah Bernhardt was passing near Rochefort and made a détour to see him. But when she reached the Rue Saint-Pierre in her specially fitted automobile that was constructed to contain the litter-like portable chair to which she was now condemned, it was too wide to pass the narrow entrance. So Loti was carried down to sit beside her for a few moments. There, in the car, Sarah and her 'Julien le Fou' made their adieux.

There was one more farewell meeting; in September 1922 Madame Adam, 'Madame Chérie', the adopted mother of his literary début, made the journey from Gif in answer to his appeal. She was eighty-six, but she did not hesitate; he wanted her, and she had never failed him yet. She found him sadly in need of her spiritual consolations, but as she left he told her he had nothing more to desire from life. She wrote later: 'he knew his son happy, he had seen his grandchild, and in leaving one mother (myself), believed at last, with a new-found faith, that he would find again that much loved other.'

All through 1922 Loti remained shut away in his austere cabin-like bedroom. On the whitewashed walls there now hung a crucifix, and a dismal picture of a monk contemplating a skull. Sometimes the pastor of the Reformed Church came to read the Bible with him, echoing those nightly readings in the old parlour of his childhood. This was no classic deathbed repentance. Loti had not lived a life that demanded any spectacular remorse (although for some time he had condemned his own books as immoral – a weight on his conscience – and regretted having written them). His domestic selfishness was outweighed by his generosity and compassion, and that silent sacrifice of the longed-for Moslem faith he had made to ensure his mother's peace of mind. Perhaps re-reading the Bible – *her* Bible – gave him the illusion of coming nearer to her once more . . . Sometimes, he still hankered after the beauty and illusions of his mosque, and then they carried him there, settling him beside Aziyadé's stele, and the tespeyhs that hung from it – hers, or Achmet's farewell gift – were placed in his weakened hand.

In the radiant early days of June 1923 there was an improvement in his condition and he announced his intention of going to Hendaye. His doctor did not advise the journey, but Loti was as wilful and autocratic as ever. In March he had been saddened by the death of Sarah Bernhardt, and Samuel believed the change would do him good. A special wagon-lit was attached to the train, and Loti was installed among the pillows and rugs.

One of the servants wished him a good journey and a safe return. It was noticed that Loti gave a curious shrug, as if disclaiming any return to Rochefort. Bakhar Etchea was at its best, the sunlight glittering over the Bidassoa, his Basque friends surrounding him as he sat on the terrace overlooking the far Spanish shore. Berthe Durutty was beside him, asking no more than to be near her Maïté Maïtia . . . 'You will stay a while, won't you?' she asked him, and again, he gave that curious shrug as reply . . . The journey had exhausted him, and sitting late on the terrace the chill night air did its work. Three days later, he was a dying man. Long ago, the celebrated voyante Madame Fraya had predicted he would die in a house overlooking the water. Had he remembered that when imprisoned at Rochefort? Bakhar Etchea was such a house: to return there was a way to bring the prophesy about, a way for him to escape his imprisoning body. Specialists were rushed from Paris, but there was nothing to be done. On Sunday, June 10th, he died without regaining consciousness, as the joyous music of fife and drum sounded across the water from a fête at Fontarabia. It was the sort of peasant festival in which he had so often taken part, among his Basque friends, Loti the world-famous author escaping into the costume and ways of the smugglers. Now he had escaped forever.

The French Government decreed a national funeral, and three warships were dispatched to transport his coffin from Rochefort to Oléron – 'the ISLAND'. By chance, though as if to mark his attachment to all things Arab, they were the *Algérien*, the *Arabe* and the *Kabyle*. Loti's body was wrapped in the French flag, 'that most incomparable of all winding sheets', he called it. For three days the flower-smothered coffin had lain in state in the Renaissance Hall, with four sailors mounting guard, and an enormous crowd of mourners filing past. Then the navy took the coffin down the Charente and across a rough stretch of water, for Loti's last sea journey. The Government, the navy, some army officers he had been with during the war, and his old friends were all gathered at the House of the Ancestors for the burial ceremony. Blanche, conventional in mourning veils, had come from Berternet. Standing rather apart was a young man who seemed much moved: it was Edmond Gainza. He had not been included in the list of mourners, 'but after all he was my father', he told Elise, and a Gainza wreath – perhaps with a message from Crucita – was placed beside the others. Among the many mourners was a Turkish delegation. They told of Constantinople's flags being at half-mast that day. As the cortège of mourners followed the gun-carriage to the Maison des Aïeulles – the ancient ancestral root – it was seen that the small streets of Saint-Pierre d'Oléron were lined with school children, all holding bunches of that simple flower *le gazon de Mahon*. Once it had grown wild along the sides of the houses there, and when an officious municipality ordered its destruction Loti, who loved its bright colours, opposed this measure, only to be overruled. Nevertheless, some of the townspeople remembered, and saw to it that these simple flowers should once more be found along his way.

There was a macabre postscript to that day of sorrow, one quite in keeping with Loti's insatiable craving for drama. He had enjoined that his coffin should be left open (as in Moslem lands) the sooner for his body to return to dust. However, the distracted Samuel had not

325

been able to overcome the opposition of both undertakers and local authorities.

Therefore, that night, he returned stealthily to his father's grave, accompanied by two of Loti's faithful sailors, armed with shovels and a pick-axe. They put aside the splendid wreaths and began the laborious task of digging. The grave was a very deep one – this too had been one of Loti's wishes – and it was past midnight when the coffin was disclosed. Then Samuel, ravaged with grief, but obedient to the last, gashed it open. Working frantically, the three men shovelled back the earth and replaced the wreaths in a seemly fashion so that no trace of their night's work should remain.

Nevertheless, they had been seen. Neighbours had heard strange sounds, and through a chink in the wall, glimpsed the sinister scene. Later it was rumoured that Samuel had wished to retrieve a valuable ring buried with his father. Aziyadé's ring, perhaps? Romantic legends surrounded Loti, to the grave, and beyond.

BIBLIOGRAPHY

Unpublished sources: The Journals and papers of Pierre Loti in possession of Madame Samuel Loti-Viaud and Monsieur Pierre Loti-Viaud. Manuscripts and papers from the collection of Colonel Daniel Sekkles.

Published sources:
Extracts from Loti's Journals, published in collaboration with his son, Samuel Viaud
Un Jeune Officier Pauvre. Calmann-Lévy. Paris, 1923
Journal Intime 1878–1881. Ed. Samuel Viaud. Calmann-Lévy. Paris, 1925
Journal Intime 1882–1885. Ed. Samuel Viaud. Calmann-Lévy. Paris, 1925
Note: Much of this material first appeared serialized in *La Nouvelle Revue, La Revue des Deux Mondes,* with short extracts published by *Figaro, L'Illustration, Le Matin, Le Temps* and others.

Juliette Adam. *Lettres de Pierre Loti à Madame Juliette Adam.* Plon. Paris, 1924
C. Wesley Bird. *Pierre Loti, correspondant et dessinateur 1872–1889.* Impressions Pierre André. Paris, 1947
Pierre-E. Briquet. *Pierre Loti et l'Orient.* Ed. de la Braconnière. Neuchâtel, 1945
Frédéric Chassériau. *Mes Souvenirs sur Pierre Loti et Francis Jammes.* Plon. Paris, 1937
Claude Farrère. *Pierre Loti.* Flammarion. Paris, 1930
———. *Cent Dessins de Pierre Loti.* Arrault. Paris, 1948
Pierre Flottes. *Le Drame Intérieur de Pierre Loti: documents inédits.* Courrier Littéraire. Paris, 1937
Marc Hélys. *Le Secret des Désenchantées.* Perrin. Paris, 1924
Raymond Lefèvre. *En Marge de Loti.* Ed. Jean Renard. Paris, 1944
———. *La Vie Inquiète de Pierre Loti.* Société Français. Editions Littéraires. Paris, 1934
R. Millward. *L'Oeuvre de Pierre Loti et l'Esprit Fin de Siècle.* Nizet. Paris, 1935
Countess Ostrorog. *Pierre Loti à Constantinople.* Fiquière. Paris, 1927
Jean Rauch. *Orages et Tempêtes dans la Littérature.* Soc. d'Ed. Géographiques Maritimes et Coloniales.

Robert Scheffer. *Orient Royal*. L'Edition Française Illustrée. Paris, 1918

N. Serban. *Pierre Loti, sa vie, son oeuvre*. Presse Française. Paris, 1924

G. Taboulet and J. C. Demariaux. *La Vie Dramatique de Gustave Viaud*. Editions du Scorpion. Paris, 1961

Odette Valence. *Mon Ami Pierre Loti*. Flammarion. Paris, 1930

Odette Valence and Samuel Viaud. *La Famille de Pierre Loti, ou l'Education Passionnée*. Calmann-Lévy. Paris, 1940

Les Cahiers de Pierre Loti. 1952–1978.

La Revue Maritime. Pierre Loti 1850–1923. Service historique de la Marine. Paris, 1950

Numerous articles:

Les Nouvelles Littéraires, La Revue des Deux Mondes, Le Temps, Le Figaro, Candide, Le Gaulois du Dimanche, La Revue de France, Cahiers Radio-Paris etc., which appeared throughout Loti's life, between his first years of fame, until his death, and later.

THE PUBLISHED WORKS OF PIERRE LOTI

Aziyadé. Calmann-Lévy. Paris, 1877
Le Mariage de Loti. Calmann-Lévy. Paris, 1880
Le Roman d'un Spahi. Calmann-Lévy. Paris, 1881
Fleurs d'Ennui. Calmann-Lévy. Paris, 1882
Mon Frère Yves. Calmann-Lévy. Paris, 1883
Pêcheur d'Islande. Calmann-Lévy. Paris, 1886
Propos d'Exil. Calmann-Lévy. Paris, 1887
Madame Chrysanthème. Calmann-Lévy. Paris, 1893
Japonerie d'Automne. Calmann-Lévy. Paris, 1889
Au Maroc. Calmann-Lévy. Paris, 1890
Le Roman d'un Enfant. Calmann-Lévy. Paris, 1890
Le Livre de la Pitié et de la Mort. Calmann-Lévy. Paris, 1890
Fantôme d'Orient. Calmann-Lévy. Paris, 1892
L'Exilée. Calmann-Lévy. Paris, 1893
Matelot. Alphonse Lemerre. Paris, 1893
Le Désert. Calmann-Lévy. Paris, 1895
Jérusalem. Calmann-Lévy. Paris, 1895
La Galilée. Calmann-Lévy. Paris, 1895
Ramuntcho. Calmann-Lévy. Paris, 1897
Figures et Choses qui passaient. Calmann-Lévy. Paris, 1898
Reflets sur la Sombre Route. Calmann-Lévy. Paris, 1899
Les Derniers Jours de Pékin. Calmann-Lévy. Paris, 1902
L'Inde sans les Anglais. Calmann-Lévy. Paris, 1904
Vers Ispahan. Calmann-Lévy. Paris, 1904
La Troisième Jeunesse de Madame Prune. Calmann-Lévy. Paris, 1905
Les Désenchantées. Calmann-Lévy. Paris, 1906
La Mort de Philae. Calmann-Lévy. Paris, 1909
Le Château de la Belle au Bois Dormant. Calmann-Lévy. Paris, 1910
Un Pélerin d'Angkor. Calmann-Lévy. Paris, 1912
La Turquie Agonisante. Calmann-Lévy. Paris, 1913
La Hyène Enragée. Calmann-Lévy. Paris, 1916

Quelques Aspects du Vertige Mondial. Flammarion. Paris, 1917

L'Horreur Allemande. Calmann-Lévy. Paris, 1918

Prime Jeunesse. Calmann-Lévy. Paris, 1919

La Mort de Notre Chère France en Orient. Calmann-Lévy. Paris, 1920

Suprêmes Visions d'Orient, en collaboration avec son fils, Samuel Viaud. Calmann-Lévy. Paris, 1921

Un Jeune Officier Pauvre, en collaboration avec son fils, Samuel Viaud. Calmann-Lévy. Paris, 1923

Journal Intime 1878–1881, ed. par son fils, Samuel Viaud. Calmann-Lévy. Paris, 1925

Journal Intime 1882–1885, ed. par son fils, Samuel Viaud. Calmann-Lévy. Paris, 1925

Note: Much of this material first appeared serialized in *La Nouvelle Revue, La Revue des Deux Mondes* and other periodicals, with short pieces published by *Figaro, L'Illustration, Le Matin, Le Temps* and others.

INDEX